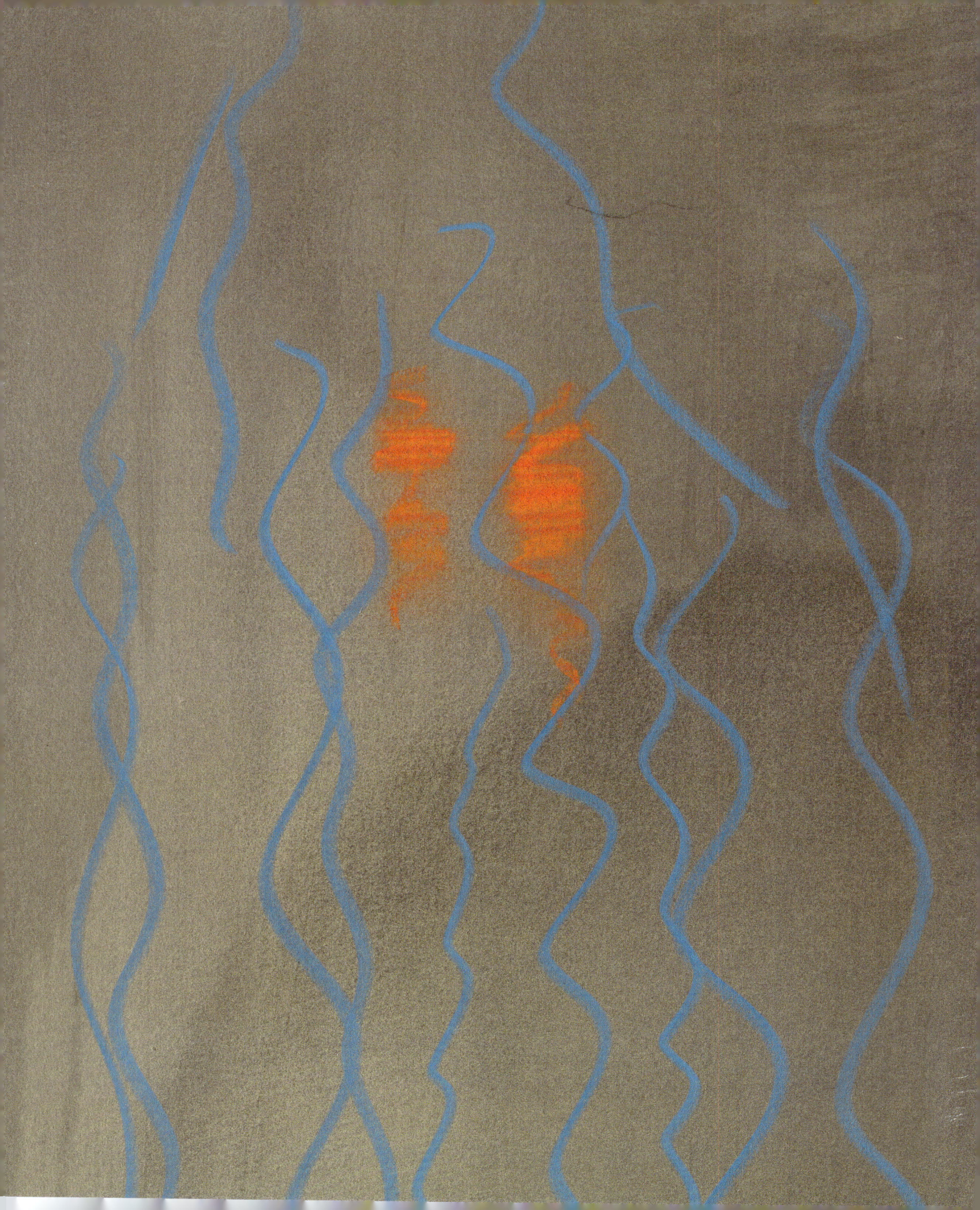

WATER'S EDGE

THE ART OF TRUMAN LOWE

Edited by Rebecca Head Trautmann

Published by
The National Museum of the American Indian
Smithsonian Institution
Washington, DC

THE SMITHSONIAN'S NATIONAL
MUSEUM OF THE AMERICAN INDIAN

VISION
Equity and social justice for the Native peoples
of the Western Hemisphere through education,
inspiration, and empowerment.

MISSION
In partnership with Native peoples and their
allies, the National Museum of the American
Indian fosters a richer shared human experience
through a more informed understanding of
Native peoples.

For more information about the Smithsonian's
National Museum of the American Indian, visit
www.AmericanIndian.si.edu.

––––––––––––––––––––

Cover:
Feather Canoe, ca. 1993. Peeled willow saplings,
feathers, copper wire, 22 x 74 x 12 in. National Museum
of the American Indian 27/607

Endsheets:
Blanket Series (Red Purple), detail, 1994. Brushed powdered
pigment and pastel on paper, 30 x 42 in. National Museum
of the American Indian 27/616

ii:
Untitled (Stream), detail, ca. 2010–15. Gesso
and pastel on paper, 30 x 11 in. National Museum of the
American Indian 27/613

Opposite:
Mimi, detail, 1979. Pine, peeled willow sticks, blue jay feathers,
leather, glass beads, 18 x 16 x 16 in. National Museum of the
American Indian 26/9773, gift of John and Meryl Lipton Lavine

viii, xi:
Stars, detail, ca. 1985–90. Pastel on paper,
22 x 30 in. National Museum of the American Indian 27/617.

Director: Cynthia Chavez Lamar (San Felipe Pueblo/Hopi/Tewa/Navajo)
Associate Director for Digital Strategy and Engagement: Ryan Dodge
General Editor: Rebecca Head Trautmann
Publications Manager: Tanya Thrasher (Cherokee Nation)
Project Editor: Alexandra N. Harris
Designer: Kevin Coochwytewa (Isleta Pueblo/Hopi)
Rights and Permissions: Wendy Hurlock Baker, Cheryl Fair
Digital Asset Management: Robin Holladay Peak, Alan Arellano
Copy Editor: Christine Gordon

Distributed by Smithsonian Books
Director: Carolyn Gleason
Senior Editor: Jaime Schwender
Production Editor: Julie Huggins
Digital Imaging Specialist: Bill Whitcher
Copy Editor: Joanne Reams
Index: Connie Binder

Library of Congress Control Number 2025017711

Printed in the United States, not at government expense
29 28 27 26 25   1 2 3 4 5

Leading support provided by Bank of America. Major support
provided by the Henry Luce Foundation. Generous support provided
by the Terra Foundation for American Art and Ameriprise Financial.

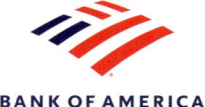

BANK OF AMERICA

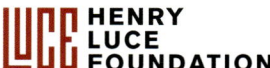

HENRY
LUCE
FOUNDATION

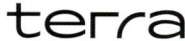

terra Foundation for
American Art

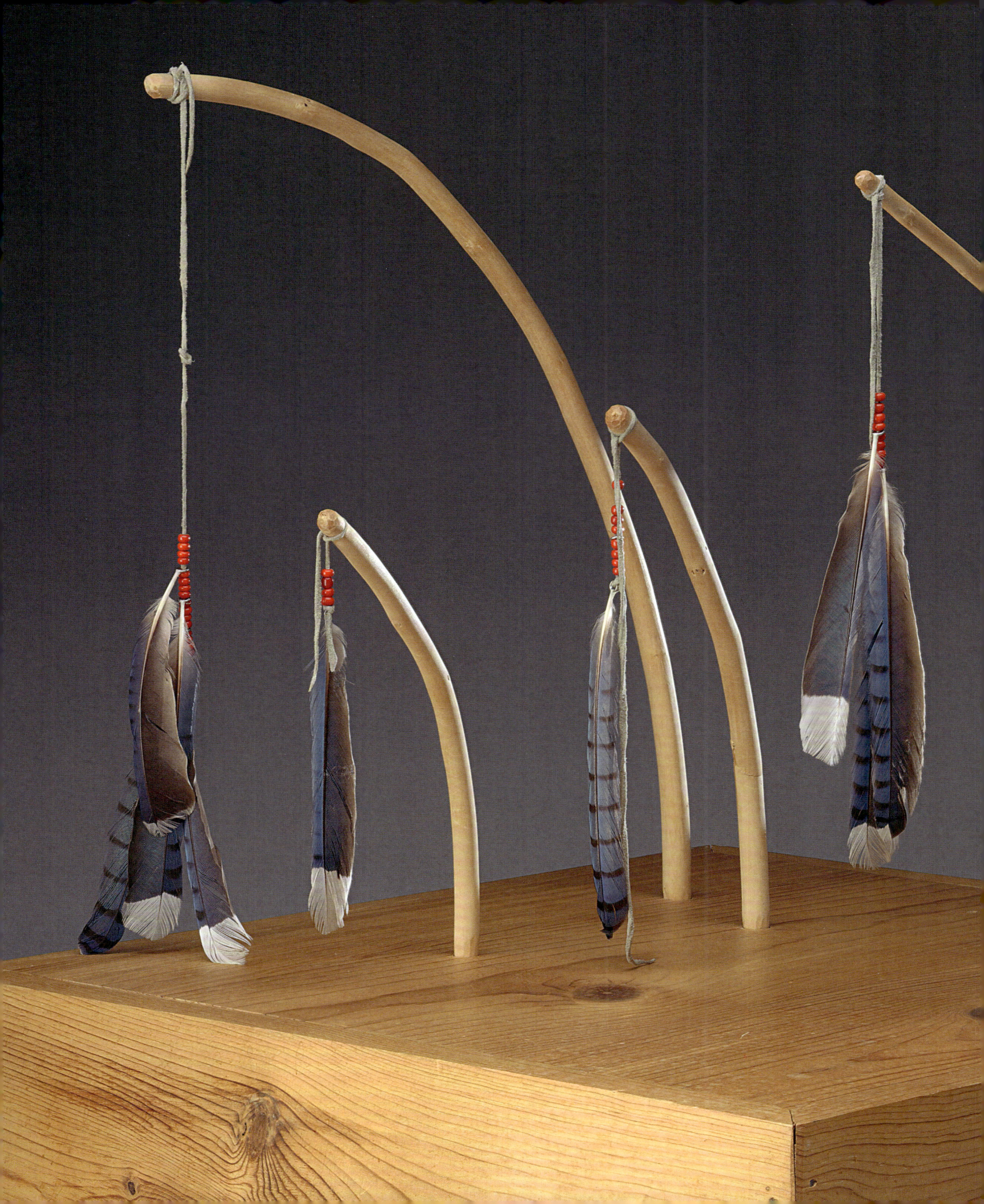

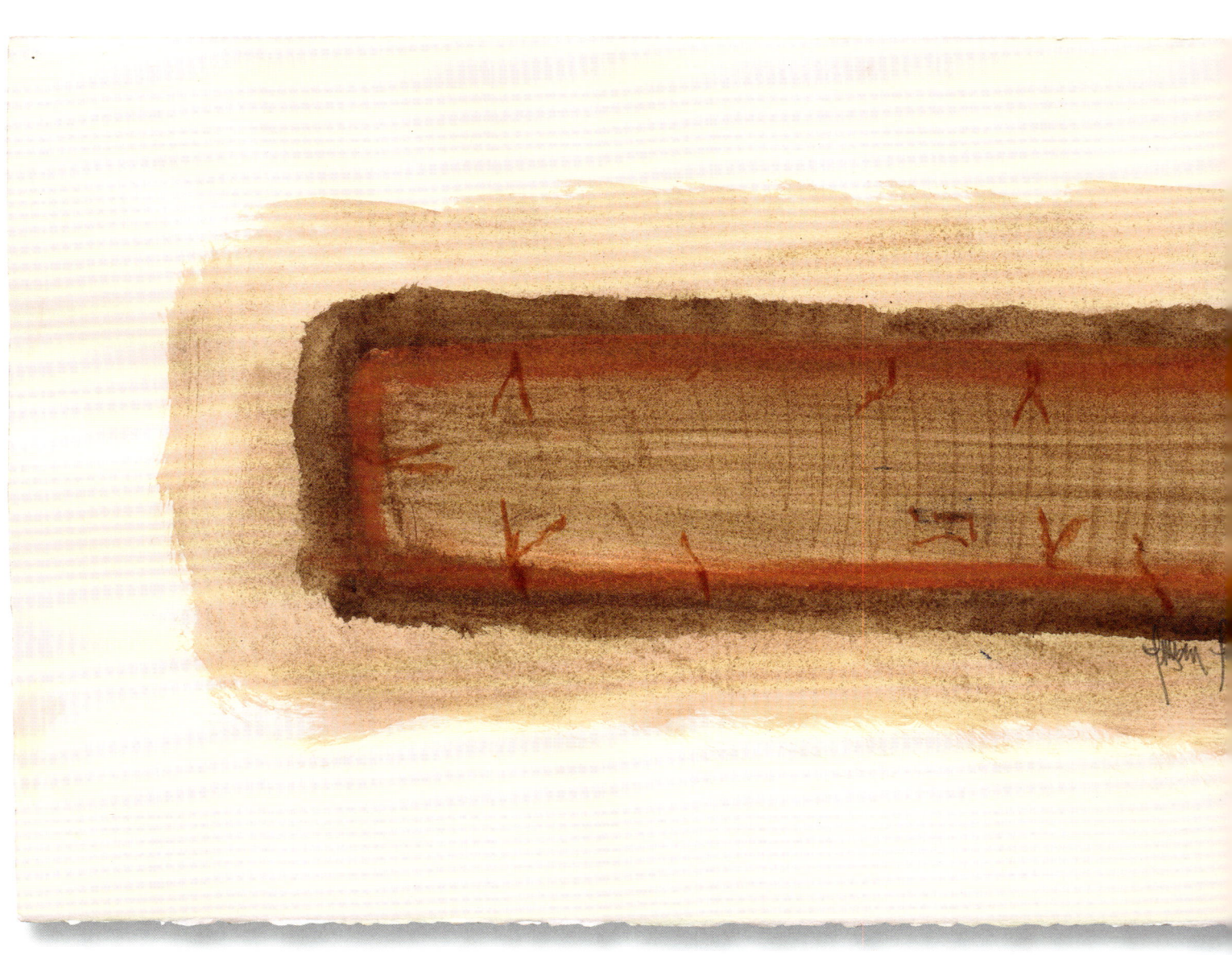

1. Untitled, ca. 2010–15. Gesso and pastel on paper, 11 x 30 in. National Museum of the American Indian 27/627

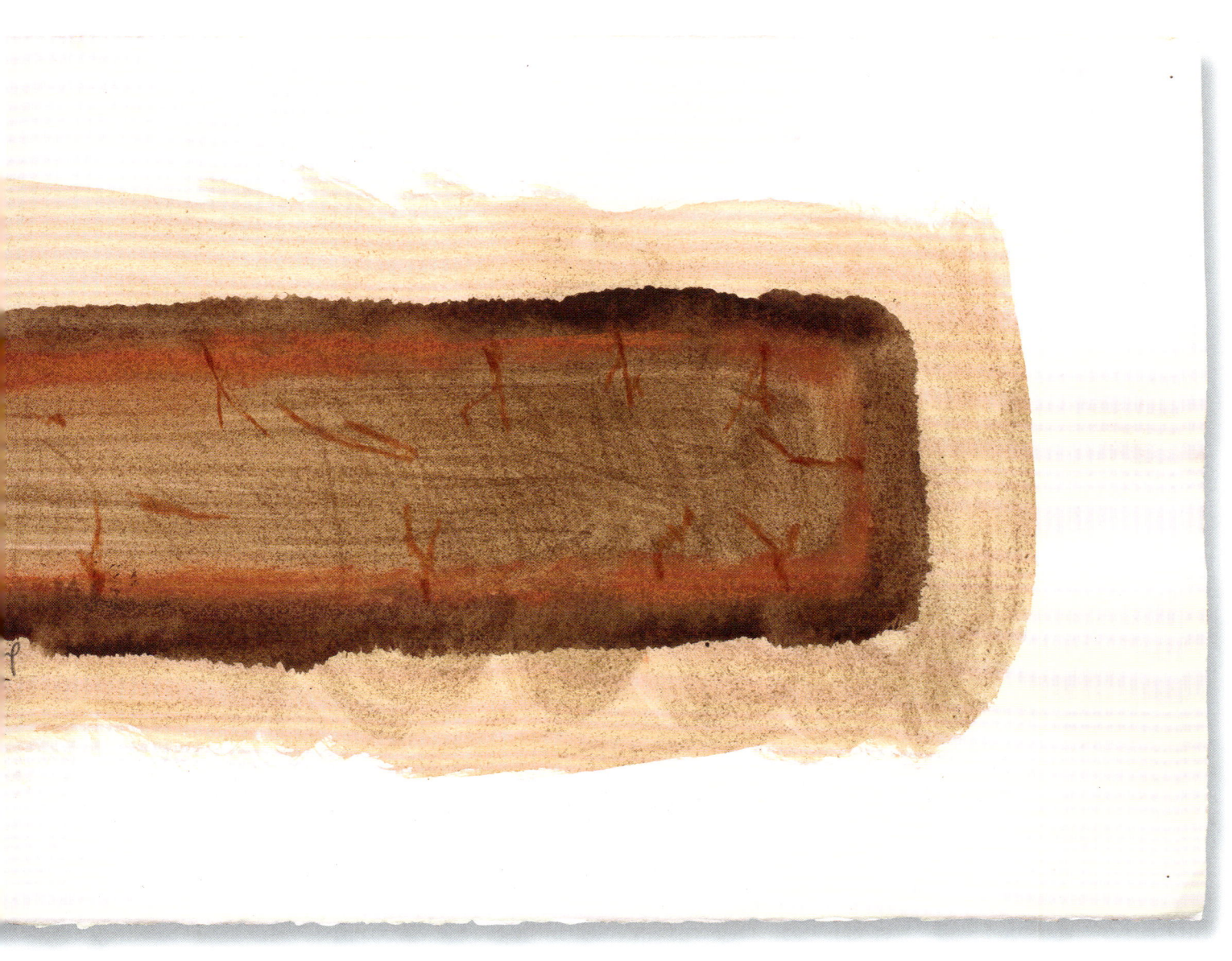

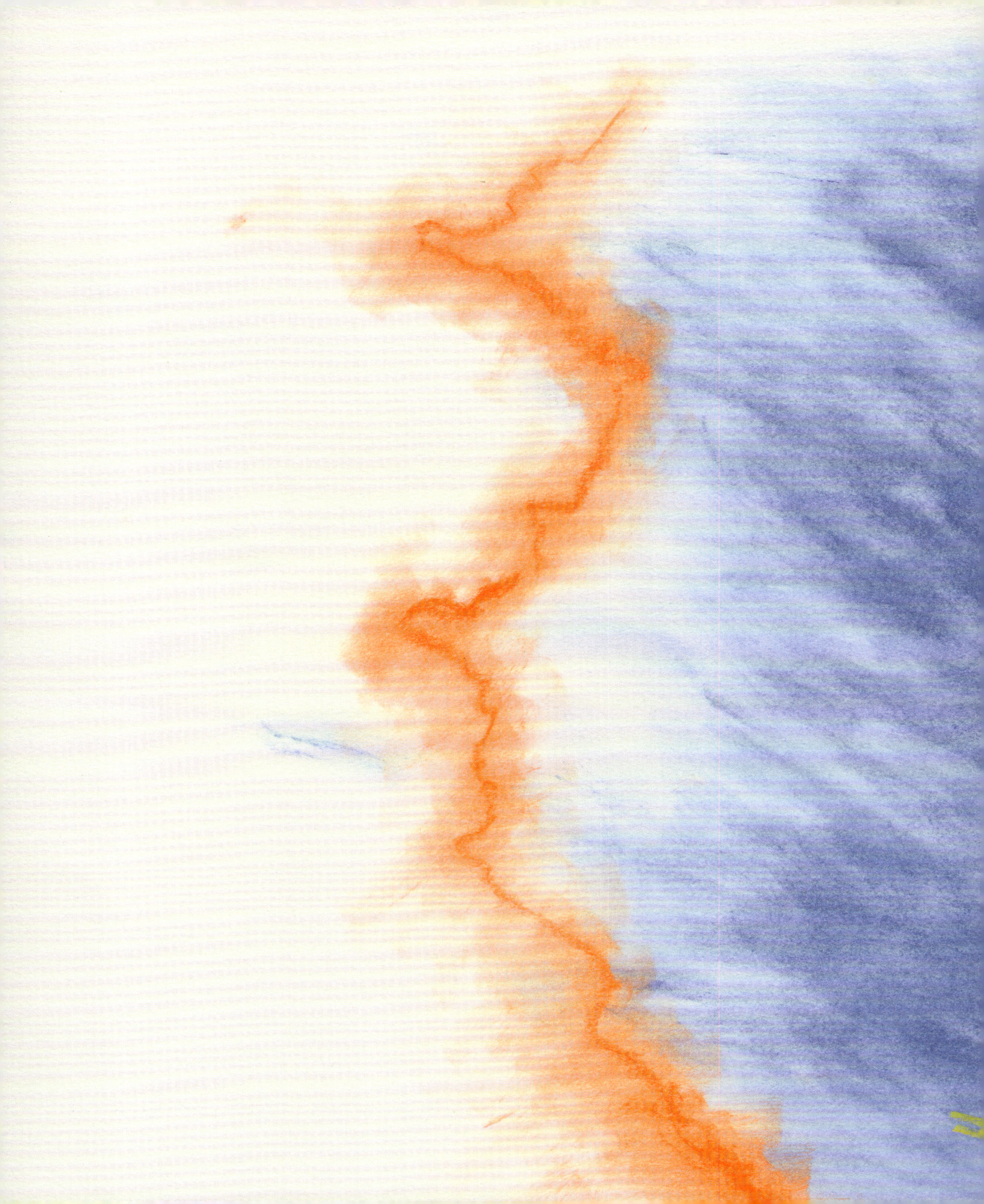

Contents

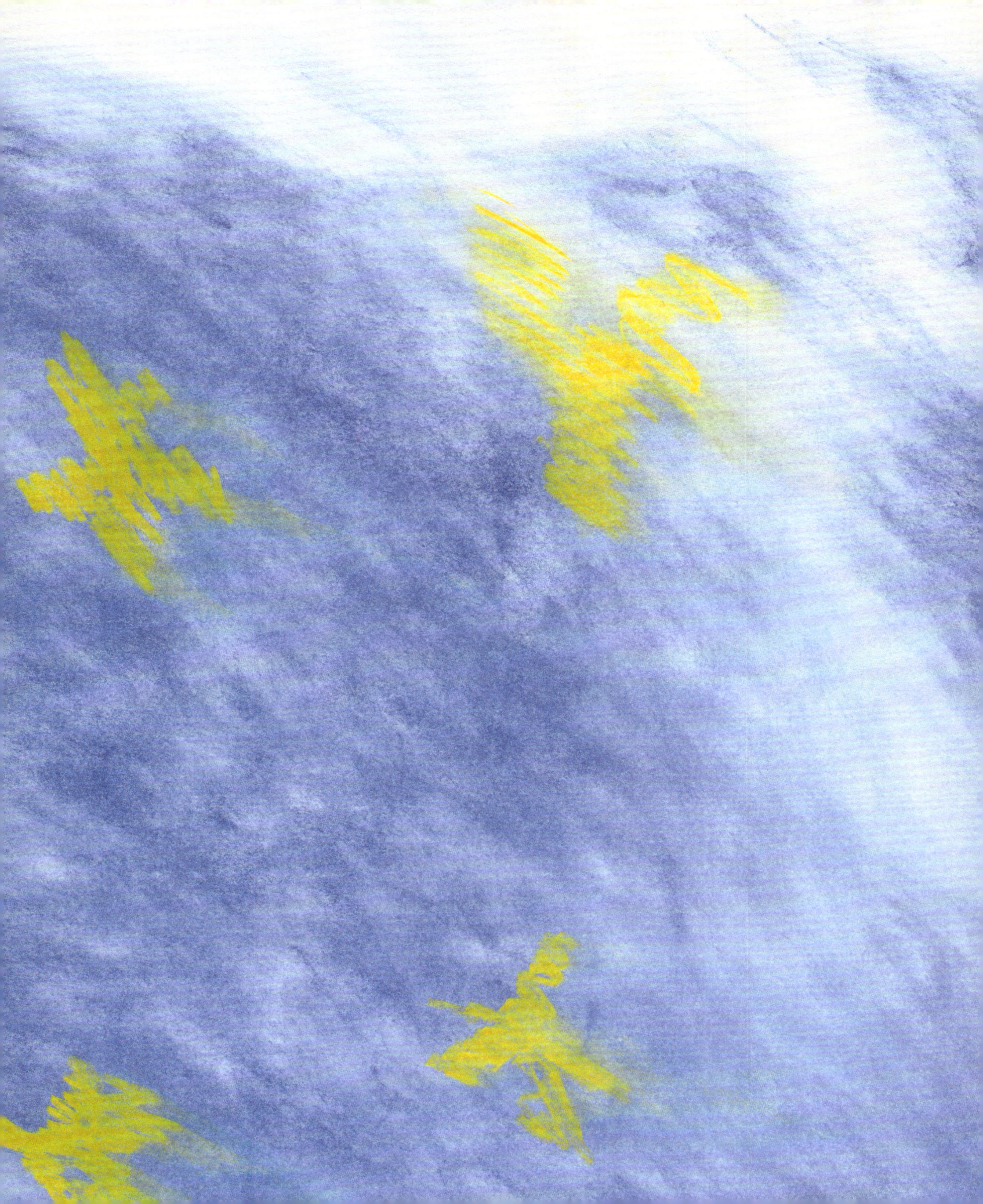

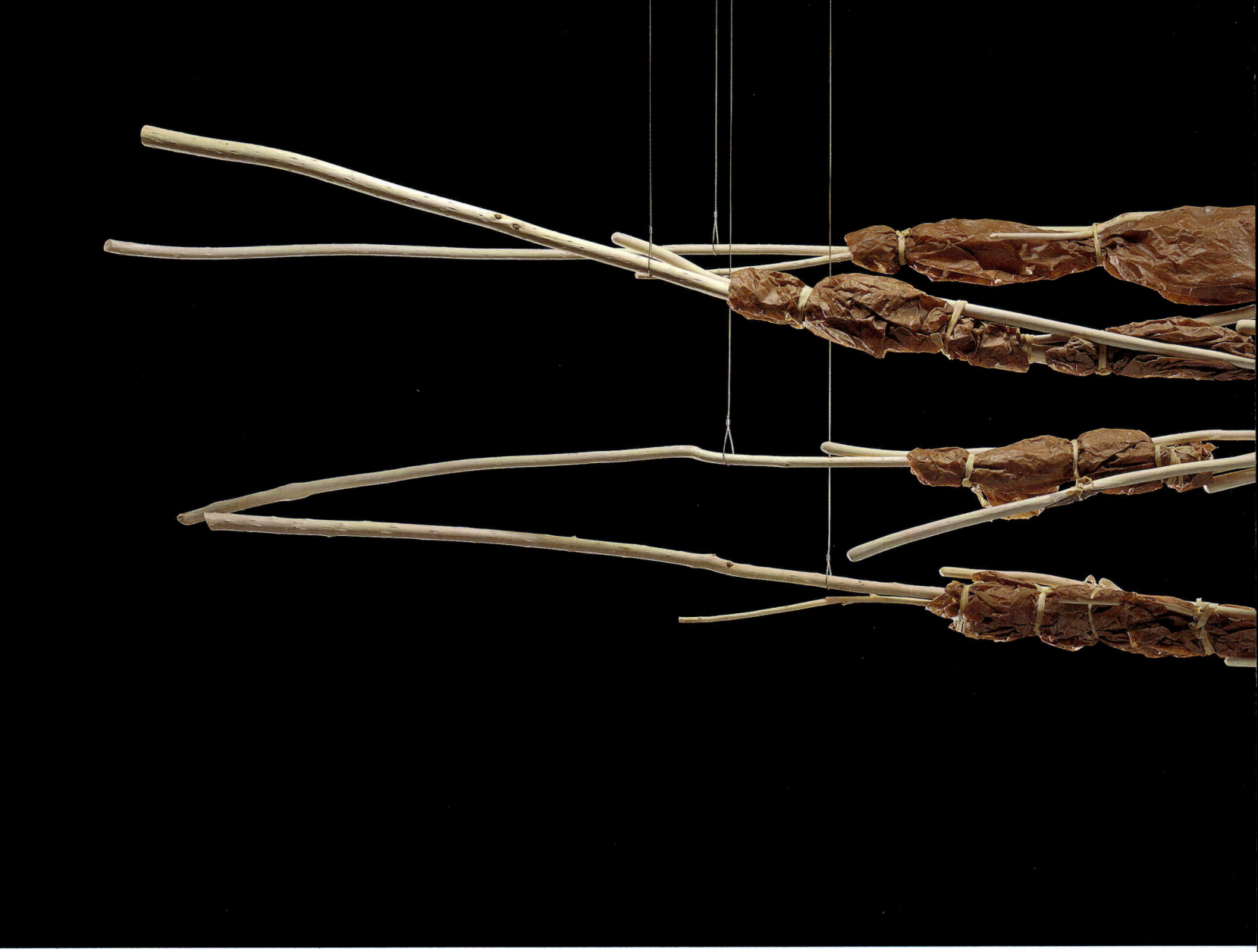

2. *Wa-Du-Sheh (Bundle)*, 1996. Peeled willow saplings, paper, wax, leather, 24 x 18 x 3 ft. National Museum of the American Indian 26/7724

Lowe made *Wa-Du-Sheh* in response to his experience of visiting an excavated ancestral mound site. He also drew on memories of his mother wrapping her belongings in a blanket in preparation for a journey. The sculpture employs the form of a bundle to address the care with which we protect the things—both tangible and intangible—that we value, carry with us, and pass on to future generations.

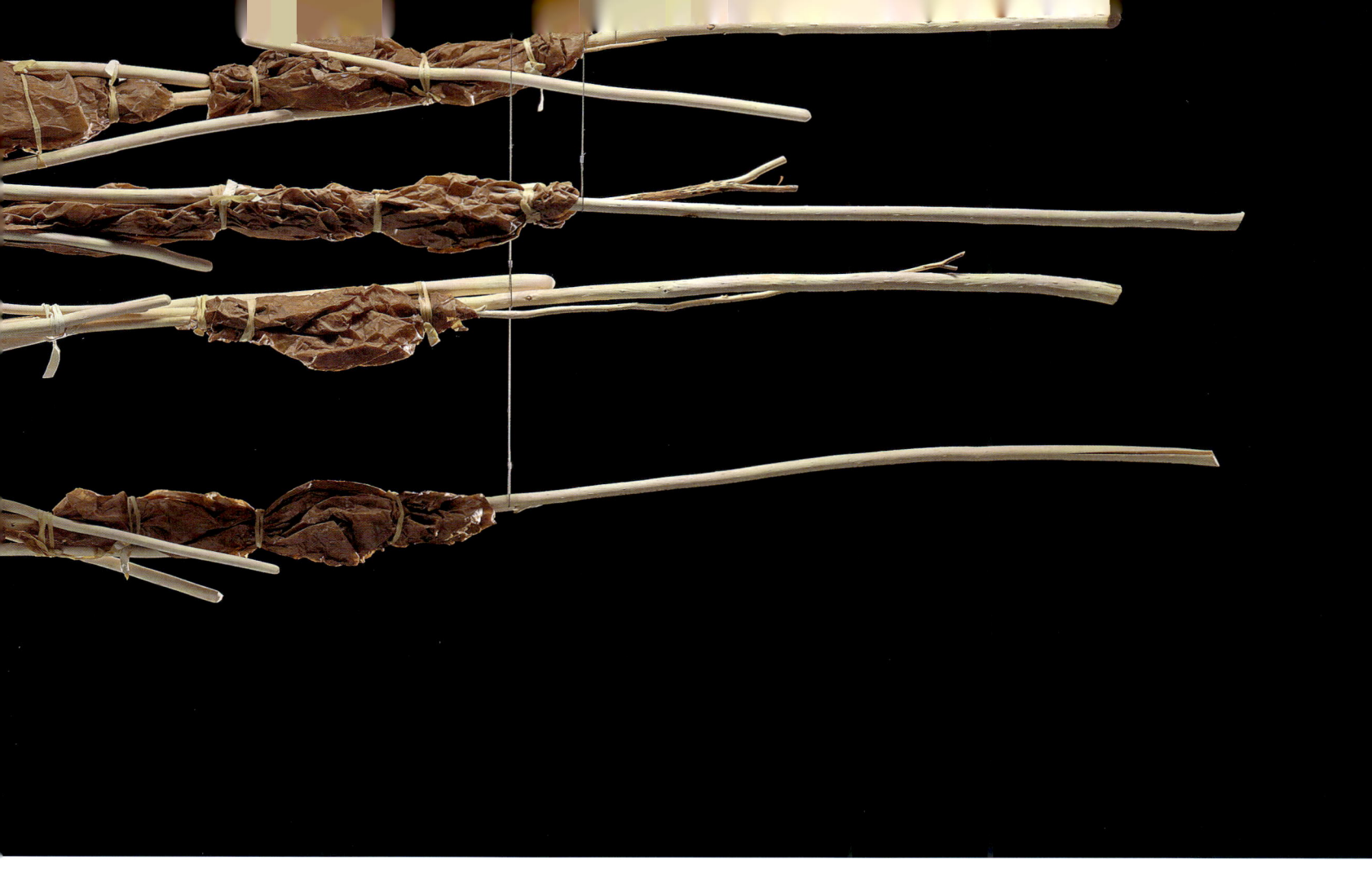

BEFORE I KNEW HIM as an influential educator and masterful artist, Truman Lowe was my mentor. When I joined the staff of the National Museum of the American Indian in 2000 as an assistant curator, it was on the rising tide of creative cultural energy that four years later would open the doors to a museum vastly different in philosophy and vision than any that had yet existed.

As a junior curator, I had the honor to work with Truman at the time he was developing *Native Modernism*, the inaugural art exhibition featuring the contemporary artwork of Allan Houser (Chiricahua Apache, 1914–94) and George Morrison (Grand Portage Ojibwe, 1919–2000), for which he was the curator. His curatorial style, like his aesthetic and even his personality, conveyed balance, calm, and serenity. In *Native Modernism* he created an immersive space, a Native space that gave voice to the artists and presence to each sculpture and painting.

Concurrently, in our Lower Manhattan location, Truman curated a complementary exhibition entitled *Continuum: 12 Artists* (2003–05), during which the museum's west gallery hosted the artists' work in pairs of solo shows. Representing the next generation of Indigenous contemporary artists, all twelve were influenced by Morrison or Houser through the elder artists' careers as creators or as educators, yet were themselves groundbreaking in their work.

While one exhibition featured key modern artists who influenced those who followed—and was the first to feature Native contemporary art on the National Mall—the other lifted younger Indigenous voices to the national stage.

Together, the two represented Truman Lowe's vision: that these two exhibitions set the framework for the National Museum of the American Indian's leading role in advancing Native contemporary art in all its diversity, continuity, and growth.

Truman was consistent in both life and in art. Like Morrison, who also called the northern woodlands home, Truman remained connected to his community and homelands. Staying true to his vision, he did not feed or bow to artistic pressures or stereotypes; his works of art were personal and full of meaning. Within his sculptures and drawings he honored Hoocąk materials and traditions of his family and community, yet also experimented—which made space for others to do so as well. In his decades as a university art educator, Truman was known as kind, encouraging, and generous, influencing new generations to find confidence not only in the grounding their heritage provided, but also in the freedom that innovation and creativity could afford. He provided the same guidance and support to me as a new curator and for that I will forever be grateful as it helped me grow as a museum professional.

Emblematic of his philosophy were the many stories he told about *Wa-Du-Sheh (Bundle)*, his 1996 installation of suspended bundles made from willow, leather, and paper (fig. 2). Of the varied inspirations for this work—from an experience at ancestral earth mounds to a memory of his mother packing travel items in a bundle rather than a suitcase—each represents the ways we protect and care for important things. Sharing knowledge and creating opportunities for others have become Truman's enduring legacy.

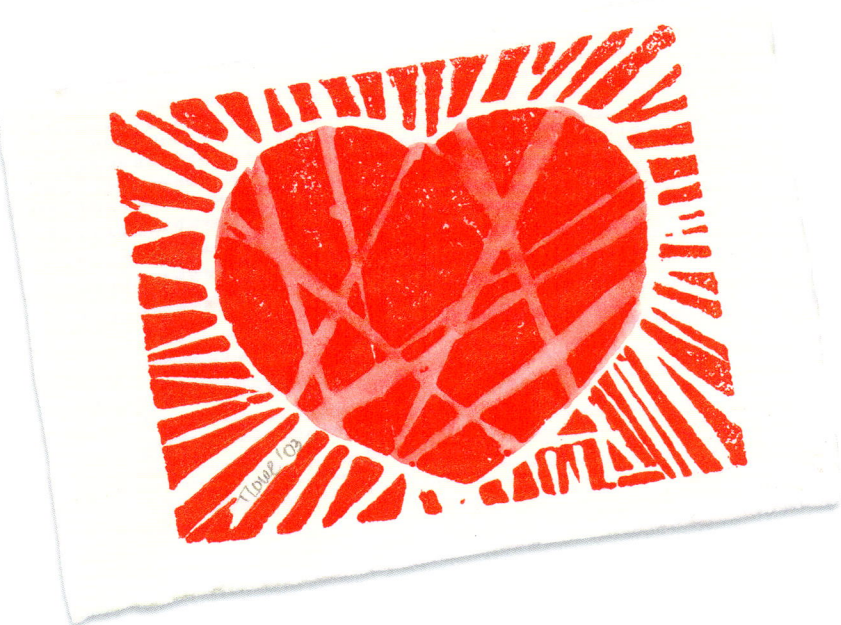

3. Lowe created this valentine in 2003 as a gift to colleagues at the National Museum of the American Indian.

When I became the director of the National Museum of the American Indian in 2022, I chose an untitled work from Truman's *Artifact Series* to share space in my office to acknowledge his impact on the museum (fig. 42). For myself and others, his presence as a mentor has endured beyond his passing in 2019. When I walk through the halls of the museum's Cultural Resources Center in Suitland, Maryland, I still see the valentines that Truman created and gifted to staff members hanging on office walls; the valentines remain treasured representations of his artistry and generosity, made each year in a different style and material (fig. 3).

In *Water's Edge: The Art of Truman Lowe* we honor not only a master sculptor, an influential teacher, and an innovative curator, but also a respected and beloved member of our museum's community. Rebecca Head Trautmann, general editor of the catalog as well as the exhibition's curator, has assembled in *Water's Edge* scholars and artists who testify to Truman's impact on the field of Native contemporary art. This first major retrospective exhibition of his work brings together nearly fifty sculptures, paintings, and drawings to tell a comprehensive story of his art and influence. The museum is proud to include in our collections so many of Truman's artworks; twenty-eight of them will be on display in the gallery and more featured in the catalog. We deeply appreciate the collaboration and generosity of Nancy and Tonia Lowe, Truman's wife and daughter, to the project. The involvement of family has amplified Truman's presence, provided important insight into his life and work, and expanded the range of artworks featured. To ensure the Hoocąk *hoit'e* (Ho-Chunk language) in this volume is respected, we give thanks to eminent speaker Wilbert Cleveland and the Hoocąk Waazijaci Language Division for their generous expertise. We further extend our gratitude to the institutions and individuals who lent their works for *Water's Edge*, and the generous donors providing critical support to our success, led by Bank of America, furthered by the Henry Luce Foundation, with generous support from the Terra Foundation for American Art and Ameriprise Financial.

CYNTHIA CHAVEZ LAMAR

(San Felipe Pueblo/Hopi/Tewa/Navajo)

Director, Smithsonian's National Museum of the American Indian

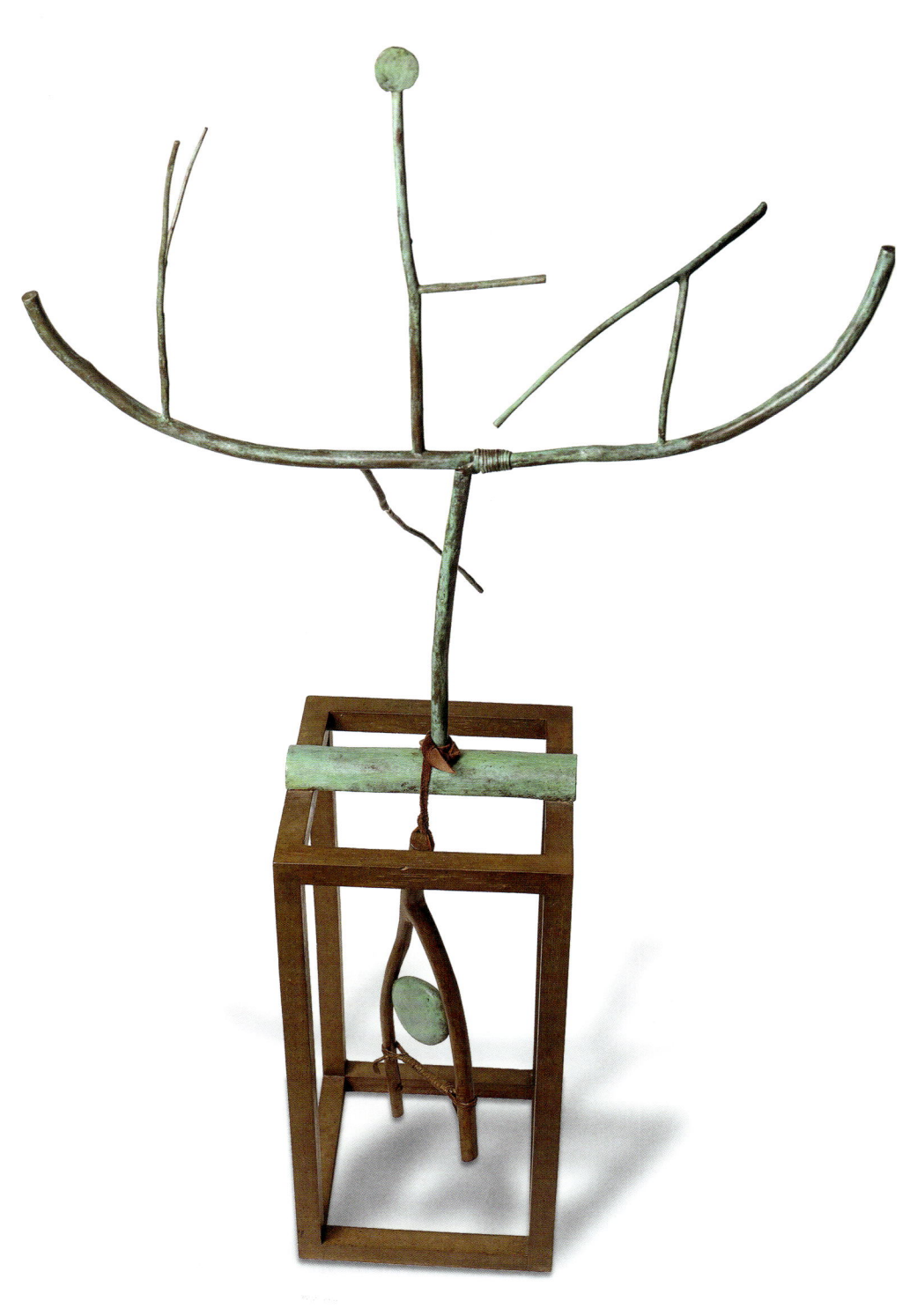

4. *Mnemonic Canoe*, 1989. Bronze and rawhide, 36 x 19 ½ x 12 ¾ in. Chazen Museum of Art,
University of Wisconsin–Madison, Frank R. Horlbeck Endowment Fund purchase, 2020.44.2a-b

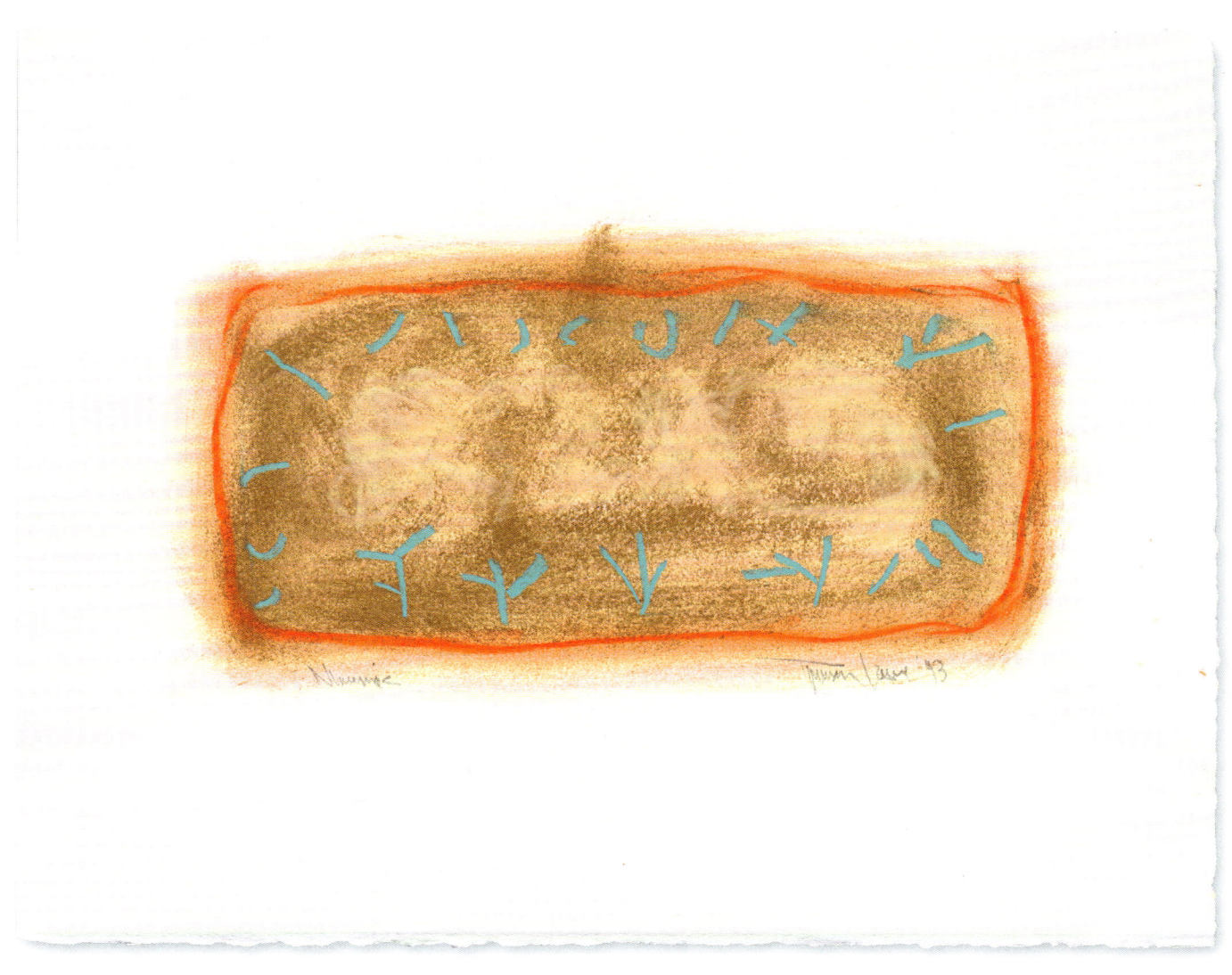

5. *Mnemonic*, 1993. Brushed powdered pigment and pastel on paper, 11 x 14 in. National Museum of the American Indian 27/626

Lowe was interested in mnemonic devices, including objects known as prescription sticks made by the Potawatomi and other Indigenous peoples of the Great Lakes region in the mid-nineteenth century. Prescription sticks are flat, rectangular pieces of wood incised with pictographic symbols around their edges to indicate plants used in preparing medicinal compounds. Made at a time when Native people were being driven from their homelands and the resources they had relied upon for generations, these objects intrigued Lowe in their roles as vessels of knowledge and memory.

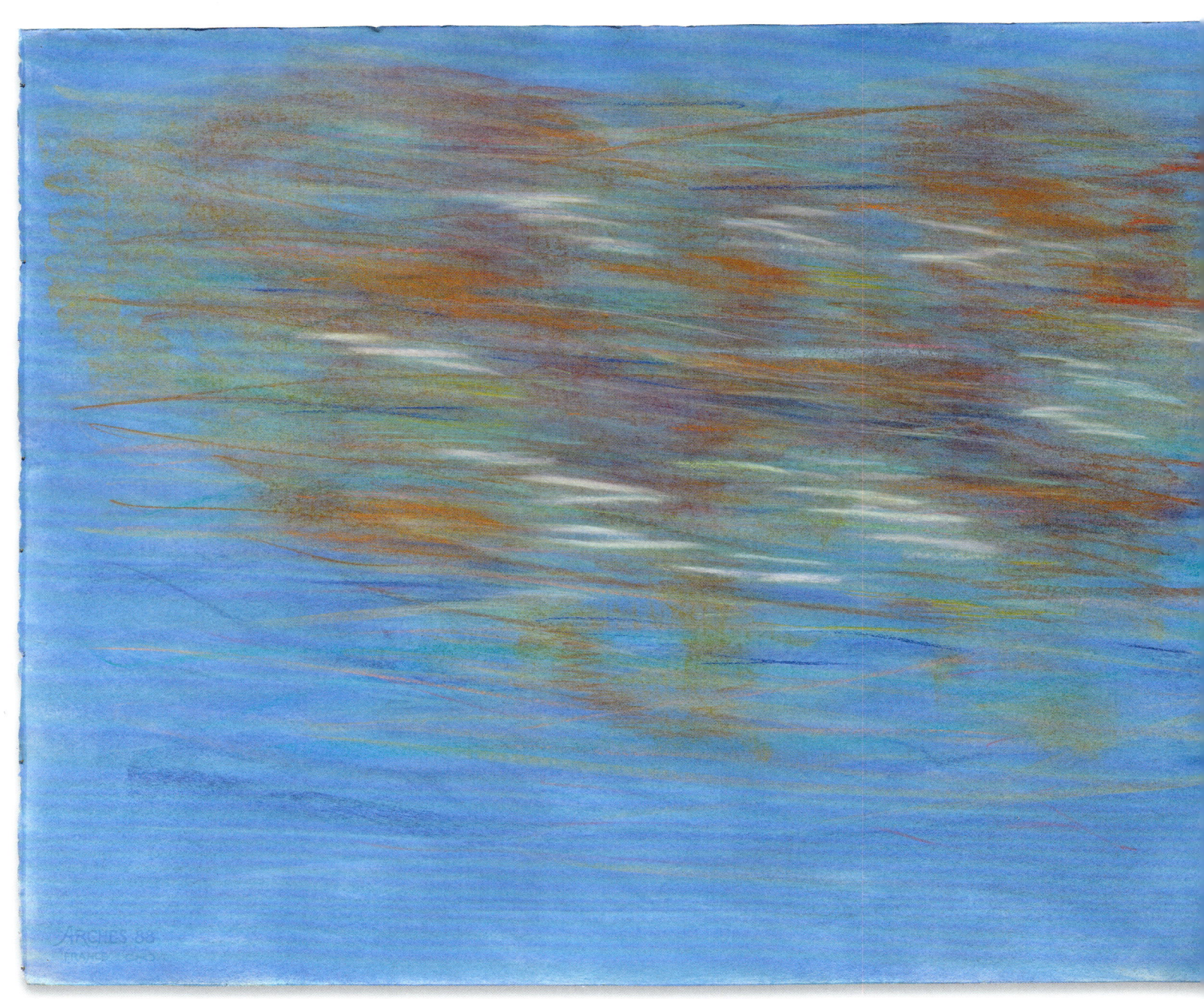

6. Untitled, 1996. Brushed powdered pigment and pastel on paper, 30 ¼ x 79 ½ in. National Museum of the American Indian 27/611

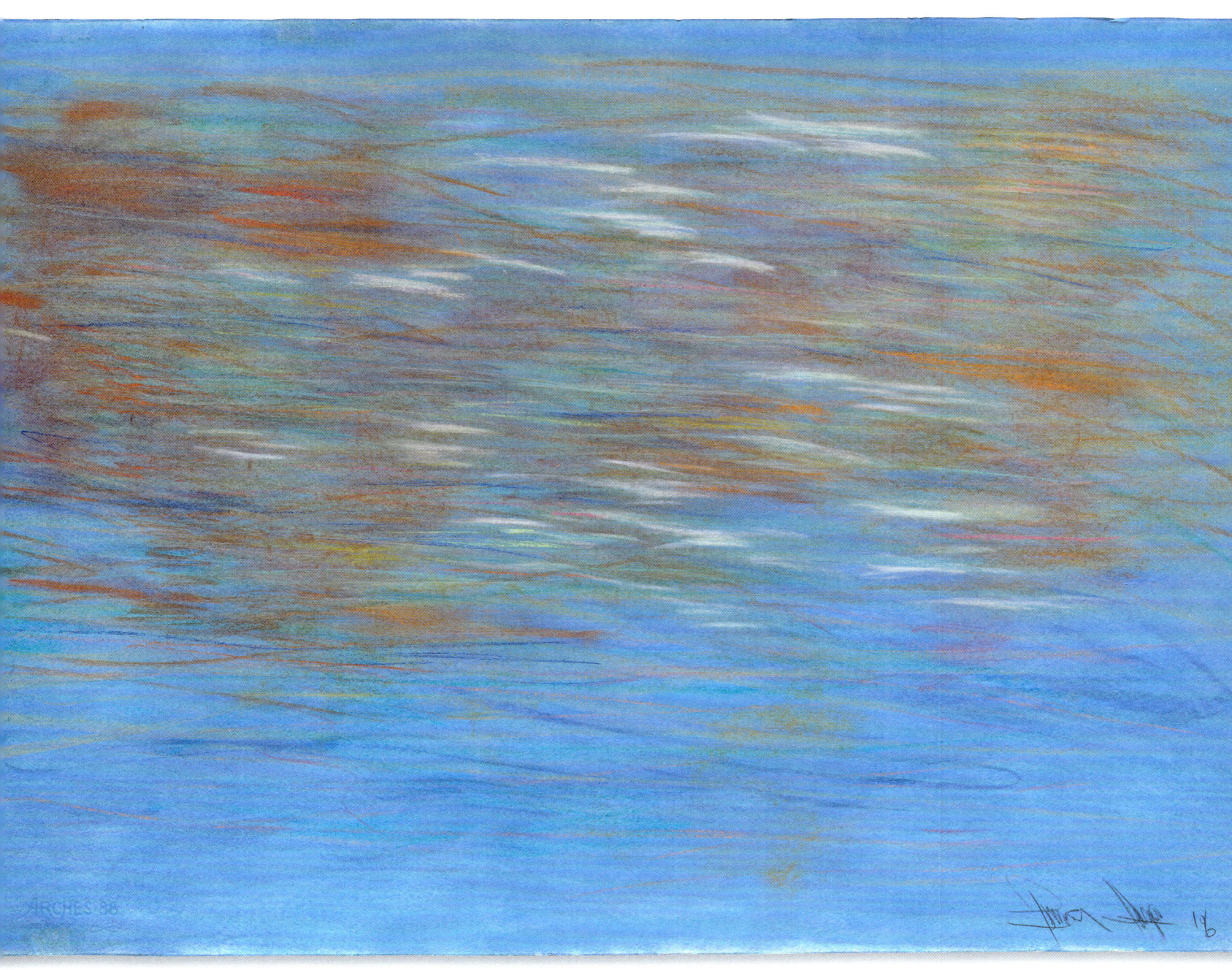

ARCHES 88

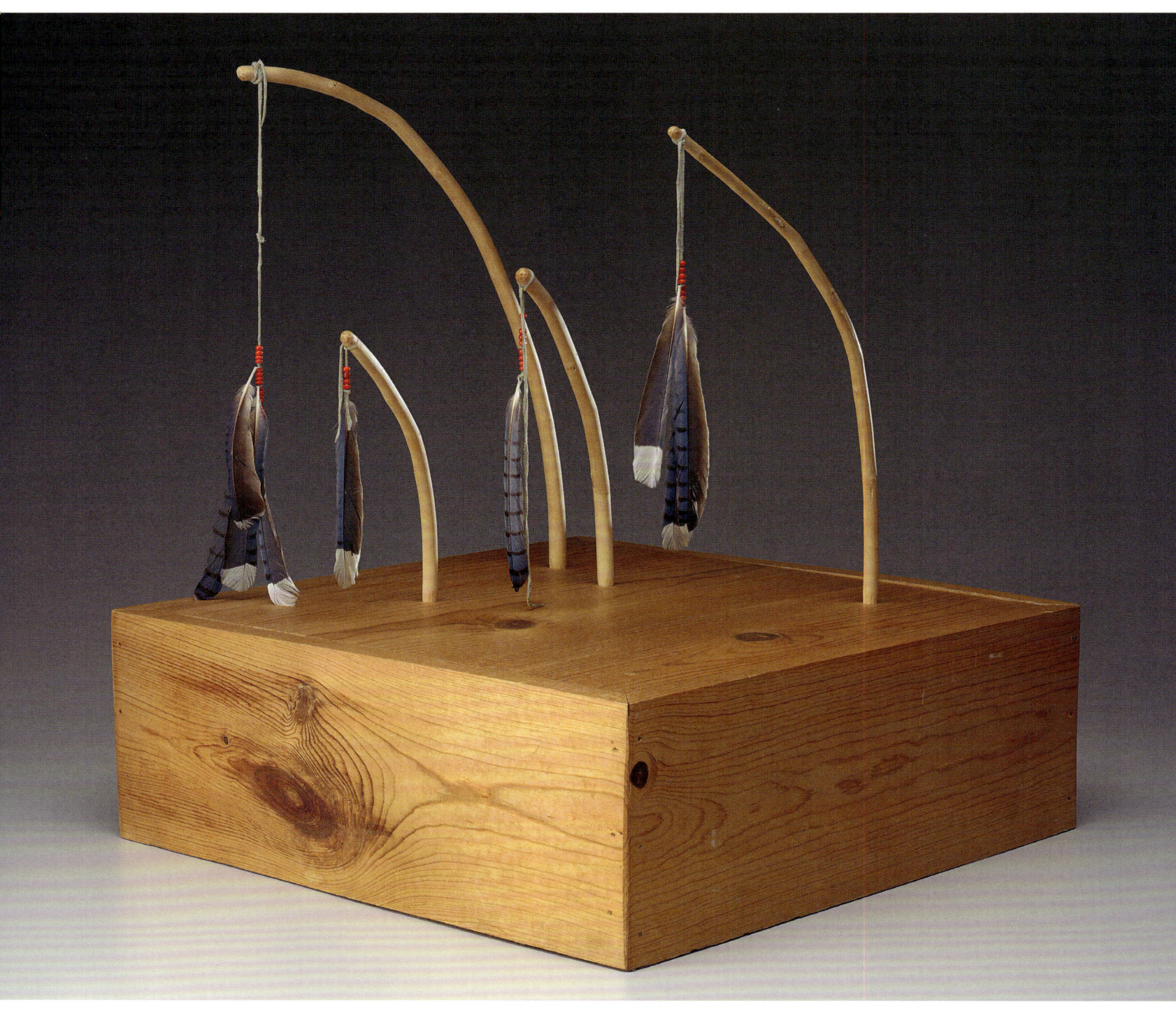

7. *Mimi*, 1979. Pine, peeled willow sticks, blue jay feathers, leather, glass beads, 18 x 16 x 16 in. National Museum of the American Indian 26/9773, gift of John and Meryl Lipton Lavine

Lowe made *Mimi* as a gift for dear friends. The sculpture, which resembles plants growing in a marsh, includes blue jay feathers gathered from around his bird feeder. Willow branches, feathers, and small red beads repeat in groups of four, a meaningful number in Hoocąk cosmology. As Lowe has explained, things that happen in fours are considered to have permanence and significance.

Rebecca Head Trautmann

"If I have a signature, it is the willows on the water's edge."

— TRUMAN LOWE, 1991

BEST KNOWN FOR HIS ELEGANT, minimalist sculptures of willow saplings, feathers, and other organic materials evoking woodland rivers and streams, canoes, dwellings, and imagined artifacts, Truman Lowe created a rich body of work that includes sculptures in aluminum and bronze as well as sensitively rendered drawings in pastels and charcoal on paper. Lowe's artistic independence, his work's deep connection to his woodland home and his Hoocąk (Ho-Chunk) heritage, and his commitment to supporting Indigenous and non-Indigenous artists and scholars have made an enduring impact on the fields of American and Native North American art. At this extraordinary and long overdue moment when work by Indigenous contemporary artists is finally being recognized, collected, and exhibited, as it always should have been, alongside that of non-Indigenous peers (something Lowe worked for in his decades as an artist, educator, and curator), it is fitting to recognize his body of work and its lasting significance in a major retrospective exhibition and catalog.

Raised at the Indian Mission near Black River Falls, Wisconsin, Lowe spent his childhood exploring the tributaries and streams of the Black River, gathering berries with his family, fishing, swimming, and using stones he found there as his first drawing materials. As an adult, he enjoyed recreational canoeing and gathered the riverine willow saplings that figure prominently in much of his work. These formative experiences contributed to a lifelong fascination with moving water. Lowe was intrigued by water's surface ripples and reflections, the hidden life and smooth, tumbled river stones within, and the relationship between the river and the land through which it

flows. Whether in his wood and metal sculptures or pastel and charcoal drawings, he frequently portrayed dramatic waterfalls, fast-moving rivers, quiet slivers of streams and marshes, and the plant life along their shores. The structural openness of his sculptures echoes the crisp, clear waters of a rock-bottom river.

An art-school-trained, cosmopolitan, contemporary artist who drew inspiration from the work of sculptors such as Constantin Brancusi (Romanian, 1876–1957), Henry Moore (British, 1896–1986), and George Morrison, Lowe remained closely connected to his cultural heritage. His sculptures and drawings reflect on the creative practices, stories, and knowledge of his Hoocąk community and family, and on human relationships to place, including the woodlands of the Great Lakes region. Canoes and other kinds of woodland structures held a particular interest for him, as did the many ancestral effigy mounds in the region.

Willow saplings were a favorite sculptural material for Lowe. "I can use southern pine because its grain and aging resins give me the sense of a breeze crossing water, that refractive or reflective texture," Lowe stated. "The reeds and willow wands are like the plants, weeds and rice, that grow out of a marsh or stream's banks. If I have a signature, it is the willows on the water's edge."[1] He appreciated their pliability when the bark was peeled away just after harvesting. The flexible stalks could then be bent into desired forms and would hold these shapes when they dried. The lightness and brightness of the interior wood appealed to him as well, as did the dark, winding trails left by burrowing insects. Willows are readily available,

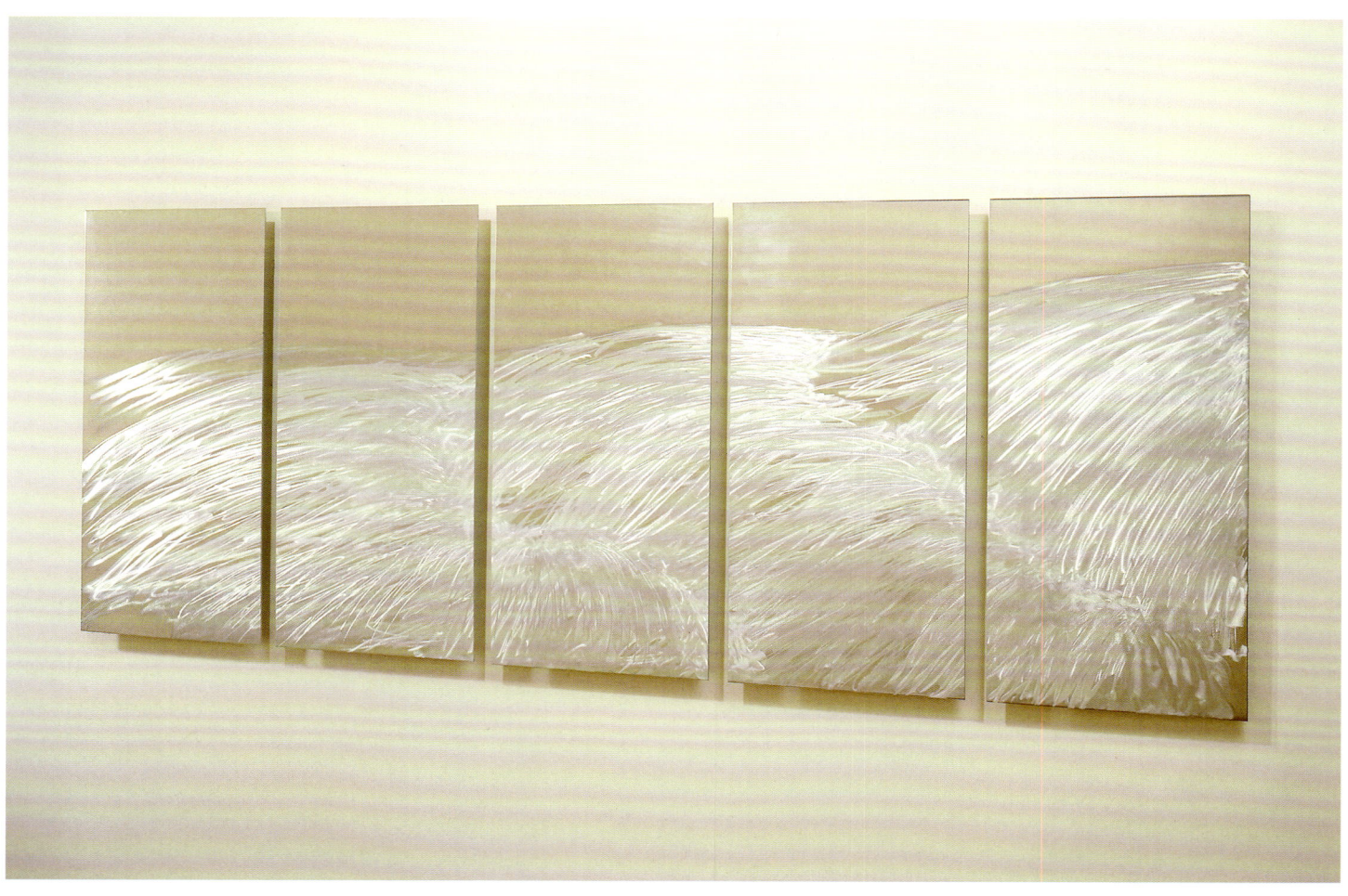

8. *Wána (Cascade)*, 2002. Aluminum, 48 x 128 x 1 ⅝ in. Northwestern University, Kellogg School of Management

frequently considered a nuisance plant, and have a deep-rooted connection to the rivers along whose banks they grow. When people marveled at his ability to transform solid wood into water, Lowe replied that the wood *is* water, describing the way liquid streamed out of willow saplings when he peeled them. His use of wood as his primary material was a link to the woodland home of his youth and his father's and community's deep understanding of wood and its properties.

Water's Edge: The Art of Truman Lowe is organized around four intersecting themes that Lowe explored and returned to throughout his career, currents that also ripple through the artworks and essays in this book: moving water, landscape and place, woodland structures, and memory and shared knowledge.

MOVING WATER

Lowe was captivated by moving water and returned to it again and again in his artwork, depicting rushing rivers, cascading waterfalls, slow-moving streams, and marshy wetlands. He viewed a river as a metaphor for life, experience, and the passage of time. He often spoke about water's importance and his concern with protecting it. In striking works in pastel on paper, Lowe portrayed the glimmering reflections and changing colors on a river's surface (fig. 6). His *Waterfall* sculptures (figs. 31, 38, 58, and 104) and the brushed aluminum work *Wána (Cascade)* (fig. 8) suggest the sometimes chaotic tumble of a river's rapids and falls. *Watermound* (fig. 10) and *Ne Pu Saka (Sand on Water)* (fig. 103) explore the ways a river's shifting course reshapes

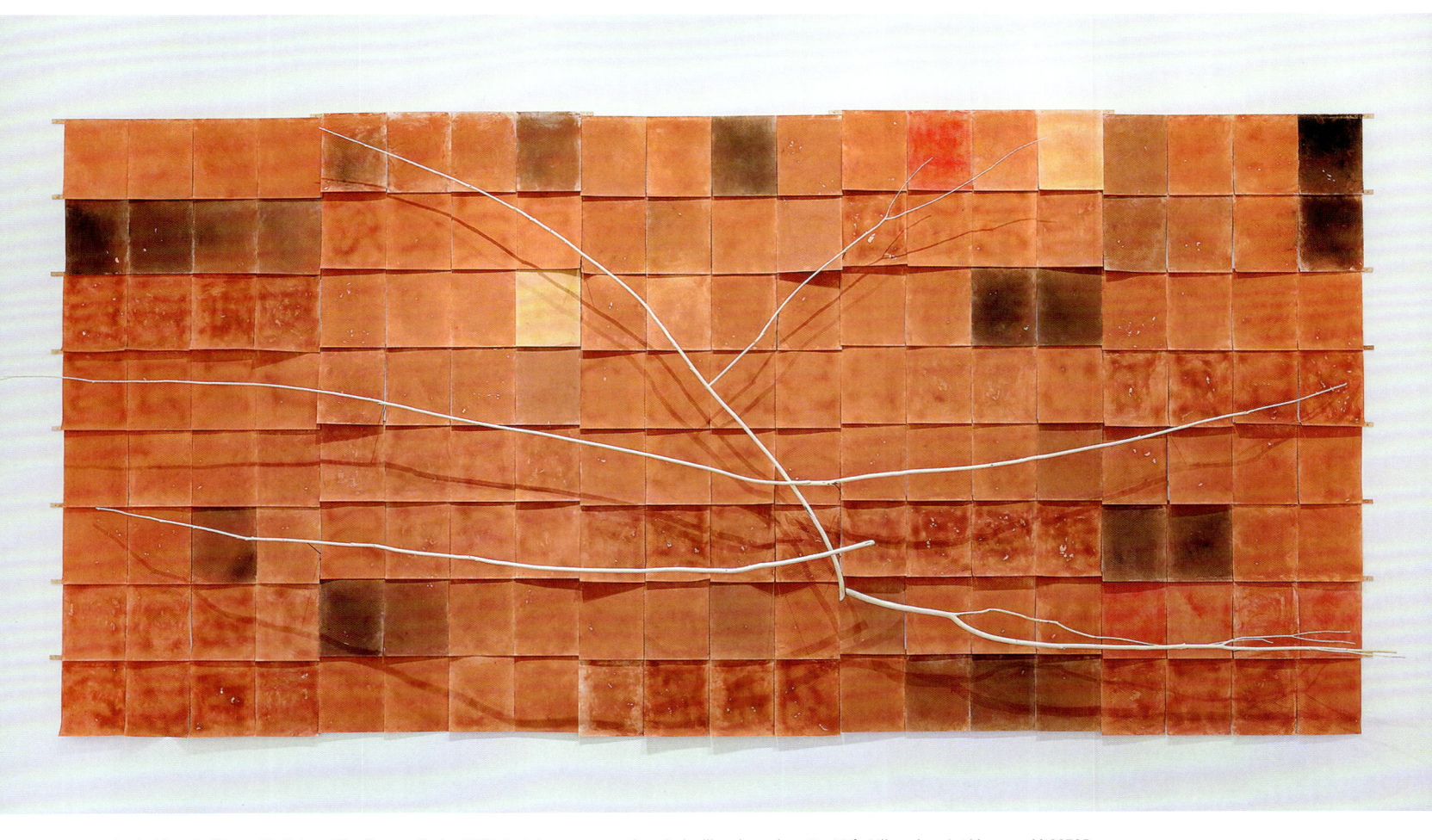

9. *Inni-chi-ru-he (Stone Wall)*, from *The Canyon Series*, 1995. Pastel on paper and peeled willow branches, 8 x 23 ft. Milwaukee Art Museum M1997.25

the earth and sand of its banks, while evoking the movement of earth into effigy mounds by ancestral Woodland peoples. Lowe's meditations on the qualities and movement of water afforded him a seemingly limitless source of inspiration.

LANDSCAPE AND PLACE

Lowe's sense of place and of home was informed by his youth in the Wisconsin woodlands, in the Hoocąk community near the town of Black River Falls, but also by stories he heard when visiting his mother's relatives in Nebraska about Hoocąk people's forced removal from and return to their homeland in Wisconsin. He spoke about the impact of his own movement away and back again, writing in a

1995 artist statement, "The landscape of the woodlands continues to be the source of my work."[2]

While works such as *Totem for Henu (First Daughter)* and *Totem for Kunu (First Son)* draw visually and conceptually on that forested landscape, others such as *Inni-chi-ru-he (Stone Wall)* (fig. 9) and *Ottawa* (fig. 38), respectively, respond to the dramatic red-walled canyons of the southwest and the confluence of three rivers—historically an important trade site for Native peoples—around which the Canadian capital was established. In other works, like the monumental sculpture *Red Banks* (fig. 67), named for the origin site of the Hoocąk people, he responded to the history and stories embedded in places in a symbolic rather than literal way. Lowe was also interested in marks left on the land by ancestral Indigenous people, including the many effigy mounds in and around Wisconsin and the art painted and carved on rock walls there and beyond.

WOODLAND STRUCTURES

As an art student at the University of Wisconsin in both La Crosse and Madison, Lowe experimented with then-current synthetic materials including plastics and resins. After completing his master of fine arts degree, he reevaluated his direction. While he saw themes in his work that he wished to continue, he became interested in working with readily available, natural materials, saying, "My father's use, respect, and knowledge of wood became my own quest and primary direction. My mother's work with color, beads, and ribbons also found their place in my work. I discovered what I wanted to do: use those natural forms and materials reflecting where I grew up."[3]

Lowe was interested in the traditional dwellings and other ingenious constructions Hoocąk and neighboring Woodland peoples made from wood. He particularly admired what he considered to be the ideal architecture of a canoe, which he observed had changed very little over time. He made abstracted canoe forms of willow branches, some filled with feathers, and at times suspended overhead. He constructed the domed frameworks of *ciiporok'e* (or wigwams, as he sometimes referred to them) from willow saplings and steel and created a series of invented artifacts using wood, feathers, and stones. His parents' black ash splint-plait basketry was a source of inspiration as well.

MEMORY AND SHARED KNOWLEDGE

Lastly, Lowe was intrigued by mnemonic devices, or the ways in which knowledge is given physical form or expression and is encoded, preserved, and communicated. These included items known as prescription sticks—flat, rectangular pieces of wood incised with pictographic plant forms to record botanical knowledge and medicinal formulas—made primarily by Potawatomi people in the mid- to late-nineteenth century, a time when they and other Indigenous peoples were being forcibly removed

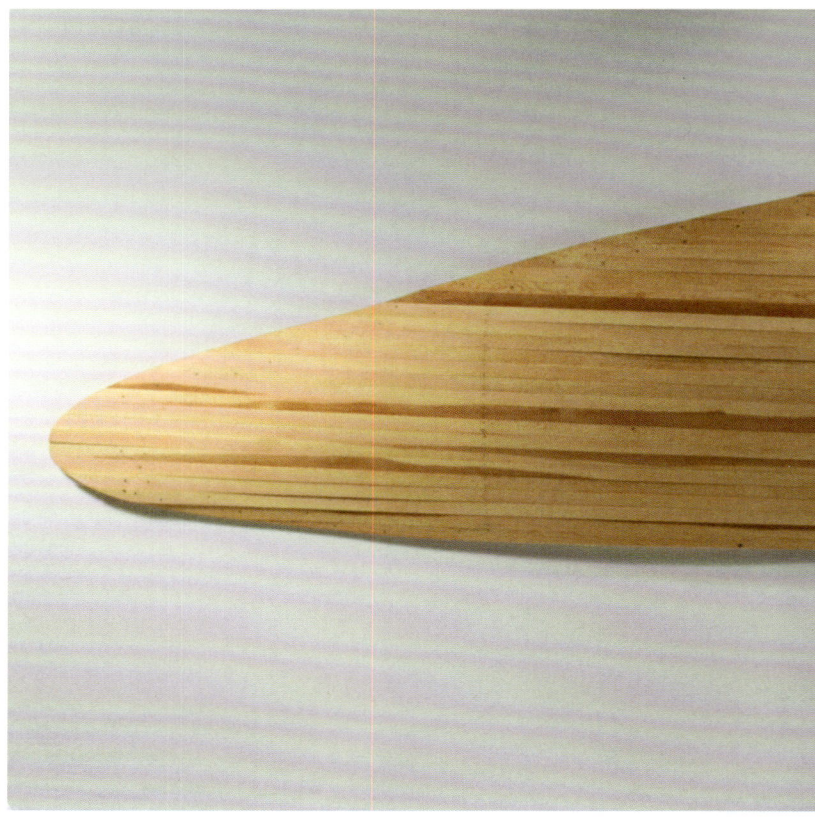

from their homelands and the natural resources they had relied upon for generations. In his *Mnemonic* series of drawings and sculptures, Lowe contemplated these tools and their makers' determination to sustain their cultural knowledge and heritage (figs. 1, 5, 54, and 55).

Lowe's exploration of memory and knowledge extended to his interest in family stories and cultural histories, the Hoocąk moiety and clan structure, and Hoocąk language and cosmology. In his sculpture *Wa-Du-Sheh (Bundle)* (fig. 2), made of simple materials—willow saplings, crumpled paper, wax, and strips of leather—Lowe meditates on the ways we protect and care for the things, both tangible and intangible, that we value and want to preserve for future generations.

Water's Edge brings together multiple new perspectives on Truman Lowe and his work by scholars and artists who

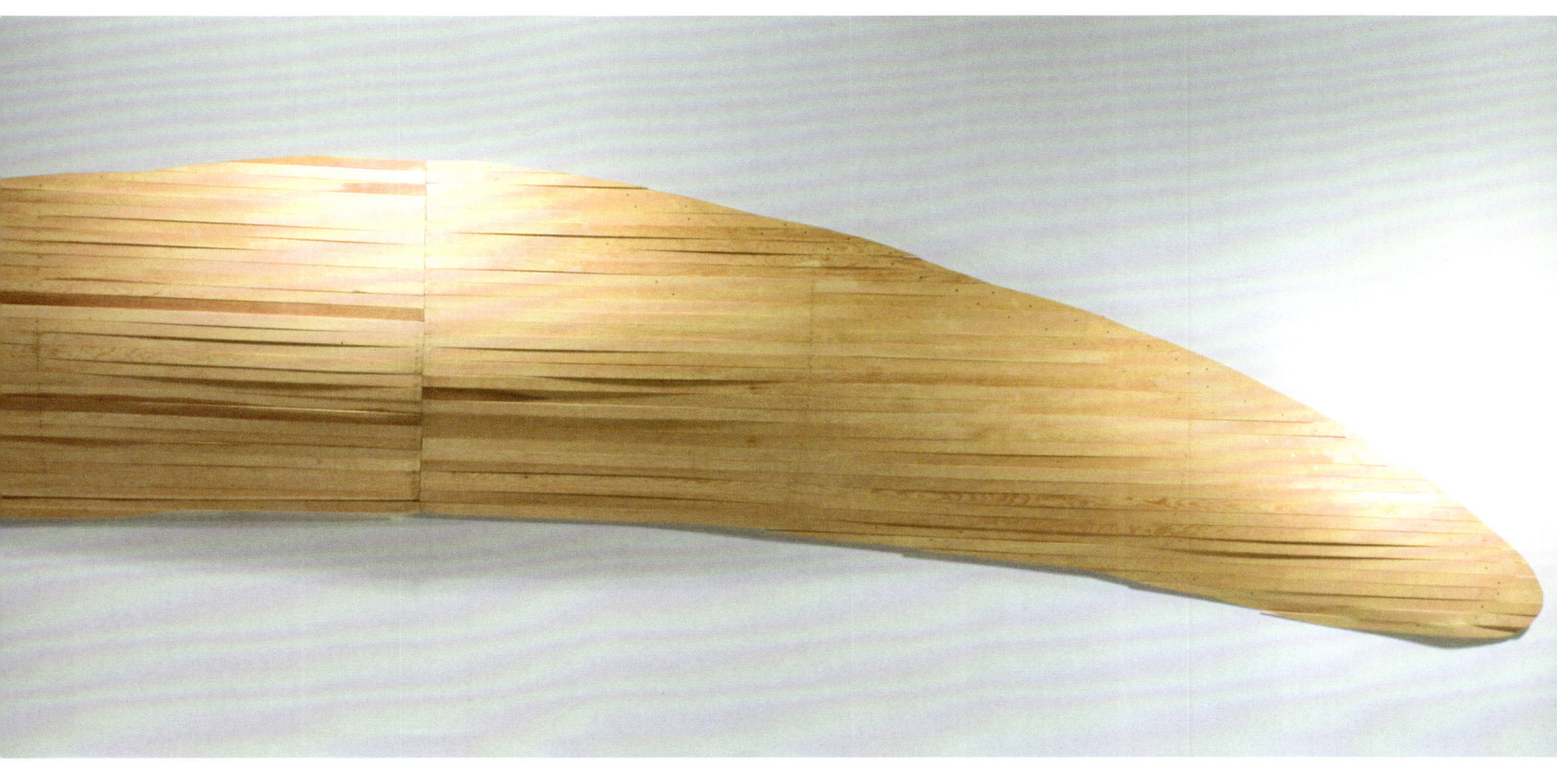

10. *Watermound*, 1993. Wood, 80 x 288 x 48 in. Eiteljorg Museum of American Indians and Western Art, Indianapolis, gift of Tonia Lowe 2007.3.1 A–B

have felt its impact. Their essays and reflections provide fresh insight on Lowe's art and its continued significance.

Art historian Jo Ortel has written extensively about Lowe's work. Her 2003 monograph *Woodland Reflections: The Art of Truman Lowe* provides a foundation on which this publication's new scholarship builds. For *Water's Edge*, Ortel traces Lowe's life and career, from his birth and upbringing near Black River Falls through his art education and development of his personal style, his thirty-five years teaching at the University of Wisconsin–Madison, and his influential work as the National Museum of the American Indian's first curator of contemporary art.

Next, David Penney reflects on his encounter with Lowe's work as a young curator at the Detroit Institute of Arts (DIA) in the early 1980s. Discussing works Lowe created for the DIA and his early *Artifact Series*, Penney describes how Lowe's highly original, improvisational approach to his work, using unexpected, ephemeral materials, confounded many viewers at the time who had never seen anything like it.

Scholar Amy Lonetree (Hoocąk) provides an overview of Hoocąk people's history, particularly their repeated removal from and determined return to their homeland in the place now known as Wisconsin. She addresses their resilience and the deep ties that bind them to their ancestral home. Her essay provides important historical context not only for Lowe's work, which is so deeply connected to the Wisconsin woodlands and to Hoocąk cultural knowledge, but for his own family as well.

With a focus on Lowe's less-known pastel and charcoal drawings, including several exhibited and published here for the first time, art historian and curator Kendra

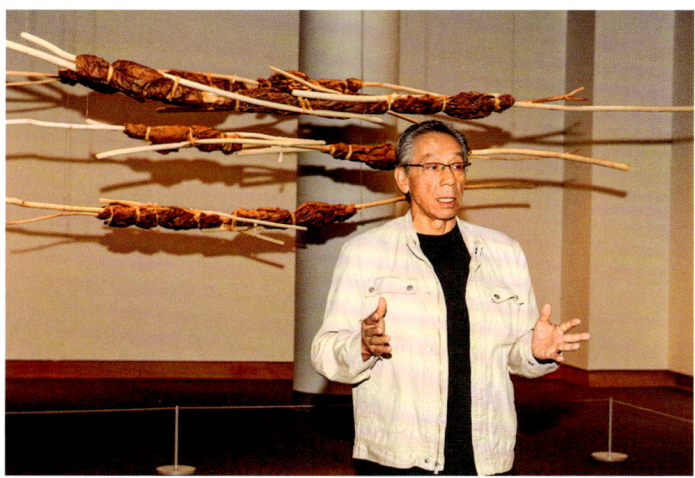

11. Truman Lowe with *Wa-Du-Sheh (Bundle)* in the exhibition *Vantage Point: The Contemporary Native Art Collection* at the National Museum of the American Indian, 2010

Greendeer's (Hoocąk) thought-provoking essay posits the development of a Hoocąk color theory in Lowe's work, linking his use of color, particularly blues and greens, to the Hoocąk homeland and cultural ways of conceptualizing and describing colors.

Patricia Marroquin Norby (P'urhépecha descent), associate curator of Native American art at the Metropolitan Museum of Art, discusses several of Lowe's sculptures in relation to the ancestral earthen effigy mounds, waters, and skies of Teejop ("Four Lakes"), the area known today as Madison, Wisconsin. She closes with Lowe's 1993 *Feather Canoe* sculpture, recently added to the Met's collection, and its central place in the 2022 exhibition *Water Memories*.

At the Smithsonian American Art Museum (SAAM), curator Karen Lemmey considers four recently acquired works by Lowe in the context of SAAM's modern and contemporary sculpture collection, describing the ways they prompt a reconsideration of sculpture as landscape or portrait, and viewing them alongside works in wood by Louise Nevelson (American, 1899–1988) and Martin Puryear (American, b. 1941).

Paul Chaat Smith (Comanche) worked closely with Lowe on several ambitious exhibitions and projects at the National Museum of the American Indian. He describes

Lowe's curatorial work, particularly the influential 2004 exhibition at the new museum on the National Mall titled *Native Modernism: The Art of George Morrison and Allan Houser*, with an eye to the way it resisted what Smith describes as a then-rising essentialism in the discourse around Indigenous contemporary art.

I'm very grateful to seven distinguished artists—peers and successors to Lowe—who reflect on his work and its deep and lasting impact on their own. These include (in order of appearance in the book) Kay WalkingStick (Cherokee Nation, b. 1935), Sky Hopinka (Ho-Chunk Nation/Pechanga Band of Luiseño Indians, b. 1984), Joe Feddersen (Arrow Lakes/Okanagan, b. 1953) with Rachel Allen (Nimiipuu/Nez Perce), John Hitchcock (enrolled member of the Kiowa Tribe of Oklahoma/Comanche/European ancestry, b. 1967), Dyani White Hawk (Sičáŋǧu Lakota, b. 1976), Michael Belmore (Anishinaabe, b. 1971), and Andrea Reynosa (b. 1962). These artists' thoughtful, poignant contributions enrich our understanding of Lowe's transformational artistic legacy.

Finally, Lowe's daughter, Tonia Lowe (Hoocąk), offers a moving and personal afterword, describing the ways her father and the lessons he imparted have shaped her life and her own relationship with water, and how her family's love of canoeing together in rivers and lakes sustained them through devastating loss.

Lowe often spoke of rivers as allegories for time and life, of standing along a river and looking upstream to see what had come before and downstream to see what was yet to come: "We embody the benefits of previous generations' work and organization, and what we will contribute is still down the river."[4] As we look back at Lowe's art and career, we consider the impact of his life's work that is visible to us today and look forward to what the future holds.

Water's Edge could not have come into being without the contributions and support of numerous people. My deep appreciation goes first and foremost to Truman Lowe for the artwork that is the subject of both exhibition and book and for his mentorship, support, and friendship. My heartfelt thanks also go to the Lowe family, particularly Truman's wife, Nancy Lowe, and daughter Tonia for their

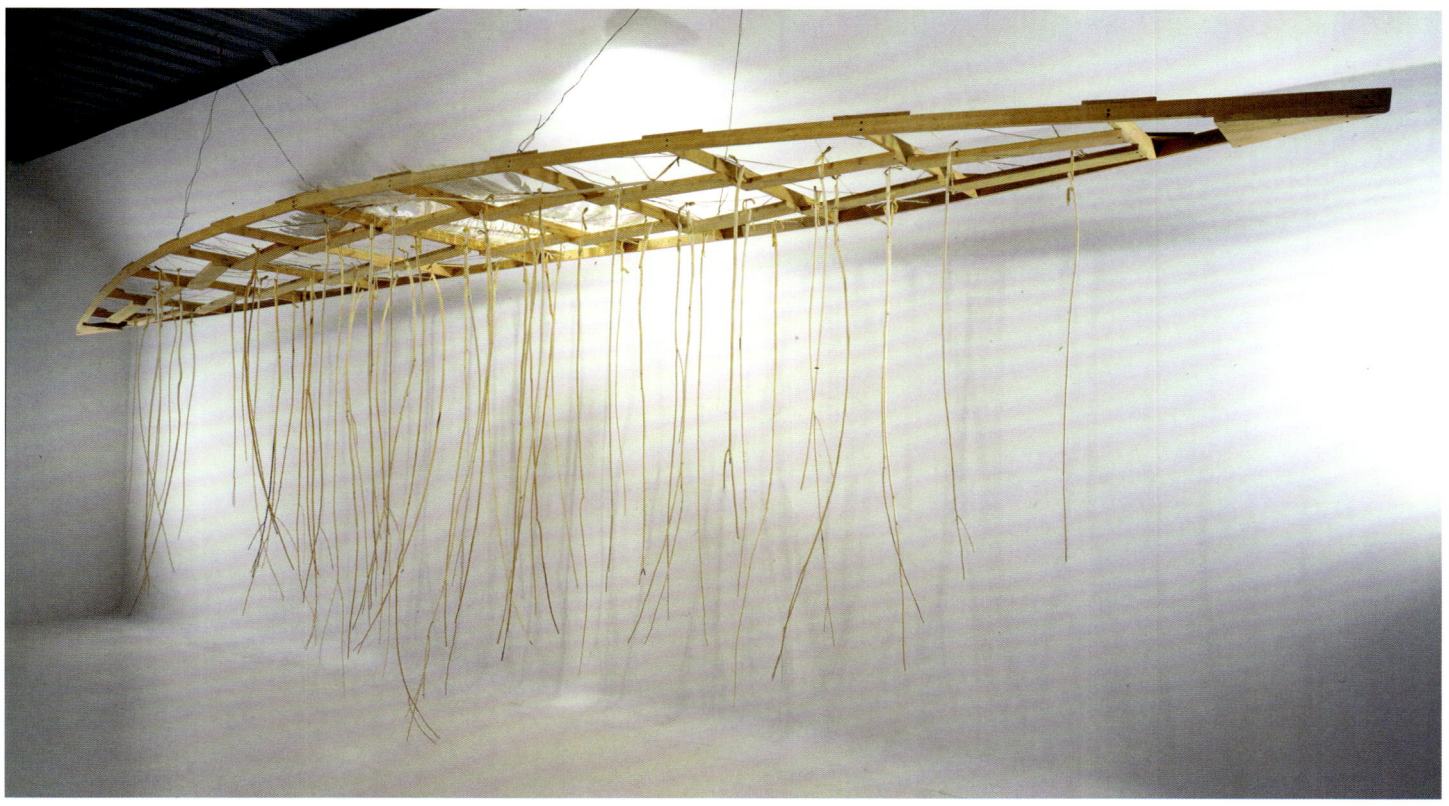

12. *Wach-Nee (Canoe Form)*, 1996, reworked 1999. Pine wood, twine, willow branches, leather, iron screws, 8 x 24 x 4 ft. Eiteljorg Museum of American Indians and Western Art 1999.6.1 A–B, museum purchase from the Eiteljorg Fellowship for Native American Fine Art

kindness, generosity, and warmth. Many thanks also to Jo Ortel, whose extensive writing and knowledge of Lowe's work have been invaluable resources, and who has advised in countless ways. I've so enjoyed and benefited from our many conversations over the years. Thank you to all of the brilliant contributors to the book and generous lenders to the exhibition, as well as to the talented and dedicated project and exhibition team. And finally, thank you to my family—my parents, David and Linda, my husband Drew and son Lukas—whose unconditional love and support have meant so much and made everything possible.

A note on language:

Truman Lowe's first language was Hoocąk (Ho-Chunk). Though he was not fluent as an adult, he often used the Hoocąk *hoit'e* (language) to title his artworks. Lowe consulted his older brother Chloris for guidance and used the phonetic spellings preferred at the time.

For *Water's Edge*, museum staff consulted with the Hoocąk Waazijaci Language Division of the Ho-Chunk Nation in Black River Falls, Wisconsin. Language speakers and instructors assisted us in ensuring that Hoocąk words are accurate and conform to their contemporary orthography. The museum is grateful for their expertise and generosity.

Hoocąk and Ho-Chunk are pronounced the same. Ho-Chunk is a phonetic spelling and remains the official name of the Ho-Chunk Nation. Hoocąk and other words in the language are written in the contemporary orthography.

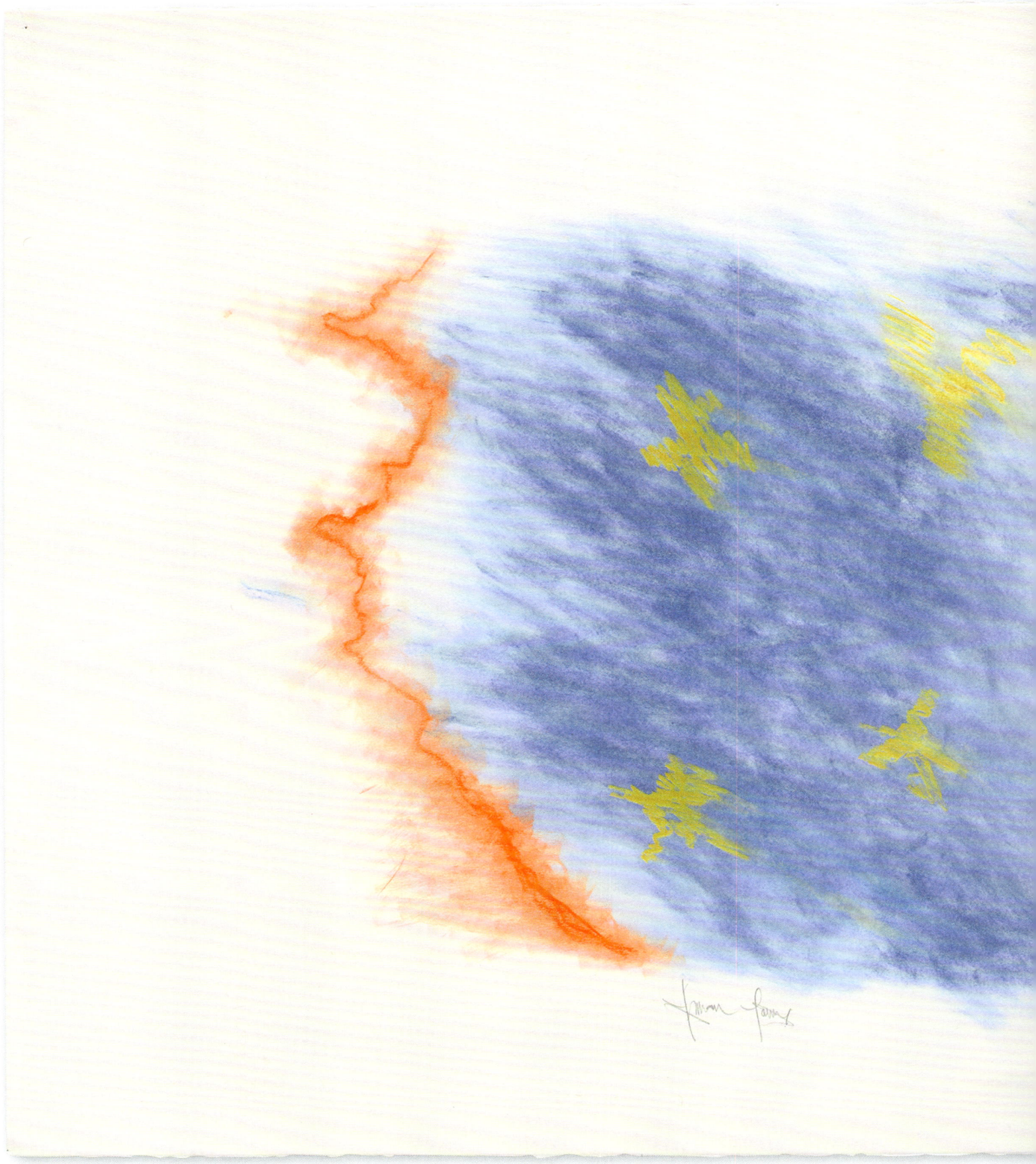

13. *Stars*, ca. 1985–90. Pastel on paper, 22 x 30 in.
National Museum of the American Indian 27/617

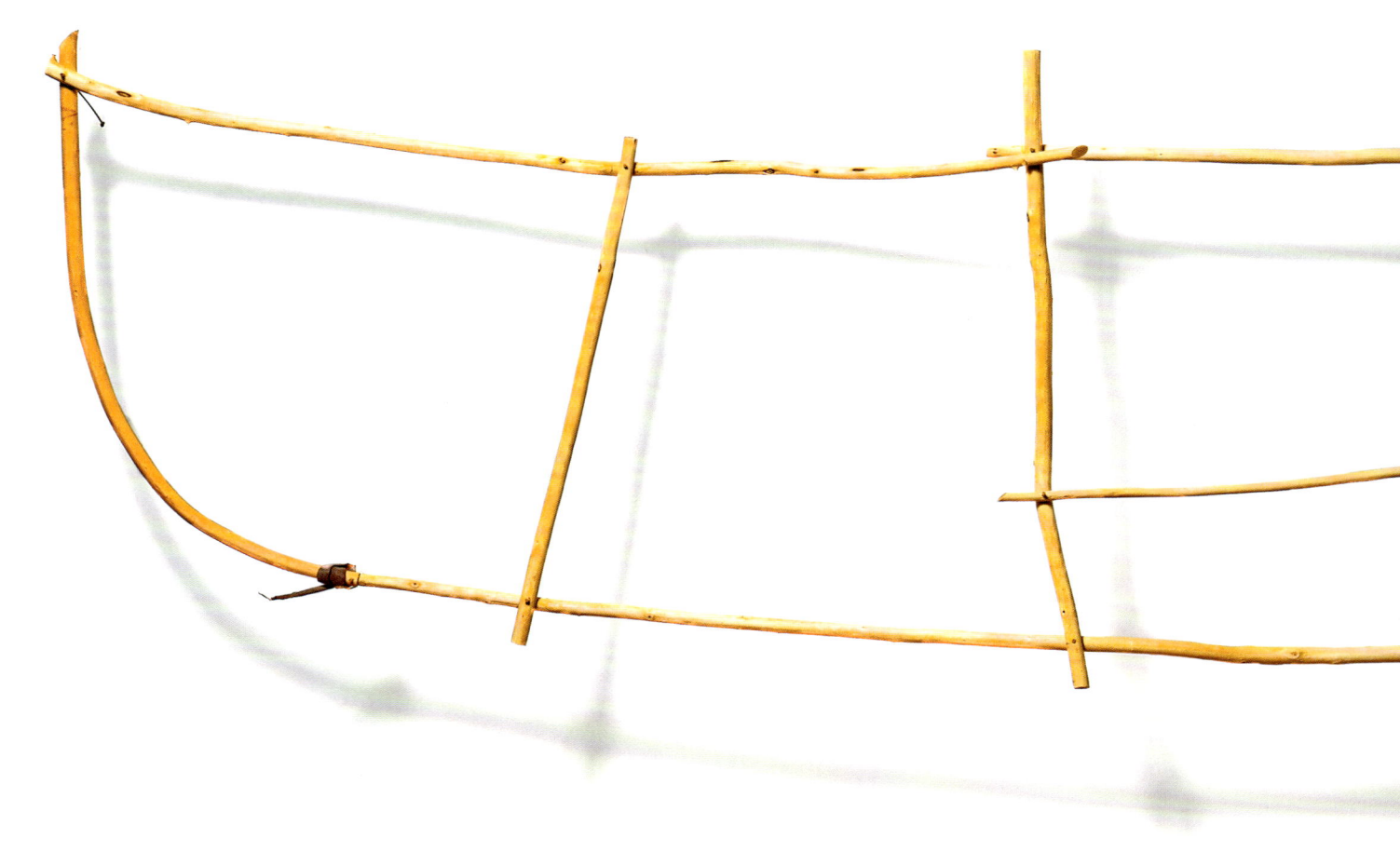

14. *Canoe (Drawing in Willow)*, 2009. Peeled willow, 30 x 99 ¼ x 2 ½ in. Museum of Fine Arts, Boston,
John Wheelock Elliot and John Morse Elliot Fund and Harriet Otis Cruft Fund, 2022.1802

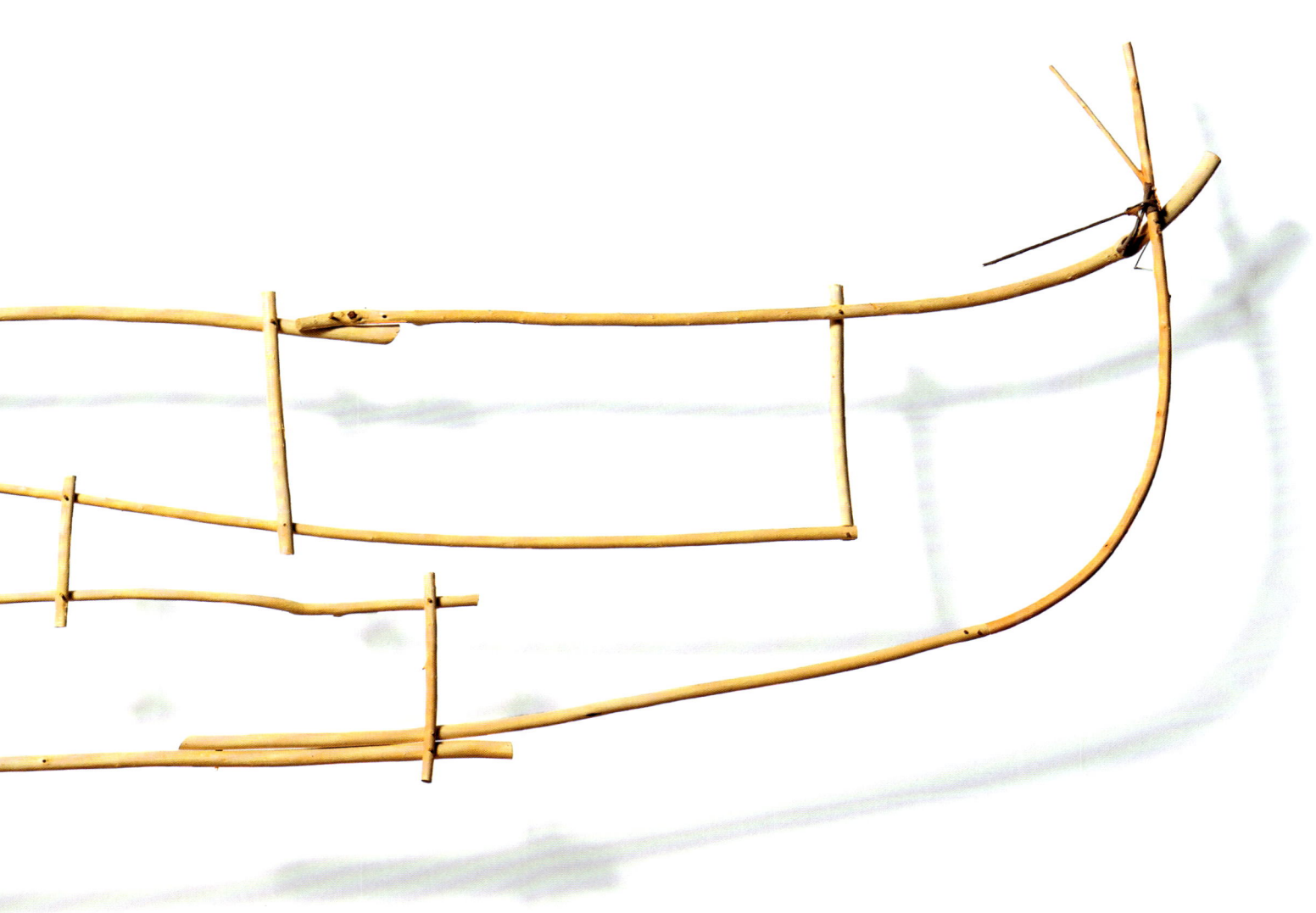

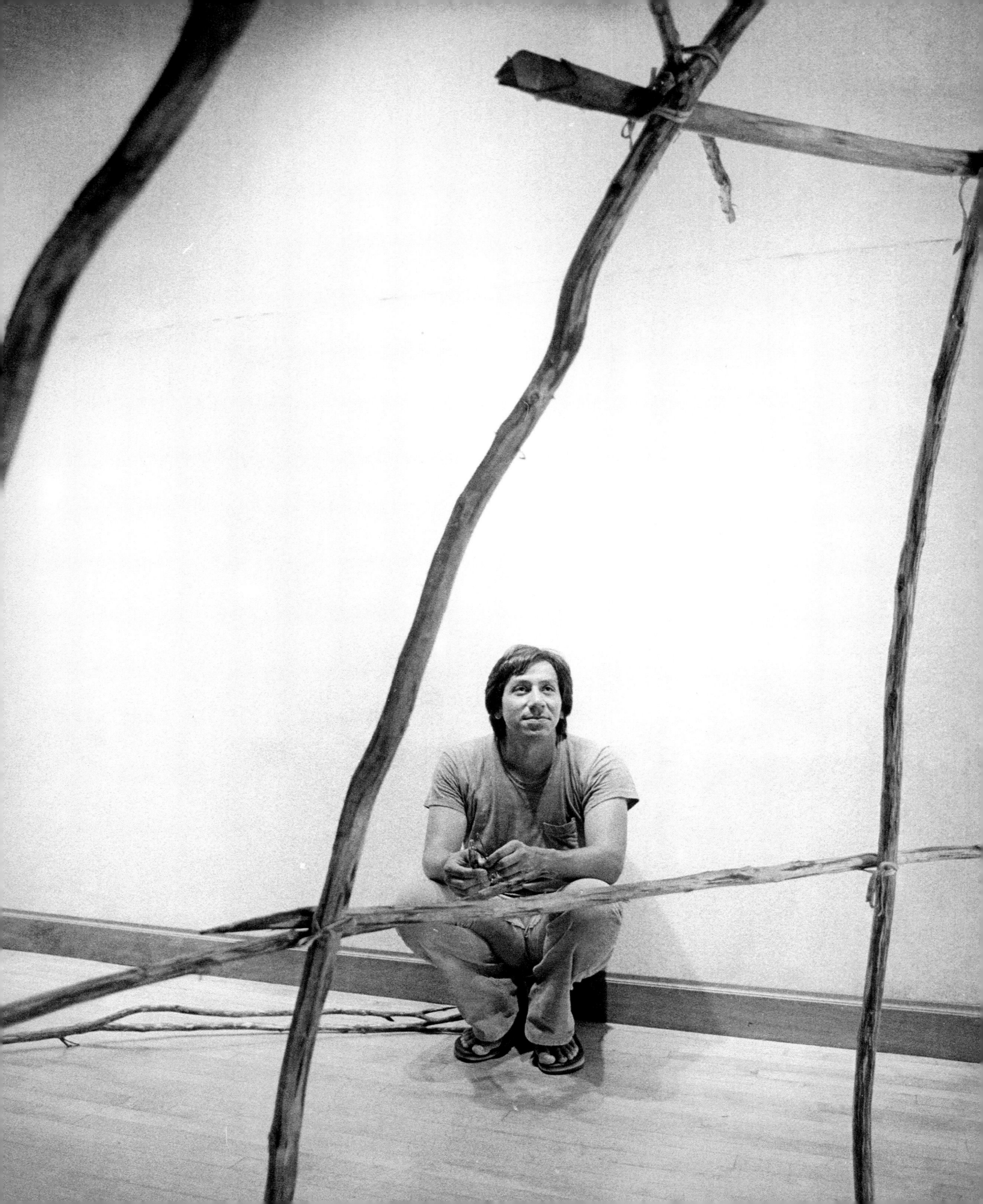

"Wood . . . Land . . . Woodland . . ."

Jo Ortel

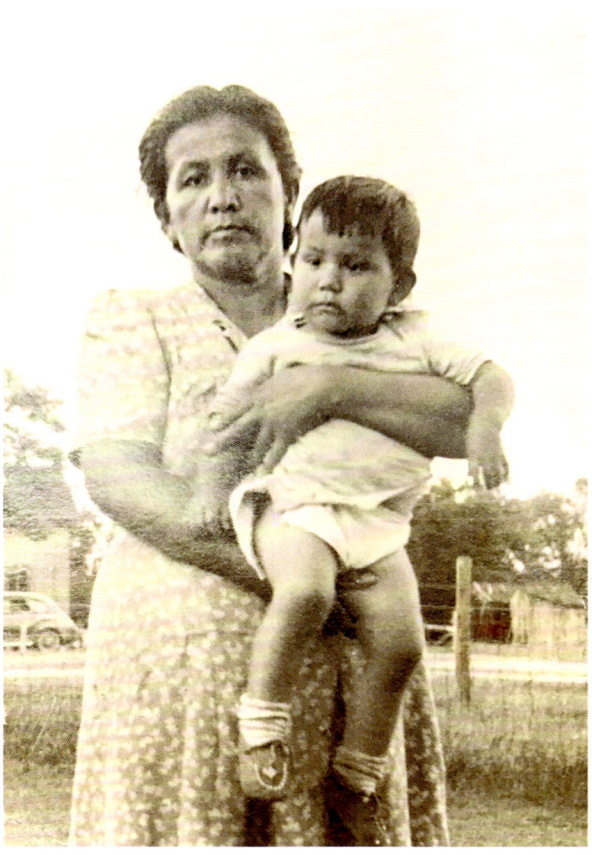

16. Mabel Lowe holding Truman, ca. 1945

15. Truman Lowe with a ciiporok'e (wigwam) sculpture entitled *Woodland Shelter*. *Constructions* exhibition at the University of Wisconsin–Madison Memorial Union main gallery, 1980. Not extant

THE ESSENTIAL SPIRIT OF CASCADING FALLS, of eddies among marshland grasses. Truman Lowe had an ability to transform careful observation of freshwater streams and woodland environments into striking sculptural forms. Often constructed with supreme delicacy, his artwork can appear provisional and improvisational, yet there is a timeless quality about it, too. It is infused with avant-garde art-world notions, and it is deeply rooted in Truman's Hoocąk heritage.

It is the responsibility of the artist, he believed, to interpret and make visual the influences of one's environment. To a large extent, his art is about the physical environment in which he grew up: the woodlands of the upper Great Lakes region. But environment can encompass many dimensions, including one's intellectual, cultural, and social milieu, as well as one's geographical surroundings. It would be impossible to catalog all the experiences and influences that were imprinted on Truman Lowe—or any artist, for that matter. But as a quiet champion of contemporary Native American art, Truman impressed upon me the value of engaging critically with Native art. In the classroom and beyond, he nurtured Native artists. With art historian colleagues like me and museum curators at the National Museum of the American Indian, Truman worked tirelessly to raise awareness about Native American art and share information about the deep wells of inspiration that feed it. Here, then, are some of the experiences and contexts that shaped him and his art practice.

Born in 1944, Truman grew up on what is familiarly called the Indian Mission, a Hoocąk community located seven miles east of Black River Falls in western Wisconsin

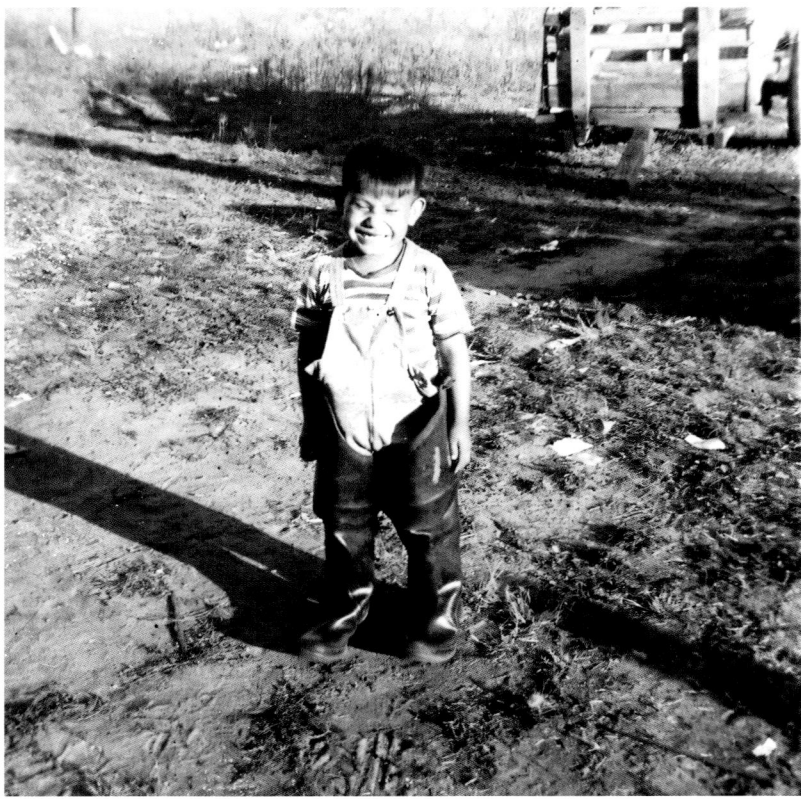

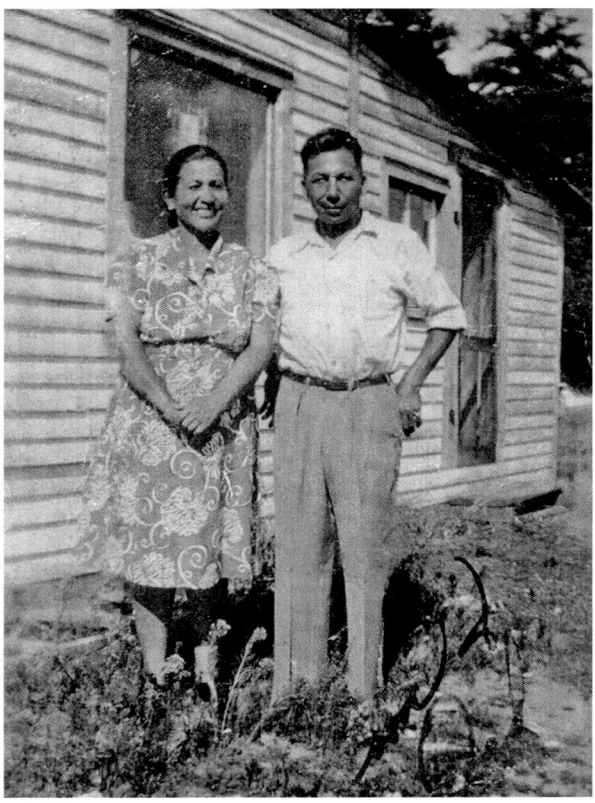

17. Truman Lowe, four years old, wearing wader boots, Black River Falls, Wisconsin, 1948

18. Truman's parents, Mabel and Martin Lowe, at the Indian Mission near Black River Falls, Wisconsin, early 1940s

(fig. 16). One of six children—and thirteen years younger than his closest sibling—he was surrounded in his youth by relatives and friends, many of whom joined the family in difficult times (fig. 17). The Lowes belong to the Thunderbird Clan, responsible for assisting others, mediating disputes, and peacefully leading the community.[5] Thus, despite their own poverty, Truman's parents, Martin and Mabel Davis Lowe, understood their role as caretakers within the community.

Clan responsibilities shaped Truman; so too did his Christian upbringing. His grandfather, George Lowe, and his family had been among the first in the community to convert to Christianity, around 1900. It was not an impulsive decision. When, in 1878, a missionary of the Sheboygan Classis of the Reformed Church arrived in Black River Falls, the Hoocąk people welcomed the assistance he offered, particularly in education.[6] Many attended Sunday services. But there were no converts to Christianity at the Mission for twenty years, likely because the missionaries

insisted that Hoocąk beliefs and traditions be forsaken. Two generations later, the Mission church was one focal point of the community. Truman's father was a devout Christian all his life. Truman and his siblings were raised in the church, while his mother was much more involved in Hoocąk traditions. His parents' conversations, respectful exchanges of interpretation, instilled in Truman a sense of tolerance and acceptance, and an understanding that there are no absolutes.

Both Mabel and Martin worked hard at various odd and seasonal jobs (fig. 18). Supplemental income came from the sale of traditional Hoocąk craft items made by the family for the tourist trade, particularly beadwork and baskets. Like his siblings, Truman helped in their production. Basket making took time and was labor intensive, involving the selection of suitable black ash and its preparation by Truman's father, followed by the dyeing of the wood strips by his mother after they had dried. Mabel, a gifted colorist, was admired for her striking color combinations, while

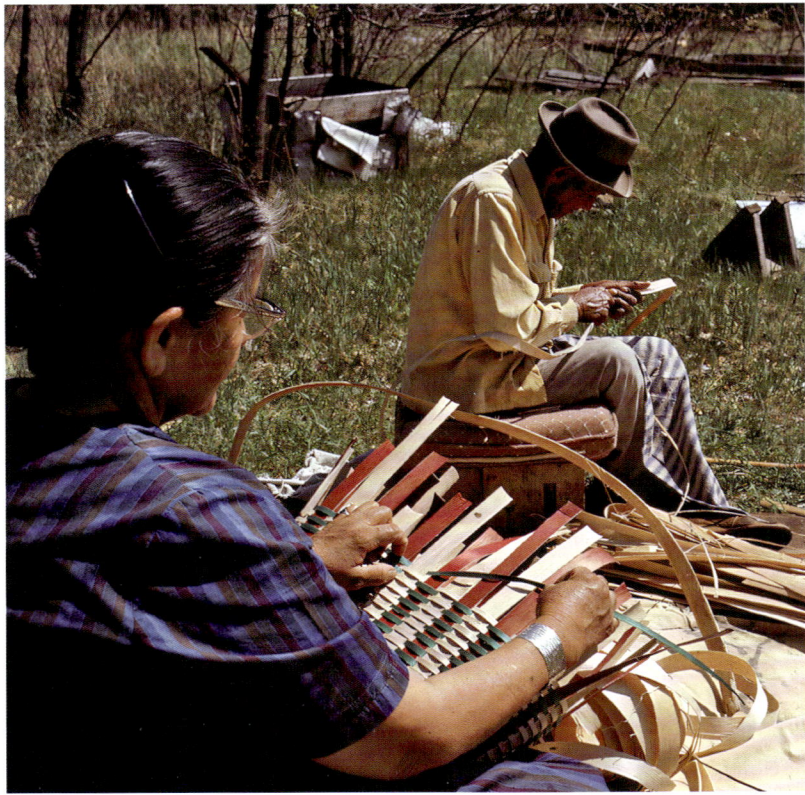

19. Mabel Davis Lowe weaves a black ash basket while Martin Lowe prepares a handle, 1967

Martin was known for the graceful bentwood handles he made for his wife's baskets (fig. 19). As a child, Truman often helped his father in the wigwam that served as a workshop behind the family house. As an adult, he often expressed admiration for his father's deep knowledge of wood and its properties. Mabel also made traditional appliqué, or ribbonwork, fashioning abstract patterns cut from colorful fabric for clothing and dance regalia.

Hoocąk was Truman's first language, which was not unusual at the time. In grade school, lessons were taught in English. He attended a two-room public school on the Mission until sixth grade. The curriculum was fairly standard for an American elementary school, though with a student body of forty children, all (or nearly all) of whom were Hoocąk, the two teachers at the Mission school also sought to encourage students' pride in their heritage.

For the upper grades, Truman and his peers were bused to much larger schools in the city of Black River Falls. Despite what has been called a quiet tension between the Native and non-Native cultures, the high school art teacher, Miss Carol Kinley, encouraged Truman's talents, gave him a key to her classroom, and let him use art supplies freely. For his senior year of high school, Truman went to live with his brother Chloris and his family in nearby New Lisbon, where he enjoyed greater opportunities and acceptance.

Like many Hoocąk people, Truman worked summers in Wisconsin Dells ("the Dells") from 1960 to 1968 (fig. 76). Long an important tourist destination in the state, the region is known for dramatic geological formations along this section of the Wisconsin River. Breathtaking scenery and boat tours were a central attraction; Indians became another, beginning in the late nineteenth century. Truman took a day job as an "Indian guide" on the boats that toured the river. He also danced in "ceremonials," programs held nightly for tourists. Today, the notion of "playing Indian" may strike us as problematic; at the time, it was one way for Hoocąk people to make decent money over a relatively short season. It was also a way to spend time with friends and relatives. Truman took his jobs seriously but wore the roles lightly.

It was a foregone conclusion that Truman would go to college; his siblings, who recognized that an education would give him advantages they did not have, made the decision for him when he was still an infant. When he enrolled at Wisconsin State College–La Crosse in 1962, it took him a few years to find his bearings.[7] Though he had been a good student through high school, his grades faltered. In his second year, he withdrew after a car accident left him briefly hospitalized. He resumed his studies in autumn 1964 but by the following June was ineligible to return.

The summer held better prospects. While working in the Dells, Truman met and fell in love with a fellow college student also there to earn money. Nancy Knabe hailed from a small town north of Black River Falls. At the end of the season, she returned to Stout State University[8] in Menomonie to finish school while Truman returned to La Crosse and took an assembly line job—work for which he soon learned he was ill-suited. The couple visited one another on weekends. Eventually, with encouragement from Nancy and his parents, Truman reviewed his college transcripts and realized that if he majored in art education, he could complete his degree in two years. He applied for readmission and recommenced his studies in 1966 with newfound focus, taking as many art classes as he could. In November, he and Nancy wed in a small church ceremony.[9]

After graduating in 1969, Truman taught art for two years in a public school in rural Wisconsin (fig. 20). He continued making his own work and even submitted some pieces to regional exhibitions. At the time, artists everywhere were exploring plastics. In 1970, for example, the Milwaukee Art Center hosted an exhibition called *A Plastic Presence*.[10] Minimalism, which sought to pare painting and sculpture down to their most essential elements, was also in vogue. Truman was aware of these trends. While at college in La Crosse, he had made a pop-inspired toaster using plastic. Now, he cut, folded, and crumpled plastic sheeting to make shapes that seemed to test the outer limits of sculpture.

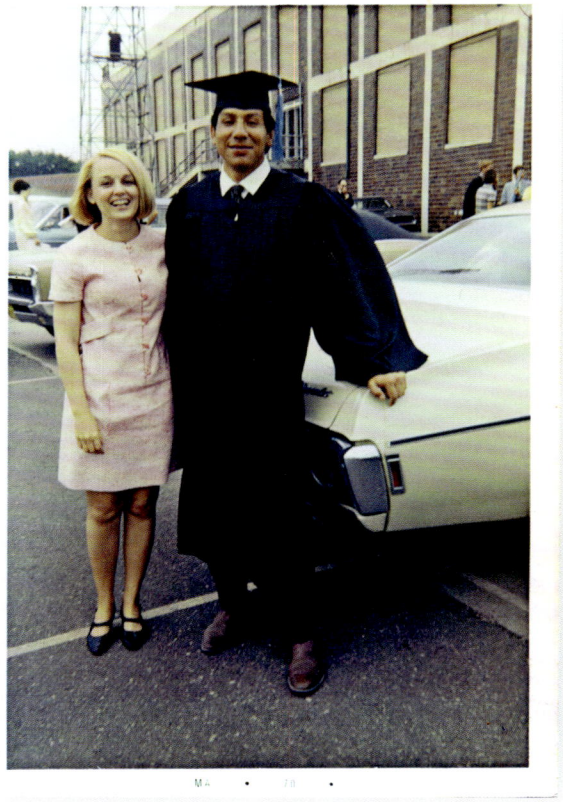

20. Truman and Nancy Lowe at Truman's Wisconsin State University–La Crosse graduation, 1969

Eager to learn more, for the sake of his students as much as for himself, Truman applied for and won a Ford Foundation fellowship for American Indians in 1971. He and Nancy, pregnant with their first child, moved to Madison where he began his graduate studies in art at the University of Wisconsin (UW) (fig. 23).[11] Daughter Tonia was born a month later.

The fellowship provided full support for Truman and his young family. In addition to art classes, he took an anthropology course, Indians of the Western Great Lakes, that held particular interest. For his final paper, he researched Native artists working in the region and interviewed Grand Portage Ojibwe artist George Morrison by phone, a connection he valued for the rest of his life.

In his own art, he continued to work with plastic sheeting (fig. 22). To his professors, it was evident he was

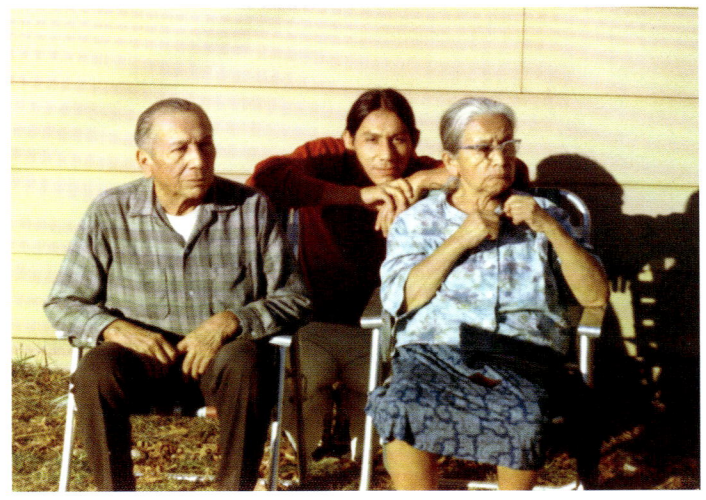

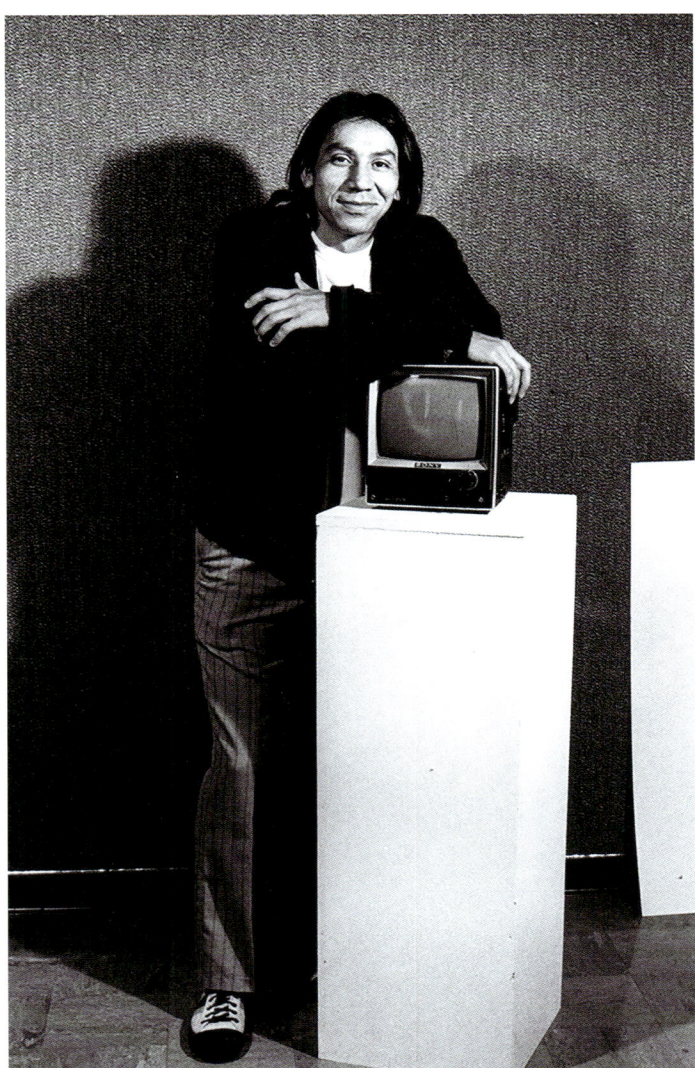

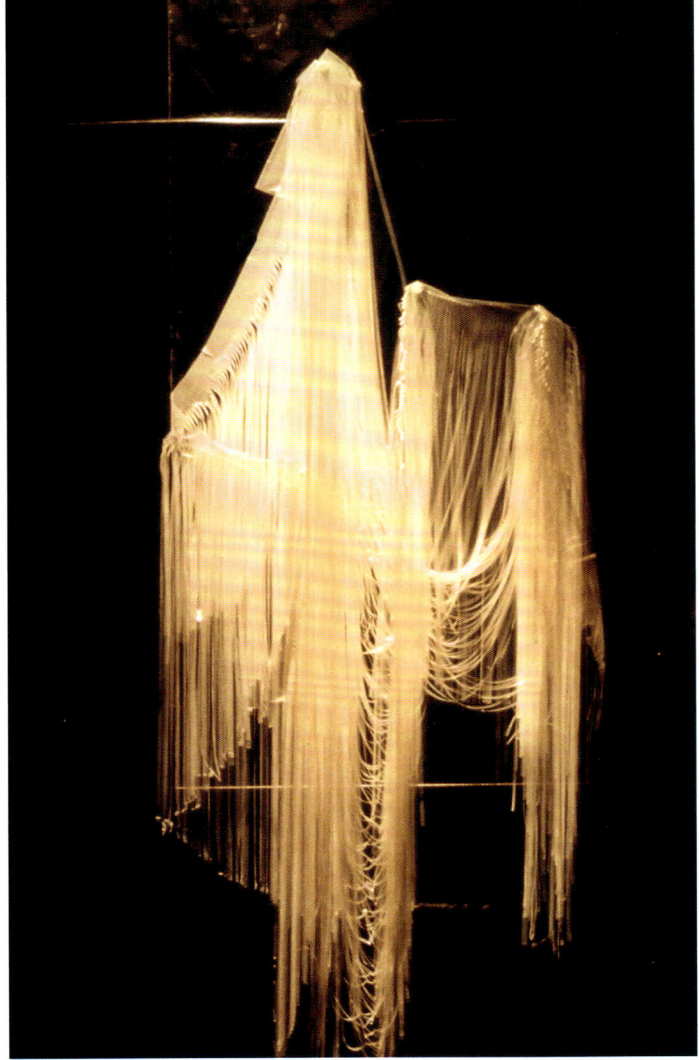

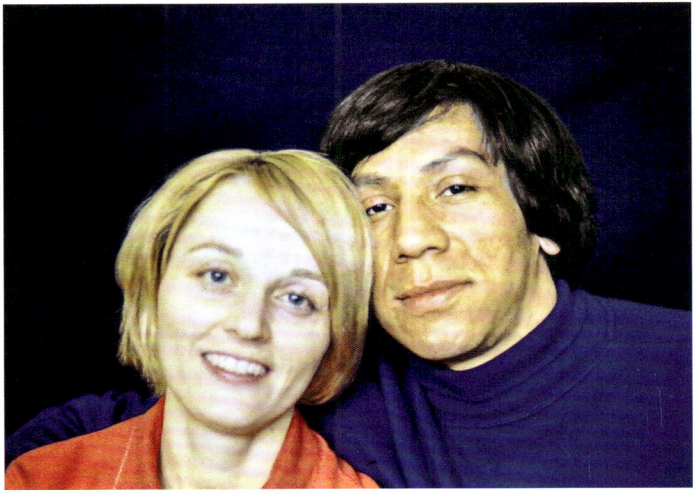

21. Truman Lowe with his parents, Martin and Mabel Lowe, 1970s

22. *Draped Fringes*, 1973. Polyethylene and plexiglass, 56 x 24 in. Not extant

23. Truman Lowe at the University of Wisconsin–Madison, 1973

24. Nancy and Truman Lowe, 1972

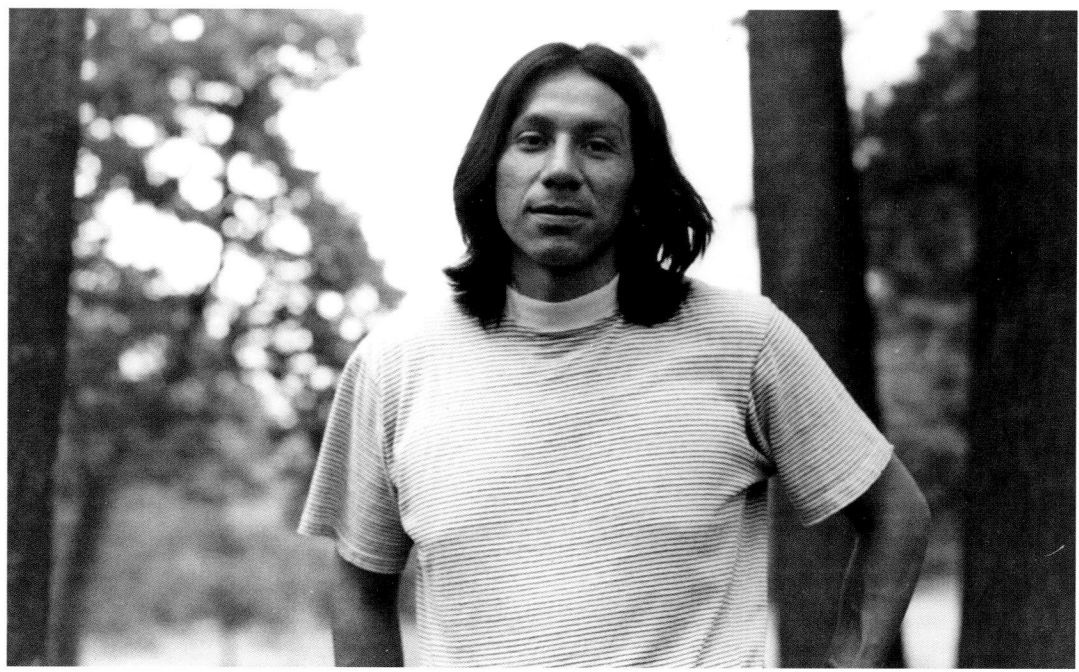

25. Truman Lowe, Black River Falls, Wisconsin, early 1970s

engaged with avant-garde ideas, including those of artist Robert Morris (American, 1931–2018) who, in an article in *Artforum* in 1968, had called for "anti-form," or artwork that drew attention to the materials used and the processes by which they were manipulated.[12]

With his master of fine arts (MFA) degree completed in 1973, the Lowes moved to Kansas, where Truman took a one-year teaching position at Emporia State University.[13] Far from home, he discovered, as he often said, that he was really a Woodland Indian—a realization that had profound implications for his art. He abandoned plastic and began working with wood and other natural materials. The family returned to Madison in 1974 when Truman was hired as assistant dean of students and coordinator of multicultural programming at the University of Wisconsin, an administrative post created to help defuse tension between students and school officials after multiple protests by students of the school's policies and sociopolitical events. When the crisis subsided, he moved into a joint

position as coordinator of the fledgling Native American Studies program and assistant professor of art.[14]

It was an eventful time at home, too. The Lowes' son Martin was born in July 1975. Though named after his paternal grandfather, he was called Kųnų (Kunu), the Hoocąk word identifying the firstborn son, to distinguish him from his namesake.[15]

At UW–Madison, Truman was the sole American Indian in a full-time faculty position, a dubious distinction he held for eleven long years. Inevitably, the academic community looked to him to speak for all Native Americans. The load lessened after Menominee activist Ada Deer joined the faculty, but he was still stretched thin.[16]

On the other hand, Truman's role within the university bolstered his confidence about the direction he was pursuing in his art. He began to combine imagery from his personal history and study of Indigenous art and culture with wood and the traditional craft techniques learned in his youth to form modern abstract sculptures and what he called "sculptural drawings." The art was not yet fully mature, but he was finding his voice.

Not long after his faculty appointment, Truman met John Lavine. A publisher of several Wisconsin newspapers, Lavine served on the UW System Board of Regents and chaired a subcommittee on minority education. With a common cause and many additional shared interests, the two men became lifelong friends. John, an avid collector of Native American art, was soon buying Truman's and creating professional opportunities for him.

Sculptors often make works that displace space; Truman preferred open forms. Beginning in the late 1970s, he found the wood he would use for the rest of his career. Willow wasn't his only material (nor the only wood type), but he liked its blond color when peeled, its ready availability, and its suppleness. Found in marshy lowlands, sandbar (or narrowleaf) willow (*Salix interior*) is considered a nuisance shrub to farmers.[17] Truman harvested saplings or branchlets in early summer, then peeled off the bark. Easily bent when freshly cut, the willow could be formed into shapes or left in its original form to dry.

He used it to build larger and larger sculptures. In 1980, he lashed arcing sticks together with leather ties to suggest the contours of that most essential form, a shelter—specifically a ciiporok'e (a Hoocąk wigwam or dwelling). "To the Indian," Truman said, "the wigwam is comfort and security."[18] For him, the ciiporok'e was a symbol of Hoocąk values and a metaphor for the efficiency and vitality of Native culture. It was a form to which he would return many times (fig. 15).

A couple of years later, Truman constructed *Totem*, a tall, latticelike structure (fig. 26). It was the first of many. The totem's form and function appealed to him, even though it wasn't associated with the Great Lakes region: "I can play in that area that archaeologists try to reconstruct, that anthropologists speculate about," he said. "I add my own notions. For example, we have no concrete evidence that Woodland Indians built totems. Perhaps they did, but none have endured or survived. I am sure we had them, though. If we did not, then I think we might need them. Totems tell us a lot."[19]

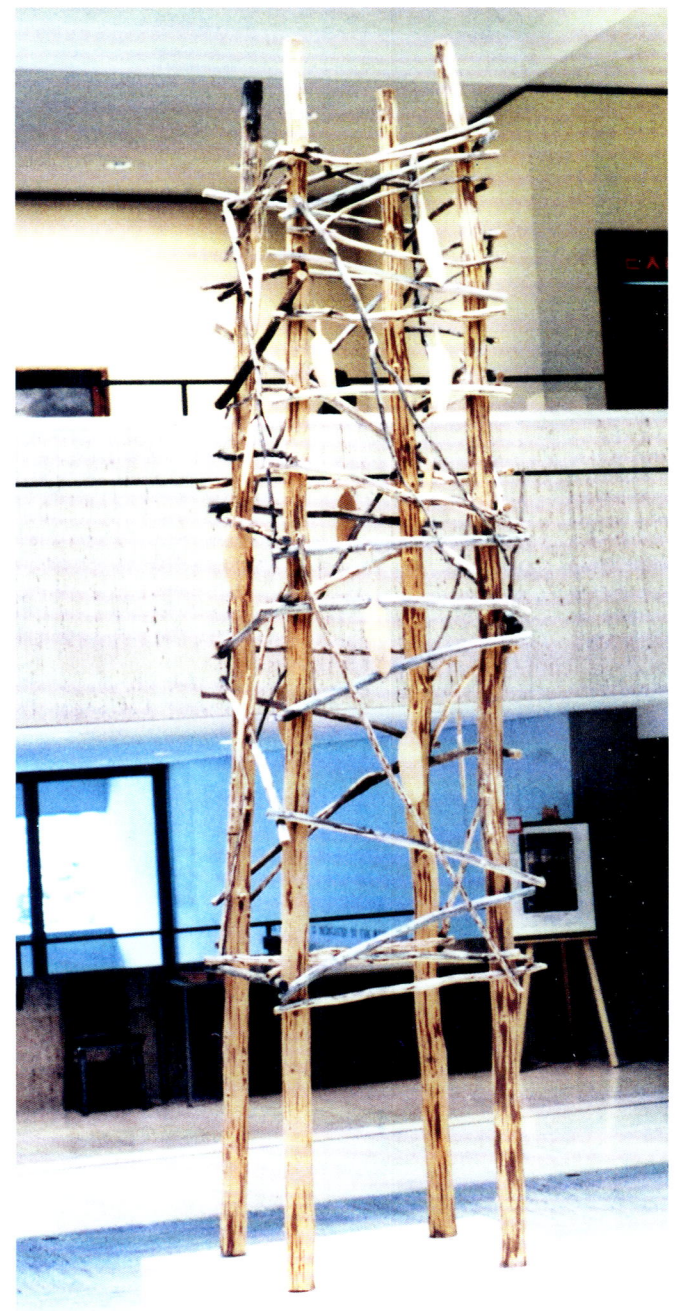

26. *Totem*, 1982. Cedar, tamarack, pine, rawhide, 156 x 48 x 48 in. Elvehjem Museum of Art (now the Chazen Museum of Art), University of Wisconsin–Madison. Not extant

As with the ciiporok'e and totem forms, Truman frequently worked in series, making more than one piece on a particular subject or motif. He did so, he said, when he wasn't satisfied with a completed work.[20] With every successive attempt, he sought to reduce his concept to its essence. "Every time I make something," he said, "I get closer to what I really want to do."[21] His canoe series is instructive. Truman canoed with his young family for recreation. Canoe camping trips were favorite getaways. He marveled at the ingenuity of the canoe form, which he asserted had remained unchanged since its invention. His first sculpture exploring the form, *Proto-Mississippian* (1984), was made with milled lumber. In its next iteration, he replaced the lumber with willow sticks tied with leather. Then in 1987, after watching ducks on a lake, he had the inspiration to fill the sculpture with white feathers, to evoke the feeling of "flying on water."[22] When he thought about the canoe form ten years later, it reappeared greatly abstracted as the *Thunder Bay* series (figs. 27 and 28).

Truman's fascination with structures included the ancient effigy and ceremonial mounds of the upper Midwest. That their original function was lost to time did not disturb him; he was captivated by their physical form. In 1985, he created *Effigy I*, his first outdoor installation, for an exhibition in Ann Arbor that coincided with a conference of the Native American Art Studies Association (NAASA), an organization formed in 1977 to encourage the ongoing study and exchange of ideas on Native American art. Truman attended the conference in 1983, and enthusiastically participated in planning and programming for the Ann Arbor meeting.

ATLATL was another Native arts collective important to Truman. Active nationally from 1974 to 2000, the organization played a critical role in nurturing a national Indigenous art community.[23] In an interview in 1986, Truman provided some context: "There are a number of us nationally who had gone to school at about the same time. We're all about the same age, in our mid-forties, and we've mostly come from fairly traditional backgrounds, growing up on reservations or in large Indian communities, entering into the public-education process, and going on to get MFA degrees. In the last five years, we've

started to . . . become aware of each other and get involved in some of the group shows that are held nationally."[24] Truman was not alone in interweaving Native and non-Native influences in his artwork. He was one of a group who helped broaden perceptions of "Indian" art. This shared sense of purpose was energizing. Lasting friendships and important connections were forged in NAASA and ATLATL, including with artists such as Larry Beck (Inuit-Chanagmiut, 1938–94), Joe Feddersen (Colville, b. 1953), G. Peter Jemison (Seneca, b. 1945), George Longfish (Seneca and Tuscarora, b. 1942), Jaune Quick-to-See Smith (citizen of the Confederated Salish and Kootenai Nation, 1940–2025), Kay WalkingStick (Cherokee Nation, b. 1935), Linda Lomahaftewa (Hopi/Choctaw, b. 1947), and Jean La Marr (Northern Paiute/Acomawi, b. 1945).

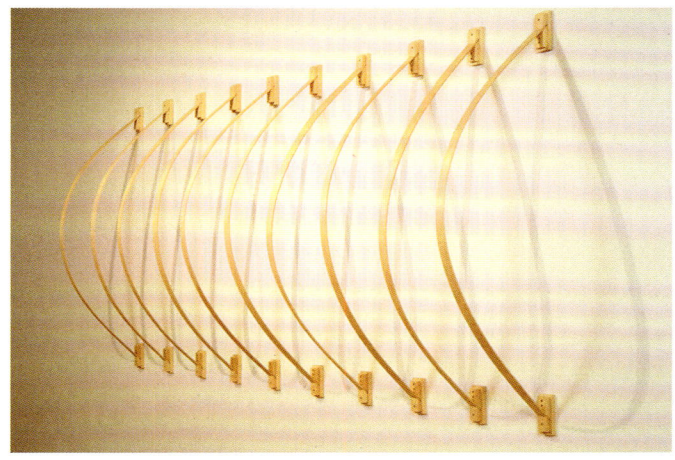

27. *Thunder Bay I*, 1999. Pine, 66 x 131 ¾ x 24 in. Museum of Contemporary Art Chicago

By the mid-1980s, Truman was perfecting the balance between his Native American imagery and his minimalist aesthetic, which reduced forms to their essence.[25] In 1987, he created another expansive installation, *Maumee Reflection*, evoking shoreline vegetation and its watery reflection. His attention turned increasingly to the streams and streambeds he knew so well (fig. 29).

He enjoyed the challenges of working large-scale and in the early 1990s had additional opportunities to do so. *Feather Tree* (1990) memorialized a moment from his

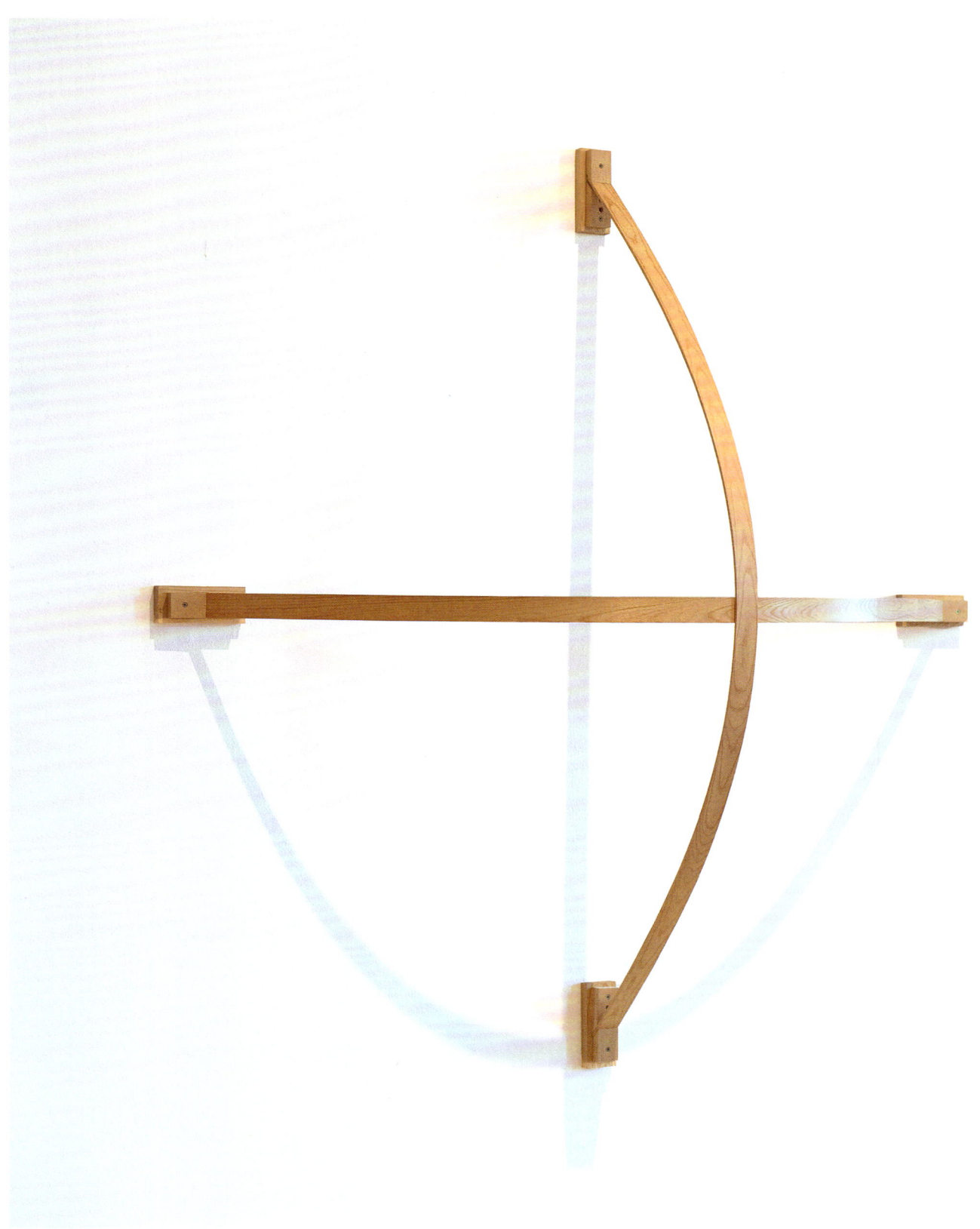

28. *Thunder Bay II*, 1997. Pine, 60 x 60 x 48 in. Madison Museum of Contemporary Art, purchase funded by Richard E. Brock

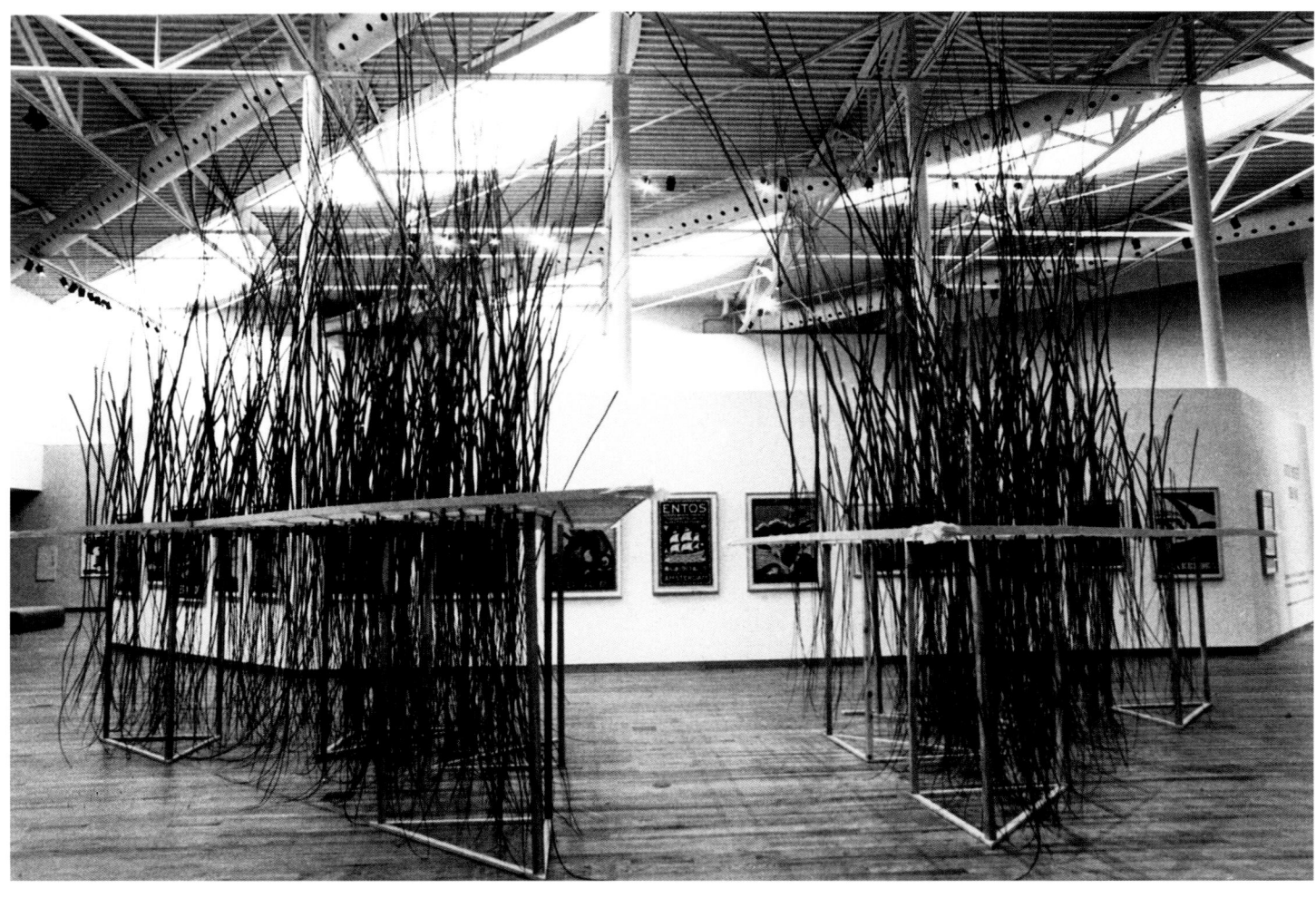

29. *Maumee Reflection*, 1987. Pine, willow saplings, 20 x 48 x 24 ft. Installation at the Fort Wayne Museum of Art. Not extant

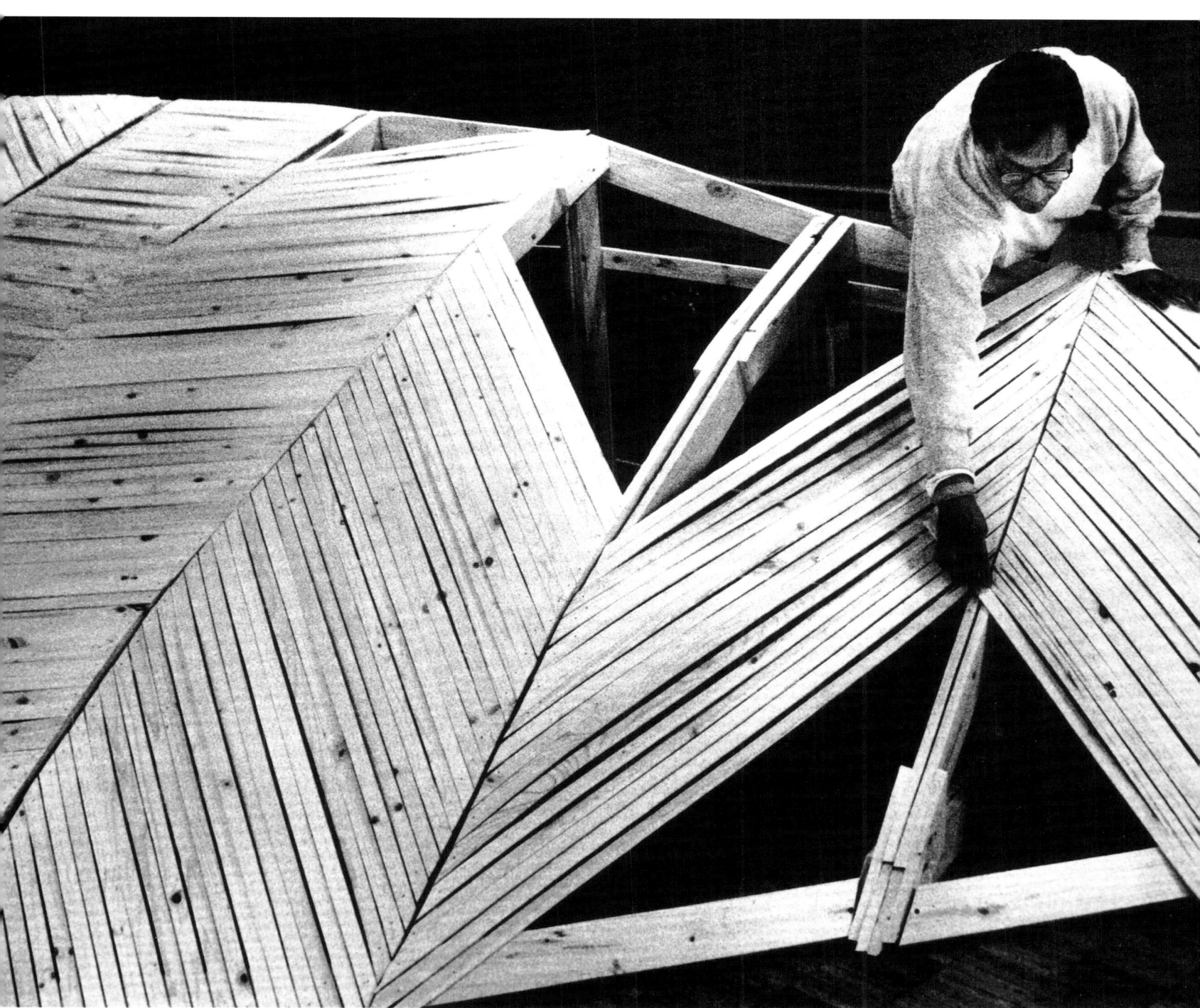

30. Truman Lowe with *Red Banks*. Lawton Gallery, University of Wisconsin–Green Bay, 1991

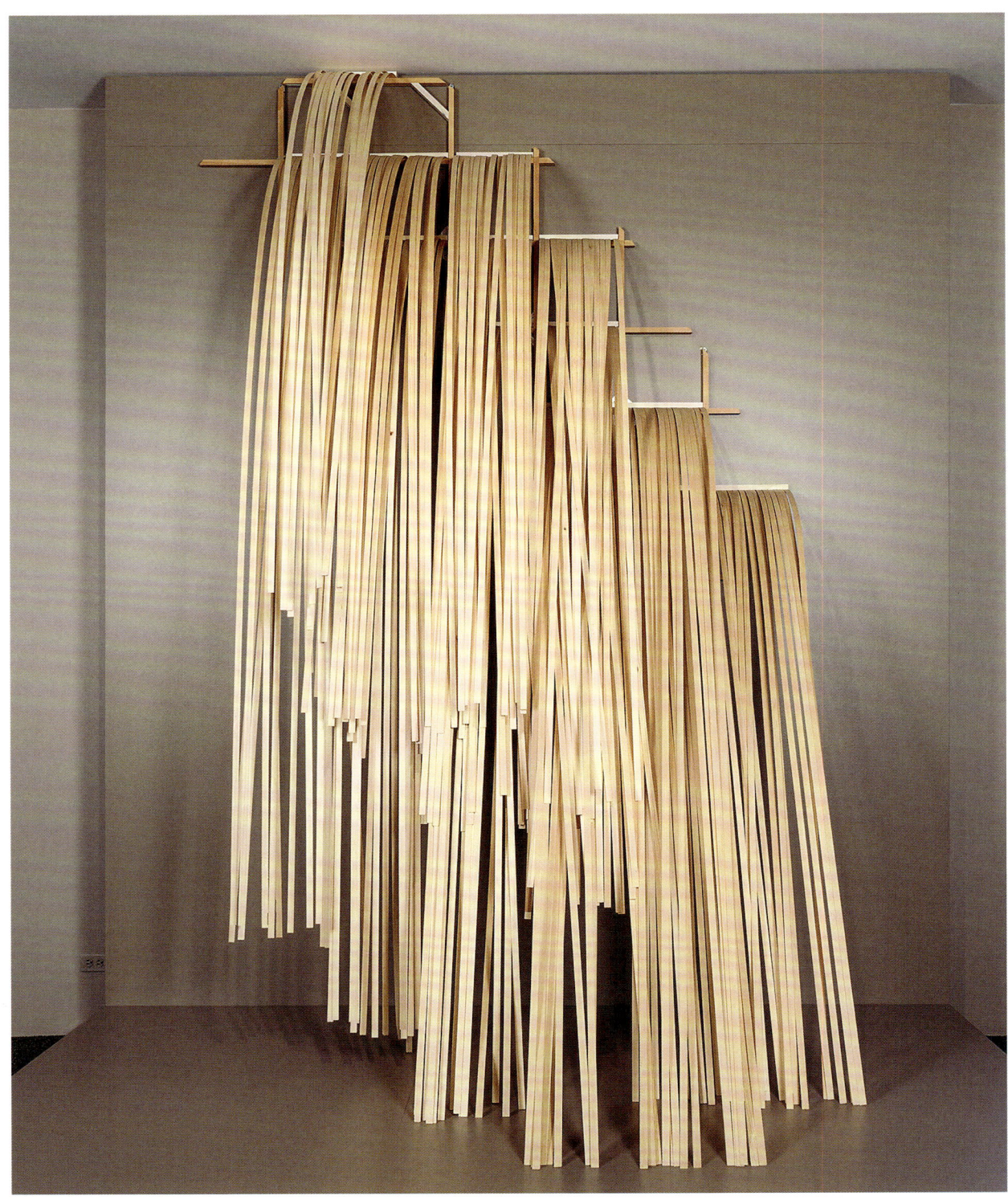

31. *Waterfall VIII*, 2011. Pine, metal fasteners, 82 x 80 x 64 in. Denver Art Museum: Native Arts acquisition fund, 2011.430A-N

Waterfall VIII was created for a 2011 exhibition at the Denver Botanic Gardens. Here, the elegance and drama of Lowe's waterfalls find their full expression.

personal history; *Red Banks* (1991) commemorated the origin story of the Hoocąk (fig. 60). *Aztalan* (1990) was inspired by the site of an ancient village, while *Red Ochre* (1991) was a visual meditation on the burial rituals of early Eastern Woodland Indians.[26]

His next major piece, *Ottawa*, was created for a landmark exhibition of First Nations contemporary art, *Land, Spirit, Power*, organized by the National Gallery of Canada in 1992 (fig. 38). On a site visit before the exhibition opened, Truman was captivated by the velocity and force of the Ottawa River, which flows through Canada's capital city. He returned home and made a cascade of monumental proportions, using wood slats arranged on an exposed armature. True to form, the piece combined a modernist aesthetic with materials reminiscent of his parents' splint-plait basketry. The next year, he tackled rushing water again and created the first of his *Waterfall* sculptures, which culminated in 2011 with *Waterfall VIII* (fig. 31).

Truman was busier than ever. From 1992 through 1994, he served as chair of the art department at UW–Madison. *Haga (Third Son)*, his first major solo exhibition, opened at the Eiteljorg Museum in Indianapolis in 1994.[27] A small show at Jan Cicero Gallery in Chicago followed, featuring two series inspired by a family trip through the American Southwest. In 1996, he participated in an artist residency at Murray State University in Kentucky, which included visits to the nearby site of an ancient Mississippian town and an outdoor art-making workshop with schoolchildren—two of his favorite activities. Additionally, Kentucky Educational Television produced a documentary, which, though somewhat romanticized, remains one of the most sensitive, revealing portraits of Truman Lowe.[28]

In 1997, twelve Native sculptors were selected to show work in the White House gardens in Washington, DC, as part of a series initiated by then-First Lady Hillary Clinton celebrating twentieth-century American sculpture. For his submission, Truman circled back to the ancient mounds to make *Effigy: Bird Form* (fig. 91). "Being from the woodlands," he said, "I wanted my inspiration to come from a culture that inhabited this area and left its mark with earthen mounds—a unique way of showing respect and living with the earth. This is my attempt to pay my respects."[29]

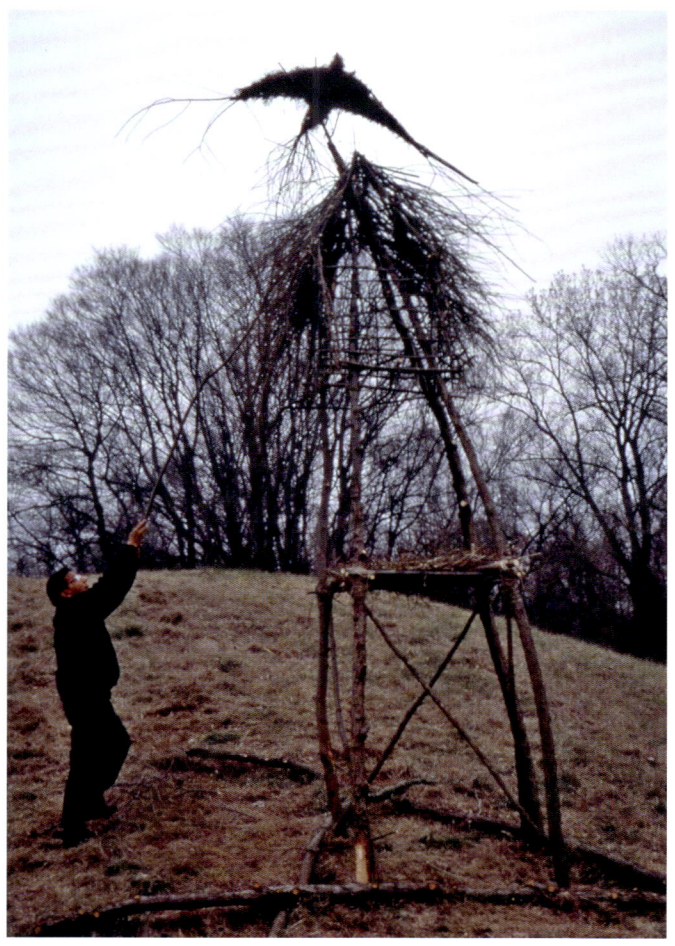

32. Truman Lowe with temporary untitled outdoor sculpture created with students at Wickliffe Mounds, Kentucky, 1996

At the end of the millennium, he was among the first group of artists to be awarded the Eiteljorg Fellowship for Native American Fine Art (1999). It was a fitting cap to the most prolific period in his life as an artist.

Of course, Truman was also teaching during these years. Both in the classroom and beyond, he mentored countless individuals (fig. 34). In addition, he worked quietly but steadily to give students, particularly those who were Native American or underrepresented, the same opportunities he'd had.[30] In his experience, what he learned in the classroom and beyond deepened his understanding of himself and the world. He wanted others to have that, too.

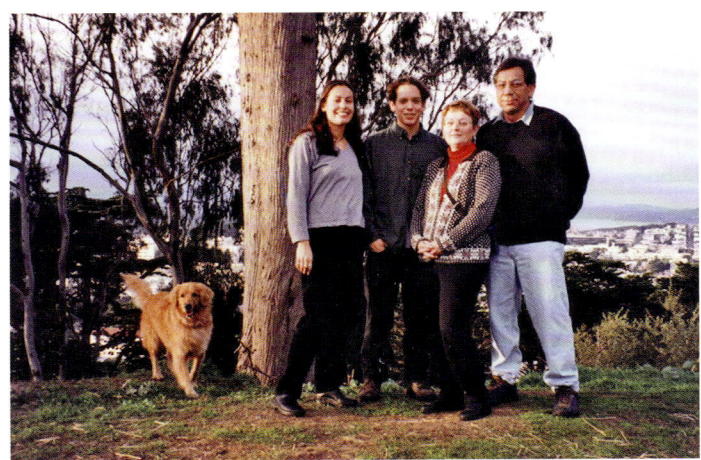

33. Tonia, Kunu, Nancy, and Truman Lowe, San Francisco, 1998

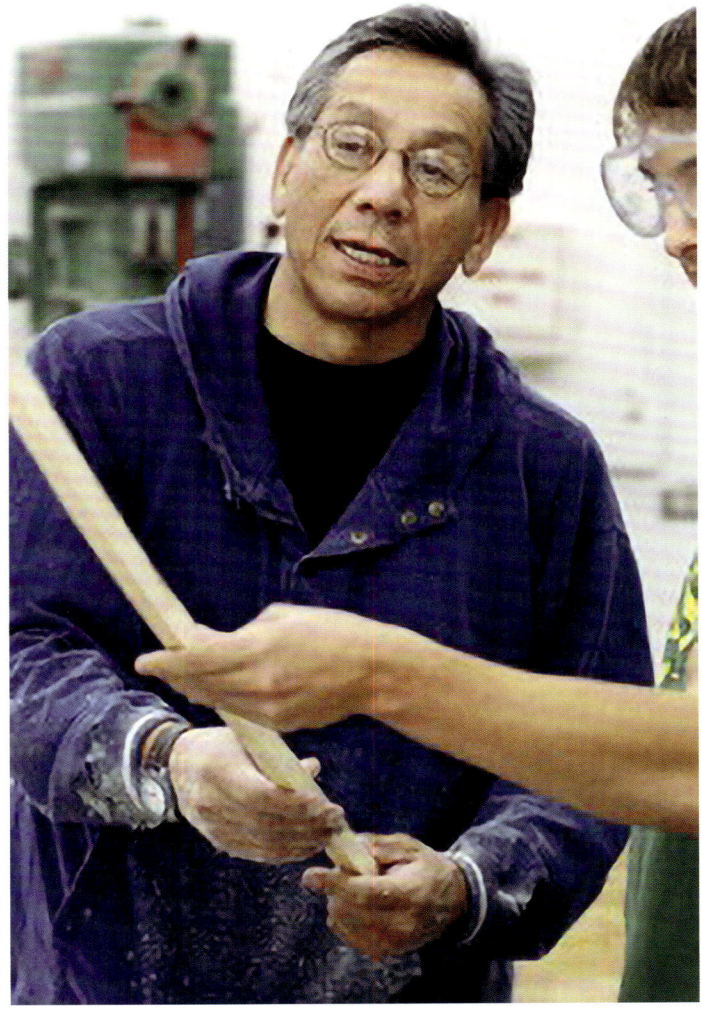

34. Truman Lowe teaches woodworking techniques during an undergraduate wood sculpture class, 2004

Four years before the opening of the Smithsonian's National Museum of the American Indian on the National Mall in Washington, DC, Truman was invited to become its first curator of contemporary art. He had participated in discussions about the new museum since at least 1990. His unique ability to imagine and articulate a vision where none had previously existed was well noted. The offer intrigued him, though it was a difficult time to leave Madison. His son was struggling with anxiety, depression, and addiction. Still, it was a singular opportunity—one he didn't feel he could pass up. He took a leave of absence from UW–Madison and accepted the position.

In DC, Truman wanted to showcase individual artists who, through their work in nontraditional media and the example of their careers, impacted the trajectory of Native American art in the second half of the twentieth century. Truman knew that the intellectual scaffolding for his program was freighted with modernist notions of art history as a linear progression of (male) artists. Still, one had to start somewhere. *Native Modernism: The Art of George Morrison and Allan Houser* (2004–05), the first exhibition he curated for the new museum, received widespread critical acclaim, as did *Fritz Scholder: Indian/Not Indian* (2008–09), the next exhibition charting a history of contemporary Native art. As he had done in all his administrative posts, Truman took the long view. Change was incremental.

While he lived in Washington, he continued to make art—mostly tiny collages and drawings, which he gave to his museum colleagues. On regular visits home to Madison, he spent time at his studio. He also accepted invitations to universities and museums where he could make large-scale pieces. He worked with students at Western Michigan University to make *Modular Wigwam: H.U.D.* (2000) (fig. 35). In 2001, he worked on-site at the University of Minnesota in Duluth for an exhibition he called *Nigachiwong (Swirling Waters)*. For a solo show that same year at the Madison Art Center (later renamed the Madison Museum of Contemporary Art), he revisited

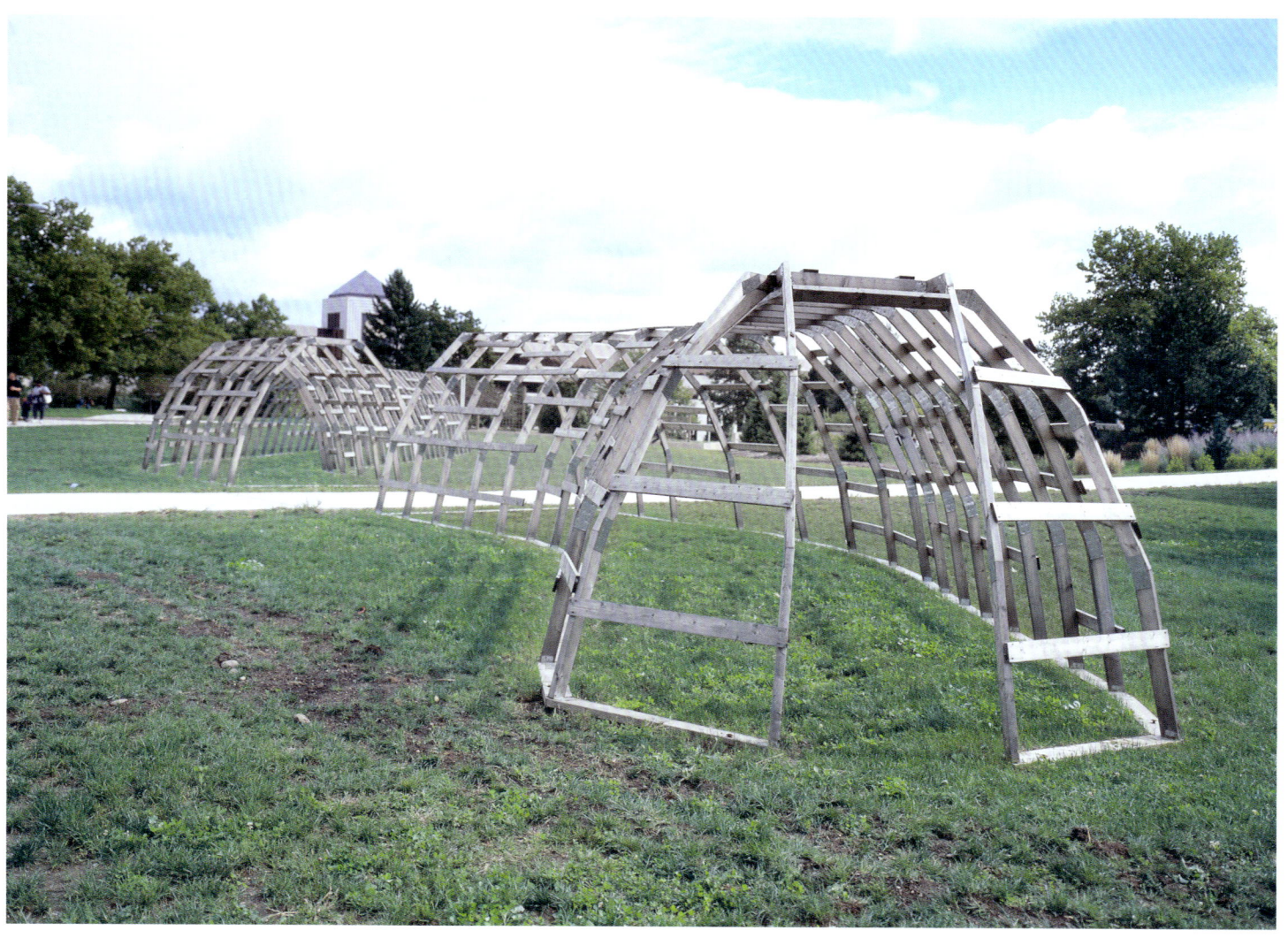

35. *Modular Wigwam: H.U.D.*, 2000. Wood, dimensions unknown. Western Michigan University. Not extant

dwellings. Industrial materials figured prominently in these installations and sculptures, as if his time in the nation's capital had shifted his thoughts about the intersection of nature and culture.

In 2005, after years of struggle, Truman's son, Kŭnŭ, had seemed to turn a corner and was building a life. Tragically, after only a brief time in a new job, he suffered a traumatic brain injury in a work-related accident and passed away shortly thereafter. Losing Kŭnŭ devastated the Lowes.

Family matters brightened considerably when Tonia married in 2009 (fig. 36). Truman had stepped down from his position at the National Museum of the American Indian the previous year, content in the knowledge that he had helped introduce countless viewers to the broad expanse—the *possibilities*—of contemporary Native American creativity. Certainly, others recognized his achievements. He received more honors, including the Wisconsin Visual Art Lifetime Achievement Award.[31] His greatest happiness, though, came when grandson Anders was born in 2010. Truman's retirement that year from the university meant he and Nancy could spend more time visiting Tonia and her family in California. He continued to fill sketchbooks with journal entries and drawings,

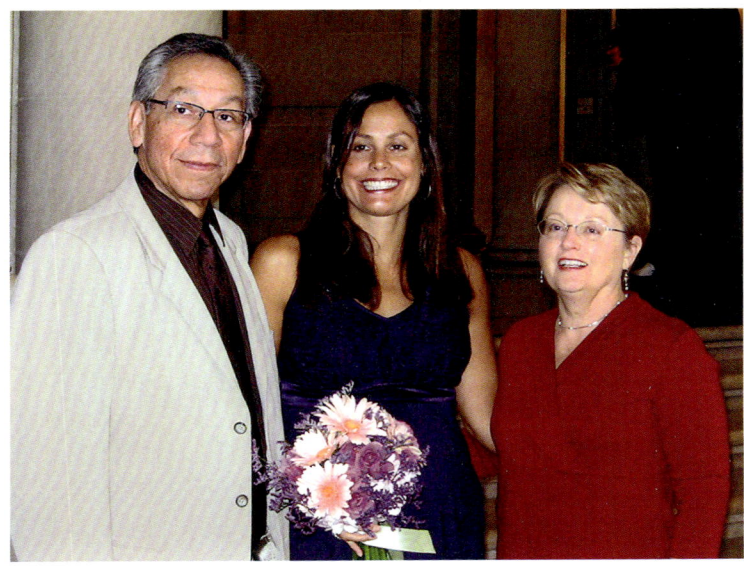

36. Truman, Tonia, and Nancy Lowe, San Francisco, 2009

visit his studio daily, and show new work, often smaller in scale. Sadly, in the fall of 2018, he was diagnosed with stomach cancer. He passed away in March 2019, surrounded by his family.

Truman's final sculpture, designed in early 2018 for an urban environmental park located just over the Wisconsin state line in Illinois, brings his art and life full circle (fig. 94). Unveiled after his death, *Ke-Chunk Ciporoke* is sited on the banks of Turtle Creek, just yards from its confluence with the Rock River and near where a large Hoocąk village called Keecąk (or Ke-Chunk, meaning turtle) had thrived until 1832. Following the influx of white settlers, the Hoocąk and other Indigenous people were forcibly and repeatedly removed from this site and other traditional lands. *Ke-Chunk Ciporoke* thus commemorates Hoocąk presence on the site even as it also speaks of a more complicated history of forced displacement. Like a drawing in three dimensions, the sculpture's spare, open form speaks of Truman's reverence for his heritage and culture and for the woodland environment with which it blends so seamlessly. As the work of a twenty-first-century Native artist, it is a testament equally to the continuing creativity and vitality of the Hoocąk people.

It can be a fool's errand to suggest how an artist's work connects to his life. Truman himself once said, "A [work of art] can embody all the influences that one person has in a lifetime." And he added, "I feel very fortunate to be able to combine so much into one piece."[32] His life was indeed filled with countless meaningful experiences and relationships forged across many different realms. He was receptive to the world around him. At the same time, he was secure in who he was. He honored his Hoocąk heritage, his Wisconsin roots. This is why I chose to borrow one of Truman's most succinct artist statements as the title for this essay. In both form and content, it captures so much of who he was, what his work was about, and where he drew much of his inspiration: "Wood . . . Land . . . Woodland . . ."[33] This was Truman in his own playful, poetic words, with his talent for finding elegant, simple solutions to complicated challenges.

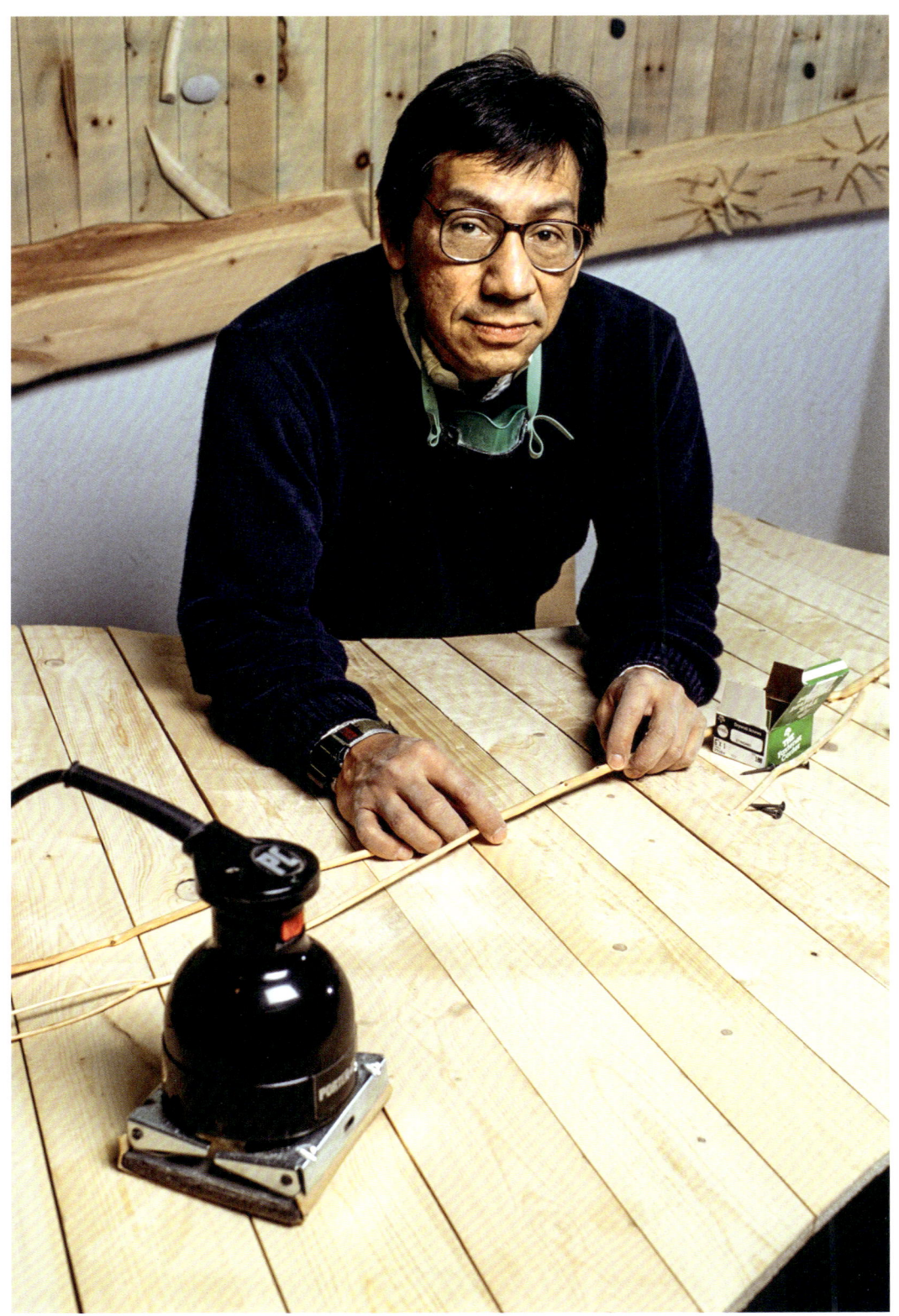

37. Truman Lowe working in his studio in Middleton, Wisconsin, with *Stream I* on the wall behind him, 1992

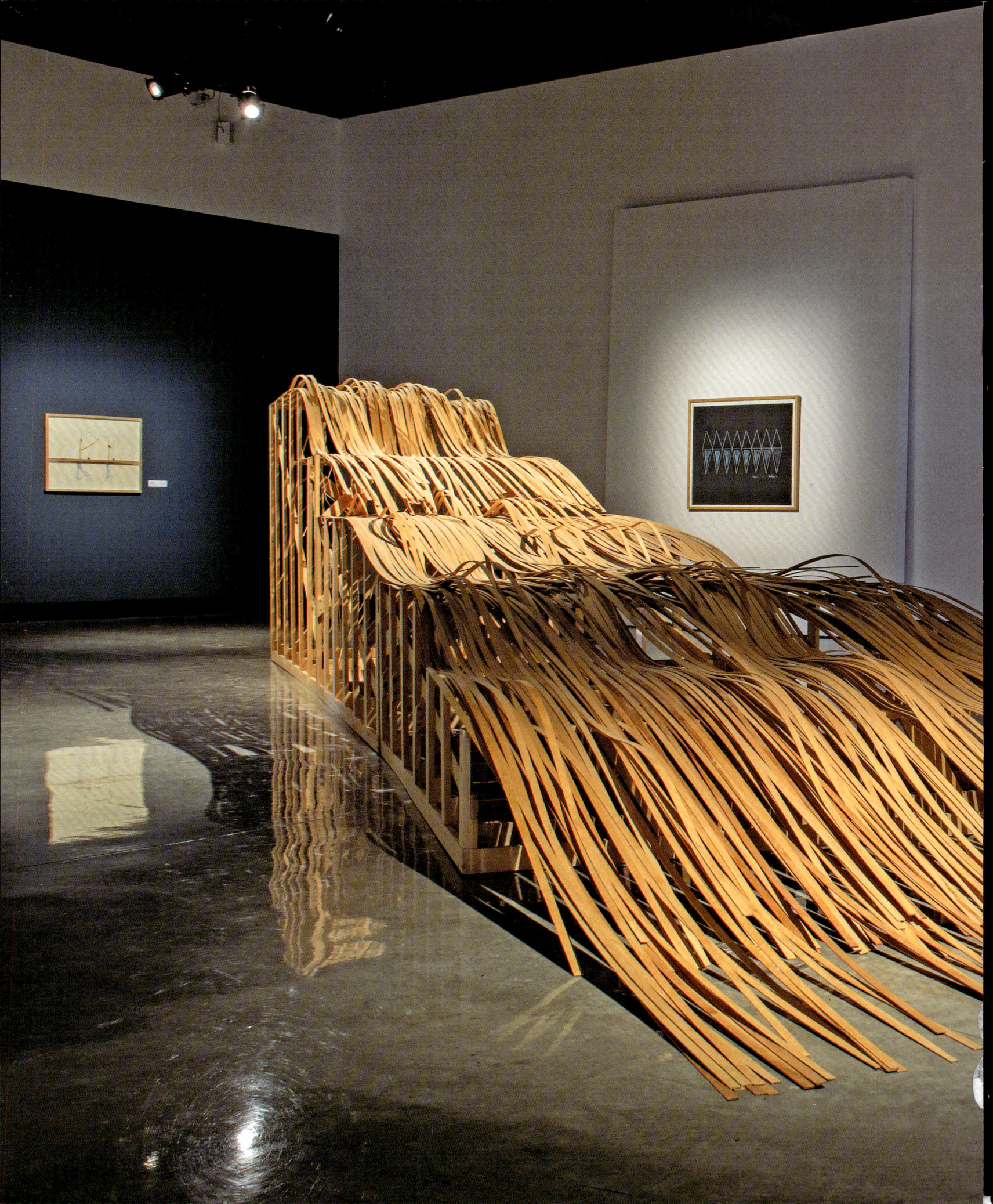

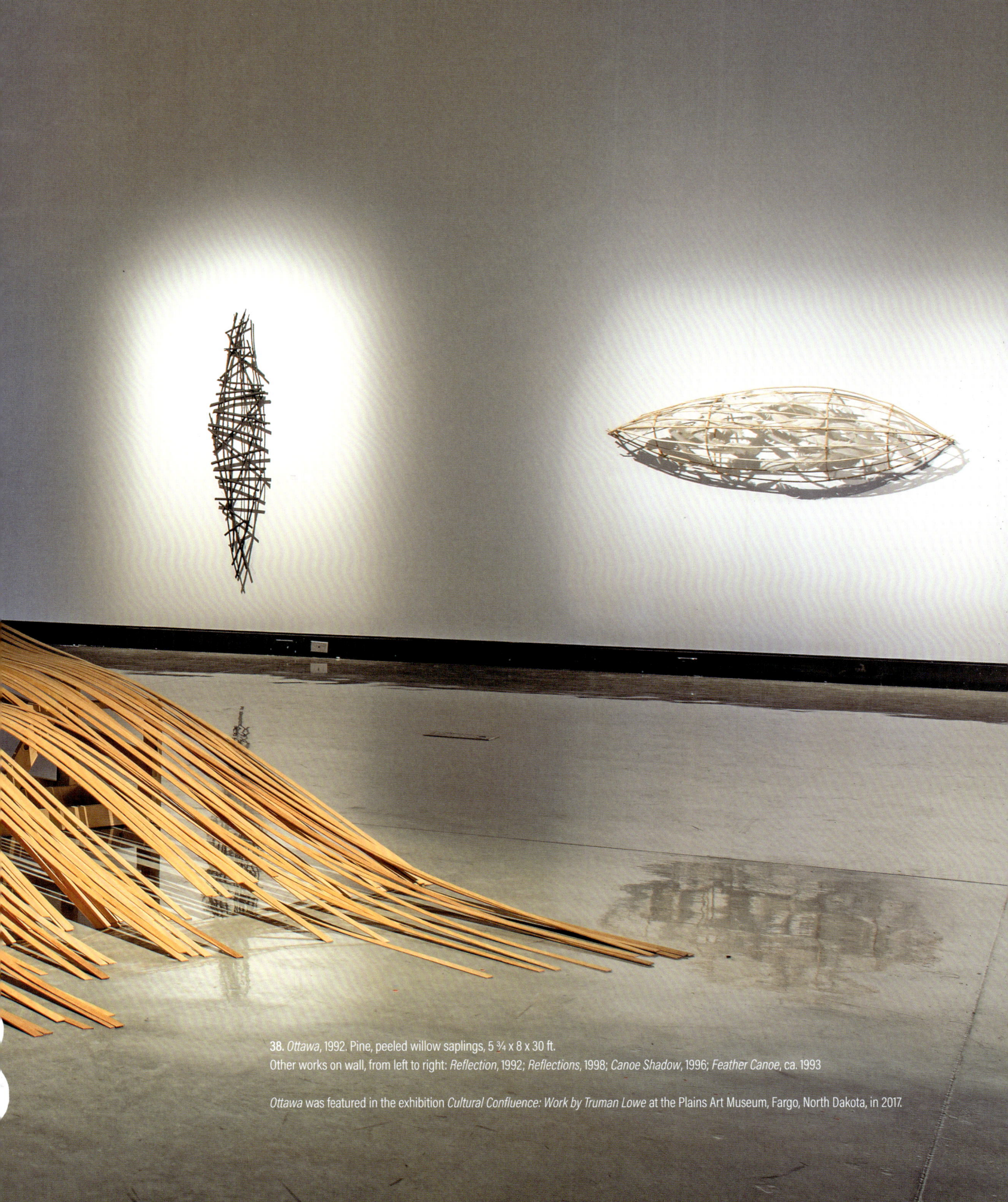

38. *Ottawa*, 1992. Pine, peeled willow saplings, 5 ¾ x 8 x 30 ft.
Other works on wall, from left to right: *Reflection*, 1992; *Reflections*, 1998; *Canoe Shadow*, 1996; *Feather Canoe*, ca. 1993

Ottawa was featured in the exhibition *Cultural Confluence: Work by Truman Lowe* at the Plains Art Museum, Fargo, North Dakota, in 2017.

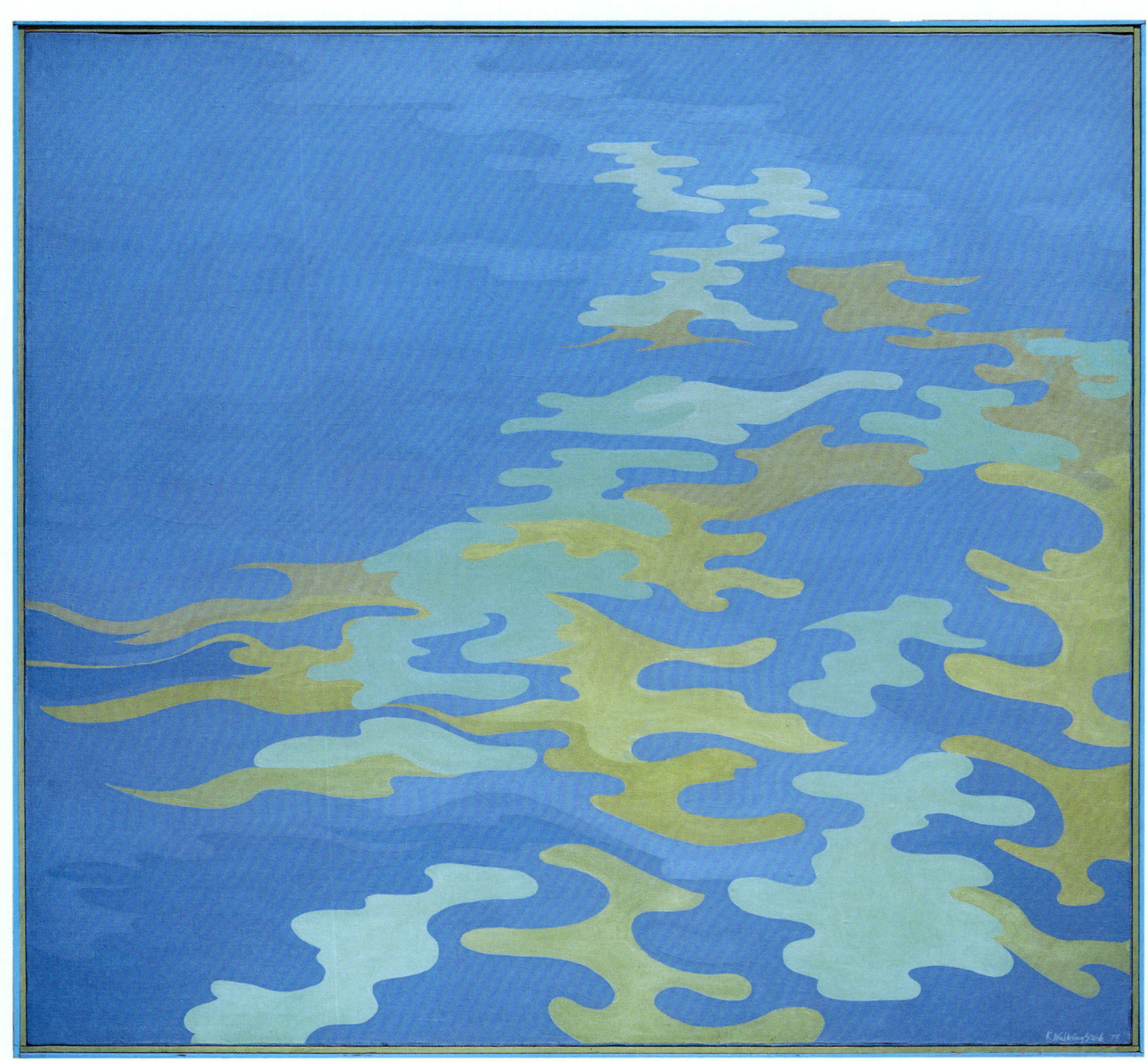

39. Kay WalkingStick (Cherokee Nation), *Hudson Reflection, III*, 1973. Acrylic on canvas, 45 x 49 in. National Museum of the American Indian 26/9793, gift of Joy WalkingStick Couch

Truman Lowe: Woodworker

Kay WalkingStick

IN 1994, I described Truman Lowe as the preeminent Native sculptor of his generation. Truman was a maker of things who loved working with wood. He joked that he "like[d] to make sawdust," but he enjoyed the entire process of wood sculpture, from walking in the woods at home and selecting the ideal wood, to the shaping of his final piece.

The fascination for me in Truman's sculptures is that he could make a solid become a liquid—the wood appears fluid and full of movement. I mentioned this to him and he said, "Well, the wood is liquid. It's full of water," a statement not unlike Michelangelo's famous remark about releasing the angel from the marble. The possibility that marble can become skin or that wood can become water is a miracle—a miracle that a sculptor performs. In Truman's hands the material remains wood and yet is transformed. This is, of course, the amazing thing in all art. That is, it is made of common material through which an uncommon idea is expressed.

The piece called *Ottawa*, which Truman made for *Land, Spirit, Power*, an exhibition organized by the National Gallery of Canada in Ottawa in 1992, is a good example (fig. 38). It depicts a grand cascade like those in the river between Ottawa and Hull. The work is made from strips of lath attached precariously to simple trussed supports. The sculpture measures approximately six-by-thirty-by-eight feet. It is huge. It is superbly elegant and almost childlike in its straightforward simplicity. Waterfalls have a special fascination for humans, which scientists have ascribed to the excess ozone they create. I think the fascination is more primal than even an ozone high. Waterfalls are powerful

natural forces that have been unstoppable for most of humankind's existence on earth. They are a metaphor for the unceasing movement of time—that irrevocable journey from birth to death. It is this overwhelming sense of the passage of our lives that this tremendous work of art conveys. Through scale and through basic wood construction, Truman has expressed the flow of our lives and of time itself. The wonder is that the passage is joyful.

Truman didn't make art that portrays traditional tribal life or contemporary tribal life either. He spoke in a contemporary voice, permitting us to see the inner life of the subject he depicted. He made abstractions that used as their source his memory of life as it was lived by the Hoocąk of Wisconsin. Although his work is not pictorial, it does depict our world. A canoe is recognizable as a canoe and a waterfall resembles a waterfall. Through his depiction there is a transformation in which these objects become more than the sum of their parts, and the canoe is all canoes, in its delicacy, fragility, and strength.

Excerpted and adapted from: Jennifer Complo, Haga (Third Son): An Exhibition of Sculpture, Drawing and Painting by Winnebago Artist Truman Lowe *(Indianapolis: Eiteljorg Museum of American Indians and Western Art, 1993): 32–38.*

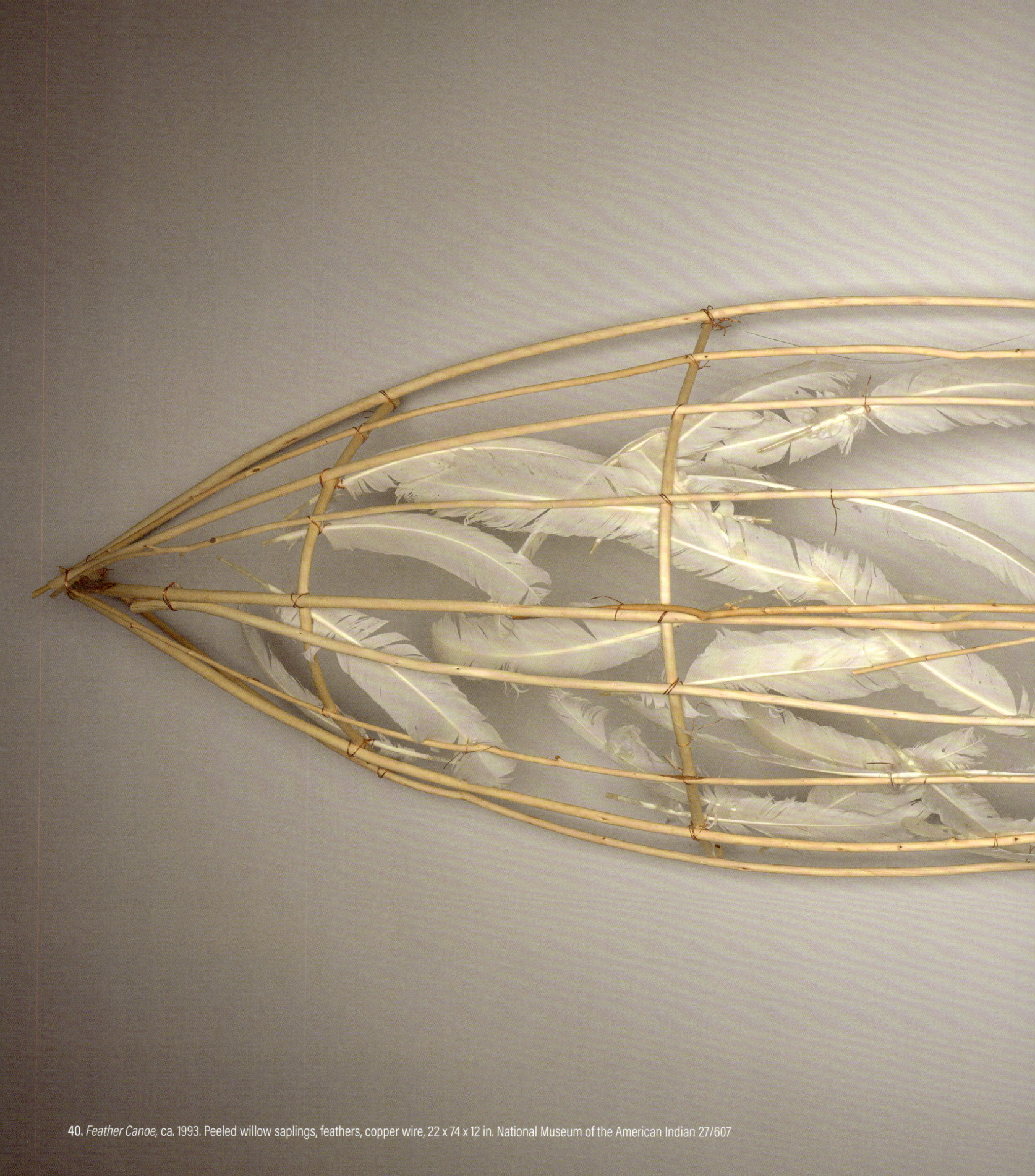

40. *Feather Canoe,* ca. 1993. Peeled willow saplings, feathers, copper wire, 22 x 74 x 12 in. National Museum of the American Indian 27/607

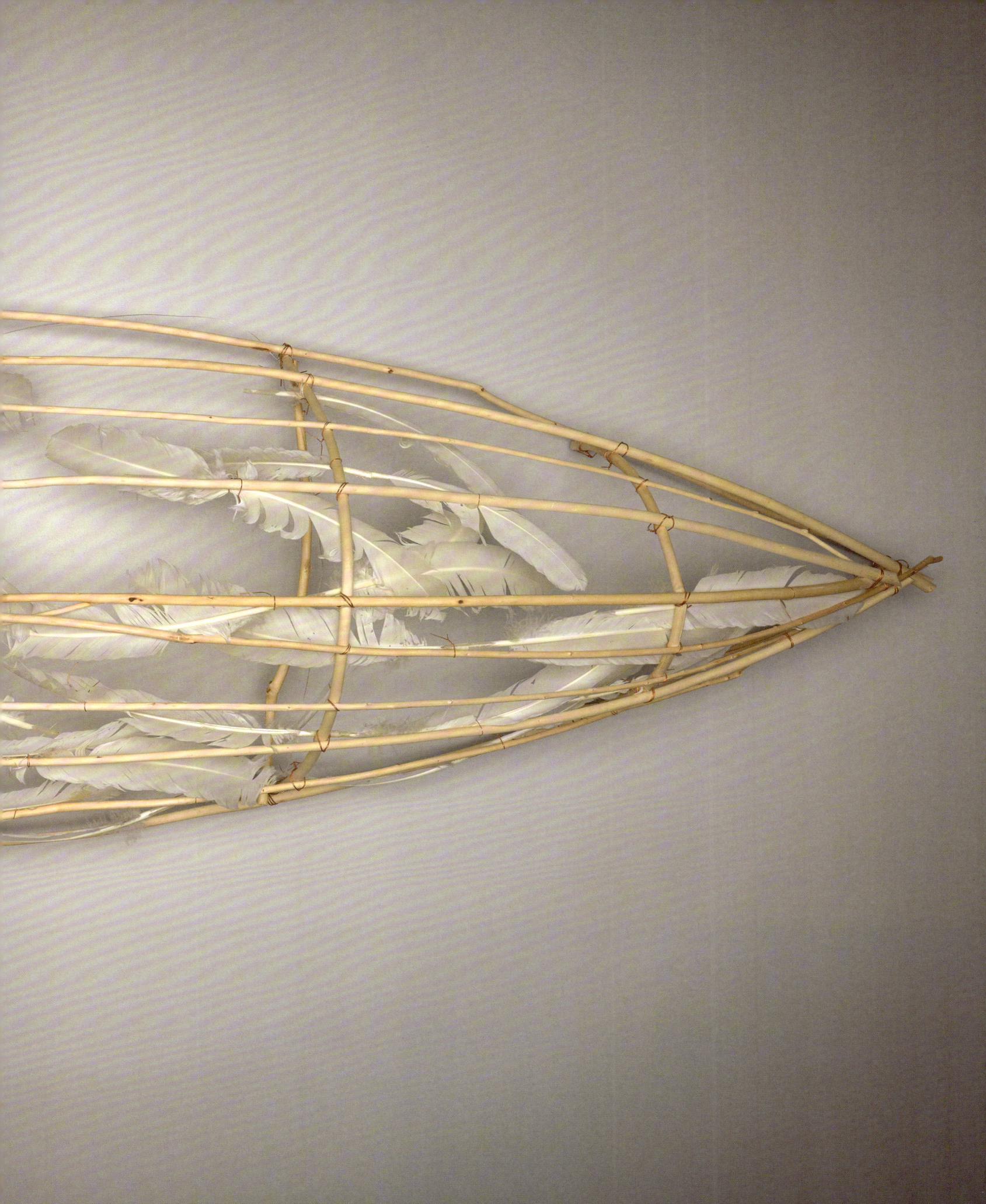

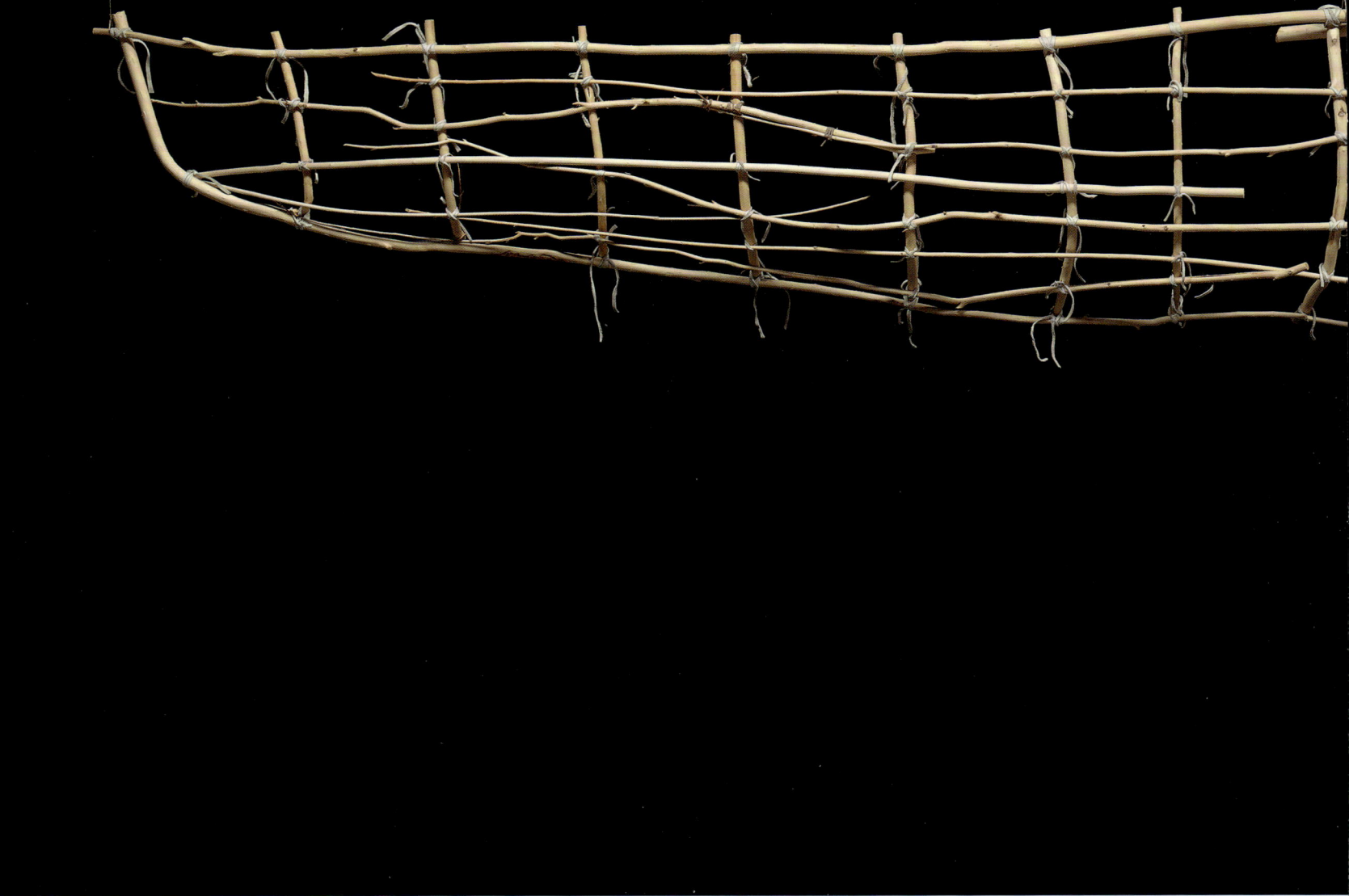

41. *Canoe Form*, 1985–90. Peeled willow saplings, leather, 25 x 191 x 25 in. National Museum of the American Indian 26/9766, gift of John and Meryl Lipton Lavine

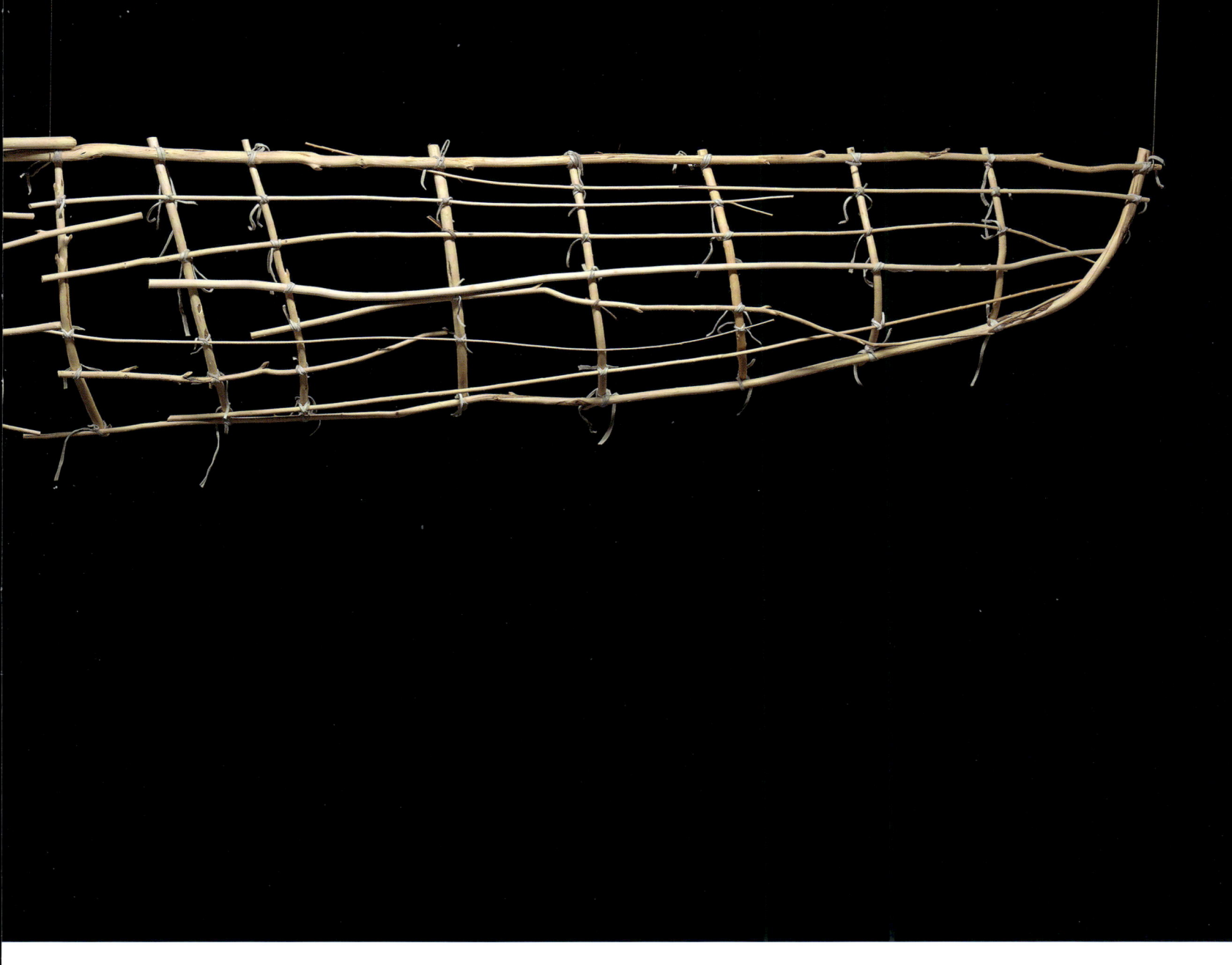

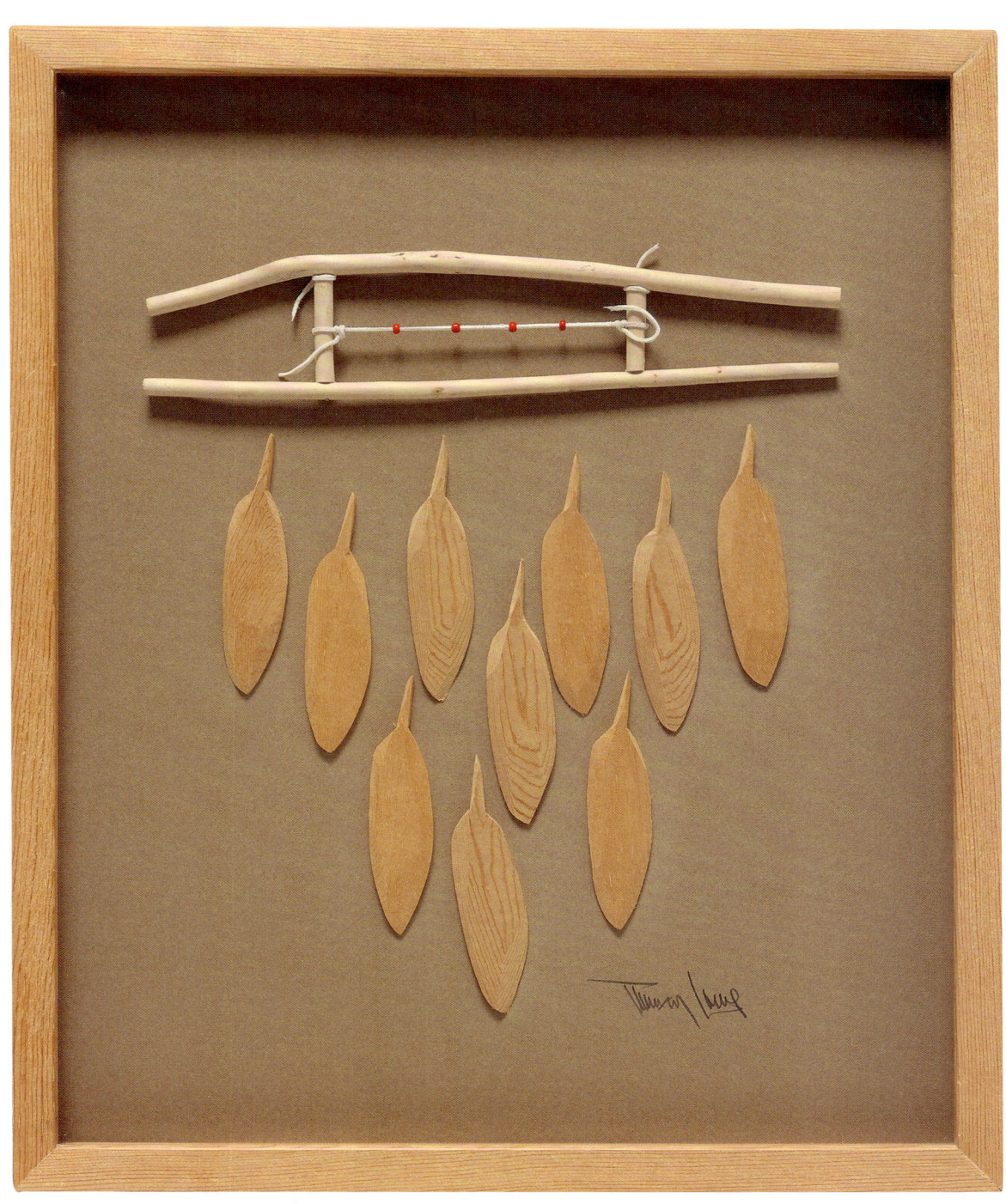

42. Untitled, from the *Artifact Series*, ca. 1980–90. Pine, peeled willow sticks, leather, glass beads on mat board, 19 x 16 in.
National Museum of the American Indian 26/9252, gift of John and Meryl Lipton Lavine

Truman Lowe: Assembling a Practice in the Early 1980s

David W. Penney

IN 1981, Truman Lowe was the coordinator of the American Indian Studies program at the University of Wisconsin–Madison and a young assistant professor of sculpture (fig. 43). Younger still, I had just started the year before as an assistant curator at the Detroit Institute of Arts. The museum had recently accessioned the Chandler/Pohrt collection, a large assemblage of Great Lakes Native arts and material culture numbering nearly one thousand individual items.[34] In an effort to publicize this collection and signal its significance for the museum, I planned a half-year-long program of visiting scholars, lectures, arts demonstrations, and a film series funded by grants from the Michigan State Council for the Humanities and the National Endowment for the Arts. Nancy Oestreich Lurie, curator of anthropology at the Milwaukee Public Museum, suggested contacting Lowe as a potential collaborator. She described him as this intelligent young Winnebago (Hoocąk) man who worked at UW–Madison and whom she knew from her fieldwork at Black River Falls, Wisconsin. In a phone conversation soon thereafter, Lowe agreed to present an arts demonstration as part of the program, although I could not have imagined what he had in mind at the time. He also agreed to serve as a consultant in selecting and reviewing films for the film series.

Lowe flew from Madison to Detroit to preview a host of short films with me, most of which I had found in Elizabeth Weatherford's *Native Americans on Film and Video*.[35] He was particularly drawn to the National Film Board of Canada's *César's Bark Canoe* (1971), an hour-long documentary wherein Cree elder César Newashish (1904–97) silently fabricates a birchbark canoe with little

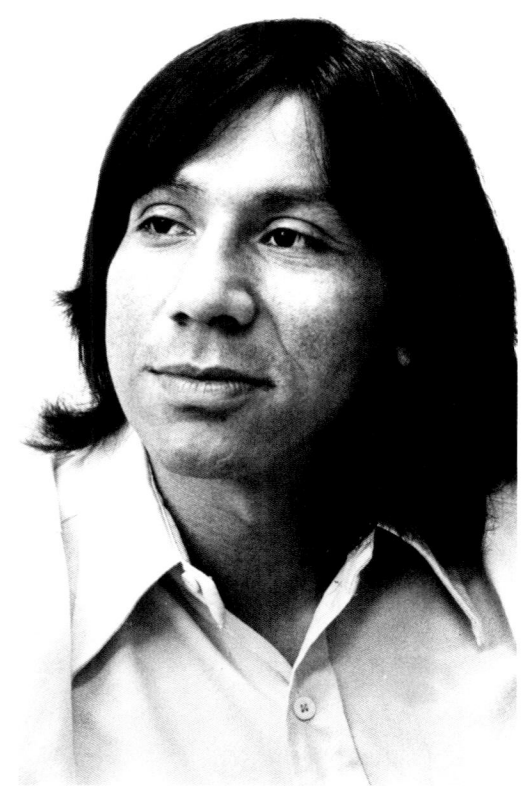

43. Truman Lowe, January 1981

more than a hand ax and a pocketknife. Similarly, *The Drummaker* (Smithsonian Folklife, 1978) documented the myriad tasks and processes necessary for William Bineshi Baker Sr. (Lac Courte Oreilles Band of Lake Superior Ojibwe, 1905–85) to create a dance drum. At one point, Baker reacts to the film crew's disappointment with the slow pace of progress, admonishing, "This is not a one-day

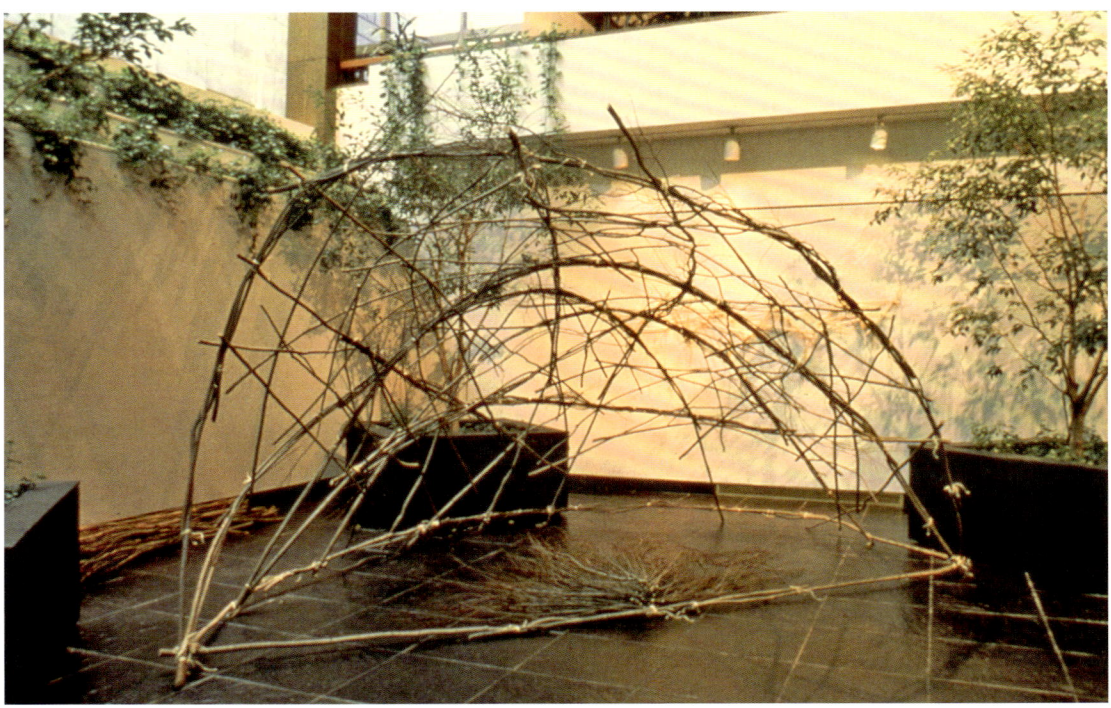
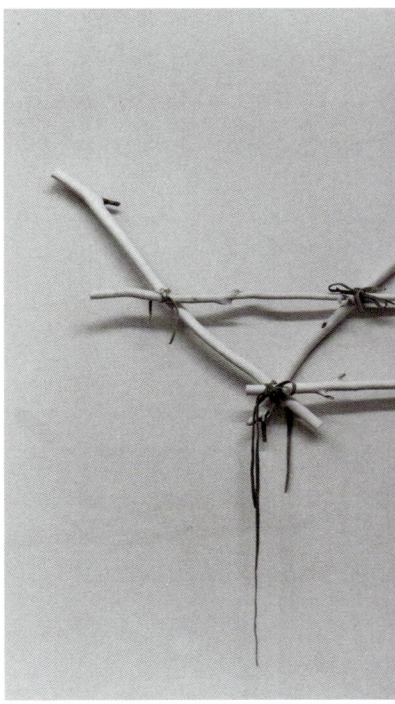

44. *Detroit River Shelter*, 1983. Willow saplings, leather, 19 x 19 x 18 ft. Detroit Institute of Arts. Not extant

job . . . not a one-day job." We looked at films available at the time about modern Native artists, such as *The Dawn Riders: Native American Artists* (1969), which featured Dick West (Southern Cheyenne, 1912–96) and Woody Crumbo (Potawatomi, 1912–89), and *Colours of Pride* (1974), wherein Tom Hill (Seneca, 1943–2023) interviews Alex Janvier (Denesuline/Saulteaux, 1935–2024), Allen Sapp (Plains Cree, 1928–2015), Daphne Odjig (Odawa/Potawatomi/English, 1919–2016), and Norval Morrisseau (Anishinaabe, 1932–2007). But the more process-driven films about making things—a canoe, a drum—seemed far more relevant to the sashes, woven bags, and wooden bowls and spoons of the Chandler/Pohrt collection, and to Lowe's own artistic process.

The Living Tradition, as it came to be called, presented six clusters of week-long public programming—gallery talk, lecture, arts demonstration, and a film with discussion—with one cluster each month scheduled over a six-month period during the fall of 1982 and early 1983. The arts demonstrations remained fairly conventional: an artist plying his or her craft and available to answer questions while seated at a table in a public space known in the museum as the "North Court," adjacent to the Native American art gallery. Don and Ida Stevens (Saginaw Chippewa; Don, 1931–2007; Ida, 1934–2017), also known as the Red Arrow family, agreed to participate and make black ash baskets. Yvonne Walker Keeshik (Odawa, b. 1946) was slated to demonstrate quillwork, but she was not able to participate. Noted sculptor Stonehorse Goeman (Tonawanda Band of Seneca, b. 1950) carved stone. Lowe's "lecture/demonstration" was scheduled for January. The promotional poster for his presentation described it as "Continuing the Tradition, One Artist's Contemporary Native Sculpture," but no one at the museum really knew what to expect.

A few days prior to Lowe's arrival in January, the museum received a crate filled with willow saplings that he had cut from the bottomlands along the Black River during an unusually balmy day after Christmas. When he arrived, he asked to borrow one of the museum's installation staff to assist him and then spent the next few days lashing the willow saplings together in the North Court

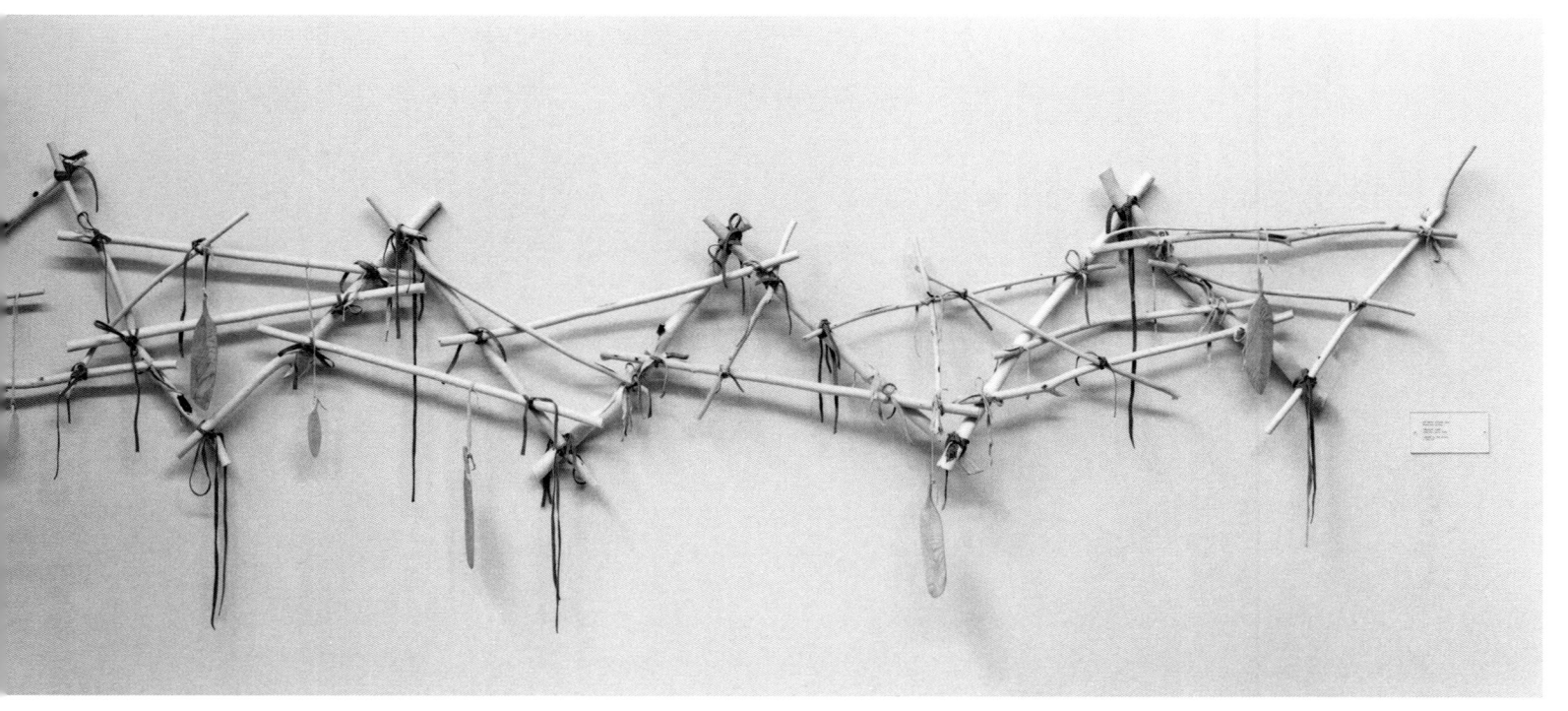

45. *Detroit River*, 1983. Peeled willow sticks, pine, rawhide, copper wire, 24 x 120 x 4 in. Truman T. Lowe Estate

to create a slightly saggy, half-domed structure he called *Detroit River Shelter* (fig. 44). It looked like a filigreed skeleton of a wigwam with a fan of twigs on the floor inside to suggest a fire or fireplace. In a backpack, Lowe also brought a collection of peeled and cut willow sticks that he lashed together with leather ties to create an angular relief wall sculpture, which he called *Detroit River* (fig. 45). While planned conceptually, both sculptures were largely improvisatory in the making. He simply tied the saplings or sticks together to create the forms he intended. *Detroit River Shelter* seemed particularly adventuresome, combining structural and formal considerations on the fly. Lowe had conceived *Detroit River* a little more thoroughly in advance, bringing along with the peeled sticks a collection of carved wooden "feathers" to hang as pendants from the wall sculpture. He was especially proud of having transported all the component pieces of *Detroit River* in a backpack, allowing him to assemble the sculpture on site.

Lowe also brought three small, framed works he wished to sell to the museum shop or to any patron who wished to buy them. Each was a simple construction

mounted on colored mat board, consisting of sticks or dowels meticulously wrapped in brightly colored thread and tied together to form squares or a simple fan shape. These then served as a scaffold for pendant feathers or, in one work, a nickel (German silver) brooch with pendant strings of glass beads. Lowe framed the mat-board constructions in varnished shadow boxes, each twenty by sixteen inches and glazed with plexiglass. The works were "experiments," Lowe told me, particularly the shadow-box presentation.

The small, framed works resemble others Lowe made about the same time and sold to Chicago collector John Lavine, who later donated them to the National Museum of the American Indian (figs. 42, 46, and 47). These too are small assemblages composed of peeled or floss-wrapped sticks, feathers (real or carved of wood), and other objects—in one instance, a small, rounded stone. There are no obvious signifiers in the sense of the ensemble representing something. Instead, they seem most analogous to a made-up artifact: different materials combined in ways that emulate craft production, such as wrapping or lashing, and Indigenous materials and symbols, such as feathers, beads, the number four, and so on. It is as if Lowe wished to reproduce the mystery and spiritual resonance of Indigenous heritage items but to avoid any direct reference or resemblance to historical artifacts. The artworks Lowe brought to the Detroit Institute of Arts in early 1983 were greeted by visitors, staff, and art enthusiasts with little more than polite curiosity and indifference. *Detroit River Shelter* occupied the North Court of the museum for a few months until a maintenance crew removed it to a dumpster. Practically speaking, it could not be transported or stored. Additionally, Lowe never intended for this to be a permanent structure—permanence wasn't part of his vocabulary. I attempted to convince the curator of twentieth-century art at the time to purchase *Detroit River* but was not successful. I retained it at the museum as a long-term loan to await a more sympathetic curator—but that never happened. I had no luck finding homes for the three small shadow-box pieces either. One professor of sculpture at a local university, whom I approached because he collected antique Native American art, complained about their "presentation," as if offering an art student critique. Recalling these events of 1983, I think it is safe to say that nobody in Detroit had seen anything like Lowe's work before, and they simply didn't understand it. It seemed too insubstantial, slapdash, and ephemeral.

If we pull back to consider the larger context of Native arts in the early 1980s, some confusion and uncertainty about what Lowe was up to make a little more sense. Born in 1944, Lowe belonged to an influential and transformative generation of Native American artists, including Jaune Quick-to-See Smith, George Longfish, Bob Haozous (Warm Springs Chiricahua Apache, b. 1943), Peter Jemison, Harry Fonseca (Nisenan Maidu/Hawaiian/Portuguese, 1946–2006), and Robert Houle (Saulteaux Anishinaabe, Sandy Bay First Nation, b. 1947), among others. These artists began their careers in the 1970s at a time when Native arts and Native artists were undergoing radical transformations. As artist Lloyd Oxendine (Lumbee, 1942–2015) put it in his very influential essay for *Art in America* in 1972, "Until quite recently, modern American Indian art was not considered authentic or valuable unless it was executed in

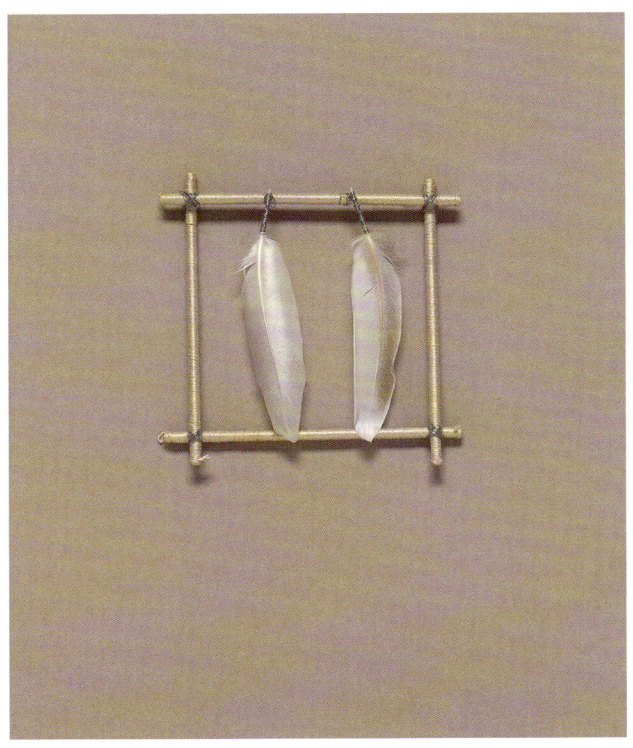

46. Untitled from the *Artifact Series*, ca. 1985–90. Feathers, wood, thread, copper wire on mat board, 12 x 10 in. National Museum of the American Indian 26/9765, gift of John and Meryl Lipton Lavine

strictly traditional Indian forms.... For the first time, a generation of articulate and well-educated Indian artists have a positive Indian identity to which they may relate. Their new solidarity focuses their art, an art that is Indian in a whole new way."[36] Edwin Wade and Rennard Strickland's (Osage/Cherokee, 1940–2021) 1981 survey for the Philbrook Museum, *Magic Images: Contemporary Native American Art*, referred to this generation as "individualists."[37] Lowe's early graduate school sculptures at UW–Madison, conceived with the *au courant* considerations of minimalism and fabricated of manipulated plastic, eschewed any overt references to his Hoocąk experiences or identity. But by the early seventies, Lowe had reconsidered that position. Like other Native artists of his generation, he began to explore how to bring his cultural understandings as a Native individual into his sculpture.[38]

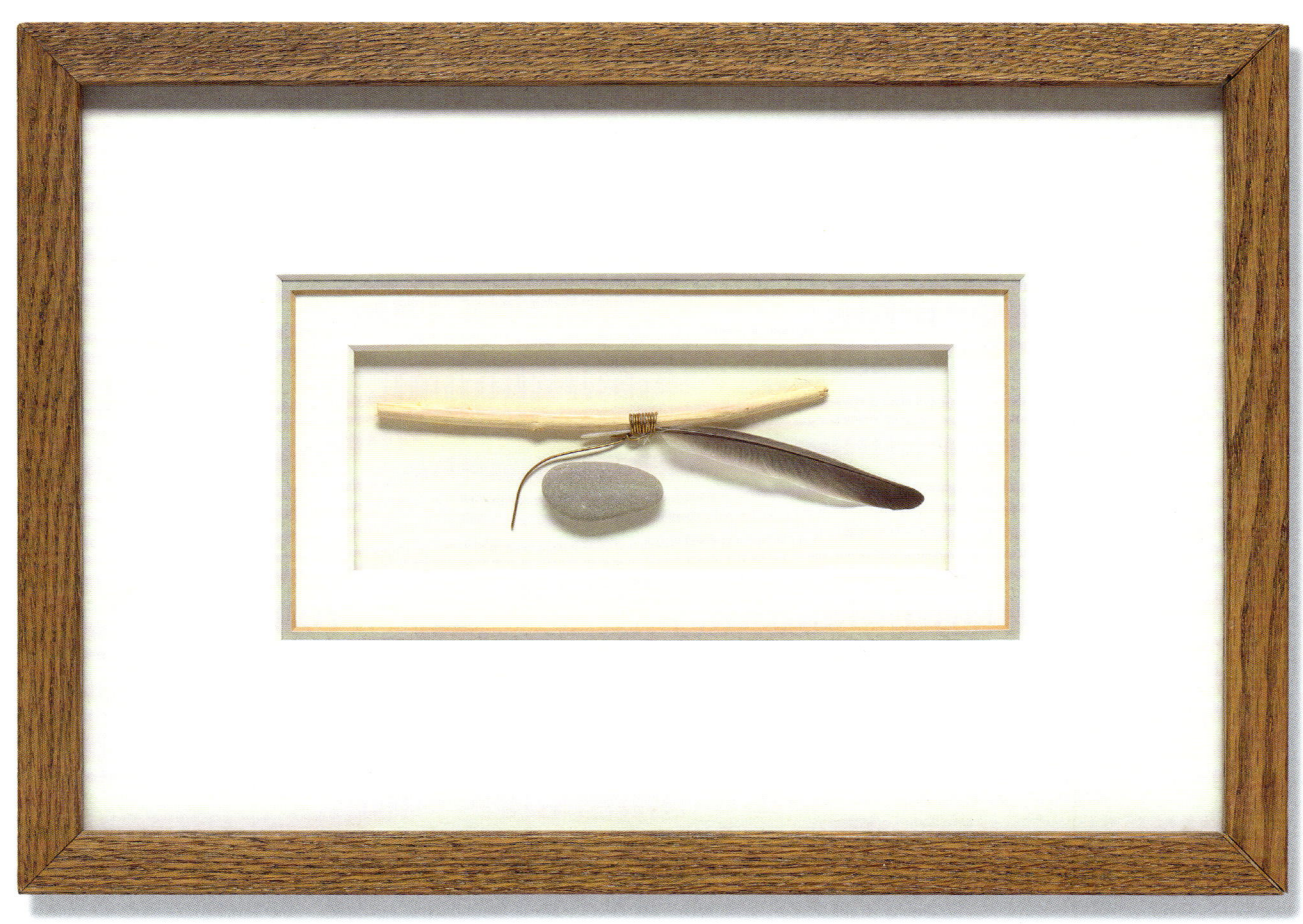

47. Untitled, from the *Artifact Series*, ca. 1985–90. Peeled willow stick, feather, stone, copper wire on mat board, 8 x 11 in. National Museum of the American Indian 26/9253, gift of John and Meryl Lipton Lavine

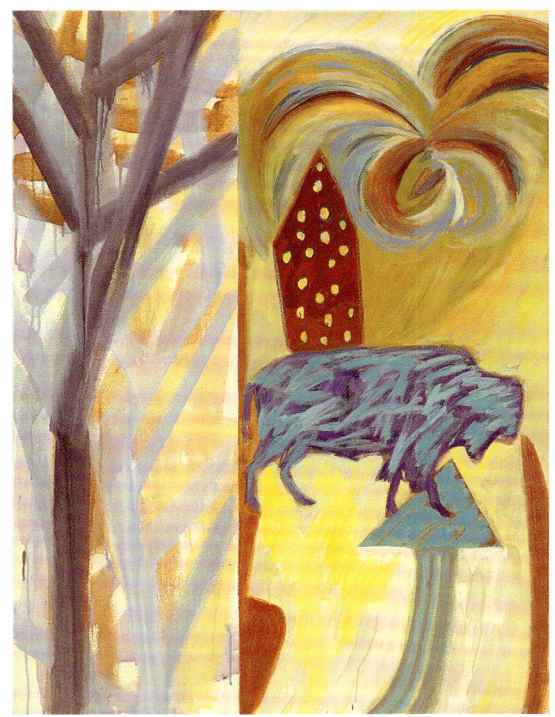

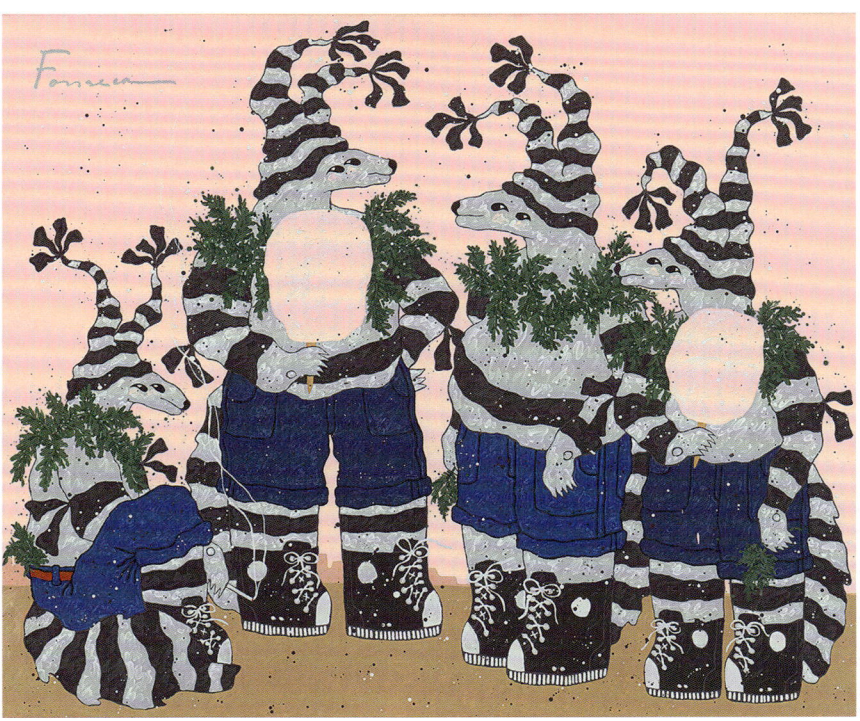

48. Jaune Quick-to-See Smith (citizen of the Confederated Salish and Kootenai Nation, 1940–2025), *Red Lake Series #5*, 1981. Acrylic on canvas, 48 x 36 ¼ in. National Museum of the American Indian 25/590, gift of Leonard D. Horodenski and Anne Pomeroy Horodenski

49. Harry Fonseca (Nisenan Maidu/Hawaiian/Portuguese, 1946–2006), *Dance Break*, 1982. Acrylic on canvas, 60 x 72 ¼ in. National Museum of the American Indian 26/8885

The problem lay in how to merge these lived experiences and cultural understandings with the late-modernist, studio disciplines of contemporary art of the time. Robert Houle, a curator and critic as well as an artist, wrote eloquently about this issue in the catalog for his group show *New Work by a New Generation* for the Norman MacKenzie Art Gallery in Regina, Saskatchewan, in 1982. When merging North American and Western European artistic traditions, Houle urged Native artists to "create an independent art relevant to contemporary Indian and Inuit life."[39] Similarly, George Longfish and his frequent co-author Joan Randall, in the introduction to *Contemporary Native American Art*, their survey of the contemporary Native scene for the Gardiner Art Gallery at Oklahoma State University in 1983, wrote that artists of their generation "talk of technique, of materials used, of problems to be solved. None of the artists concern themselves with how 'Indian' their work appears."[40]

The challenge, when it came to critical and popular reception of Lowe's work at the time, was that no one else was doing anything like it. Most of his generational contemporaries were painters drawing upon the critically celebrated traditions of gestural abstraction, like Jaune Quick-to-See Smith (fig. 48); large-scale minimalism, like Robert Houle; or pop art—think of Harry Fonseca's coyotes (fig. 49). Lowe's rough-hewn, raw wood assemblages corresponded to little else in the emerging world of contemporary Native arts of the 1980s, or the contemporary art world more broadly speaking. But their unique character is their genius.

In his statement for the Gardiner Art Gallery catalog, Lowe wrote, "The origin of my work stems from a personal investigation into the history of the woodland Indians of the Western Great Lakes region. Traditional craftsmen of this area utilized materials from their environment to produce their crafts, such as black ash splint-plait basketry, birch bark containers and shelter coverings, cattail reed mats and porcupine quill decorations."[41]

Lowe frequently acknowledged his parents and his upbringing as a wellspring for his art. His mother and father collaborated to make black ash baskets. The technique is labor intensive and requires deep knowledge of the materials, the environment that nurtures them, and the seasons of their growth.[42] The best ash wood comes from an environment that fosters generous and evenly spaced growth rings so that when the ash log is pounded, the rings split into even, pliable, and fine-grained slats or "splints," as Truman called them. The slats are trimmed to size and then further worked by the meticulous and repetitive motions of weaving and finishing.

Similarly, Lowe's process for the exhibition in Detroit began with the gathering and preparation of materials: the willow saplings harvested from the Black River bottomlands in December for the construction of *Detroit River Shelter*, or the carefully cut and peeled willow sticks and carved wooden feather pendants for *Detroit River*. Lowe often talked about his father's knowledge of wood and how the character of its growth in certain environments informed his selection of materials for basket handles. The construction of Lowe's *Detroit* works involved skilled, repetitive motions like those used when weaving a basket. But his lashing together of saplings and sticks required a far more intuited and improvised process than basket weaving. Those improvisatory and gestural characteristics joined Lowe's process to more contemporary studio practices.

Lowe introduced visual and material signifiers of Woodlands Native culture to his art but in a reductive fashion. In the late 1970s, he borrowed the traditional war shield and even a baby carrier as motifs for a few small works.[43] In later sculptures his referents become far more basic and generalized. Feathers became a recurring motif, for example. I remember Lowe commenting on the poor quality of commercial feathers—turkey, mostly—which he used for some early works to avoid problems with the Migratory Bird Treaty Act of 1918. As an alternative, he carved feathers of wood for use as pendants or other components of assembled works, their surfaces smoothed and sanded to heighten the feather-like grain of the wood (fig. 50).

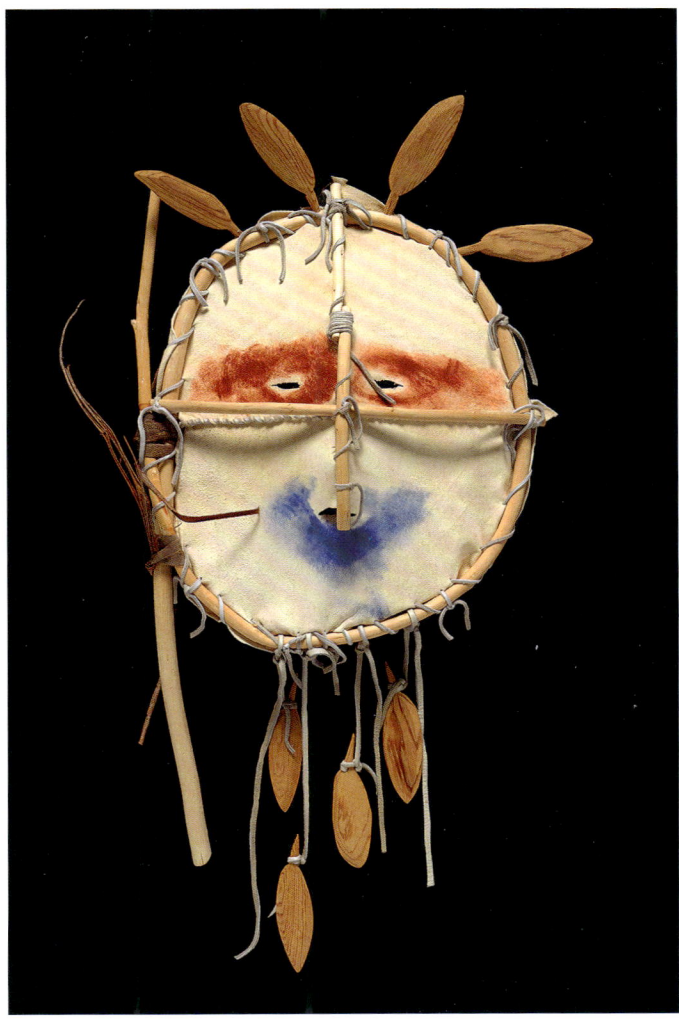

50. *Mask*, 1985–90. Leather, pine, peeled willow sticks and bark, brushed powdered pigment, 26 ½ x 12 x 2 ½ in. National Museum of the American Indian 26/9255, gift of John and Meryl Lipton Lavine

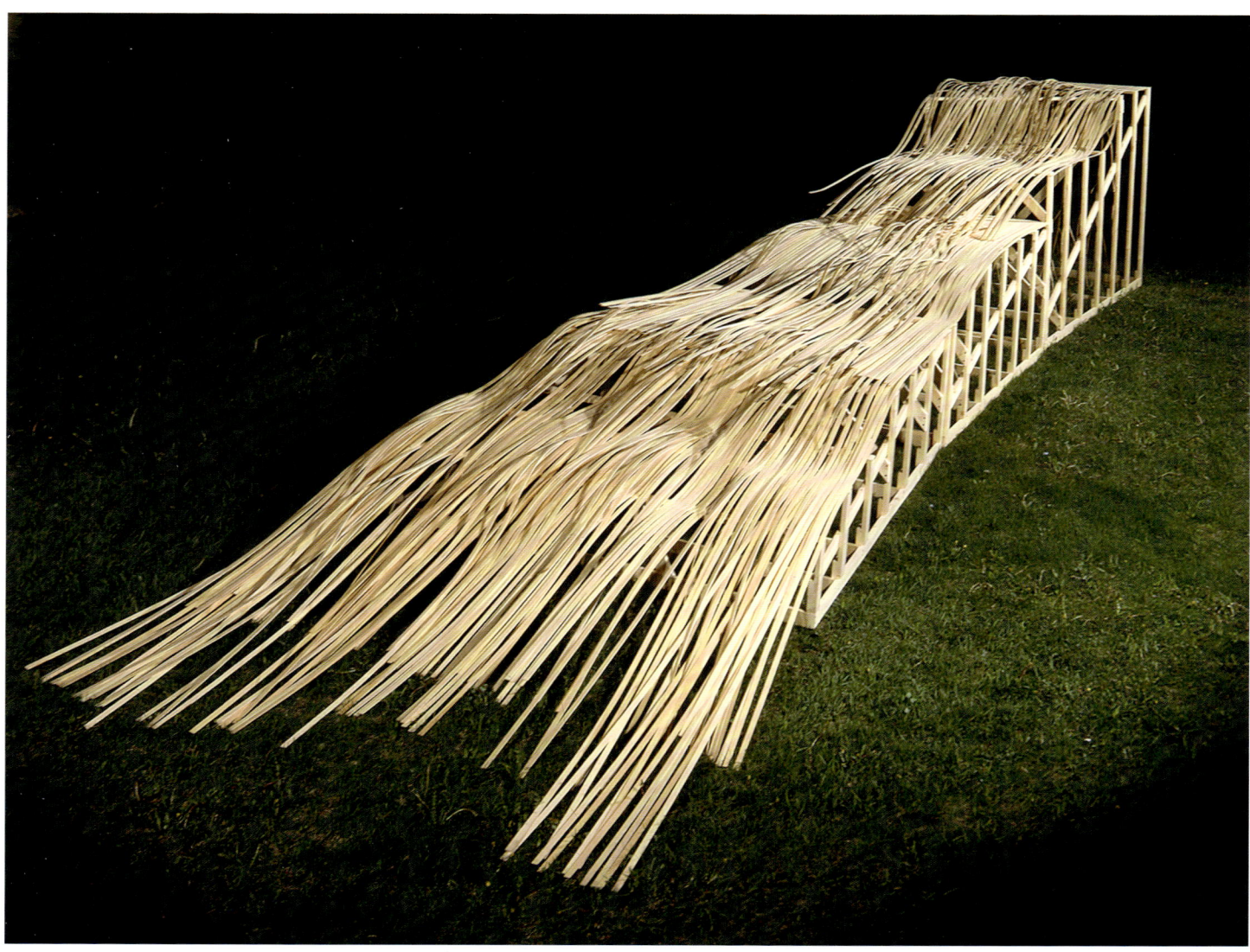

51. *Ottawa*, 1992. Pine, peeled willow saplings, 5 ¾ x 8 x 30 ft. Truman T. Lowe Estate

Rebecca Head Trautmann, the curator at the National Museum of the American Indian who worked with Lowe, recalled his speaking of the deliberate use of the number four in composition: four feathers, four beads strung on a pendant, the four sides to a square, the four directions—a traditional Woodlands Indian cosmological and symbolic concept. "Whenever anything happens in a sequence of four in our traditional Winnebago culture, it can be considered significant," he claimed.[44]

When Lowe created works for the Detroit exhibition, he focused on its particular qualities of place, and more specifically, the city's origins and setting on the Detroit River. The meaning of the French term *le détroit* is "strait," referring to the strait between Lakes Erie and Saint Clair (the smallest of the Great Lakes system). The site for the original settlement, which grew into the major city of today, was chosen for its strategic location on this critical waterway. Water, rivers, and streams were a recurring focus for Lowe.

Ten years later, when invited to create a work for the landmark 1992 exhibition *Land, Spirit, Power: First Nations at the National Gallery of Canada* in Ottawa,[45]

Lowe responded similarly with a work titled *Ottawa*, but this time summoning the distinctive, local features of the Ottawa River (fig. 51). The sculpture is a monumental construction of raw wood lath that suggests the movement of water descending in an undulating cascade or rapids. The referent is undoubtedly Chaudière Falls, a violent rapids and one of the most salient features of the city site, where the Ottawa River narrows between rocky escarpments and small, starkly vegetated islands. Samuel de Champlain commented when he portaged around the rapids in 1613, "This cataract produces such a noise in this basin that it is heard for more than two leagues." De Champlain also observed what he referred to as a "customary ceremony" at the foot of the falls, where Natives accompanying him offered tobacco with songs and dancing.[46] Lowe's work no doubt responds to these histories and stories.

Throughout his career, Lowe continued exploring the "structural elements of shelters" that he wrote about in his 1983 statement for the Gardiner Art Gallery catalog. In many ways, *Detroit River Shelter* anticipates his final public work, *Ke-Chunk Ciporoke*, a commission for Nature at the Confluence, a conservation site and park in South Beloit, Illinois (fig. 94). He started the sculpture just before his death in 2019, and it was installed by students and friends. A Hoocąk town called Keecąk occupied this site at the confluence of Turtle Creek and Rock River until 1832. The sculpture itself presents a domed framework of a small wigwam, here in painted steel but echoing the willow sapling construction of *Detroit River Shelter*.[47] Both commemorate Native presence associated with waterways by referencing traditional domiciles and construction (necessarily mimicked in metal for the permanent outdoor sculpture).

In the late 1970s, very early in his career, Lowe established and thereafter expanded a studio practice to pursue his "fascination with woodland culture, symbolism of rituals, [and] use of natural materials."[48] His themes, forms, motifs, and materials stem from his investigations and lived experiences as a part of Woodlands Native culture. "As a woodland Indian," he told curator Diana Nemiroff, "I can't ignore my environment, and I think that's what my work reflects. It comes from the land that I'm most familiar with."[49]

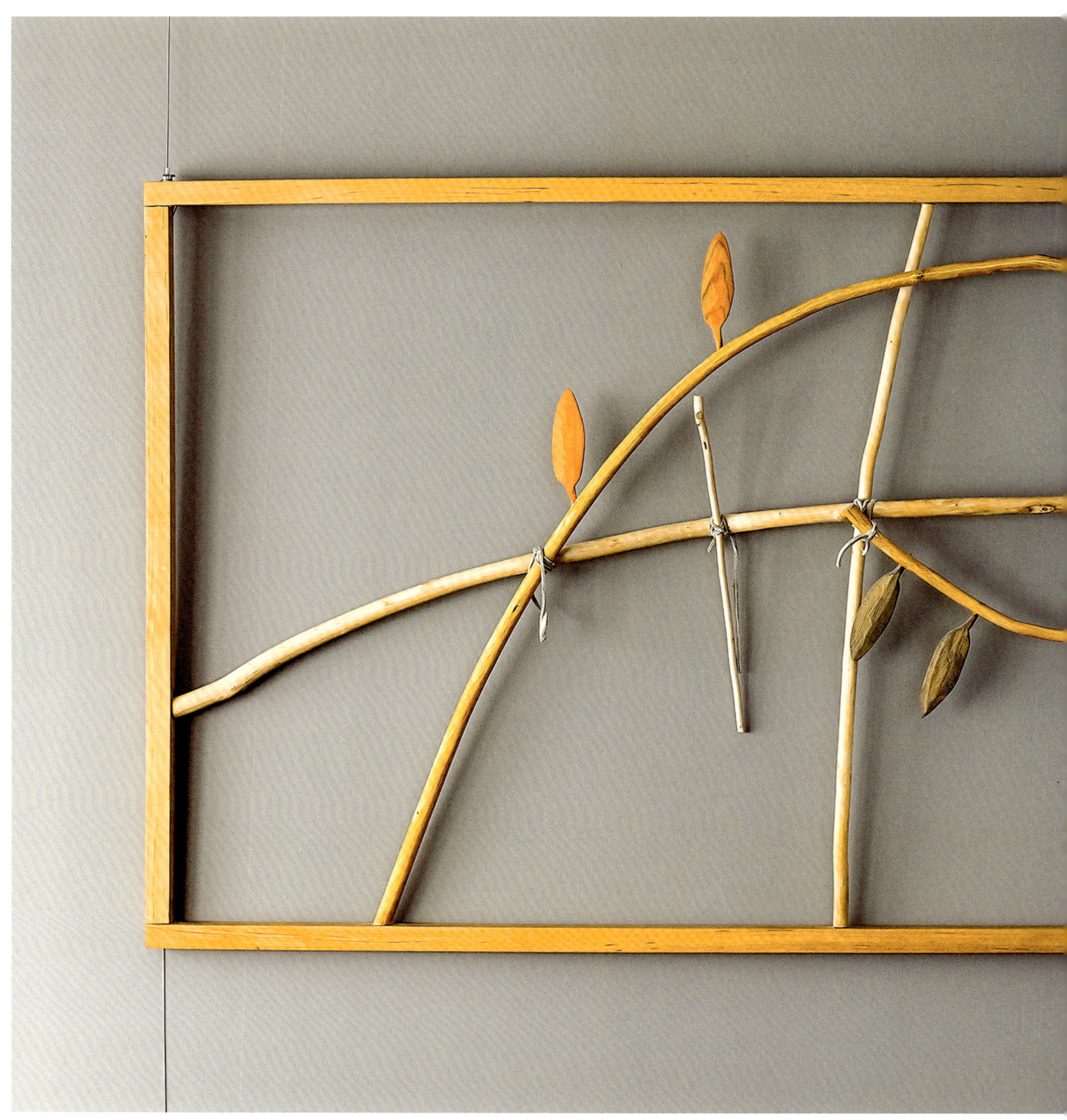

52. *Skychart III*, 1986. Pine, peeled willow saplings, leather, watercolor, 24 x 60 x 4 in. Collection of Linda Nix and Neil Short

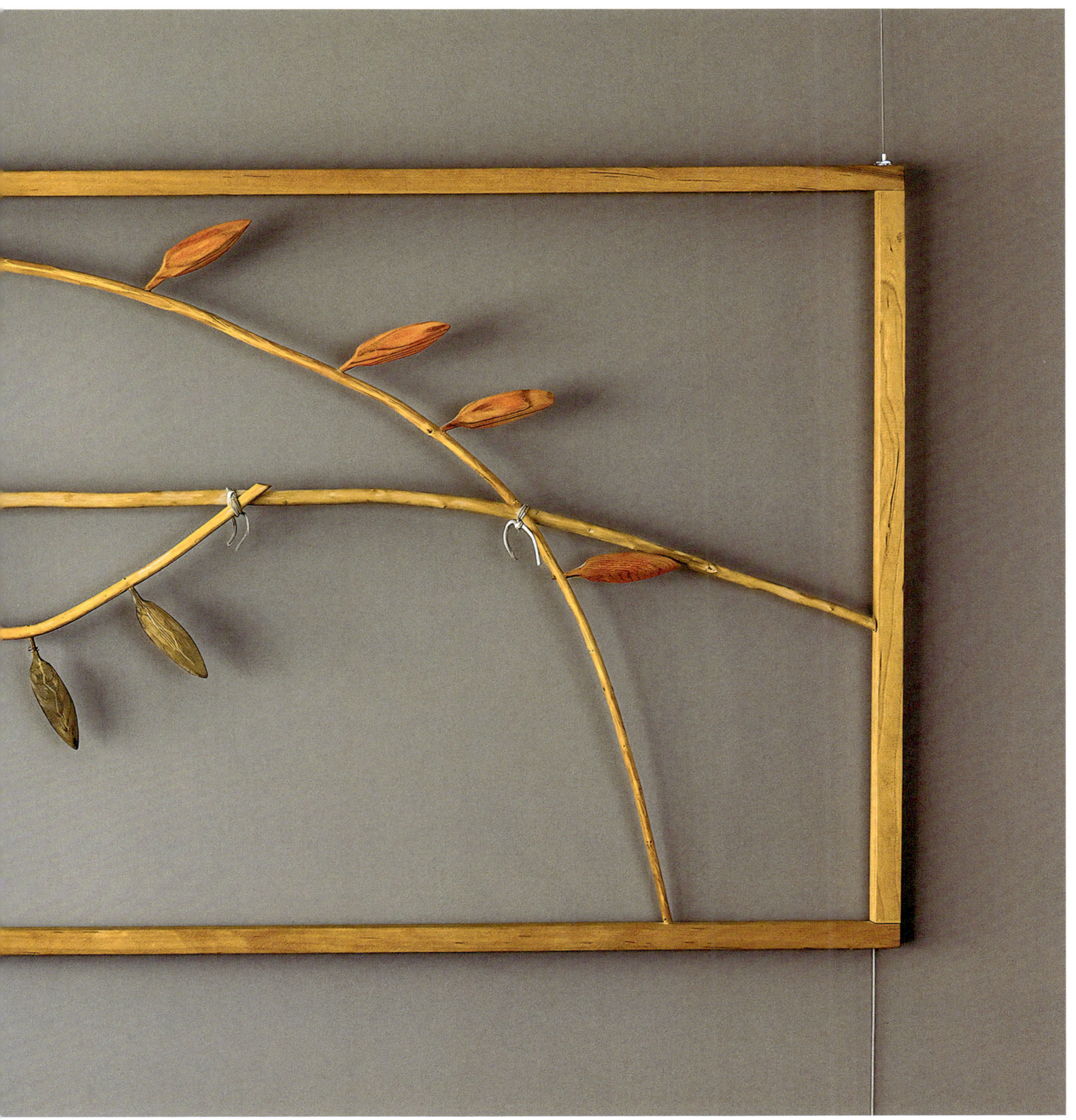

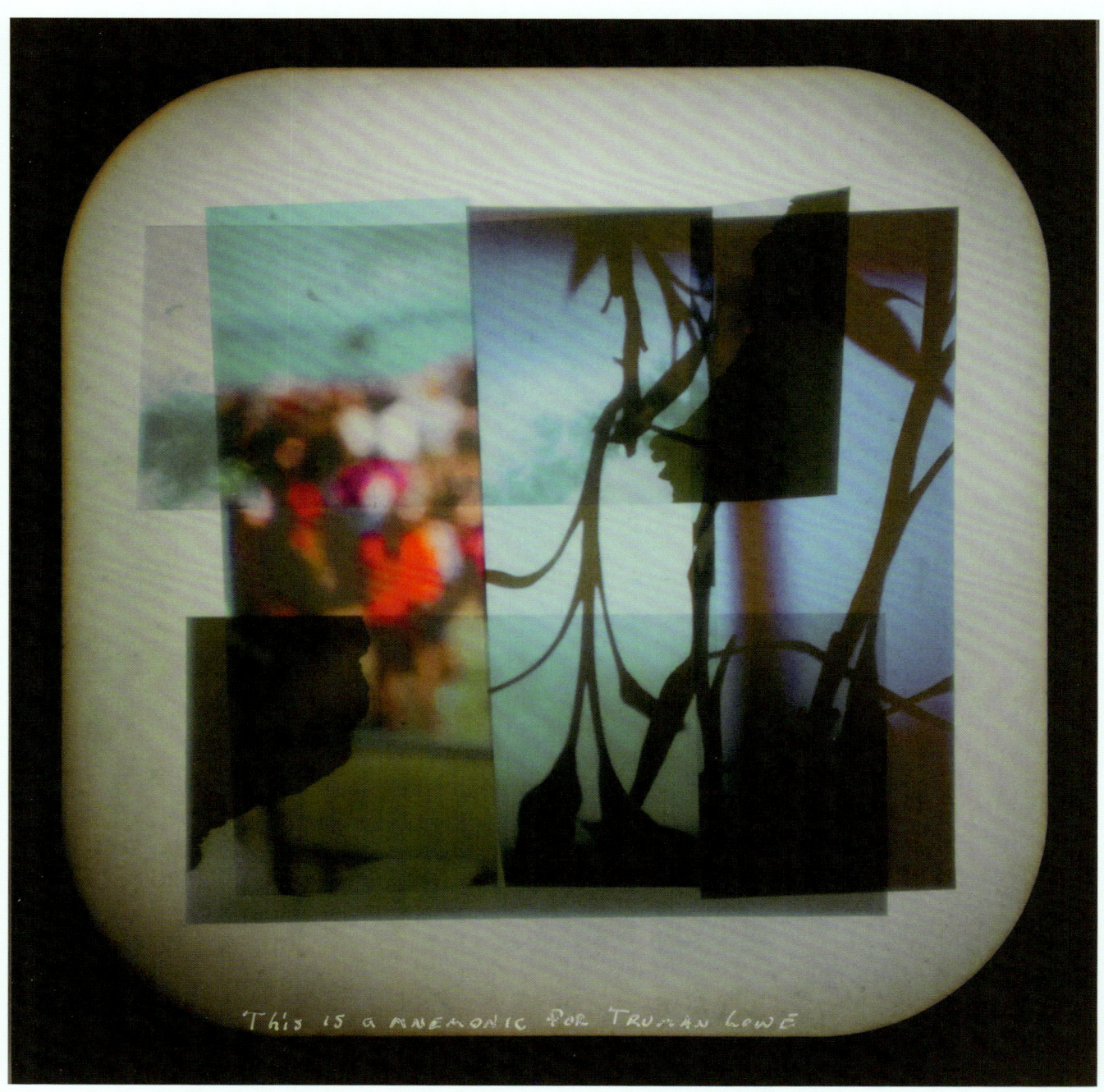

53. Sky Hopinka (Ho-Chunk Nation/Pechanga Band of Luiseño Indians), *This is a mnemonic for Truman Lowe*, 2019. Inkjet print, etching, 13 x 13 in. National Museum of the American Indian 27/776

This is a mnemonic for Truman Lowe

Sky Hopinka

THE PHOTOGRAPH *This is a mnemonic for Truman Lowe* really began about a decade before it was made, when I first saw Truman's work in his *Mnemonic* series, hanging on a wall at an artist's house. I thought it was beautiful. Small branches, twigs, and little objects from our homelands—objects that instilled a sense of meaning and grounding and representation in their assemblage. Representation for a history that I felt connected to. Even though I grew up in the Pacific Northwest, Wisconsin is still my homeland and carries the connection to my father, my grandmother, and all the family. It is a connection through my name and my namesake: my great-grandfather, Blue Sky.

Whenever I'd see Truman's work, I would always feel a sense of understanding and learning and knowing and mystery. It wasn't a learning of everything, a knowing of what I couldn't know but, rather, a familiarity and a warmth that invited me in. A familiarity that spoke of family and earth and breath. It was an introduction and a welcome into a world that one can be a part of by birth and by birthright. A world that had no place for assimilation tactics; for choices that were made by my father, my grandmother, and my grandfather; or for the choices that were made for them.

The series this photo is from is called *The Land Describes Itself* and is about listening to the landscape and listening to a language you might not know but can still understand. When I started putting the photos together that make up this series, and assembling the transparency cutouts, I began by arranging them in different configurations. I was guided by what felt right, what was

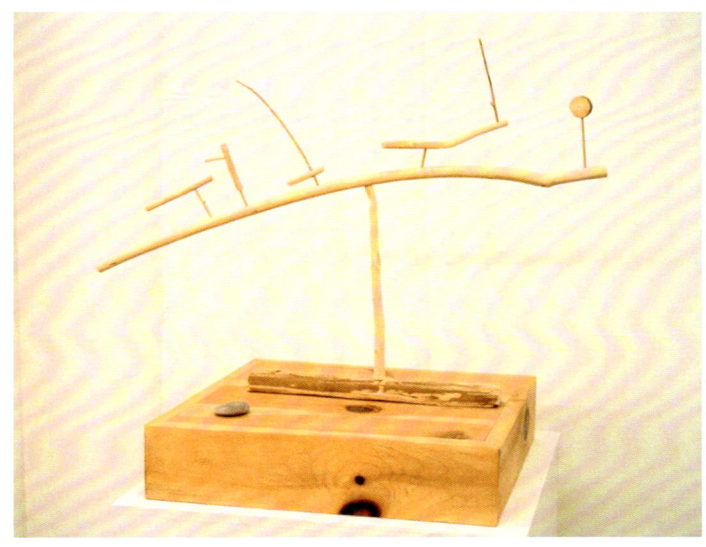

54. *Mnemonic*, ca. 1988. Peeled willow, stone, pine base, 19 ½ x 24 ¼ x 8 in. Not extant

intuitive, and into things that reminded me of a memory or a place or an impossible description.

The text etched on the bottom of each photograph is meant to be an evocative descriptor of the thing that you're seeing, taking you beyond the purely representational aspects of photography and the indexical instincts that arise when you recognize what you know. With this one in particular, I had thought of Truman and his mnemonics. He had just passed away some months before I made this, and there was something about the configuration that felt like a mnemonic for something and someone back home, drawn from a time that is circular, weightless, and repeating.

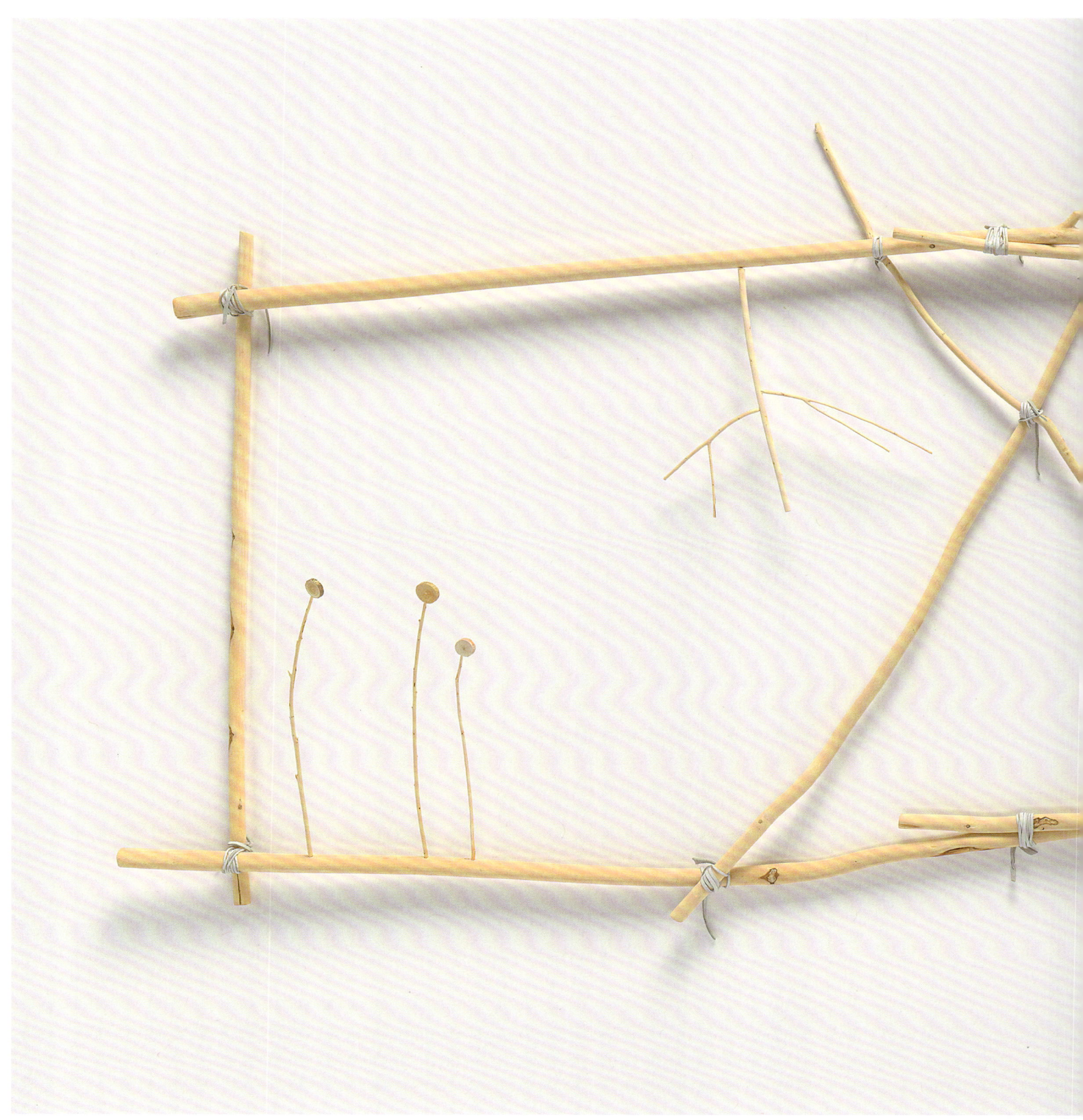

55. *Mnemonic*, ca. 1985–90, 2013. Peeled willow, leather, paper, 37 x 90 x 3 in. National Museum of the American Indian 26/8988, gift of John and Meryl Lipton Lavine

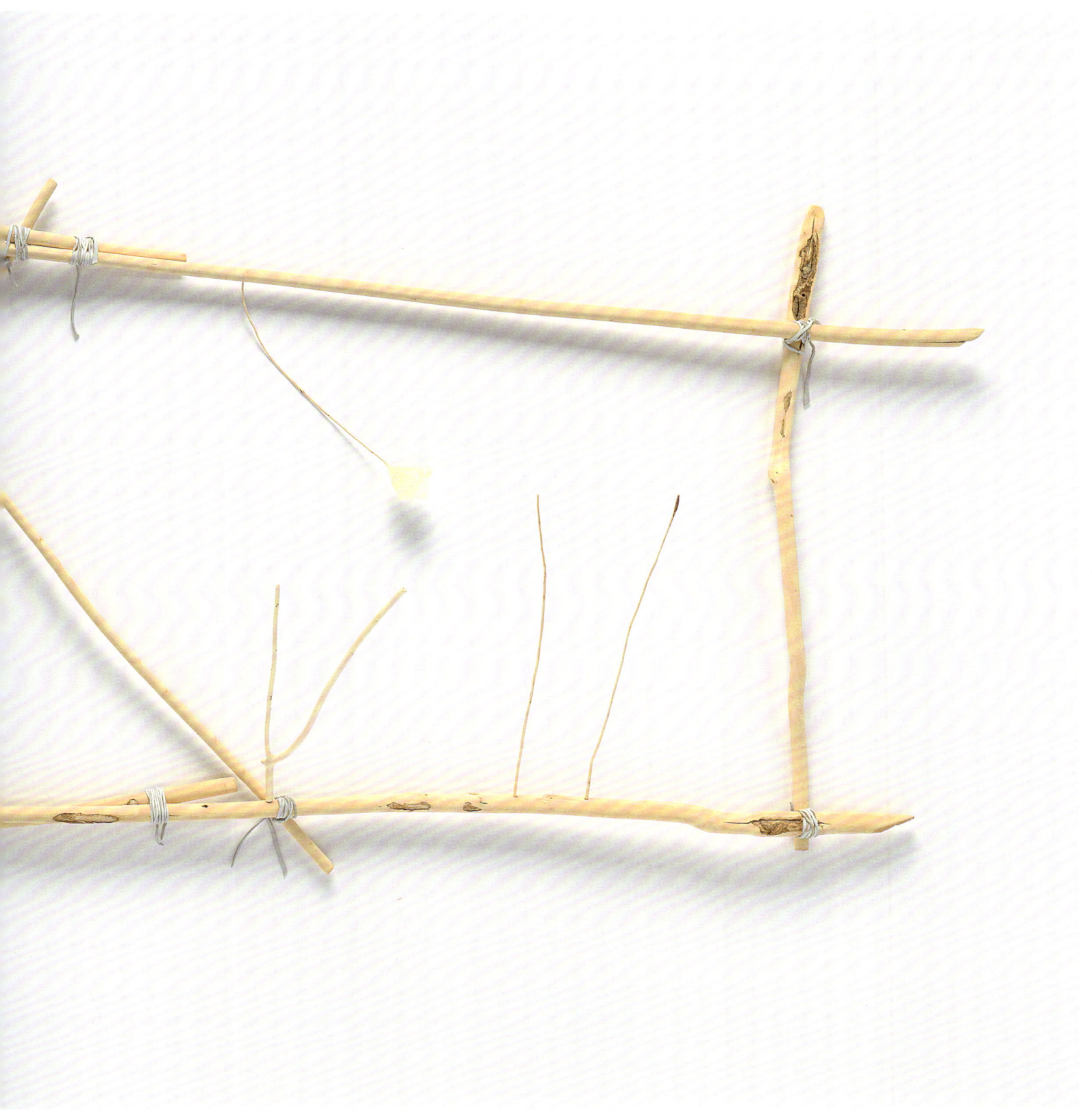

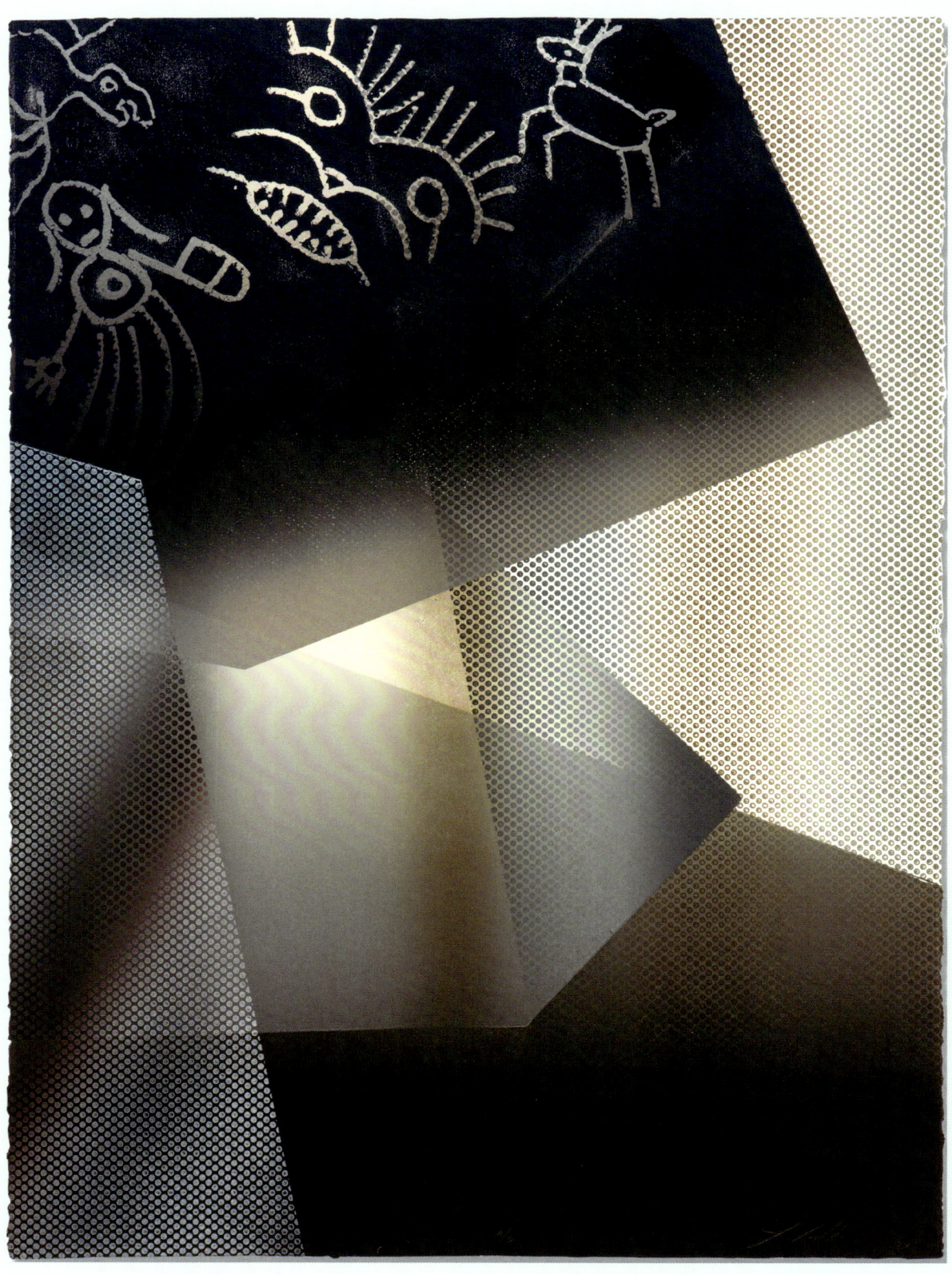

56. Joe Feddersen (Confederated Tribes of the Colville Reservation), *The Changer II*, 1992. Ink relief print on paper, 30 x 22 in. National Museum of the American Indian 26/4325, gift of R. E. Mansfield

Land Acknowledgments

Joe Feddersen with Rachel Allen

IN PLATEAU CULTURE, First Ceremonies mark seasonal cycles as well as collective connection to place. When the first salmon of the run migrate upstream, when the first roots of the season are gathered, or when a new hunter harvests a deer for the first time, protocols direct us to share these gifts with the community before taking part ourselves. This act echoes the generosity of plants and animals who gave themselves first. As recipients of generosity, we ensure each other's survival through giving. To me, Truman Lowe embodied the spirit of First Ceremonies in his pathfinding career.

As in First Ceremonies, Lowe used his esteemed faculty position at the University of Wisconsin–Madison to recruit and mentor a vibrant community of students. I first met Lowe in Seattle in 1983, when artists convened with curators and scholars at the Native American Art Studies Association conference. There, Lowe invited me to pursue a master of fine arts degree with him, which I later accepted. During this MFA program, my peers and I received mentorship that helped us understand who we wanted to be as artists. Lowe encouraged me to make work free of allegiances to specific mediums, where I could combine processes to make my creative practice. This allowed me to develop my work as a painterly printmaker who was more concerned with gestural mark making. Additionally, I was free to experiment with nascent digital technologies and glass casting. Throughout the program, Lowe modeled a community-based practice where everyone helped each other with the necessary tasks to complete their work, such as pouring bronze or casting aluminum. Beyond the classroom, Lowe facilitated a community by inviting students to dinner, canoeing, or powwows. From this experience, Lowe and I developed a lifelong friendship.

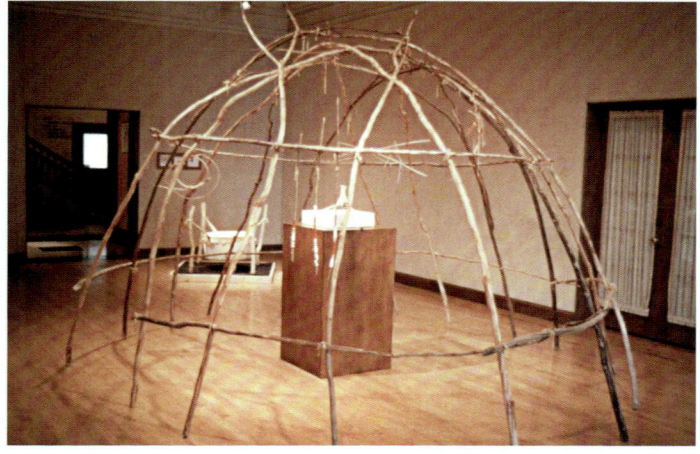

57. Lowe's *Constructions* exhibition at the University of Wisconsin–Madison Memorial Union main gallery, 1980.

Our brotherly bond revealed our common approaches to art making. I believe that each artist tells the history of a place: Lowe of the Great Lakes region and myself of the Plateau. Culture is woven into artists' works, addressing important aspects of the land and how it is viewed by our respective communities. Lowe responded to the mounds and dwellings of his homeland; likewise, I look to ancient petroglyphs ubiquitous to my region for inspiration. Each of us has built on a layered history as part of a continuum that predates American art history. In this way, these landscapes can be seen as land acknowledgments. Paramount to me is the spiritual relationship to the land and culture evident in Lowe's work. Lowe's commitment to the community fostered the careers of many artists, and the cycle continues through his former students in their generosity and mentorship of the next generation.

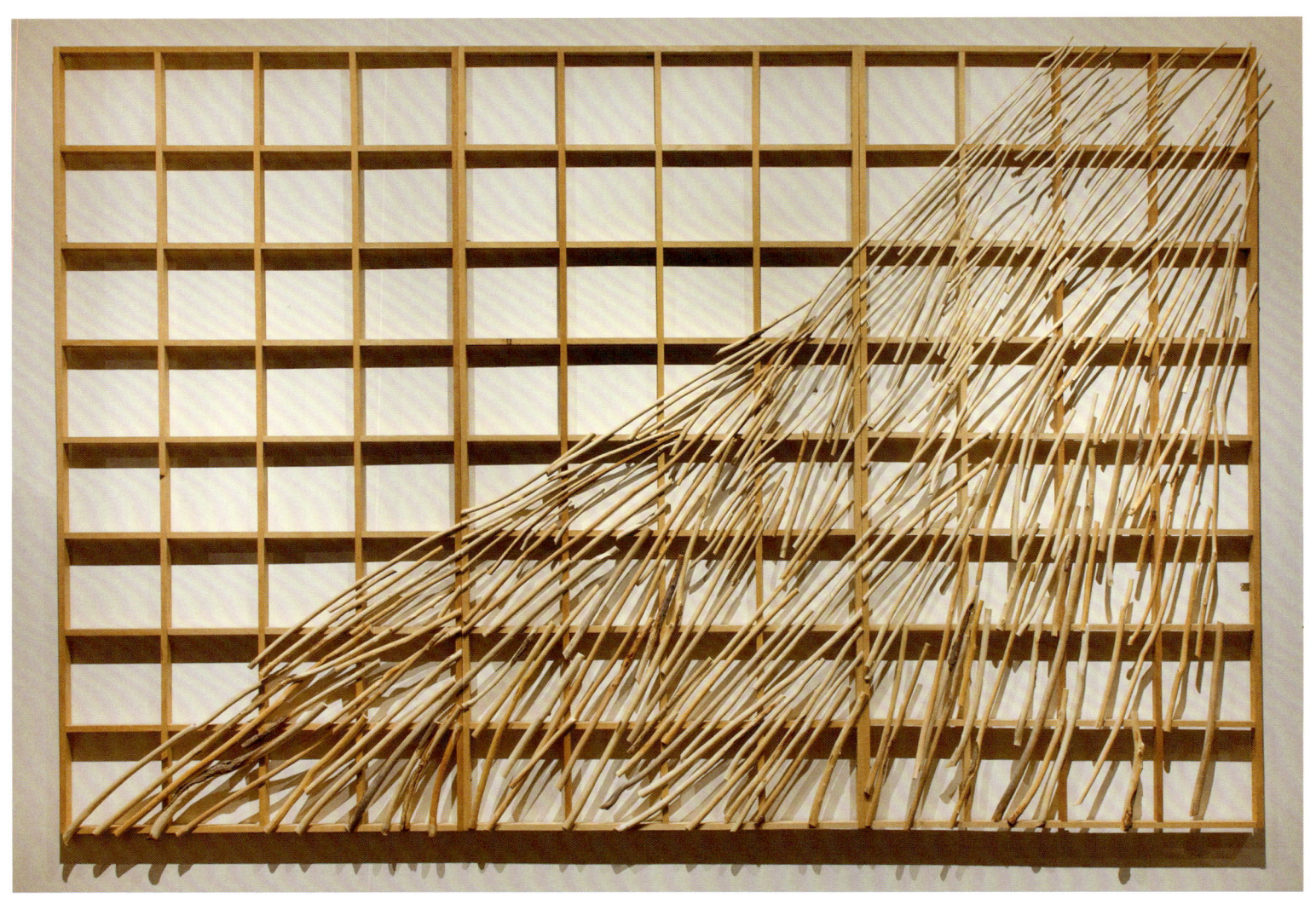

58. *Waterfall '99*, 1999. Pine, peeled willow saplings, 96 x 144 x 4 in. Eiteljorg Museum of American Indians and Western Art 1999.6.4
A-C. Museum purchase from the Eiteljorg Fellowship for Native American Fine Art. Additional funding provided by Mike and Juanita
Eagle, Roger and Mindy Eiteljorg, Stan and Sandy Hurt, Arnold and Carol Jolles, Jay Peacock, and Carolyn Kincannon

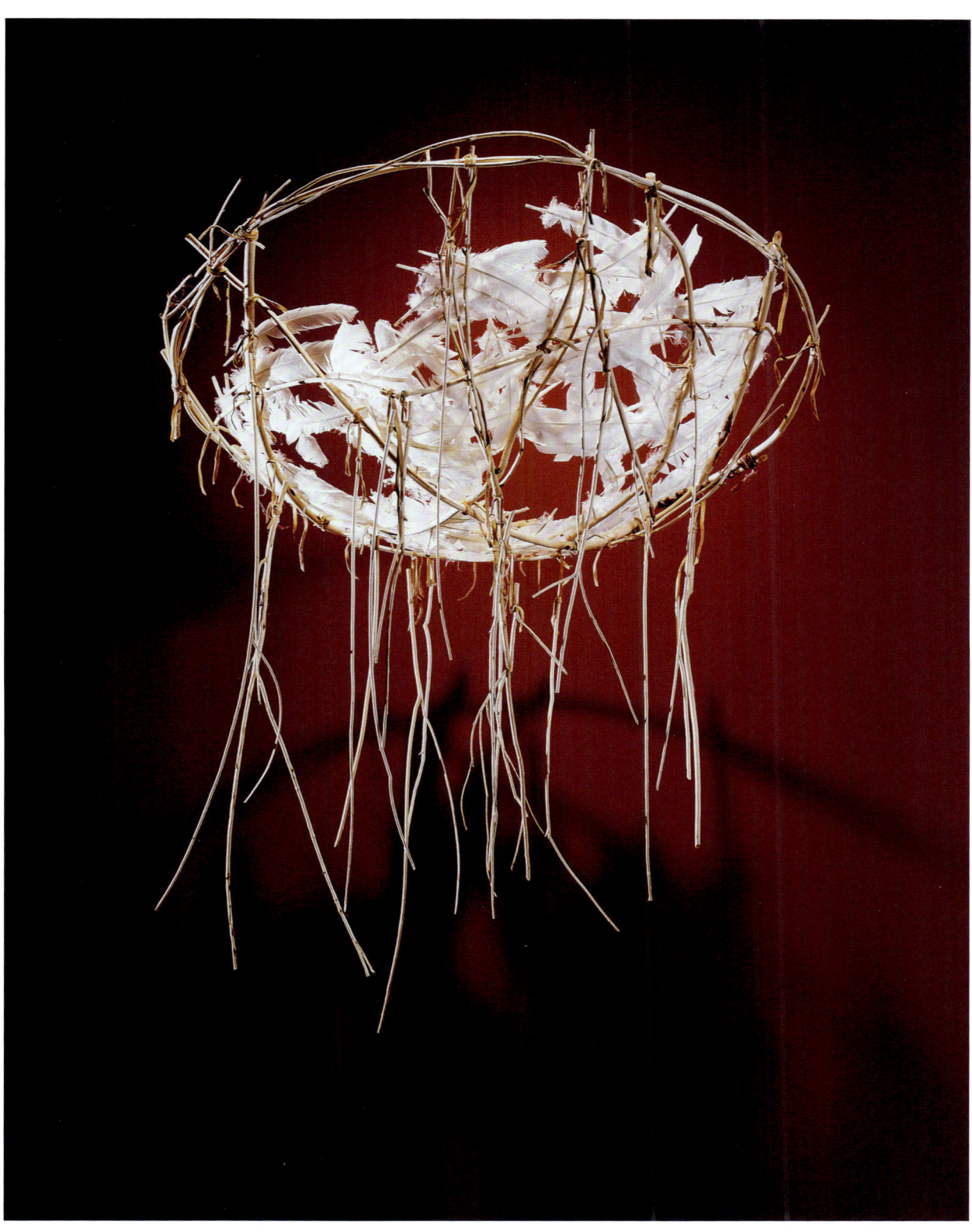

59. *Feather Basket #2*, 1994. Willow, feathers, buckskin, 60 x 80 x 24 in. Denver Art Museum, Native Arts acquisition funds, 1994.469

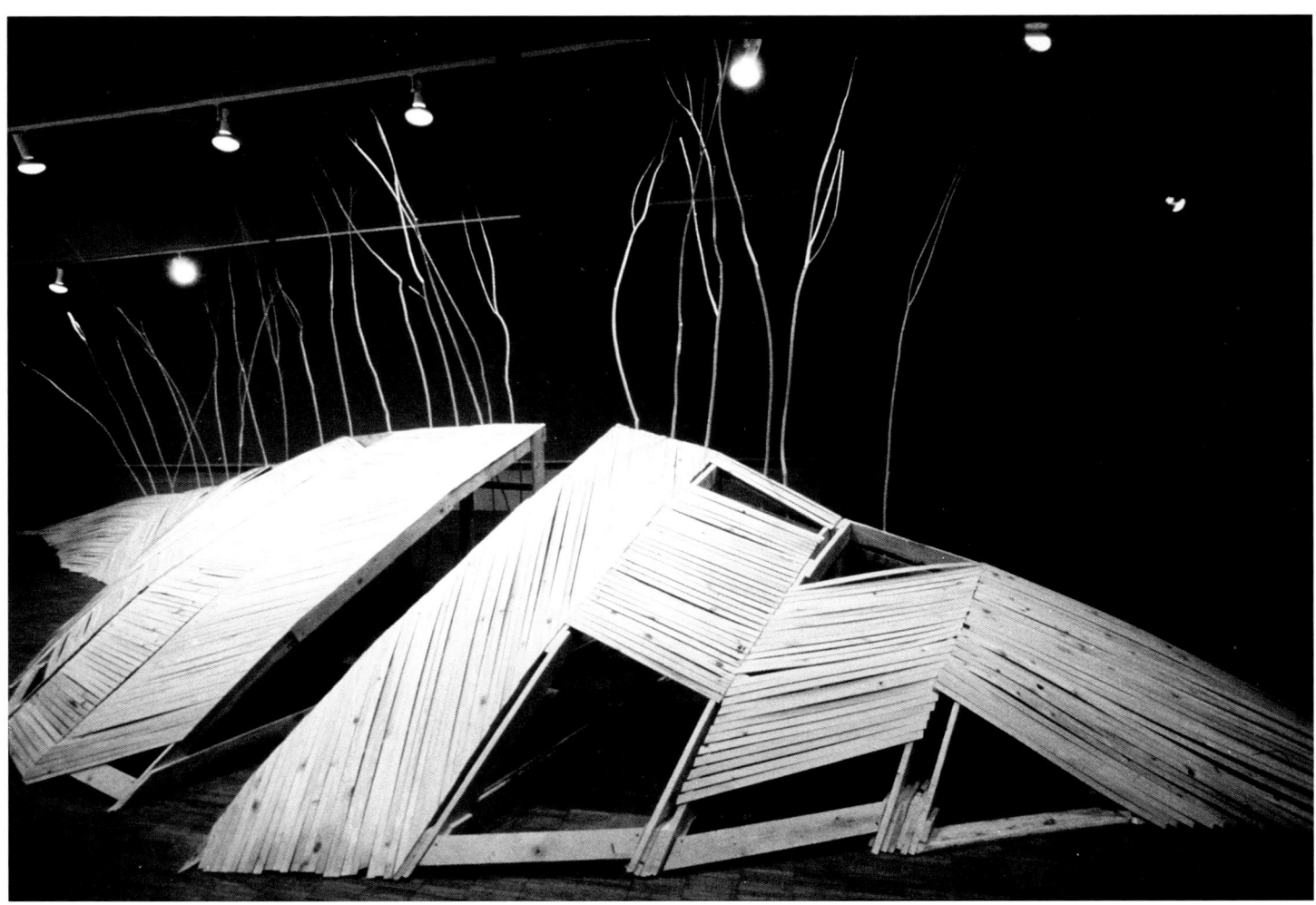

60. *Red Banks*, 1991. Pine, peeled willow saplings, 12 x 37 x 8 ft. Installed at Lawton Gallery, University of Wisconsin–Green Bay. Not extant

Truman Lowe and a Hoocąk Heritage of Resilience

Amy Lonetree

BORN AND RAISED NEAR BLACK RIVER FALLS, Wisconsin, Truman Lowe created sculptures and installations inspired by and intrinsically linked to his Wisconsin homelands. As a full professor at the University of Wisconsin–Madison, Lowe was the first Hoocąk (Ho-Chunk) citizen to hold that rank at one of this country's most prestigious academic institutions. UW–Madison was built on the ancestral homeland of the Ho-Chunk Nation, a place known to the tribe as Teejop, or Four Lakes. Teejop has been home to the Hoocąk for thousands of generations and will forever remain Hoocąk homelands.

Lowe spent most of his distinguished career at UW as a professor and later chair of the art department. He brought honor to the Ho-Chunk Nation through his artistic production, teaching, curatorial work, and mentoring. An exceptionally talented artist who blazed new trails for other artists to follow, he is finally receiving the recognition that he deserves with this career retrospective exhibition at the Smithsonian's National Museum of the American Indian. It is fitting that this is happening there, given Lowe's connection to the museum and his contributions as a curator in the early 2000s when he guided the development of the inaugural exhibitions and contemporary art program. His primary focus in preparation for the opening of the museum was the development of the contemporary Native American art gallery, which featured the work of George Morrison and Allan Houser.

In the summer of 2000, while serving as a research assistant at the museum, I had conversations with Lowe regarding his decision to focus on those two talented artists in the inaugural art exhibition. He expressed the great respect he held for them as teachers, artists, and mentors, and for their lasting contributions to the art world. He believed it was time to celebrate their achievements on a national stage. More than twenty years later, it is now time to recognize and honor Truman Lowe in the same exhibition space that he helped launch in 2004, and I am honored to join those contributing to this volume reflecting on the contributions and legacy of this extraordinary Hoocąk artist.

Lowe's commitment to advancing Hoocąk history and culture extended beyond his art to support other projects, including *People of the Big Voice: Photographs of Ho-Chunk Families by Charles Van Schaick, 1879–1942*.[50] *People of the Big Voice* is a coauthored volume written collaboratively with Hoocąk artists, scholars, non-Native allies, and historians. It features close to three hundred historic images of Hoocąk people, along with three essays contextualizing the photographs. I was one of five coauthors of this book, which explores the unique and rich collection of studio portraits taken by photographer Charles Van Schaick of Black River Falls, Wisconsin, in the late nineteenth and early twentieth centuries. Unlike those of famed photographer Edward Curtis, who sought to document a "vanishing race," Van Schaick's were photographs that Hoocąk people commissioned for their own personal use. The powerful images are viewed today as examples of Indigenous self-representation during a period when Natives were rarely controlling the representation of their communities and culture. Those who worked on *People of the Big Voice* were grateful and honored to include Lowe's perspective on the significance of the project in the foreword to the

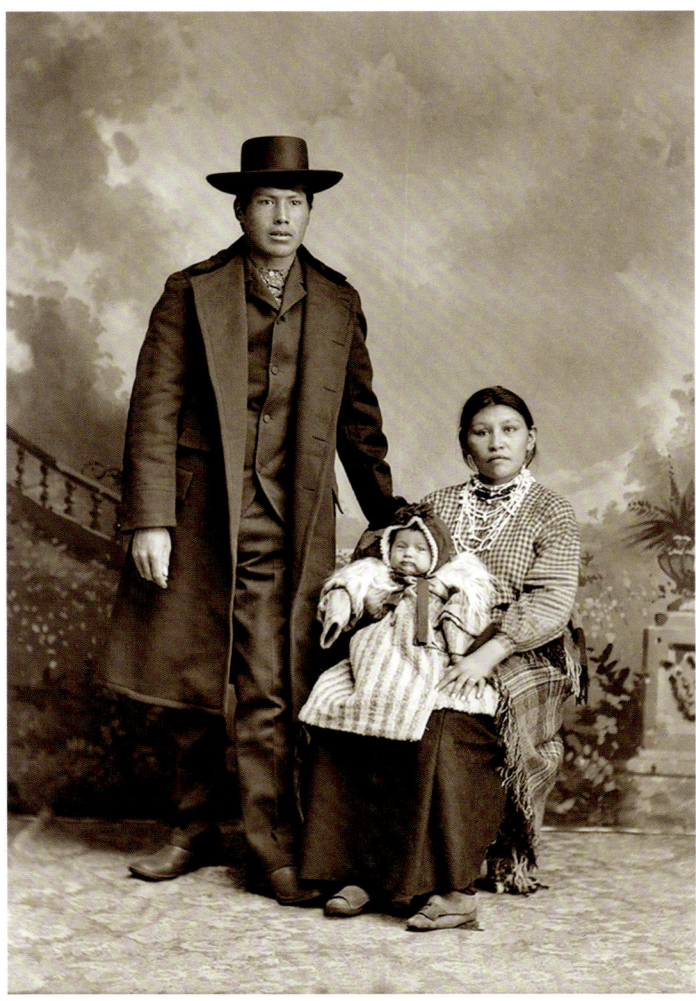

61. Studio portrait of George (Lyons) Lowe (Ahaziiga, Brown Skinned Arm), his wife, Lena Nina Marie Decorah (Lyons) Lowe (Ahusgaawiga, White Wing Woman), and their infant son Martin (Mą́ąxįsgaaga, White Cloud), Black River Falls, Wisconsin, ca. 1895.

book, in which Lowe centers his connection to this treasure trove of historic images of Hoocąk families, explaining that "they depict the place where I grew up and individuals whose children and grandchildren I know."[51]

The Indian Mission where Truman Lowe was raised profoundly shaped his life and later artistic production. He came of age "in a climate of creativity" at the Mission, surrounded by his parents, relatives, and a close-knit Hoocąk community.[52] Like many Hoocąk people during this period, Lowe's parents worked hard at multiple jobs: Martin Lowe was a farmer and often took seasonal positions, while mother Mabel worked as a cook at the local

school and at a laundromat, among other occupations. Both of his parents supplemented their wages with work in the tourist industry. His mother created beautiful black ash baskets for sale in the tourist town of Wisconsin Dells, and his father was known for making excellent bentwood handles for the baskets.[53] Nurtured by a community that valued creative practices, Lowe would later credit his family for instilling in him an "aesthetic ideal" that he would carry for the rest of his life, through his undergraduate and graduate education and his later career as an artist, professor, and curator.[54]

Lowe's family is well represented in the Charles Van Schaick collection currently housed at the Wisconsin Historical Society in Madison. His paternal grandfather, George (Lyons) Lowe (Ahaziiga, Brown Skinned Arm), grandmother Lena Nina Marie Decorah (Lyons) Lowe (Ahusgaawiga, White Wing Woman), and their son, Martin Lowe (Truman's father, Mą́ąxįsgaaga, White Cloud), are featured prominently. In one image, George is standing tall next to his family in the clothing of the day against a typical Van Schaick studio backdrop with his wife, Lena, holding their infant son (fig. 61). This is a striking image of a lovely Hoocąk family. Truman Lowe's maternal relatives also appear in the book, including his grandfather, John Davis (Kerejusepsgaaga, White Blackhawk), who is standing next to other Hoocąk men in a panoramic shot taken at a powwow (fig. 62). In one image his grandmother, Minnie Pigeon Whiteotter Blowsnake Davis (Ahugišiniwiga, Shiny Wing Woman), gazes directly at the camera, first with Emma Blowsnake Battise Goodbear Walking Priest Littlejohn Mike (Caaxšepwiga, Eagle Woman), and in another image with a larger group of Hoocąk people dressed in her Hoocąk regalia (figs. 63 and 64).

In order to understand these Hoocąk photographs, every engagement with the images should begin with the recognition that you are not just looking at Indians but at survivors whose presence in the frame speaks to a larger story of Hoocąk survivance.[55] These images are powerful representations of Hoocąk family and tribal nation history and, as such, reflect a heritage of resilience. Lowe's family, like my own, is part of this narrative of Hoocąk survivance. We are both citizens of a tribal nation whose steadfast

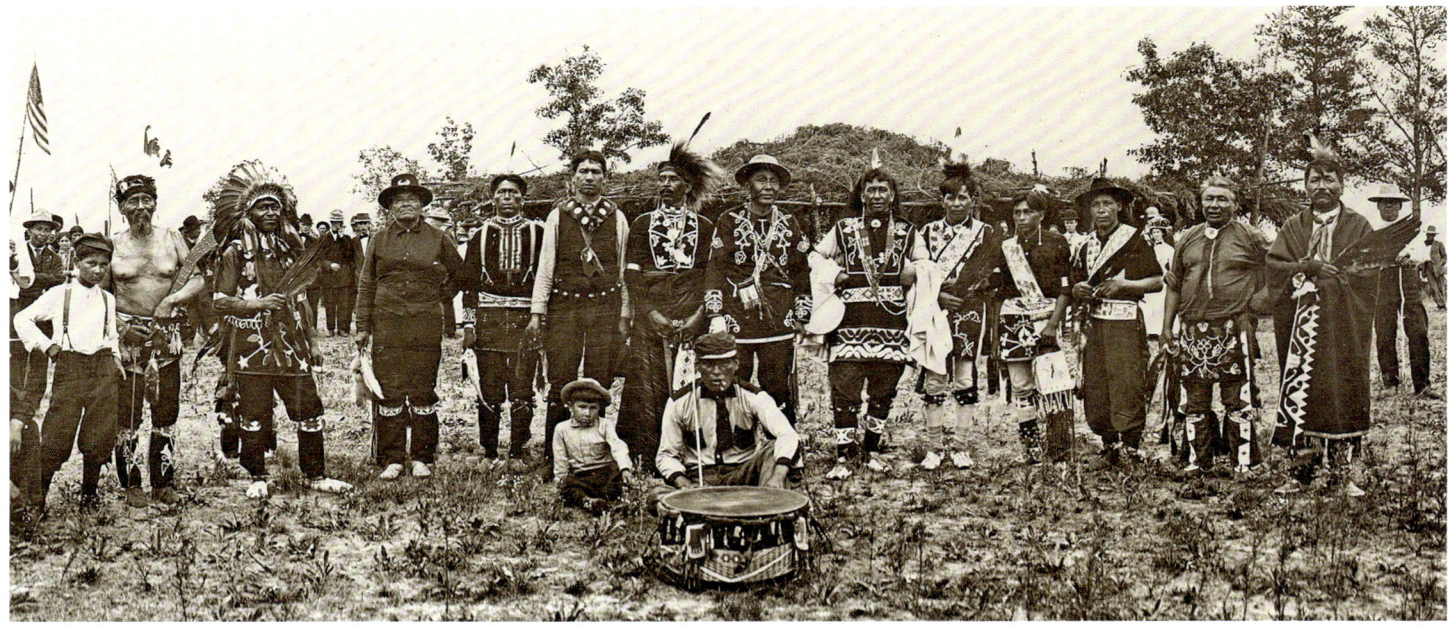

62. Hoocąk powwow participants, early twentieth century. John Davis (Kerejusepsgaaga, White Blackhawk) is sixth from right.

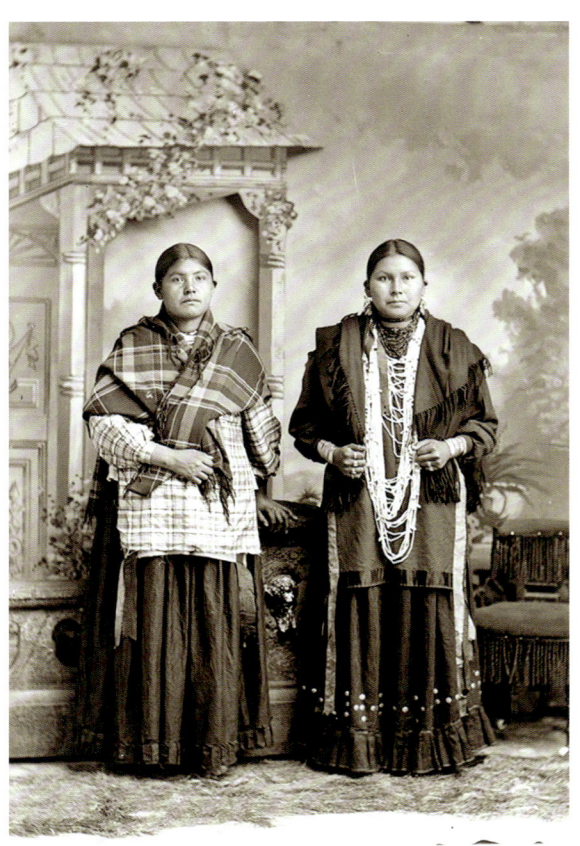

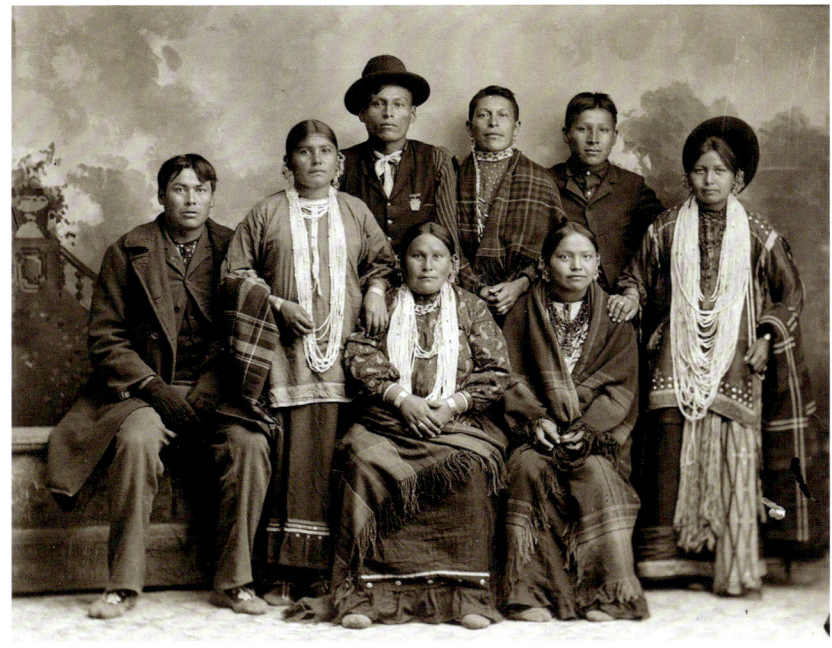

63. *(above)* Studio portrait of Hoocąk men and women, Black River Falls, Wisconsin, ca. 1895. Minnie Pigeon Whiteotter Blowsnake Davis (Ahugišiniwįga, Shiny Wing Woman) is second from left.

64. *(left)* Studio portrait of Minnie Pigeon Whiteotter Blowsnake Davis (Ahugišiniwįga, Shiny Wing Woman) and Emma Blowsnake Battise Goodbear Walking Priest Littlejohn Mike (Caaxšepwįga, Eagle Woman), Black River Falls, Wisconsin, ca. 1902. Photos by Charles Van Schaick

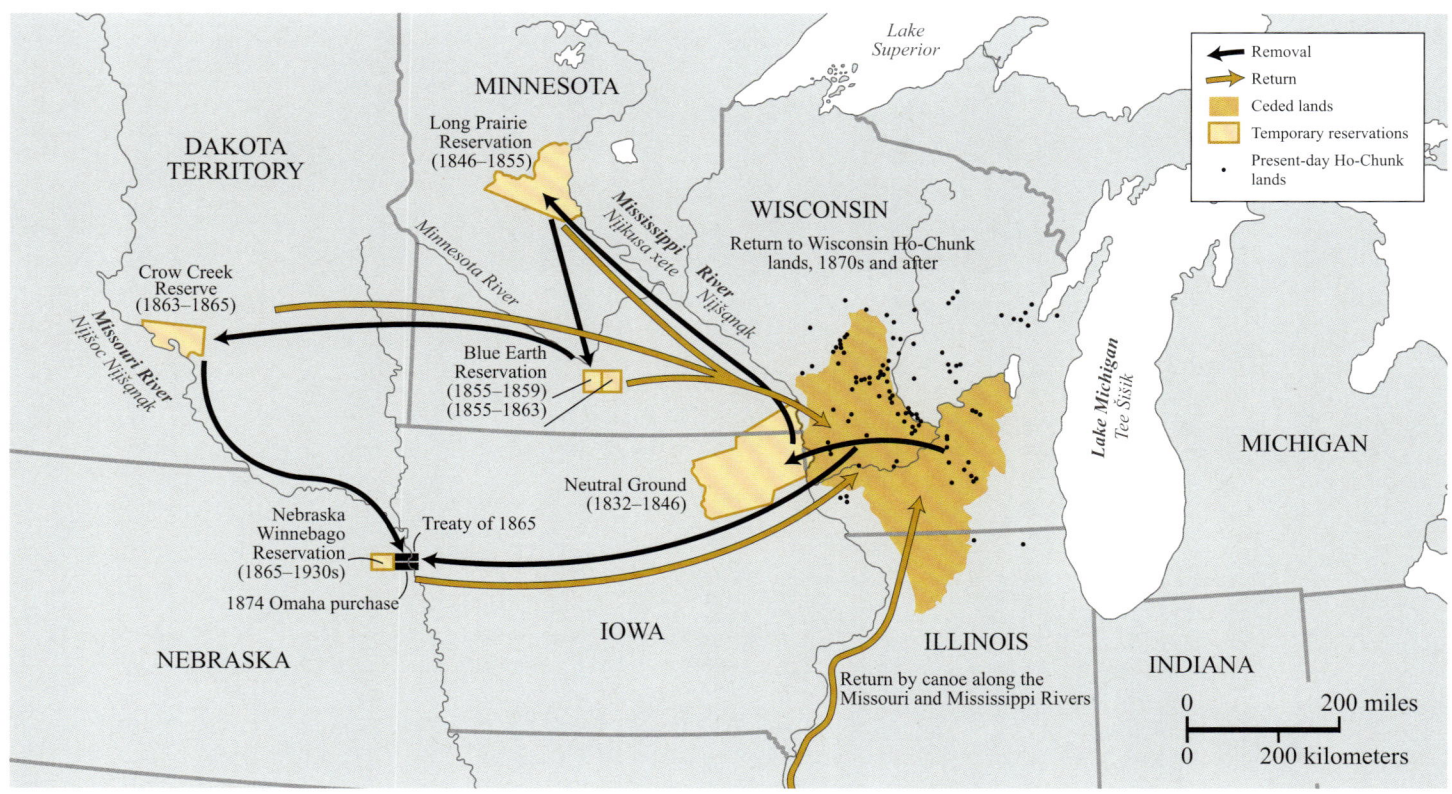

65. The Hoocąk people were removed from Wisconsin to a series of reservations in the nineteenth and early twentieth centuries.

determination to remain and persevere in our ancestral homelands is central to who we are as a people. We are descendants of those members of the Ho-Chunk Nation who resisted and fought for the right to exist as a nation in our Wisconsin homelands. The Charles Van Schaick studio portraits provide visual testimony to the ongoing presence and persistence of Hoocąk people in Wisconsin in the aftermath of colonial invasion, violence, and the devastating forced removals of the nineteenth century.[56] As we know, family history is tribal nation history, and Lowe's family is part of this rich story of Hoocąk survivance. It is this history that informed his unique and singular vision as an artist.

HOOCĄK HISTORY AND THE WORK OF TRUMAN LOWE

Truman Lowe's work is deeply inspired by his connection to his homelands and to Hoocąk history. The Hoocąk (formerly known as Winnebago) are indigenous to present-day

Wisconsin, and before the invasion of their homelands and the multiple land cession treaties in the nineteenth century, they occupied more than ten million acres of land in what is now Wisconsin and northern Illinois.[57]

By 1837, the Hoocąk had been forced to relinquish all aboriginal lands in Wisconsin and northern Illinois. After acquiring the land, the US government initiated a series of removals across four states that proved devastating, resulting in profound suffering and death. There were multiple removals for the Hoocąk, more than five in an approximately thirty-year period (fig. 65). The first official order to remove the Ho-Chunk Nation to what was called "the Neutral Ground" in Iowa occurred in 1840. A majority of the tribe was forced from ancestral territory, and close to one thousand people died as a result of the horrific journey and the poor living conditions on the Iowa reservation.[58] The tribe's time on the Neutral Ground proved to be short-lived as a result of white encroachment onto the Iowa reservation lands, and the Hoocąk

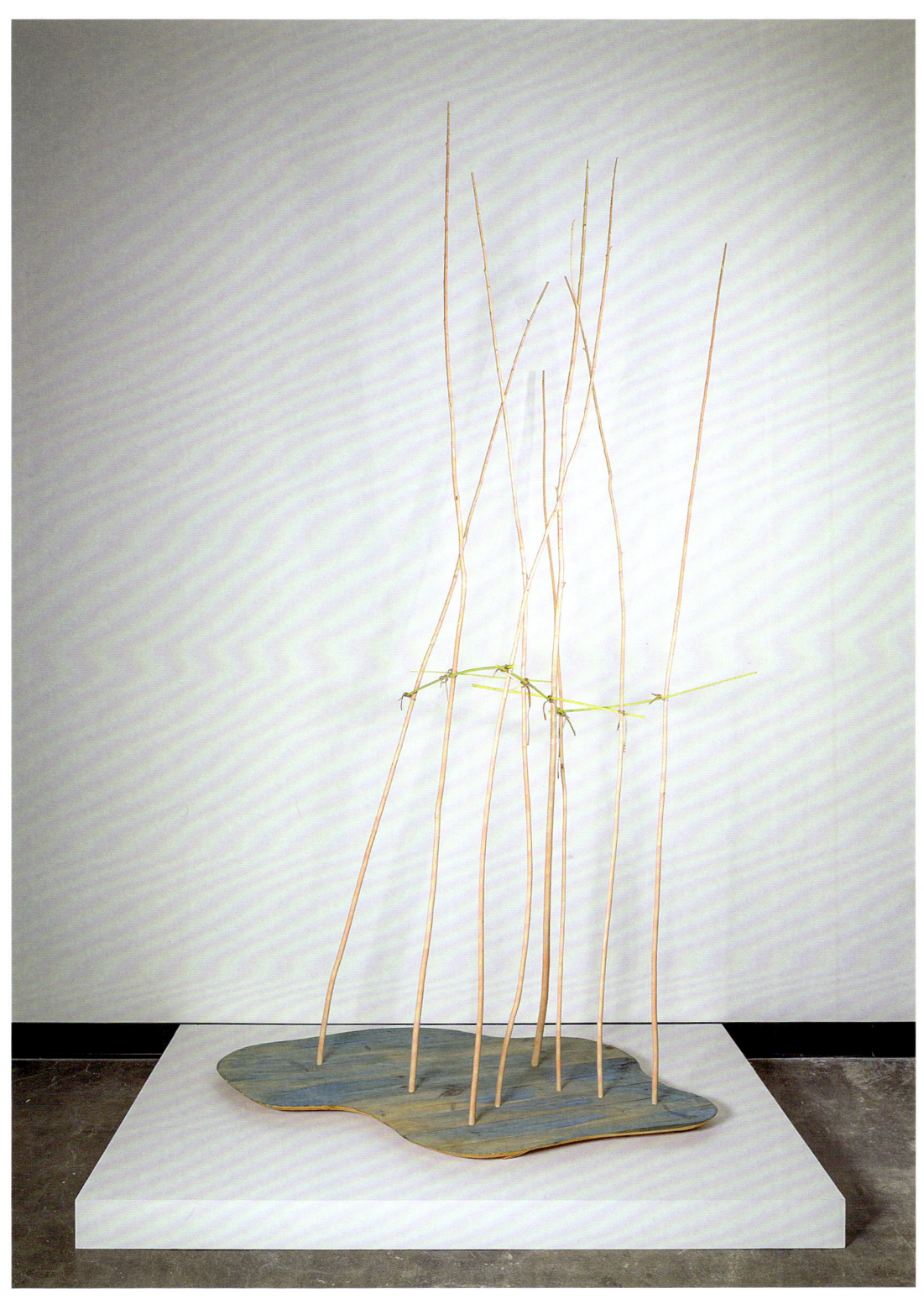

66. *Water Spirit #1*, 1991. Pine, peeled willow saplings, watercolor, leather, 94 ¼ x 49 ½ x 32 in. Milwaukee Art Museum, gift of Jan Serr & John Shannon

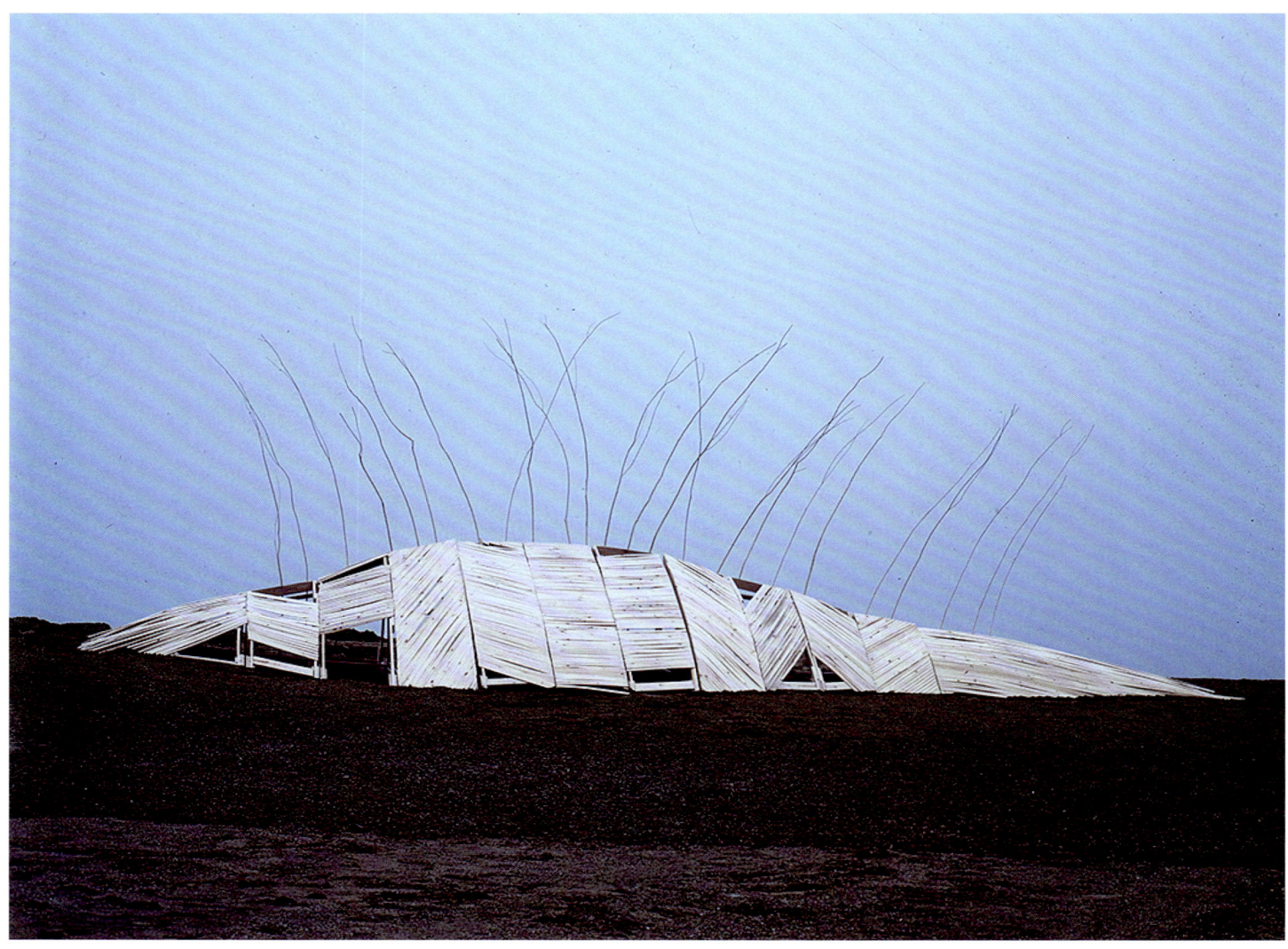

67. *Red Banks*, 1991. Pine, peeled willow saplings, 12 x 37 x 8 ft. Not extant

were then removed to the Long Prairie Reservation in northern Minnesota following the signing of the treaty of 1846. Dissatisfied with the poor farming conditions there, the Hoocąk negotiated for a new reservation beginning in 1853.[59] In exchange for Long Prairie, the Hoocąk received more suitable farming land near the Blue Earth River in southern Minnesota in 1855. For the most part, they were satisfied with the reservation but faced serious attacks by white citizens in the area, most notably a vigilante group called the Knights of the Forest, who had organized for the sole purpose of seeking Hoocąk people's further removal from the state of Minnesota.[60]

Efforts to remove the Hoocąk from the southern part of the state only intensified after the US–Dakota War of 1862. Although a majority of the Hoocąk people remained neutral and did not participate in the war, Minnesota's ethnic-cleansing policy called for the removal of both the Dakota and Hoocąk tribes from the southern part of the state. In 1863, they were sent to the Crow Creek Reservation in Dakota Territory. Close to two thousand Hoocąk made the brutal journey, and hundreds of people died on a forced migration out of the state of Minnesota. In 1865, to escape the horrible conditions at Crow Creek, the survivors crafted canoes and traveled down the Missouri

River to a new reservation in Nebraska near the Omaha Nation. This would become the tribe's last reservation.

Throughout these removals across four states, groups of Hoocąk persisted in returning to Wisconsin, even though it meant living as fugitives in ancestral territory. Between 1840 and 1874, the government made various attempts to remove these determined ancestors to the Hoocąk reservation of the moment.[61] Finally, in 1874, the US government abandoned efforts to expel the Hoocąk from their homelands. In 1881, legislation was passed that "allowed" the Hoocąk to remain in Wisconsin. That same year, the government authorized the creation of a census roll of Hoocąk people living in the state. This roll has become the "base roll" according to which citizenship in the Ho-Chunk Nation is determined today.[62] There are two federally recognized Hoocąk communities: the Ho-Chunk Nation in Wisconsin and the Winnebago Tribe of Nebraska. Lowe can trace his ancestry to those Hoocąk people who survived the ethnic cleansing policies of the nineteenth century and those who fought to remain on ancestral homelands in the aftermath of settler colonial violence and forced removals.

RED BANKS

Of all of Lowe's work, his sculpture *Red Banks* represents most clearly Hoocąk history, the oral tradition and origin story, and also vividly captures the love and deep connection the artist had for his homelands (fig. 67). According to oral tradition, the Hoocąk world began at Moogašuc (Red Banks) near present-day Green Bay, Wisconsin. In a powerful wood sculpture from 1991, Lowe recognizes and honors the tribe's deep and long-standing connection to this territory, a place that has been home to the Hoocąk since time immemorial. With this monumental piece, Lowe is honoring the oral tradition that privileges our truths regarding the origin story of the Ho-Chunk Nation. As he stated, "the real traditionalists [in the tribe] say that human beings were put down on earth . . . at Red Banks. Instead of the Bering Strait theory or even the evolutionary perspective, our myth indicates that this is where the Great Spirit decided to put us. I have always respected that tradition."[63]

The respect Lowe showed for Hoocąk people—our stories, our truths, our histories, and our rich heritage of resilience—comes through powerfully in *Red Banks* and in his other artistic works. I am grateful for the legacy of achievement and beauty he has left with us that will continue to inspire current and future generations.

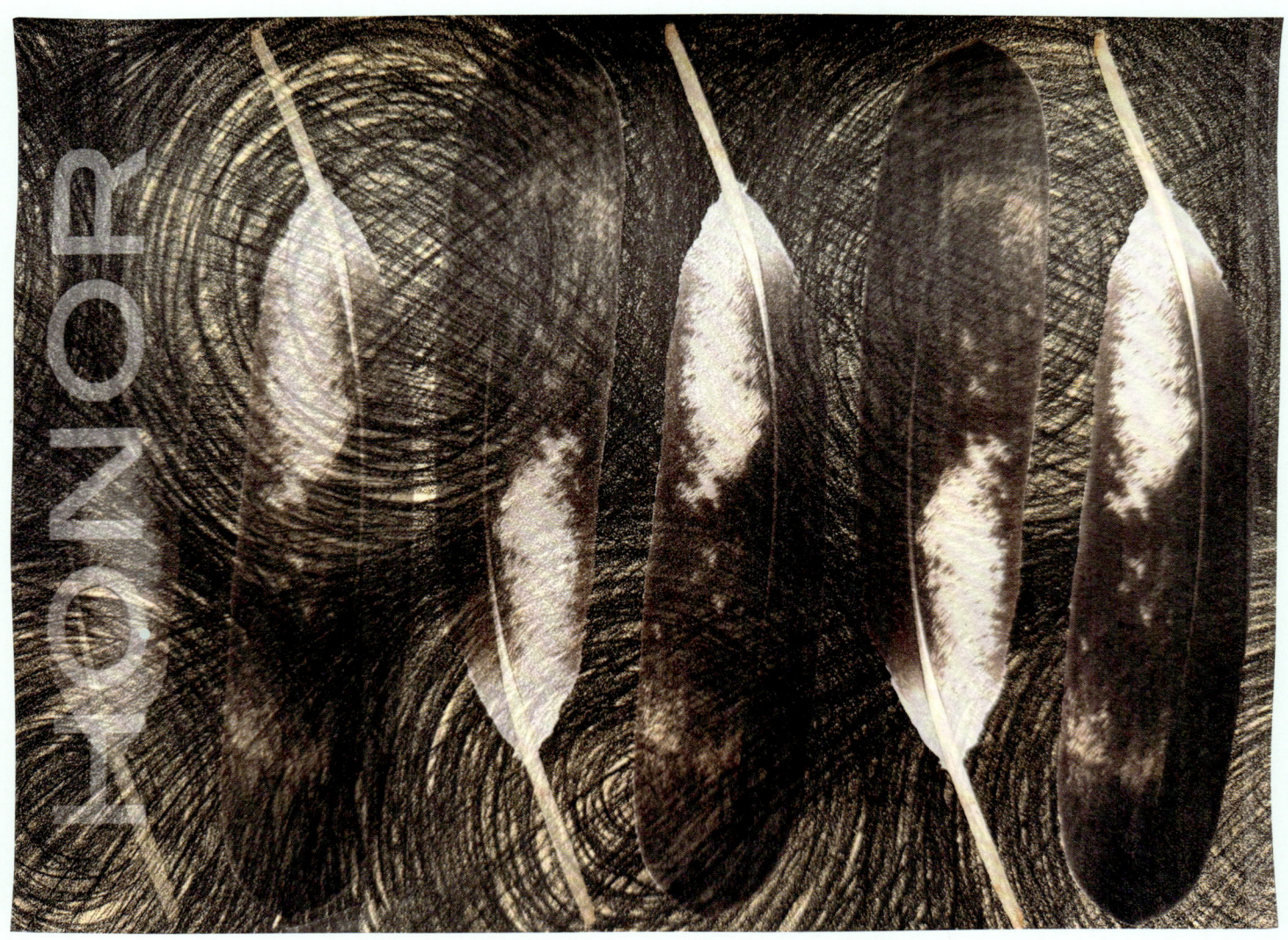

68. Truman Lowe and John Hitchcock (enrolled member of the Kiowa Tribe of Oklahoma/Comanche/European ancestry), *Honor*, 2002. Digital print, 10 ½ x 14 ½ in.

Lowe and Hitchcock made this collaborative print, with eagle feathers overlaid against an abstract landscape, to honor graduating Indigenous MFA and PhD students at the University of Wisconsin–Madison.

Sustained Resilience

John Hitchcock

PROFESSOR EMERITUS TRUMAN LOWE, also known as Wakąjahųkga, is regarded as the preeminent Native American sculptor of his generation. For me, Truman was also a distinguished artist, curator, educator, and mentor at the University of Wisconsin–Madison where we worked as friends and colleagues in the department of art.

Truman was born in Wisconsin and grew up within the Hoocąk traditions of his parents, learning basketry, ribbonwork, beadwork, and a deep appreciation for the natural world. His sculpture presents ancestral Hoocąk belief systems through the lens of contemporary art. Truman's art engages with the land through the use of milled lumber and commercial metals combined with bent tree limbs and traditional wood carving.

I was born in Oklahoma and grew up on the Comanche land of my Kiowa/Comanche grandparents, where I helped them host powwows in their field; corral horses, cows, and pigs; and even try to fence a buffalo. One of my first experiences after arriving in Madison in 2001 was visiting Truman's site-specific sculptural installation *Remembrance* at the Madison Arts Center (now the Madison Museum of Contemporary Art). He had constructed two large architectural sculptures at the entrance of the gallery, each akin to a bentwood Hoocąk family dwelling called a ciiporok'e (fig. 69). As I walked in and around the formed wood, I was reminded of my own family and community. Today, the Hoocąk community still build ciiporok'e structures, which are known to be a ten-thousand-year-old tradition.

In *Remembrance*, however, Truman's choice of materials struck me as unexpected and resourceful. Instead of woodland tree limbs and branches, Truman built this community dwelling place using readily available milled lumber. I could even read the lumber grade stamp left behind as evidence of Truman's intention to speak in the present moment with his choice of factory materials. As Native people, we adapt. Tradition is not static but is constantly changing and evolving. We build and create with materials in the present, honoring and reinforcing our innovation and strength from the past.

Later in my career at UW–Madison, Truman and I were each invited to install our work as part of an outdoor exhibition titled *Native / Invasive*. Our site-specific artwork would be viewed in the state forest near Minocqua, Wisconsin. Although today this land is managed by the Wisconsin Department of Natural Resources, the forest is the traditional territory of the Menominee, Ojibwe, Potawatomi, and Hoocąk people. Truman asked if I could deliver his artwork for the project. Since I was familiar with his large-scale sculptural pieces, I asked if I needed to get a cargo van to transport his work. He said, "No, just bring your car." When I arrived at his house, he greeted me at the door with two drawstring camouflage bags and these instructions: "When you get to the Northwoods, go out and find two rocks, wrap one in each bag, and leave them in the woods." I smiled back at him and got on the road.

As I made the drive a few hours north with his work beside me, I found myself smiling and laughing at his brilliant installation. Truman had constructed each bag with commercial camouflage fabric sewn into a pouch that could be tightened around the rocks with a drawstring cord. This powerful act would hide and protect a *native*

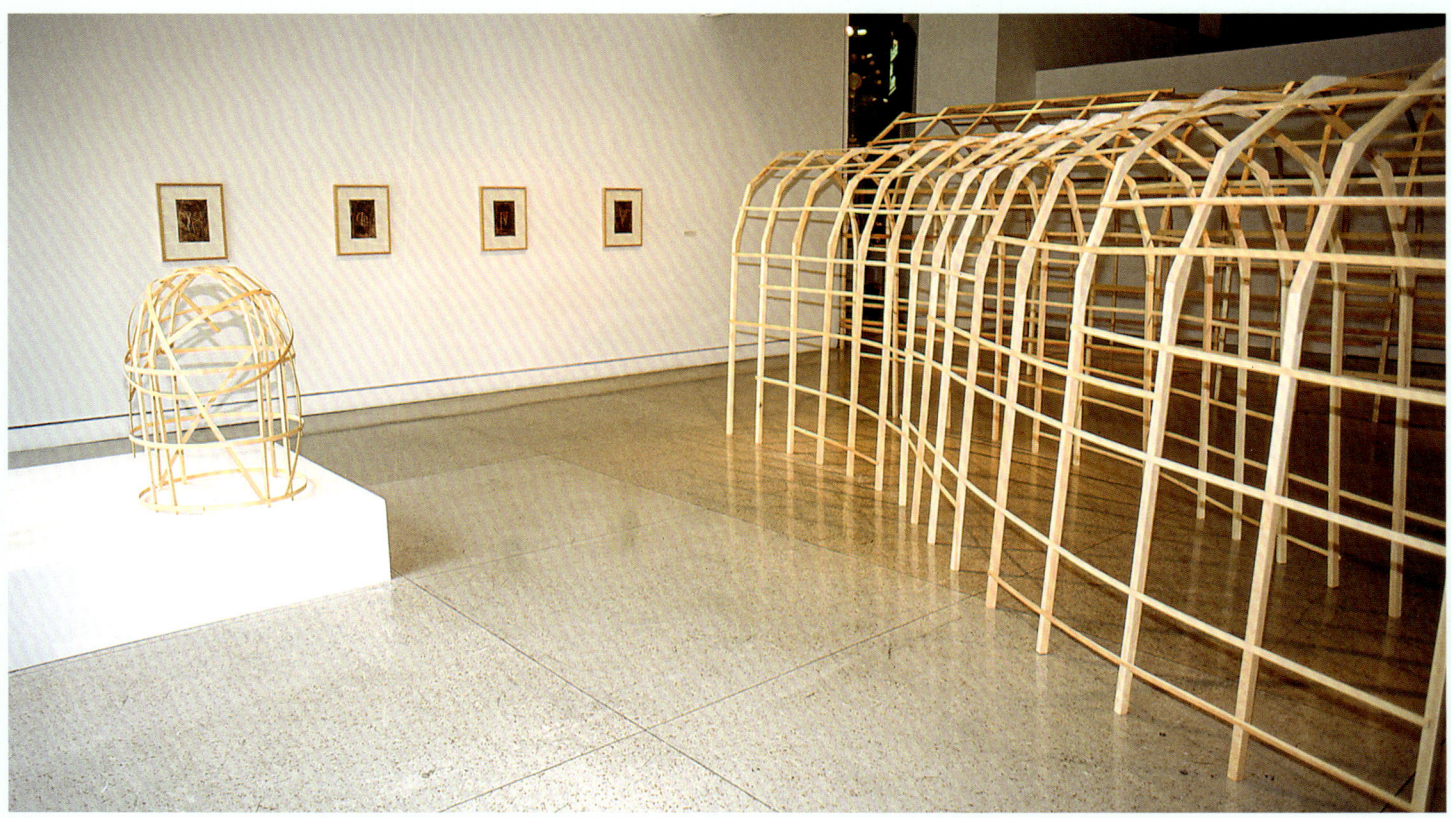

69. *Truman Lowe: Remembrance* exhibition installation, 2001. Madison Art Center (now Madison Museum of Contemporary Art)

rock on Indigenous land from the *invasive,* colonized practice of land extraction.

My own response to the *invasive* behavior toward my *Native* community has been the desire to shield my people from the continued land extraction, control, and attempted erasure of our lifeways. When I was a kid, several academics from the University of New Mexico repeatedly visited our home on tribal land for anthropological interviews. I listened as my grandparents were asked insensitive and painful questions to explain their Kiowa and Comanche ancestors and histories. Truman's camouflage drawstring bags made manifest the instinct to protect my family and my culture.

After Truman retired from the art department, I missed our humorous and meaningful exchanges. Every time Truman saw me on campus he would ask, "What have you been working on in your art?" Then he would smile really big in delight as I told him. When I was recovering from a brain surgery that nearly destroyed my eyesight, Truman

and his wife, Nancy, visited me in the hospital. Truman brought me two books for my rehabilitation. The first book was *Seven Days in the Art World*, by Sarah Thornton, and the second was a blank sketchbook. When he gifted me the sketchbook he said, "Time to draw your way out of it." Right then I committed to his sketchbook a "drawing a day" for the entire year. As my vision healed, I felt connected to Truman's strength, protection, and a shared understanding of our Indigenous perspective.

Truman's contribution to knowledge and culture continues through his artwork, named scholarships, and educational centers. His innovation, strength, and sustained resilience remains an inspiration to me and the new generation of Native artists he mentored. I see Truman's lifework as having shaped new traditions. His Indigenous perspective calls to the past and protects ancestral knowledge while his innovation through contemporary resources informs our Native future.

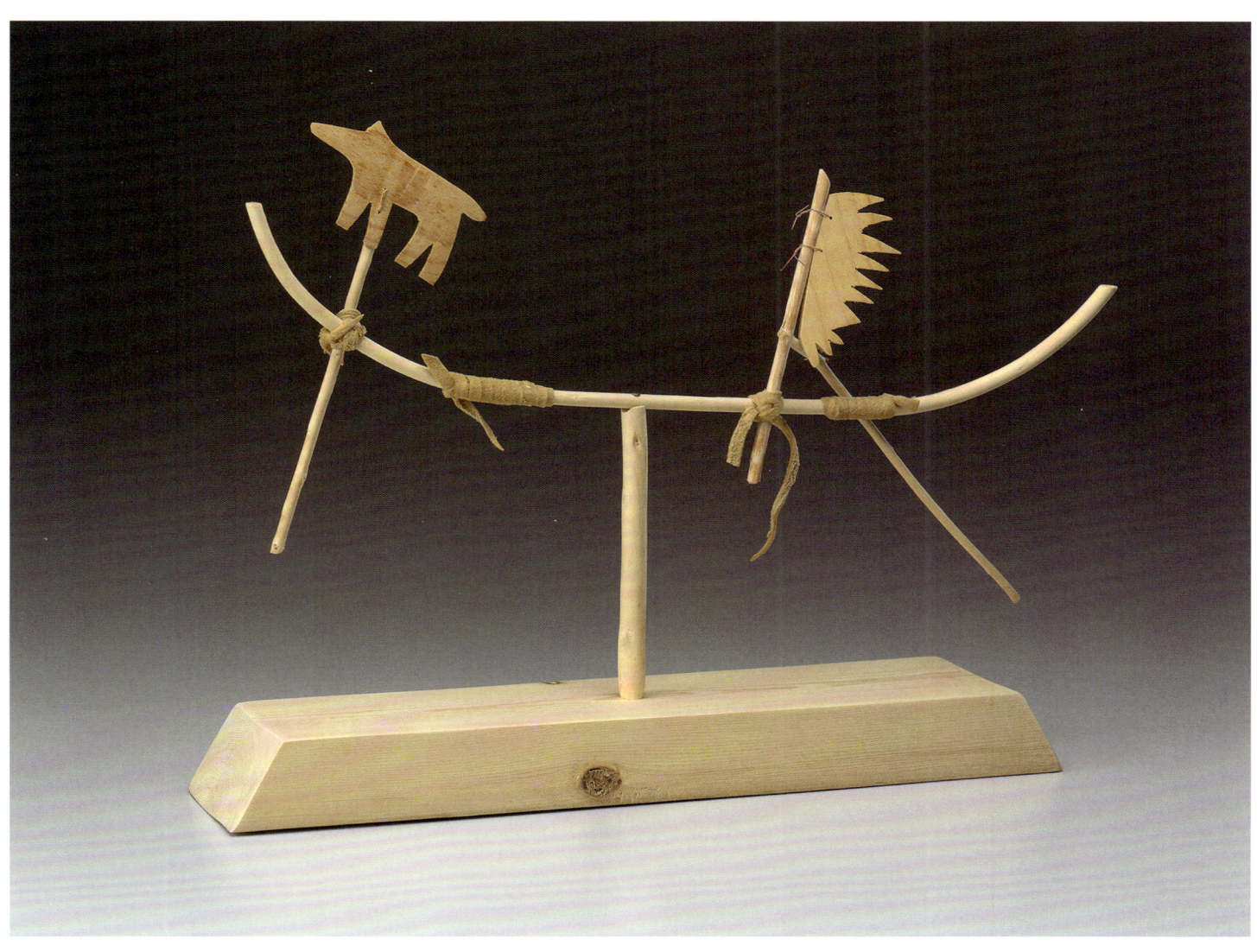

70. *Chief Takes His Dog for a Ride*, 1989. Pine, peeled willow sticks, leather, copper wire, brass nails, 11 ¾ x 16 ½ x 3 ⅜ in. National Museum of the American Indian 27/609

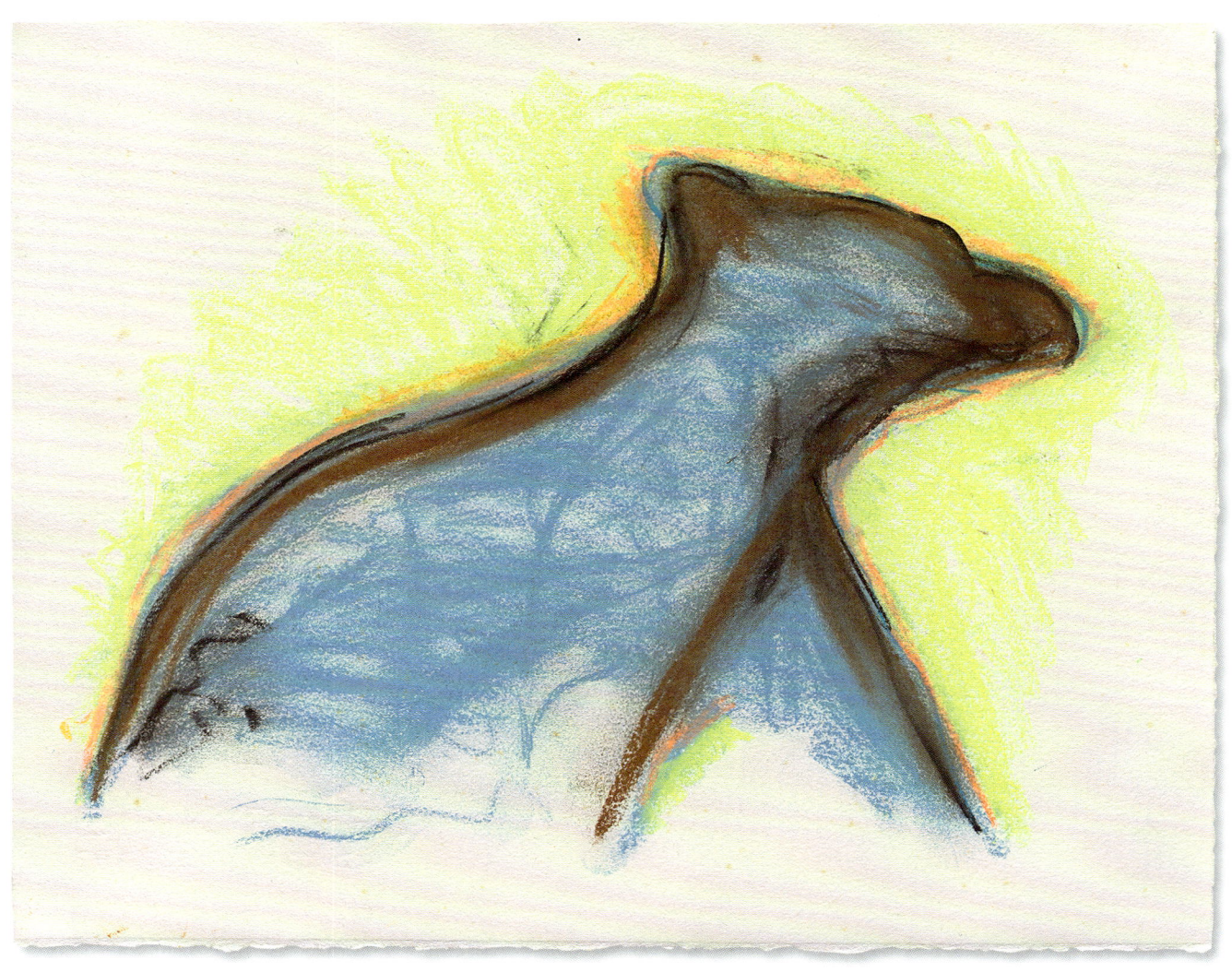

71. Untitled (Sauninga), n.d. Chalk pastel on paper, 11 x 14 in.
National Museum of the American Indian 27/619

Sauninga (or Sąąnejga, meaning "Shining One"), was the Hoocąk name
of Lowe's mother, Mabel Davis Lowe. The name derives from a story told
by Hoocąk elders of a bear that was seen walking on a hill or ridge with
the sun shining from behind so that it seemed to glow. Bears were a
frequent subject of Lowe's work, as were other references to his mother.

72. *Hoounch II*, 1992. Pine, peeled willow, leather, powdered pigment,
and ink, 75 x 72 x 3 ½ in. Museum of Wisconsin Art, gift of James and
Judith DeStefano

Lowe's playful *Hoounch* (or "bear") sculptures draw inspiration from
bearskin rugs, their construction suggesting they might be rolled or
folded. They also call to mind effigy mounds or, when hanging on a
wall, fantastical flying bears.

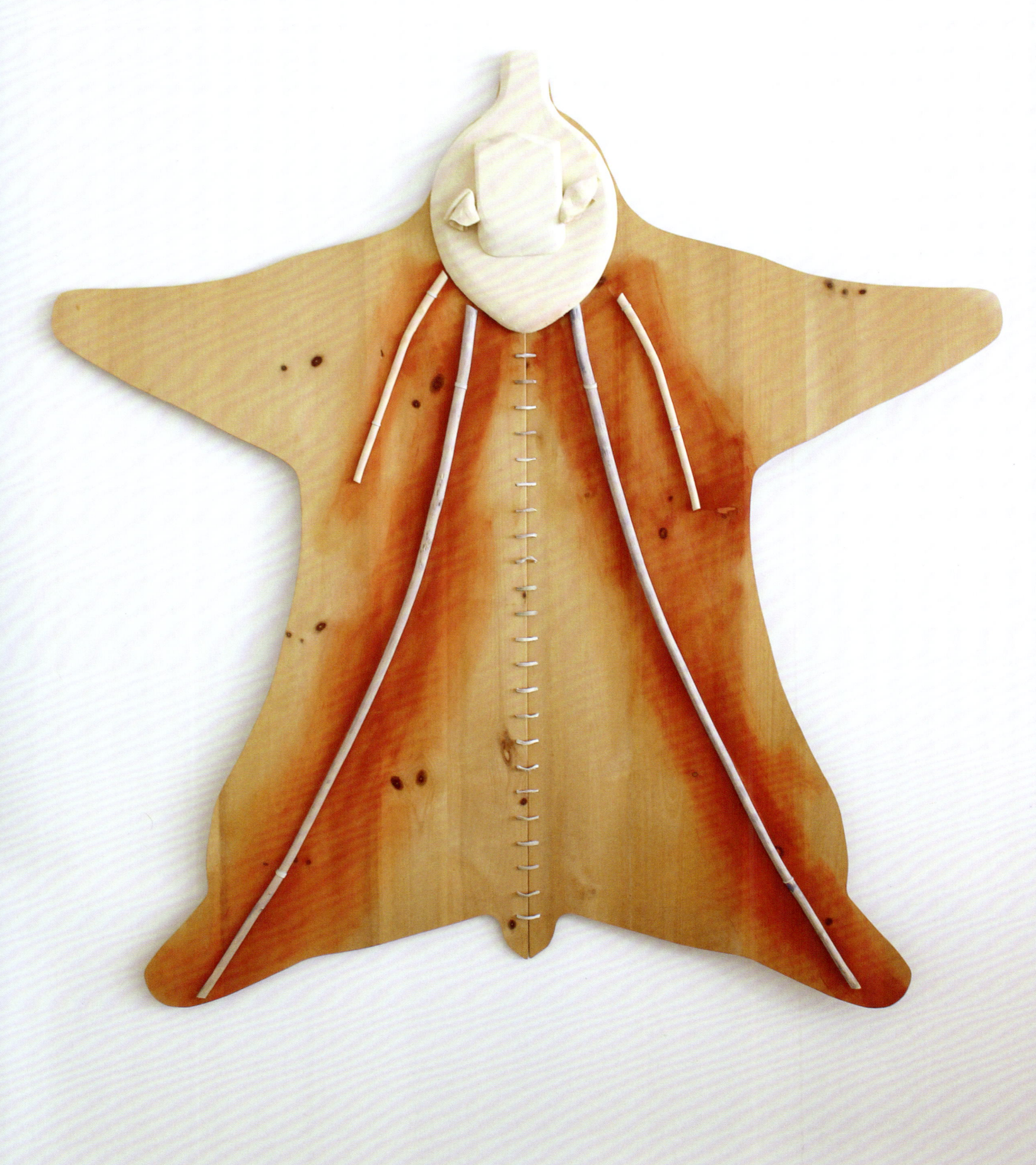

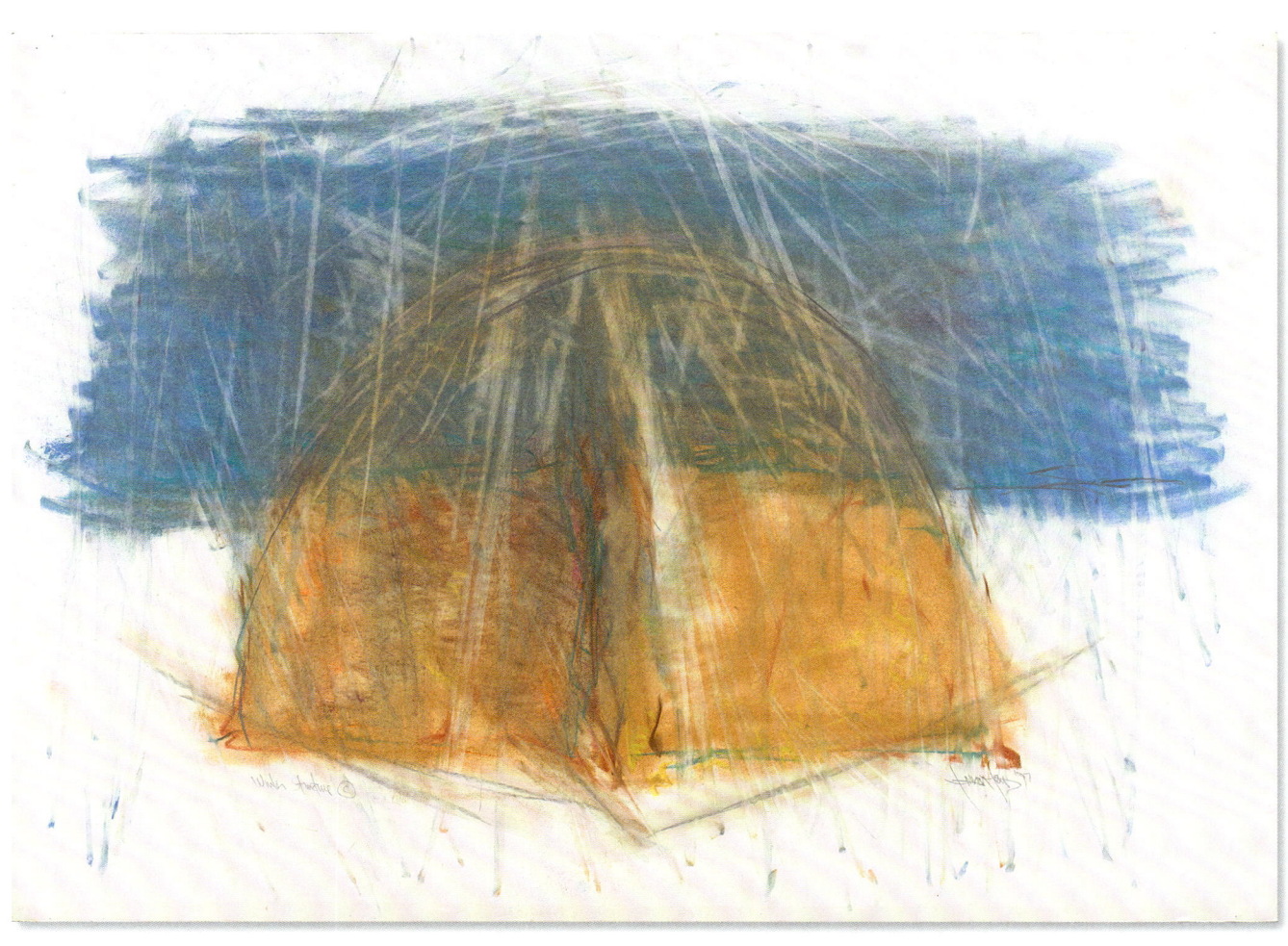

73. *Winter Structure*, 1997. Pastel on paper, 30 ¼ x 42 ¼ in. National Museum of the American Indian 27/618

Nurturing *Coo*: Conceptualizing a Hoocąk Color Theory in the Work of Truman Lowe

Kendra Greendeer

THE PASTEL DRAWING *Winter Structure* (1997) depicts a ciiporok'e, or a traditional Great Lakes covered bent wood structure, outlined in primary colors (fig. 73). In the background, subtle erasures and smudges mimic the snow-covered trees beyond this home. With each mark, color is spread to areas of the paper that one could assume are snow covered. Instead of a quiet setting of untouched snow resting on the earth, the movements created by artist Wakąjahųkga (Thunder Chief), known to most as Truman Lowe, capture a colorized, active glimpse in an otherwise still moment.

As a Hoocąk (Ho-Chunk) woman, I am reminded of home when I view Lowe's artworks. Within each of his works, there is a consideration for the brief moments of nature's beauty—in the ripples of movement suggested in drawings of water, his rendering of a delicate snowfall, the careful smoothing of willow and pine, and the subtle motifs decorating two-dimensional surfaces. As we contemplate Lowe's depictions, we find ourselves in a place where we are both connected to and preoccupied with our own memories of witnessing these ephemeral moments of nature's mysteries.

In all of Lowe's work, he exemplifies the Hoocąk connection to our tribal homelands, an area that initially spanned from east of the Mississippi River to the cities presently known as Green Bay, Wisconsin, and Saint Louis, Missouri. Today, most of the Hoocąk communities are dispersed across southern Wisconsin. While our tribal lands are now limited, Lowe's art retains a powerful sense of presence, reflection, and belonging, drawing upon keen observation and memory. Each of his creations

becomes a notation of the beauty of the western Great Lakes. The landscape of the Hoocąk homelands comprises an ecology of woodland flora, the earth covered in endless green beneath a sky of a particular shade of blue. When I consider how the natural landscape of home looks, I understand why words within our language conflate the colors of blue and green. It gives me a greater appreciation of the complexity of Lowe's work, an insight into his informed understanding of ancestral land, and a glimpse into his approach to a Hoocąk color theory.

When I first encountered a large body of Lowe's work, I was struck by his subtle use of color. Considering that he was an artist known for a minimalist approach, Lowe's choice of colors felt significant and intentional, especially when compared to other artists working in a similarly narrow color range. Although I was never able to ask him about his distinctive color palette, I feel that I can relate to the choices he made. Each time I return to Wisconsin after a lengthy absence, when I see the green-covered hills and bountiful trees scattering the landscape, I know that I am home. Understanding that Lowe's career also took him to distant places and back home again, these moments of recognition so easily taken for granted offer a level of comfort. The familiar shades of color in the landscape create a sense of tranquility and ancestral kinship with this place.

I am examining the drawings of Truman Lowe and his use of color, especially green and blue, which both translate to *coo* (cho) in the Hoocąk language. Lowe's depiction of fragments of the beauty found in his homeland creates a connection to the Hoocąk worldview and illustrates the

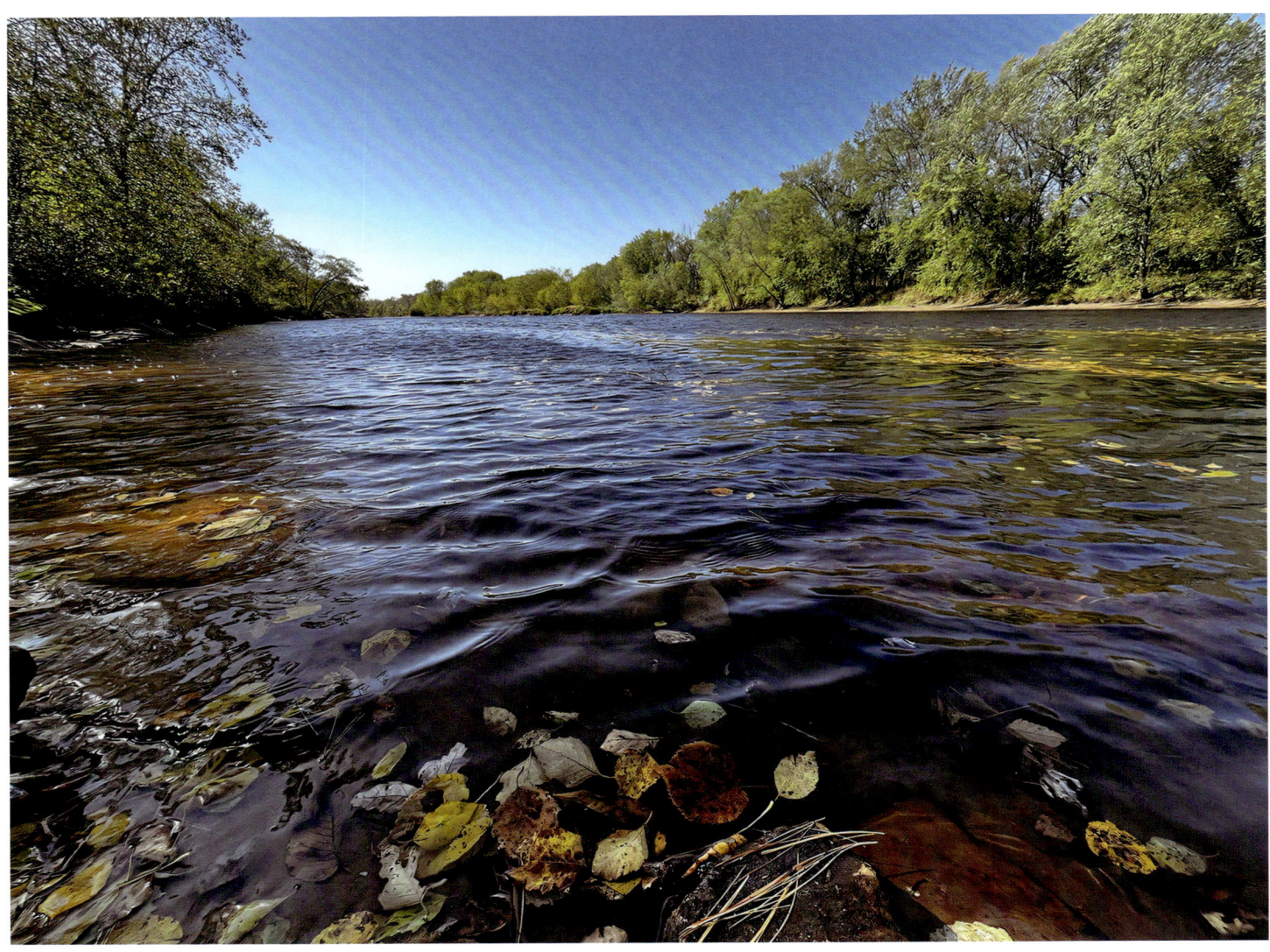

74. Black River, Wisconsin, 2024

use of Hoocąk color theory in contemporary artworks. Coo is used interchangeably to describe blue or green. Interestingly, the inclusion of color in proper names is also common in the Hoocąk hoit'e (Ho-Chunk language), including my own family name, Caacoo (Green/Blue Deer). So, with this meaning in mind, Hoocąk understandings and color descriptions of the land are embedded in a space enveloped in coo.

Lowe grew up on the banks of the Black River in Wisconsin and, like many other Hoocąk, assisted his parents in making art (fig. 74). His mother, Mabel Davis Lowe, a renowned artist in the community, was best known for her ribbon appliqué and as a notable colorist of basket wood splints. His father, Martin Lowe, made the best basket handles.[64] He also assisted Mabel with harvesting *noixga* (black ash) and making the handles and ears, the finishing pieces that would then fasten to the black ash woven body of the basket. While they lived near the river, the boy was told by his parents not to play there. Yet, he constantly watched the water flowing by, which surely nurtured his lifelong fascination with moving water. As a youth, he used smaller rocks along the Black River as pastels, scraping them against the larger rocks.[65] These stones shaped by the water became his first sketchbook.

In the pastel drawing Untitled (Stream), wavelike blue lines float alongside random splashes of orange in varied opacity, all overlaying a gesso background (fig. 75). The gesso surface adds an element of fluidity. Lowe's reverence for the movement of water and its properties is uniquely represented in this minimalist piece, with color applied to further parse his study of a stream in motion. Lowe's goal is to communicate the importance of water; it is a heavily contemplated theme in his work. As he explains, "I want to create enough interest in water through my work that others will begin to share the same beauty and the same understanding that I have about moving water."[66] He expressed his reverence for water with the techniques of minimalism and simultaneously highlighted the subtle iconography of place, Hoocąk culture, and the ephemerality of art within the culture. Hoocąk art forms share similarities with neighboring western Great Lakes Indigenous communities. Ribbon appliqué work is one form that is emblematic of the region and its historical settler-trade history. The appliqué, arranged as a continuously folded and sewn piece of ribbon, is often used to create abstracted designs of plants and flowers arranged as interconnected forms or a glimpse of the natural surroundings.

Ribbonwork appliqué designs connect us to specific communities and families and, most important, reflect a maternal love that envelops clothing, blankets, and any other surface that can incorporate a design. For Lowe and many other Hoocąk of the twentieth century, seasonal employment could be found at the Stand Rock Indian Ceremonial of Wisconsin Dells. Lowe served as a tour guide and greeted tourists dressed in traditional Hoocąk clothing. Mabel raised Lowe and his siblings and cared for her grandchildren and many other relatives. Throughout this time, she sewed clothing for her family to dance in at Stand Rock. In a photograph of Lowe, he is posed overlooking the Wisconsin River, dressed in a ribbon shirt with a matching apron and a beaded medallion, headband, and belt (fig. 76). While Lowe wore a traditional men's outfit with ribbonwork motifs, women would have been dressed in a skirt embellished in ribbon appliqué (fig. 77). Over his long career, Lowe had extensive experiences in the larger art world. However, an enduring inspiration continued

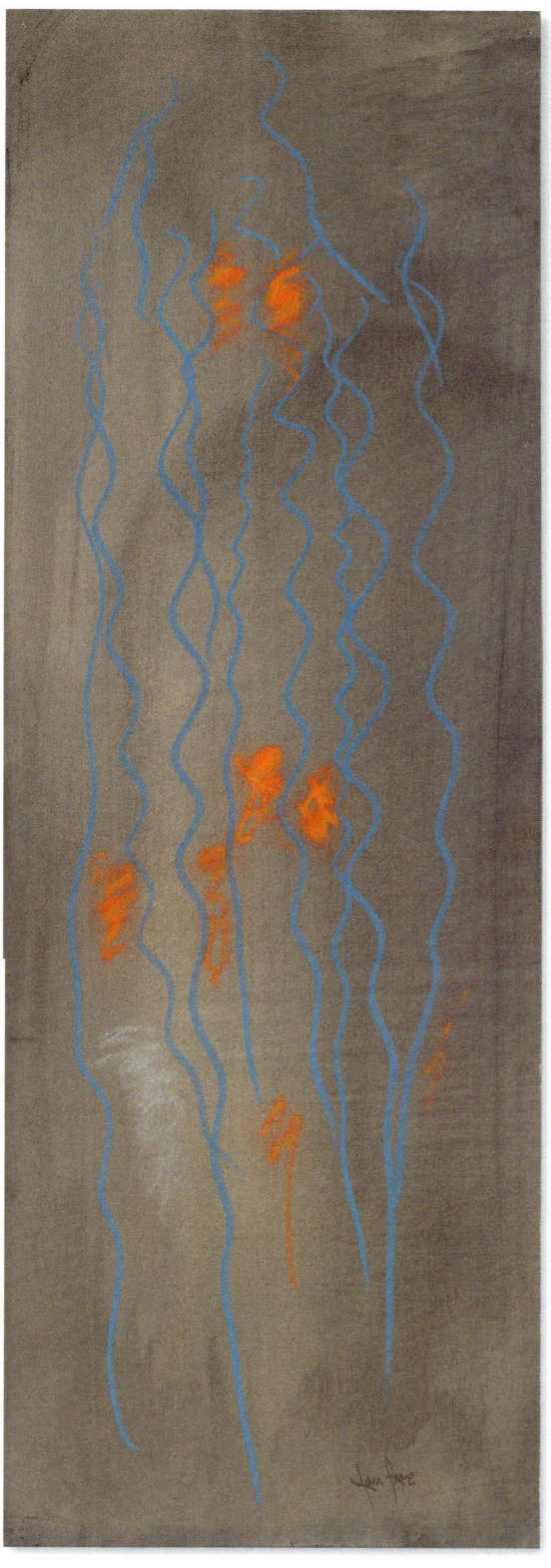

75. Untitled (Stream), ca. 2010–15. Gesso and pastel on paper, 30 x 11 in. National Museum of the American Indian 27/613

to be his mother's art practices—grounded in traditional Indigenous arts and the use of material significant to Hoocąk people.

The role of appliqué within a series of drawings by Lowe reveals his connection to the western Great Lakes and, in particular, the influence of Hoocąk art on his contemporary artistic practice. In Untitled (Ribbonwork) and *Ribbon Appliqué*, Lowe uses his mother's appliqué designs as inspiration and deftly adapts this "traditional" art into a contemporary medium: pastel (figs. 80 and 81). He depicts these particular designs arranged in a mirroring layout atop complementary colors, just as they would be in Hoocąk clothing. Mabel's ribbonwork designs were based on cutouts from materials like paper bags and flour sacks (Mabel's preference) that were then adhered to boards as reference designs for Lowe and other family members.[67] While these two pastels by Lowe featuring appliqué honor and memorialize his mother and her art, they are also ways in which he further explores the element of water, reflection, and how Hoocąk design fits into an aesthetic worldview or an expression of the natural world.

While both parents influenced Lowe's art, he honored his mother with various works, including a pastel drawing entitled *Sauninga* (1992), based on her Hoocąk name, Sąąneįga or Shining One (fig. 82). The outstretched bearskin rug—or an effigy-mound-like form—is outlined in red with blue and green lines that imply a spatiality to the otherwise flat medium as well as an echo of the mound and rug it depicts. Lowe continually explored his understanding of space and place within his works by referencing them in his compositions. Likewise, memories surrounding his mother and his deep attachment to the homelands have been recurrent themes in his work.

Lowe's mother gave her child a sketchpad in the winter when he was interested in drawing snow on trees.[68] She encouraged him to continue perfecting his drawing skills and to capture the snow that coated the branches. This experience continued to resonate in Lowe's later works, such as Untitled (Spring Branches), a drawing on translucent paper that features organic graphite lines of budding branches with green and rubbed-white pastel (fig. 83). This minimalist illustration capturing the mistaken

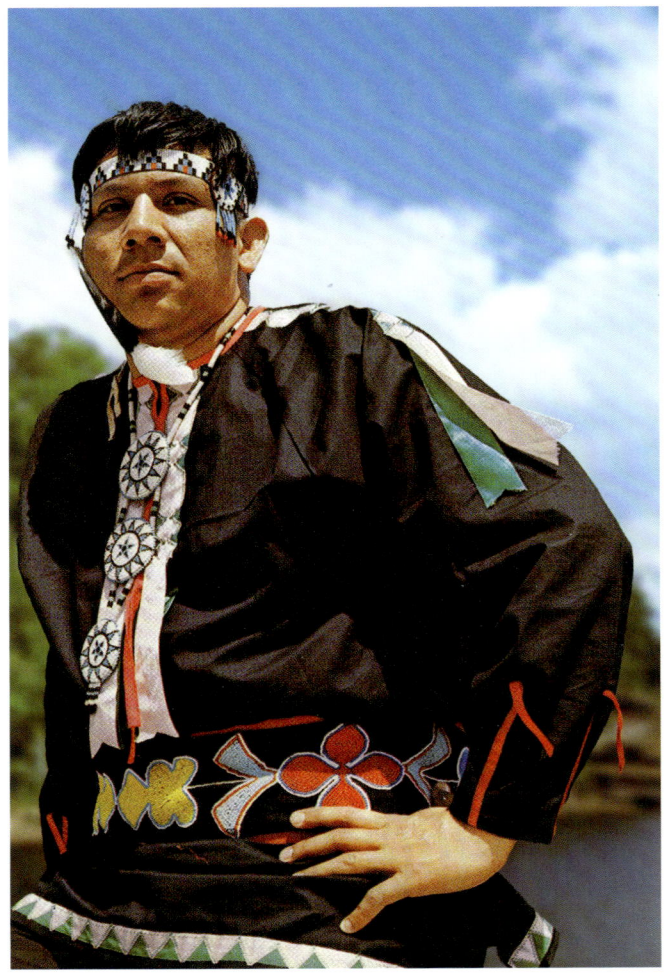

76. Truman Lowe depicted on a postcard from the Wisconsin Dells, ca. 1968. The caption reads, "Young Hawk. Full blood Winnebago Indian. Wisconsin Dells, Wisconsin."

end of winter signals a moment of the opposition within nature and in this environment. This connection of wood to water echoes Lowe's use of wood strips in other works to convey water's movement. One can sense his appreciation for the element of water and its relationship to a tree—the growth, manipulation by, and ultimate lack of power against the relentless force of water. Lowe reveals a profound understanding of wood, likely informed by watching his father prepare pieces for weaving and carving. It was work that required a deep grasp of the properties of various types of wood material and was grounded in generational knowledge.

Considering the ancestral history of Hoocąk removal and return to the homelands, it is perhaps not surprising that, while Lowe ventured to other places, he recognized how significant the Black River was to him and felt a deep loyalty to his Hoocąk heritage. One of Truman's nephews, Joe Keenan, recounted what Truman, or Uncle Tru as they knew him, had described in their conversations: "He used to say, 'I feel like I'm getting more Hoocąk every day.' Then I realized what he was talking about: the Ho-Chunk Nation culture is a bottomless pit for artists to tap into. There's always new ideas somewhere."[69] For Lowe, the Ho-Chunk Nation was a place interwoven with teachings, artistic inspiration, and, most of all, a community worth preserving and nurturing.

Lowe imbued his work with the Hoocąk experience of place and how "movement" can be articulated differently by an Indigenous person. One form that Lowe often revisited in drawing and sculpture is that of the canoe—a vessel of transportation and an ancestral form through which humans rely on the waterways of movement—honoring and respecting the purpose and place of humankind alongside an entity of greater importance. Lowe was a quiet advocate for nature, especially with respect to the beauty and significance of water. The work *Shadow Canoe* emphasizes Lowe's use of both Hoocąk color theory and a worldview influenced by the approaches and modernist reimaginings of cultural arts (fig. 78). We see a continued fascination with ribbon appliqué designs, the use of a mirrored image, and the subtle touches of color. The layered drawing of charcoal and pastel on paper depicts a series of alternating, sporadic branches or sticks in the shape of a canoe, suggesting the frame of a lodge or a ciiporok'e. While shadow and grayscale appear to be the primary use of color, underneath the extensive layers of charcoal are shades of blue and accents of yellow and red. There remains an inseparability of the color; even within a shadow rests the vivid relation to life and the dynamic colors it includes.

While Lowe often depicted real-life scenes, he rarely portrayed humans or humanlike forms, perhaps because when it came to depicting beauty, the nonhuman held more in its subtlety. When depicting water or a flowing river, Lowe stated, "No one is really ever going to stop a

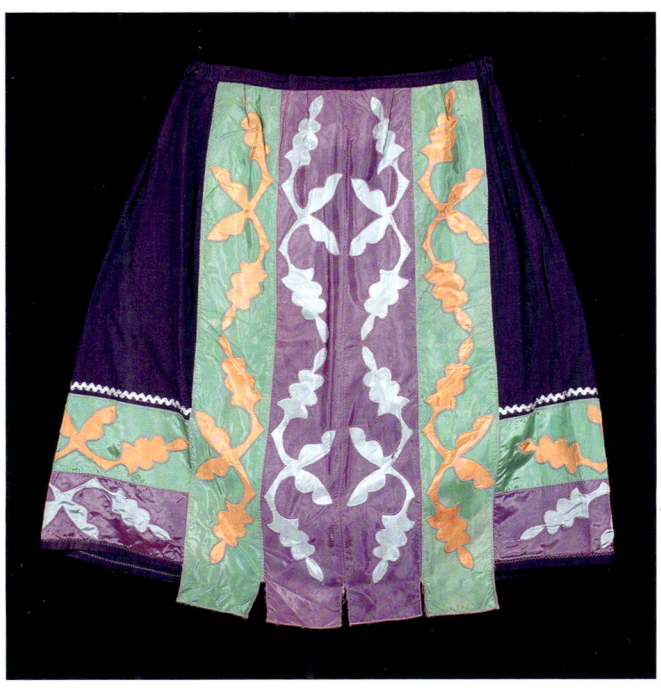

77. Mabel Davis Lowe, ribbon appliqué skirt, ca. 1950. Cotton, grosgrain ribbon appliqué, 30 x 23 in.

Mabel Davis Lowe made this ribbon skirt and a pair of matching leggings that were worn at dances by Shirley Lonetree of Madison, Wisconsin. The Wisconsin Historical Society purchased the skirt and leggings in 1981.

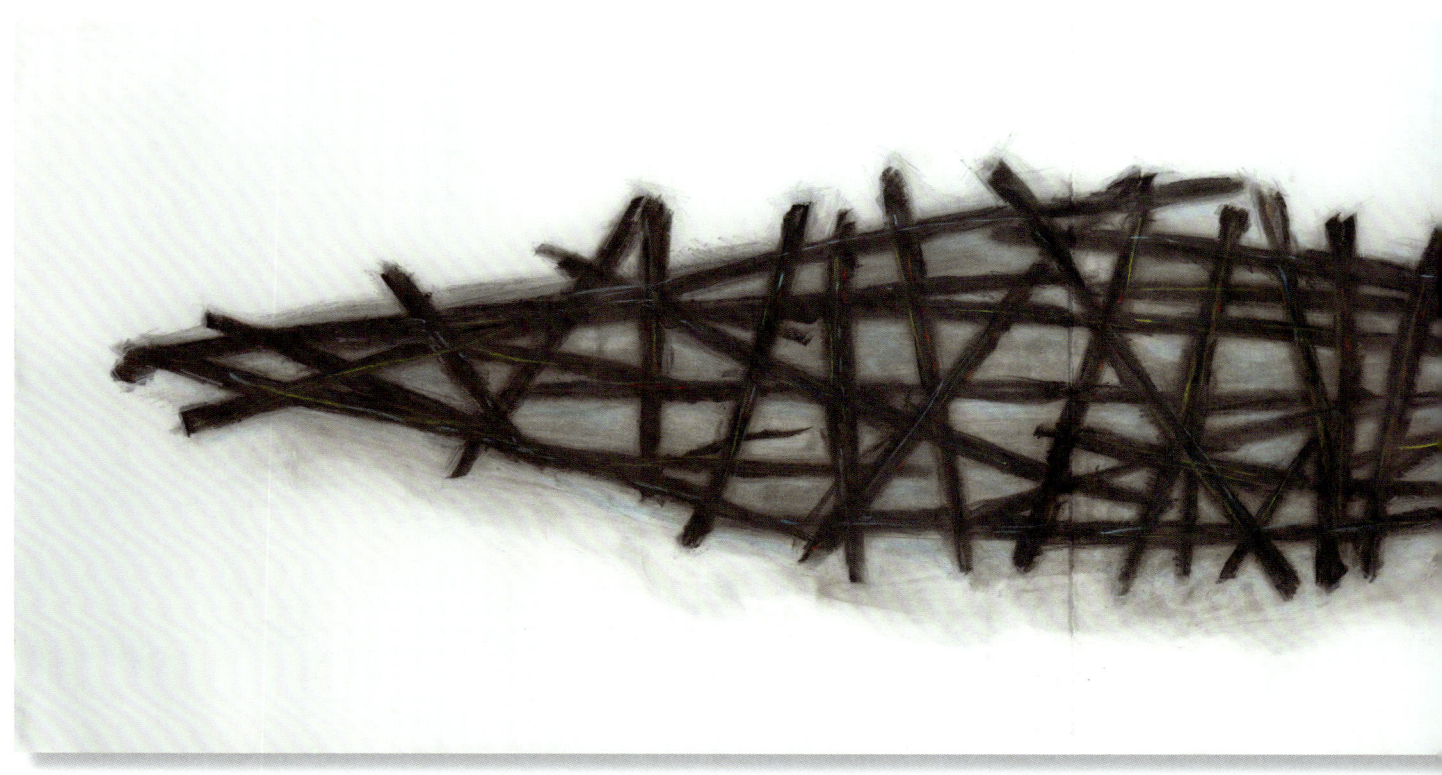

78. *Shadow Canoe*, 1996. Charcoal and pastel on paper, 30 x 80 in. National Museum of the American Indian 27/615

79. Untitled, n.d. Charcoal and graphite on paper, 11 x 30 in. National Museum of the American Indian 27/612

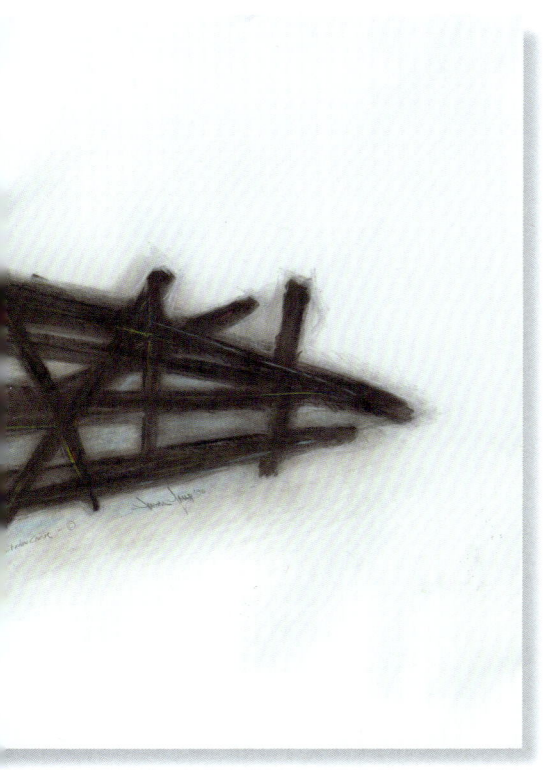

river . . . it's going to continue."[70] In this way, Lowe was incorporating traditional Hoocąk teachings that recognize humankind's position within nature, in that the river is an ultimate power and being that surpasses the power of a mere human. Lowe's aesthetic preferences and approaches to portraying water also recognize and memorialize the ongoing perseverance of the Hoocąk culture embedded within the forms and concepts he created.

He was a man with a gentle demeanor—described by family as somehow going with the flow just like the water he so often depicted—and was exploring himself, his culture, and his home within what might be considered representative and conceptual portraits of water.[71] Lowe and his use of blue and green suggest home, and the lands enshrouded in coo that can be found in the rivers, forest, and sky. His drawings depart from the space-creating focus of the large-scale sculptural works most often associated with his art practice. While some of his sketches retain the sculptor's thoughts and concepts similar to those reflected in his canoes, others, with the use of pastel, remain more delicate and are on a smaller scale. Like his sculptures, Lowe's drawings remain committed to depicting his ancestry and, most of all, exploring his uniquely shaped understanding of the land he grew up on and how he could bring this into contemporary art.

When I look at Truman Lowe's work, I am transported home. He had such a profound impact on many Hoocąk, especially artists and makers, that today I see a new community of artists coming of age across our Hoocąk homeland. He shaped contemporary Hoocąk arts just as the water shapes the land, and he imparted his love for water in motion, which came to symbolize his deeply rooted connection to his ancestral heritage. Within each minimalist work is an assembled display of Lowe's mastery as an artist, grounded in the teachings and philosophies of culture, worldview, and a reawakened Hoocąk color theory.

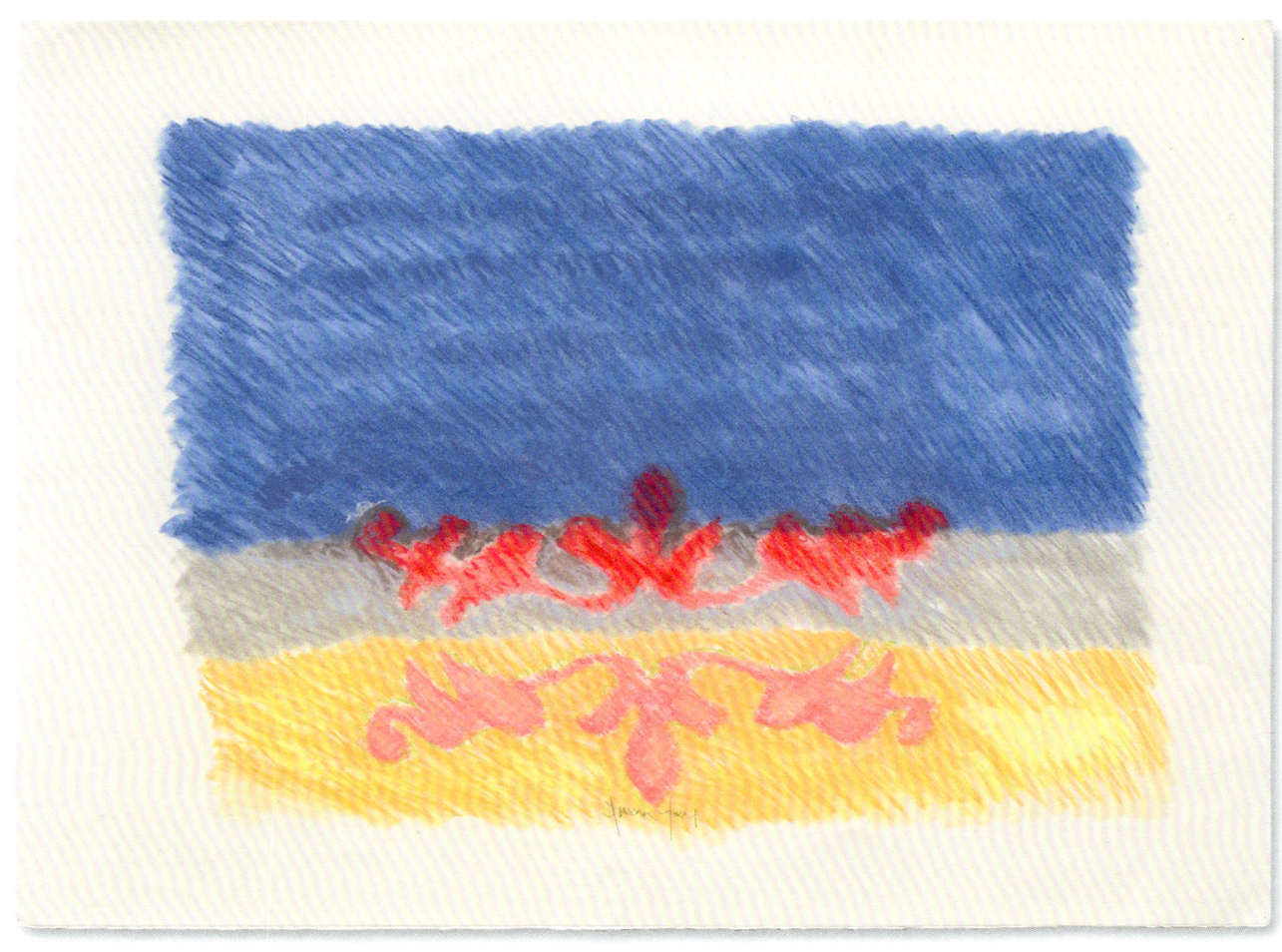

80. Untitled (Ribbonwork), ca. 1980. Pastel on paper, 22 x 30 in. National Museum of the American Indian 27/622

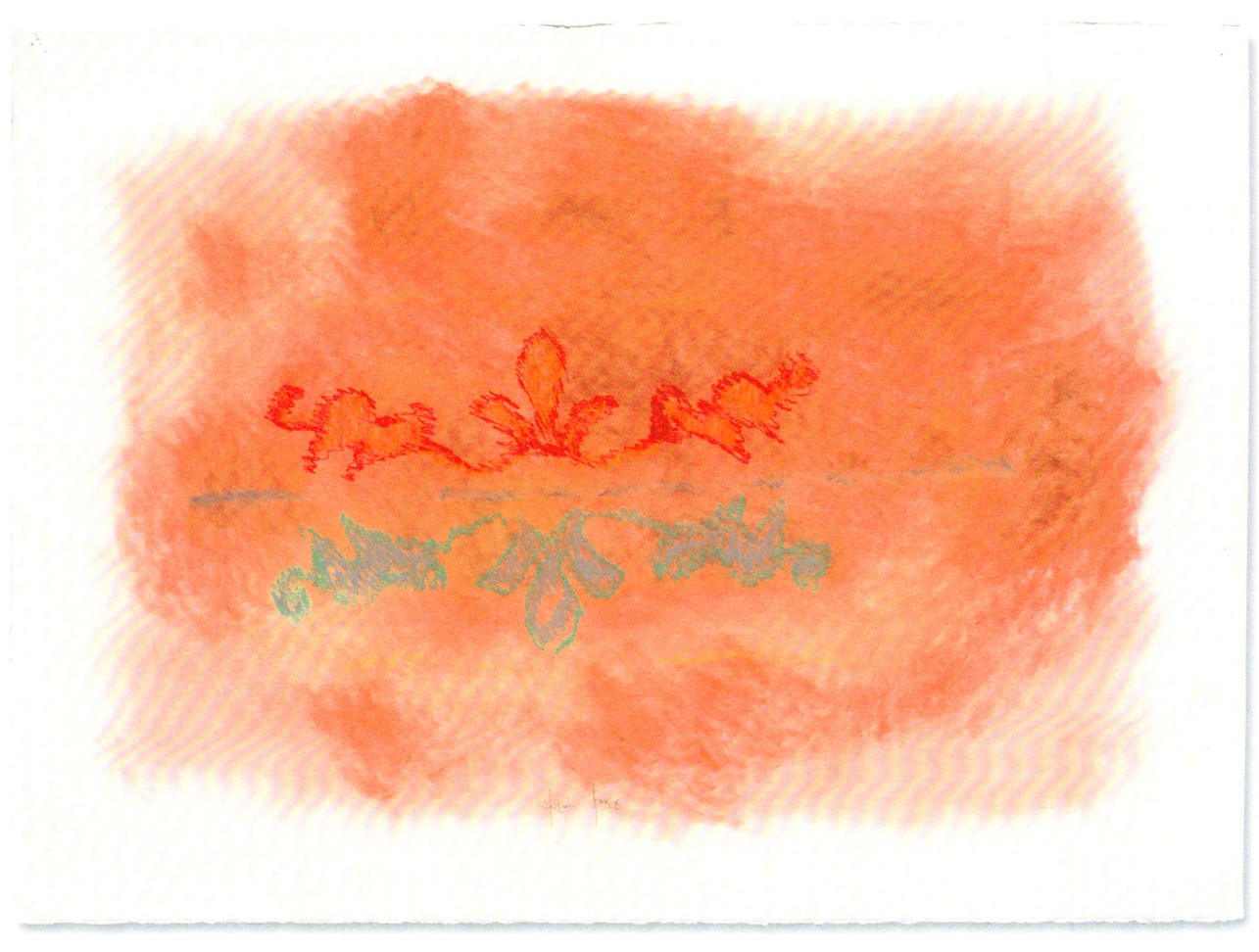

81. *Ribbon Appliqué*, ca. 1980. Pastel on paper, 22 x 30 in. National Museum of the American Indian 27/621

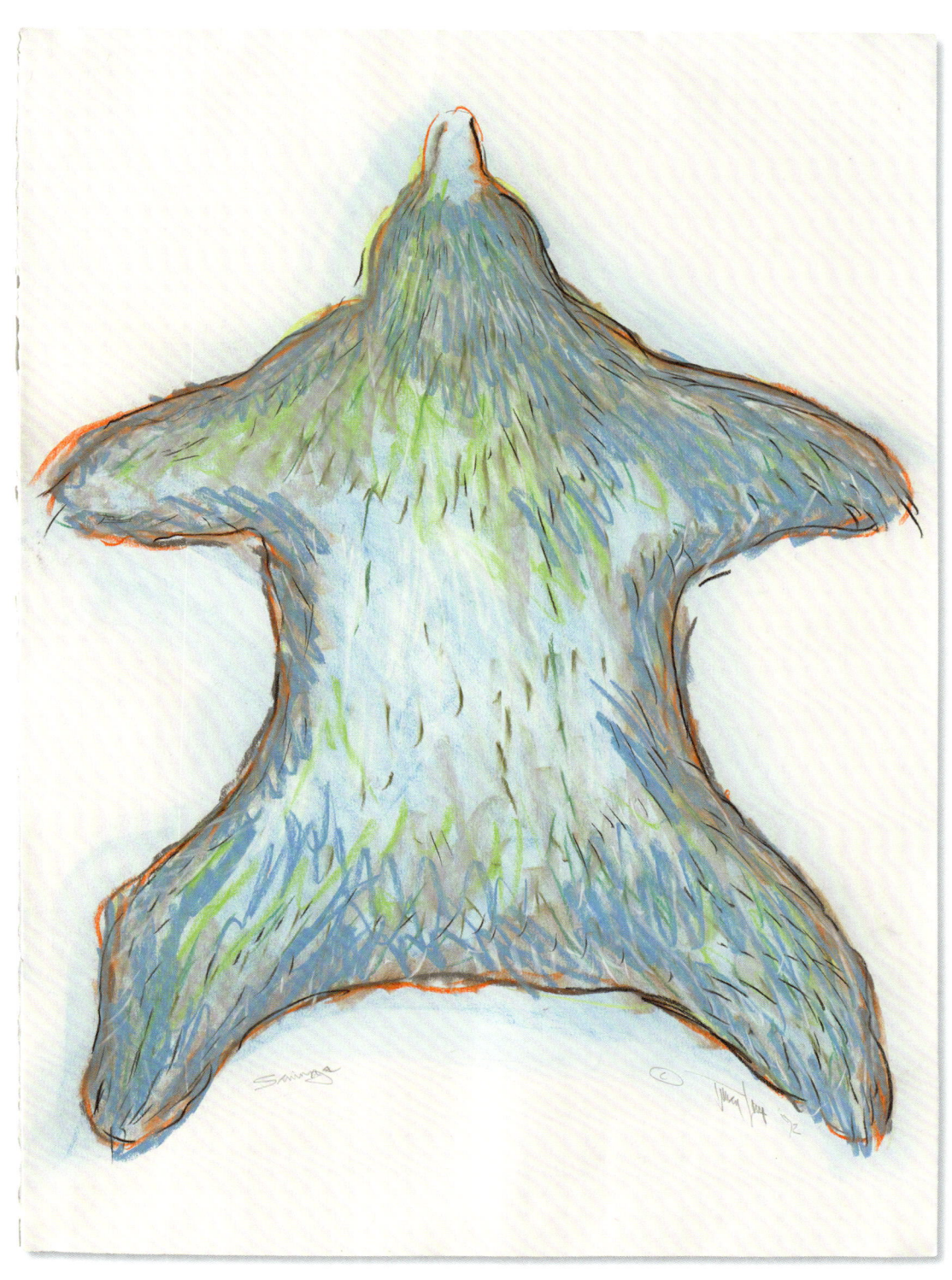

82. *Sauninga*, 1992. Pastel on paper, 30 x 22 ¼ in. National Museum of the American Indian 27/628

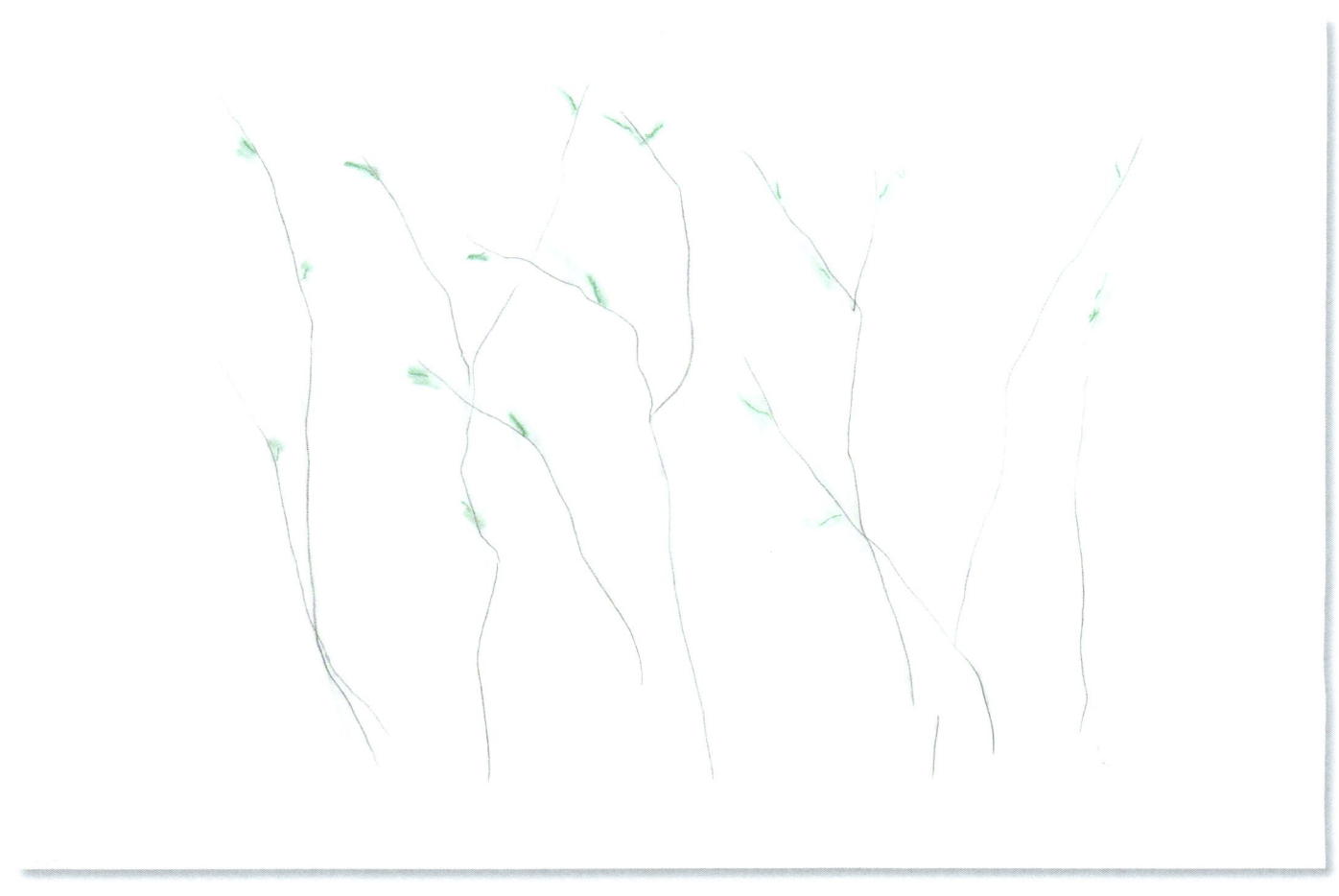

83. Untitled (Spring Branches), 2010–11. Pastel and graphite on paper, 24 x 36 in. National Museum of the American Indian 27/625

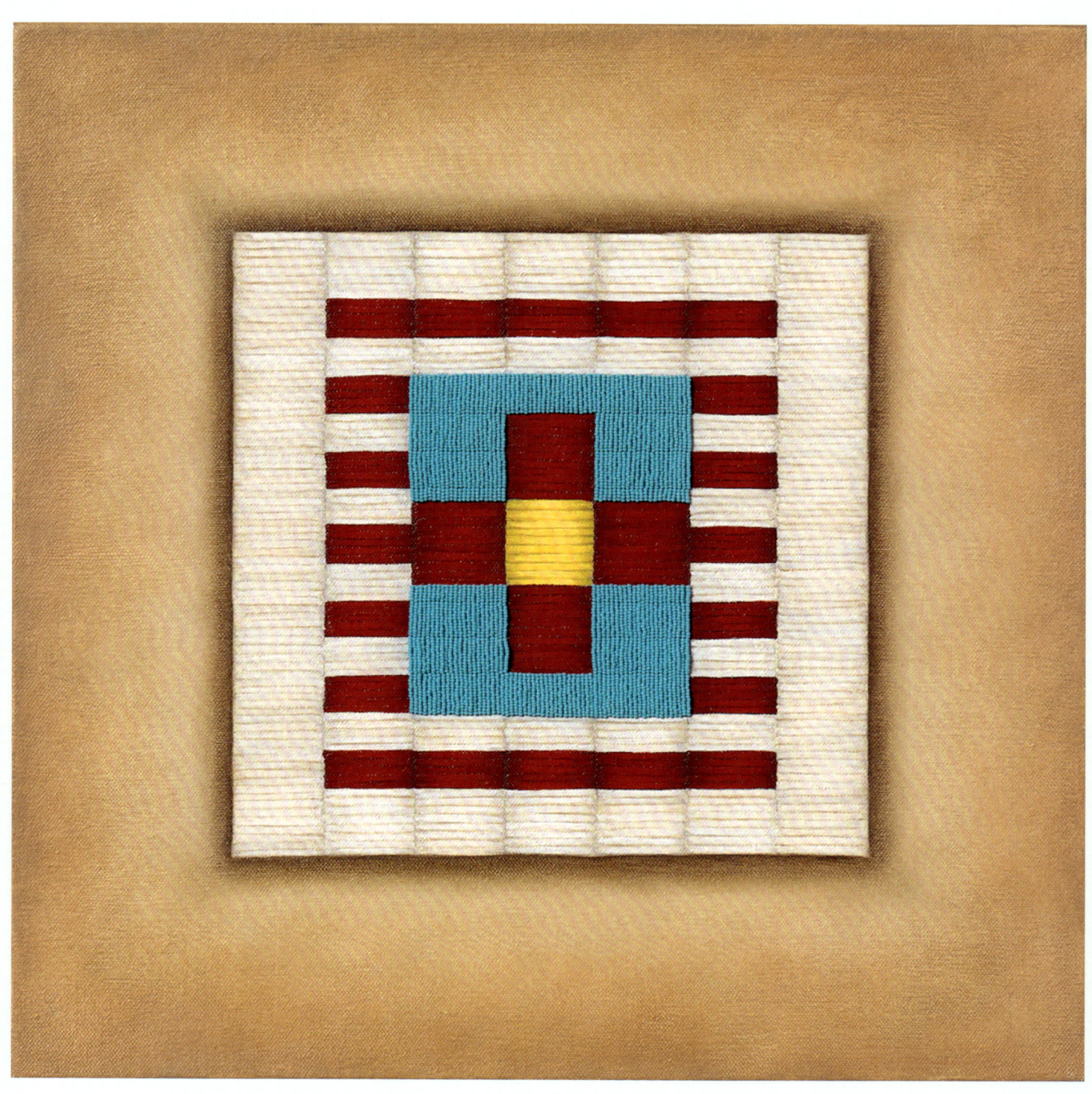

84. Dyani White Hawk (Sičáŋǧu Lakota, b. 1976), Untitled (Cross), 2014. Acrylic, oil, glass beads, and thread on canvas, 14 x 14 in. National Museum of the American Indian 26/9334

A Moment of Disruptive Truth

Dyani White Hawk

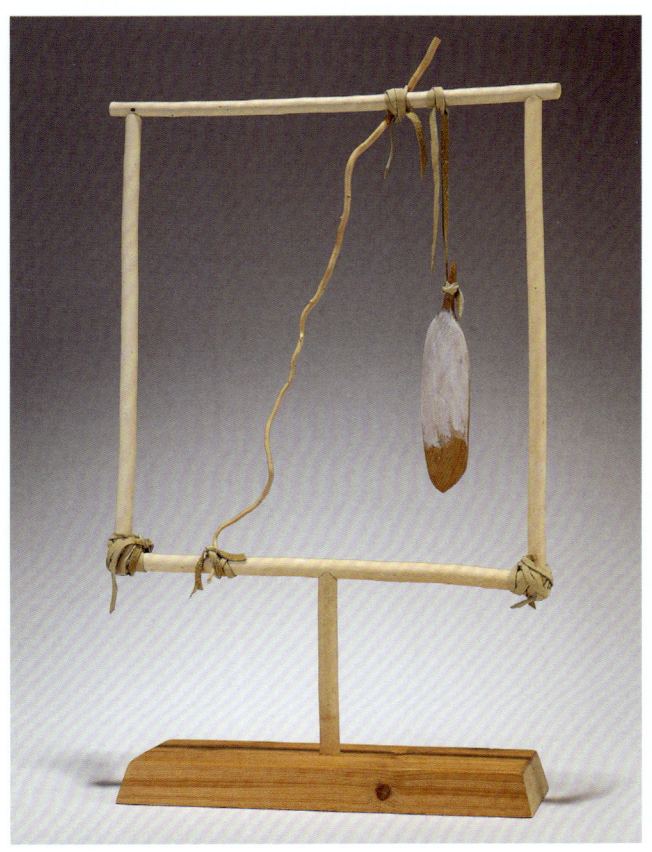

85. *Feather and Lightning*, 1995. Pine, peeled willow sticks, leather, paint, 26 ¹⁵⁄₁₆ x 16 ¾ x 1 ⁷⁄₁₆ in. Milwaukee Art Museum, gift of Jan Cicero Gallery M1997.55

TRUMAN LOWE'S WISE WORDS came at a critical moment in my education. I had just entered graduate school after six years of tribal college. I was tasked with delivering a PowerPoint presentation on the ways our life experiences informed our artistic expression. I am Lakota, German, and Welsh American. I grew up in the city, deep in hip-hop, rave, skate, and snowboarding youth culture. My life story was affected by the adoption era and the long lineage of destructive policies affecting Native people. Raised within the urban Native community, I learned how to bead before I learned to paint. My point of view is characterized by multiple modes of education, creative expression, and cultural experience.

As I reviewed written critiques submitted anonymously by my peers, I was dismayed to find that a few of my peers revealed prejudicial views. Their comments questioned the validity or worth of exploring my experiences as a person of mixed cultural background. The course's professor led the group critique, pushing hard against the conceptual basis of my work. In a condescending manner he asked, "What if all my art was about me being Polish?" as if there was no value in unpacking and reflecting upon my lived experiences as a Native woman. This particular type of targeted scrutiny of identity was not part of any of my peers' discussions on their presentations.

I asked Truman to meet me for lunch. Truman's presence was always so soothing; he emanated tranquility. After showing him the written critiques and telling him about the class discussion, Truman responded with gentle authority and assuredness. He shook his head, and he told me, "Dyani, don't give these people any of your energy." While I was caught in a tumultuous cycle of internal debate and hurt, he argued that their opinions on my story, my life, and my work were inconsequential.

This moment of disruptive truth allowed me to forge some of my strongest arguments as to why my artistic voice is important, valid, and needed in the thread of Indigenous, United States, and global artistic histories. Many of these arguments continue to be foundational in my artistic practice today. With his unshakable composure, Truman exemplified the strength of sitting wholly and comfortably in one's personal truth.

On the night of my MFA exhibition, I approached Truman as he stood in front of one of my paintings. We took in the work together silently, and he handed me a little tin box that he had sanded down to a beautifully brushed surface. Inside was a perfectly formed bed with just enough room to lay a single quill. With warm and solemn serenity, he told me, "You never have to quill again if you don't want to." He didn't mean that I shouldn't. That gleaming box dedicated to a solitary quill demonstrated the validity and strength of my painting and the legitimacy of its connectivity to our cultural continuity. In that single gesture, he exemplified to me the concrete truth of the very arguments that I had to formulate in order to defend my work and navigate a mainstream academic environment.

Truman's presence was a gift. I cried when I learned of his passing, knowing how much we would all miss his good energy and leadership. But then I went out, I put my tobacco down, I prayed for his journey, and I thanked him deeply for all he had done. *Wopila tanka,* Truman. The blessings shared through your generosity of spirit are immeasurable.

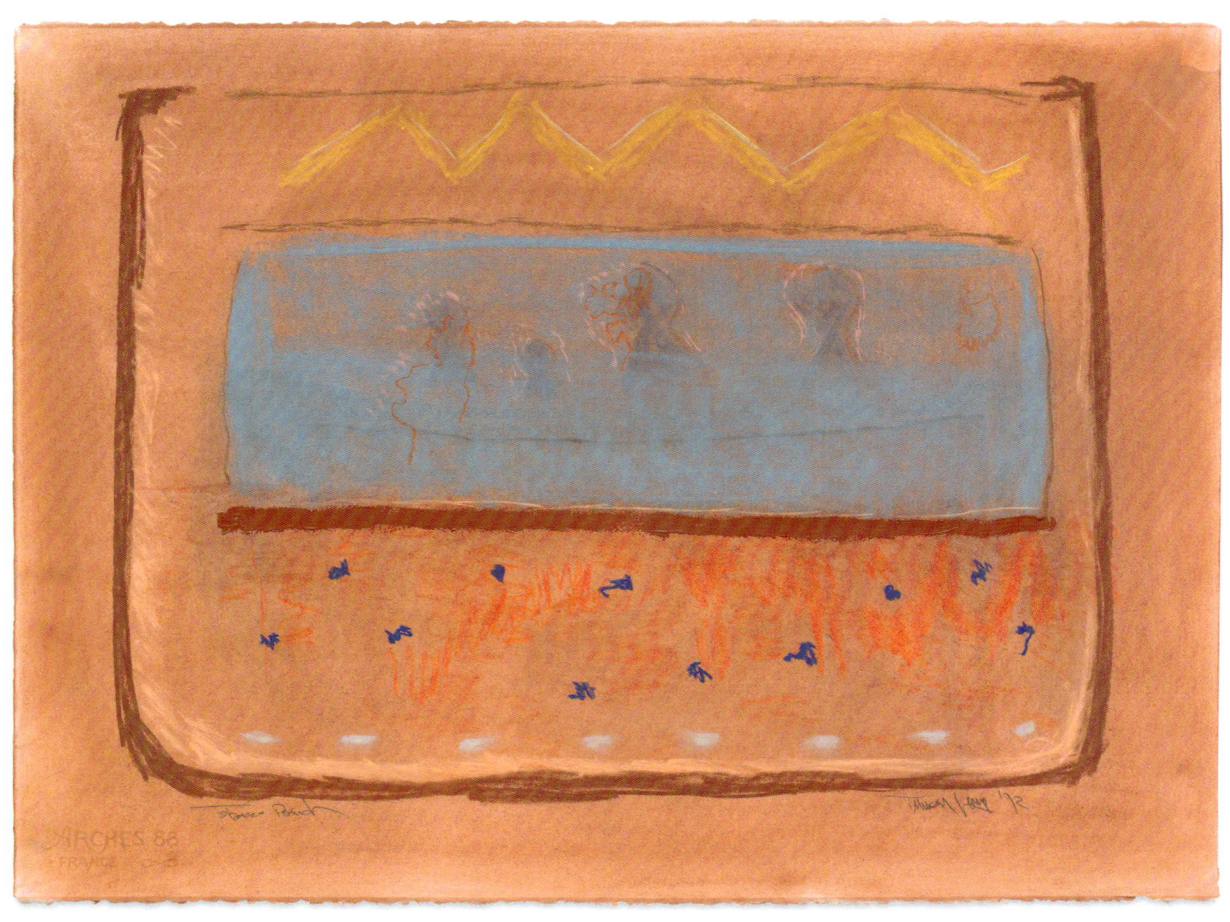

86. *Tobacco Pouch*, 1992. Chalk pastel on paper, 30 x 22 ½ in. National Museum of the American Indian 26/9771, gift of John and Meryl Lipton Lavine

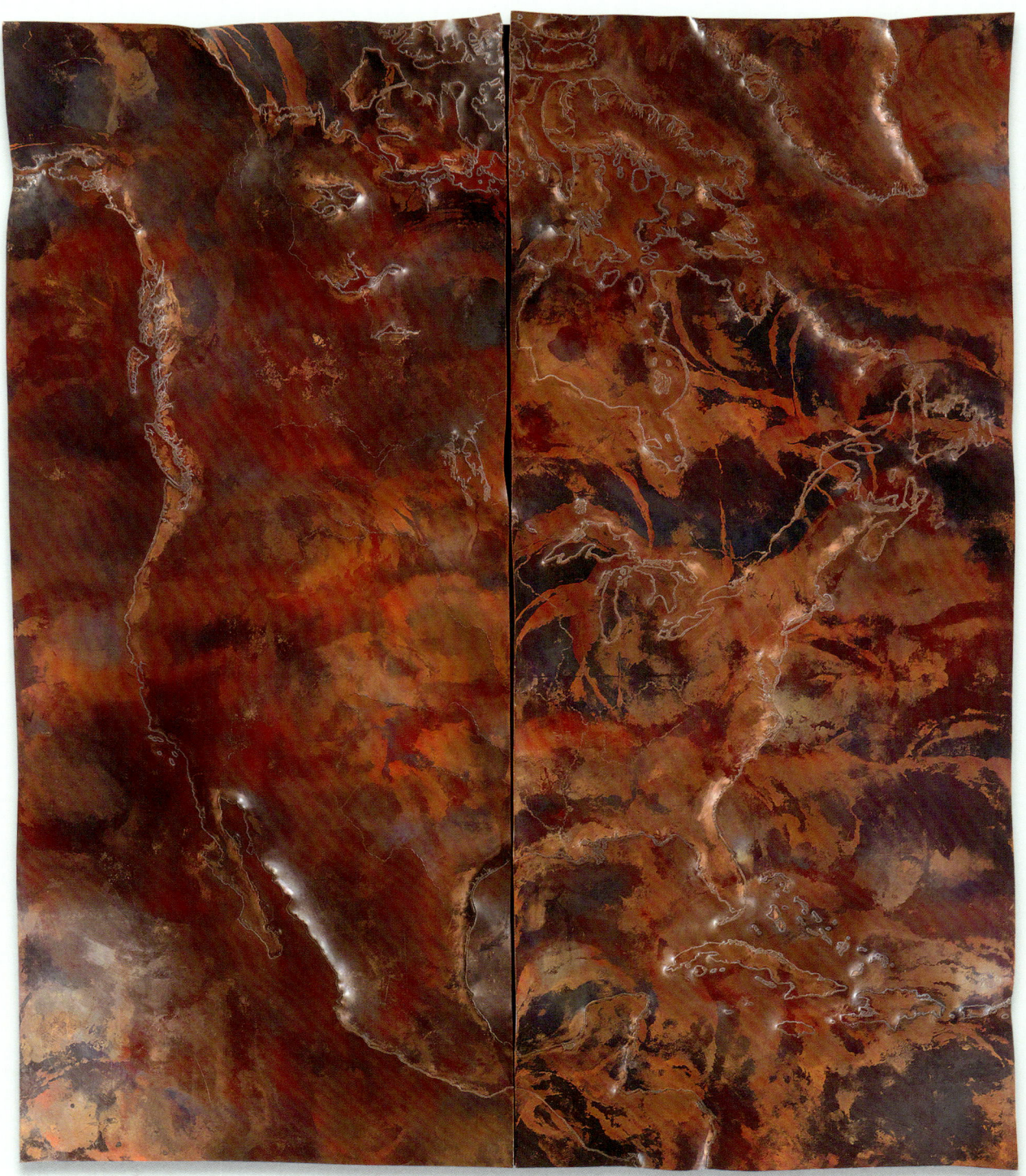

87. Michael Belmore (Anishinaabe), *Shorelines*, 2006. Copper, 84 x 36 ¼ x 3 in. National Museum of the American Indian 26/8459

That's Good Work

Michael Belmore

I AM GRATEFUL FOR THIS OPPORTUNITY to acknowledge Truman Lowe as a teacher and mentor. More than any contemporary artist, he has greatly influenced me through a conversation we did not have in person but one that I continually return to in my practice. We crossed paths a handful of times over the years. The first occasion was in 1992, when some were celebrating the five hundred years since Columbus had discovered the Americas. Among the events planned for that celebration was the exhibition *Land, Spirit, Power: First Nations at the National Gallery of Canada*, a first of its kind. Until then only a handful of works by First Nations people had ever been exhibited or collected by the institution. Following the opening of *Land, Spirit, Power*, I joined in a late-night gathering of artists. We were triumphant with our presence in the white box yet wondering if we would be invited back. Was it a one-time thing? I approached Lowe to sign a copy of the exhibition catalog. He wrote, "I appreciate your interest in my sawdust –Truman." The subtle yet poignant use of the word "sawdust" stays with me. With one word, he acknowledged that our work is not like that of our parents or grandparents. Sawdust, a by-product of an introduced practice that was unknown to our ancestors, points to an ever-evolving relationship to material and making.

Lowe's work taught me to see that seemingly small things—simple things—inspire: the swing of a hammer, a bend in a thin piece of wood, the warmth of a fire, the persistence of waves on a shore. Through the insinuation of these actions, a much larger consequence may be inferred. Materials such as water, wood, and stone have a voice.

They speak a language and have a history of conversation that extends well beyond our fleeting human existence. In our attempts to enter into this exchange, materials offer a voice to speak about the past and the future, about our connection to land and its ever-changing reality.

Lowe often relates the experience of standing on the shore of a river as a metaphor for how we travel from life toward death. We see the water move toward us; we watch as it moves away, witnessing a small glimpse into the whole. We are limited in our ability to understand the totality of what this world offers.

I have a memory, or collection of memories, which I will share as I think it illustrates the poetics of Truman's work. I am standing on a beach of tumbled stones, varying in color: reds, whites, blacks, grays, with a smattering of green, extending out for a mile in both directions. I watch as the foam dances on the surface of the water between the crashing waves. Through the roar of water and wind I hear the subtle clink, clink, clinking sounds of rocks as the water recedes. It is this action, of water continually pressing against the shore, that has informed the place where I stand. Rounded and worked together over the millennia, these stones bear witness to the persistence of nature. The sheer physical world, which we as people inhabit, is at times humbling.

Truman used to say, "That's good work," which to me was the ultimate compliment. I think about this often and the meaning of "good." "Good" meaning not perfect but carrying a smile in your heart, one that is humble and sincere.

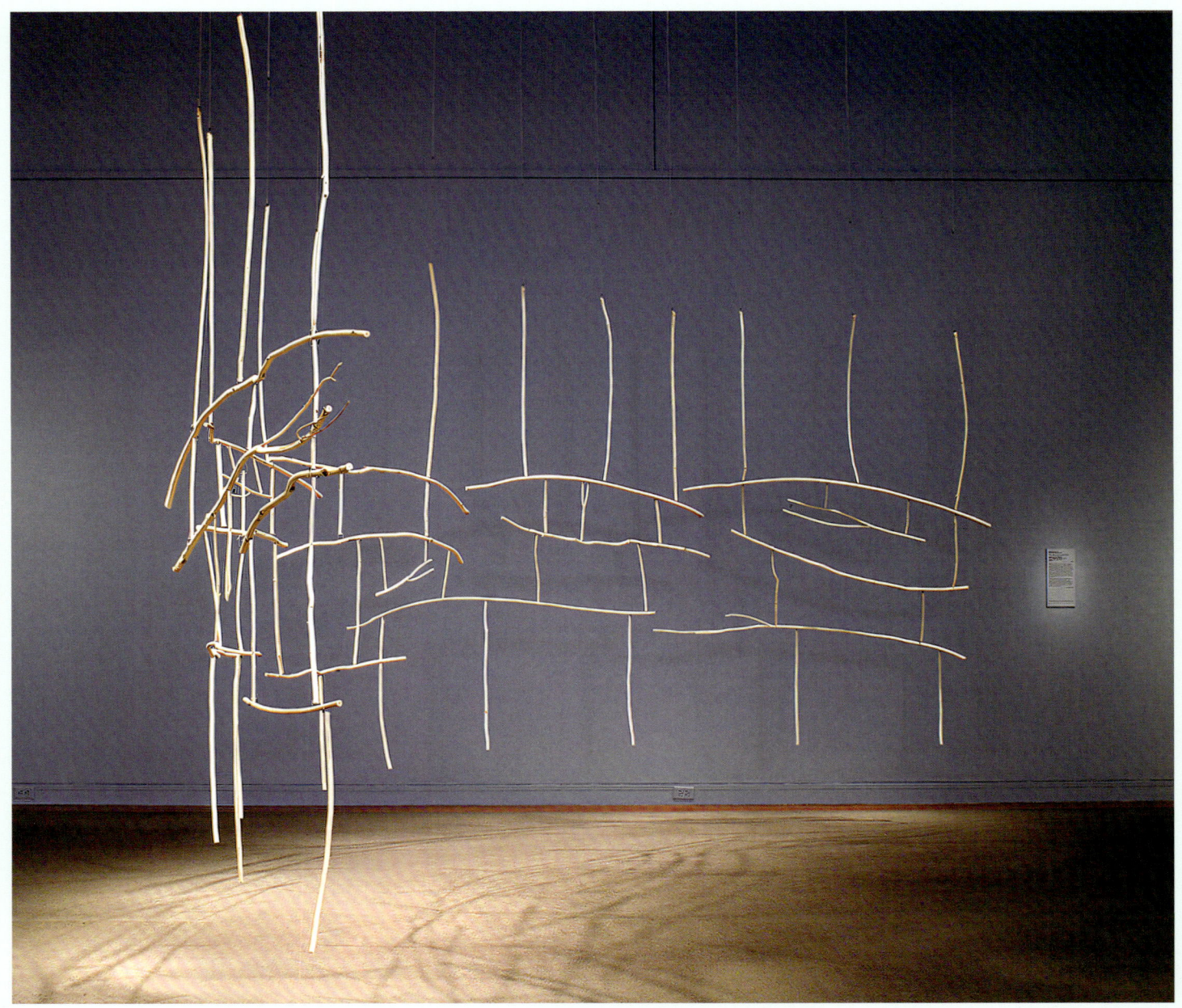

88. *The Seine of Journeys*, 2003. Willow, monofilament, and metal, 120 x 228 in. Peabody Essex Museum, museum purchase made possible by the Edward Daland Lovejoy fund, the Anna Pingree Phillips fund, and the Docent Fund, 2005, E302691

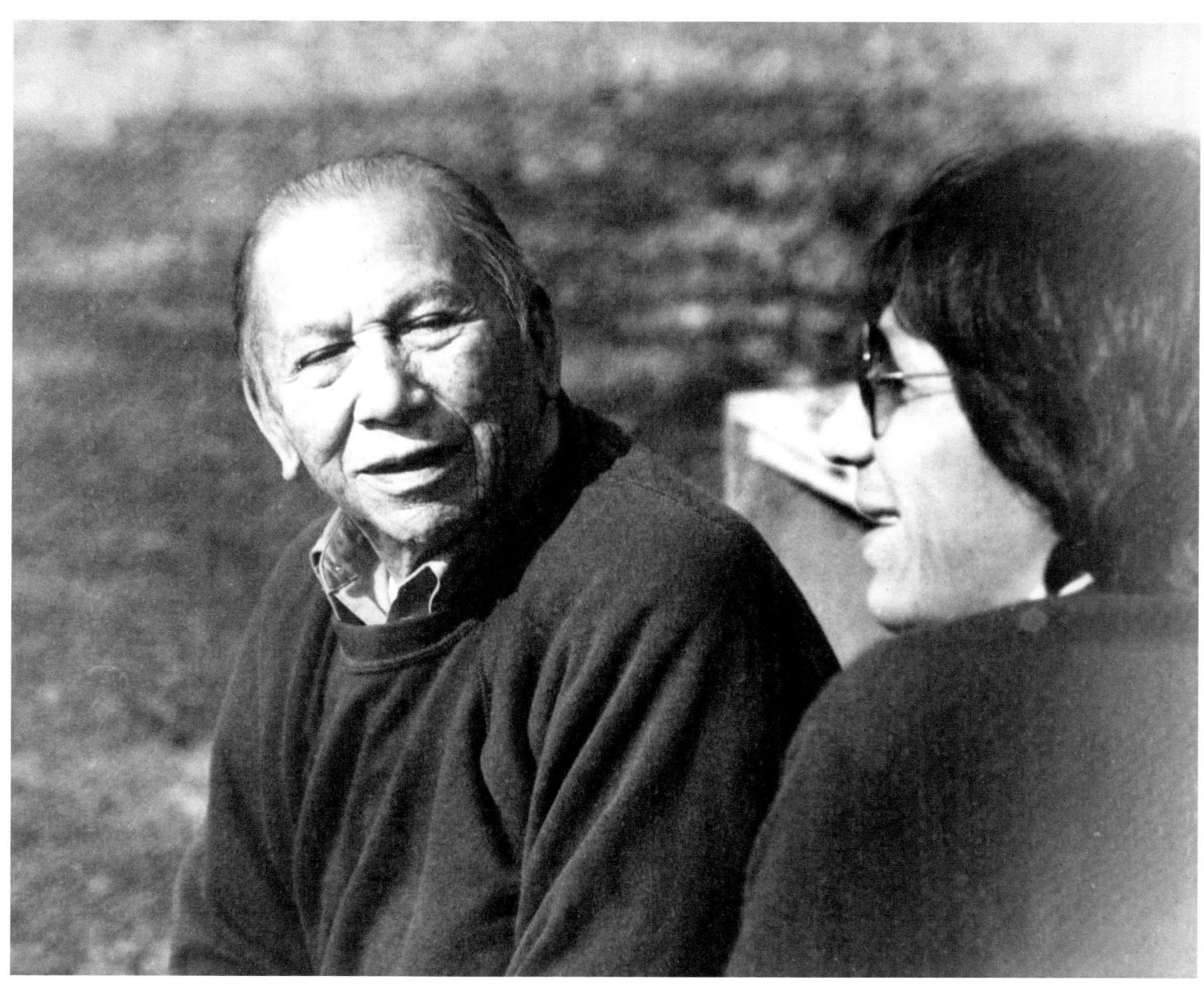

89. Truman Lowe *(right)* with his father, Martin, Black River Falls, Wisconsin, ca. 1980

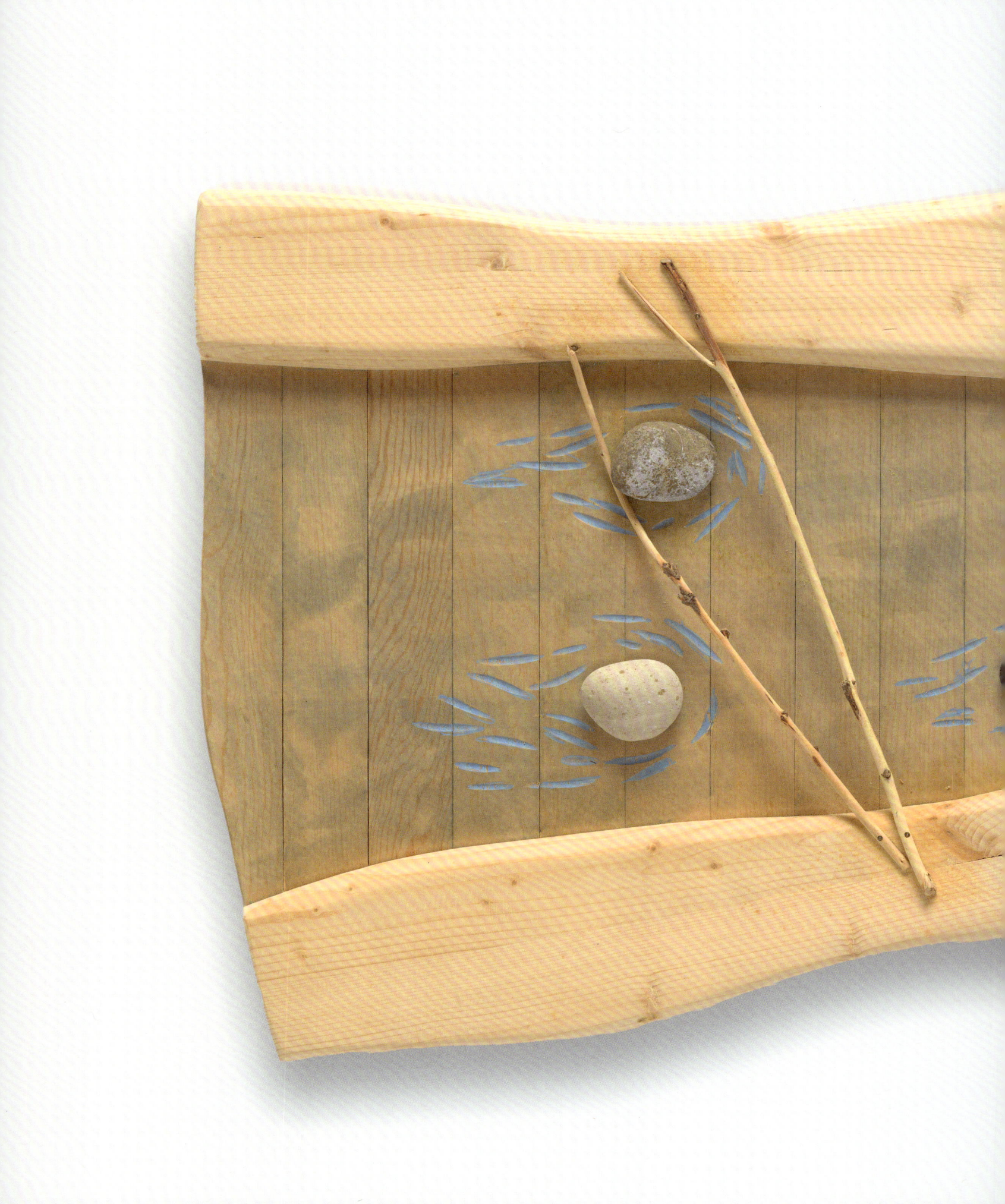

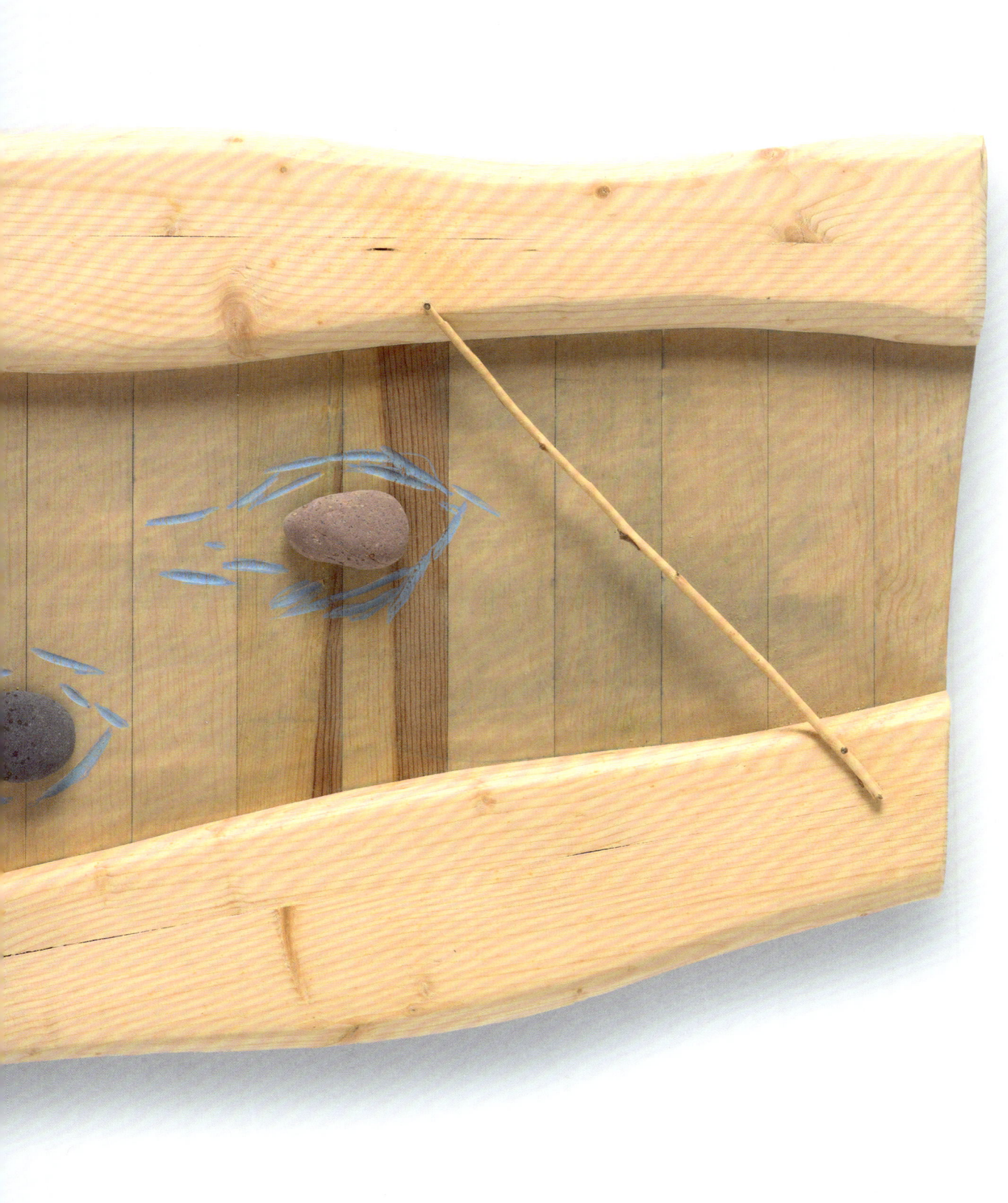

90. *Stream II*, ca. 1990–91. Pine, peeled willow sticks, watercolor, stones, pastel, 18 x 32 ¼ x 1 in. National Museum of the American Indian 27/608

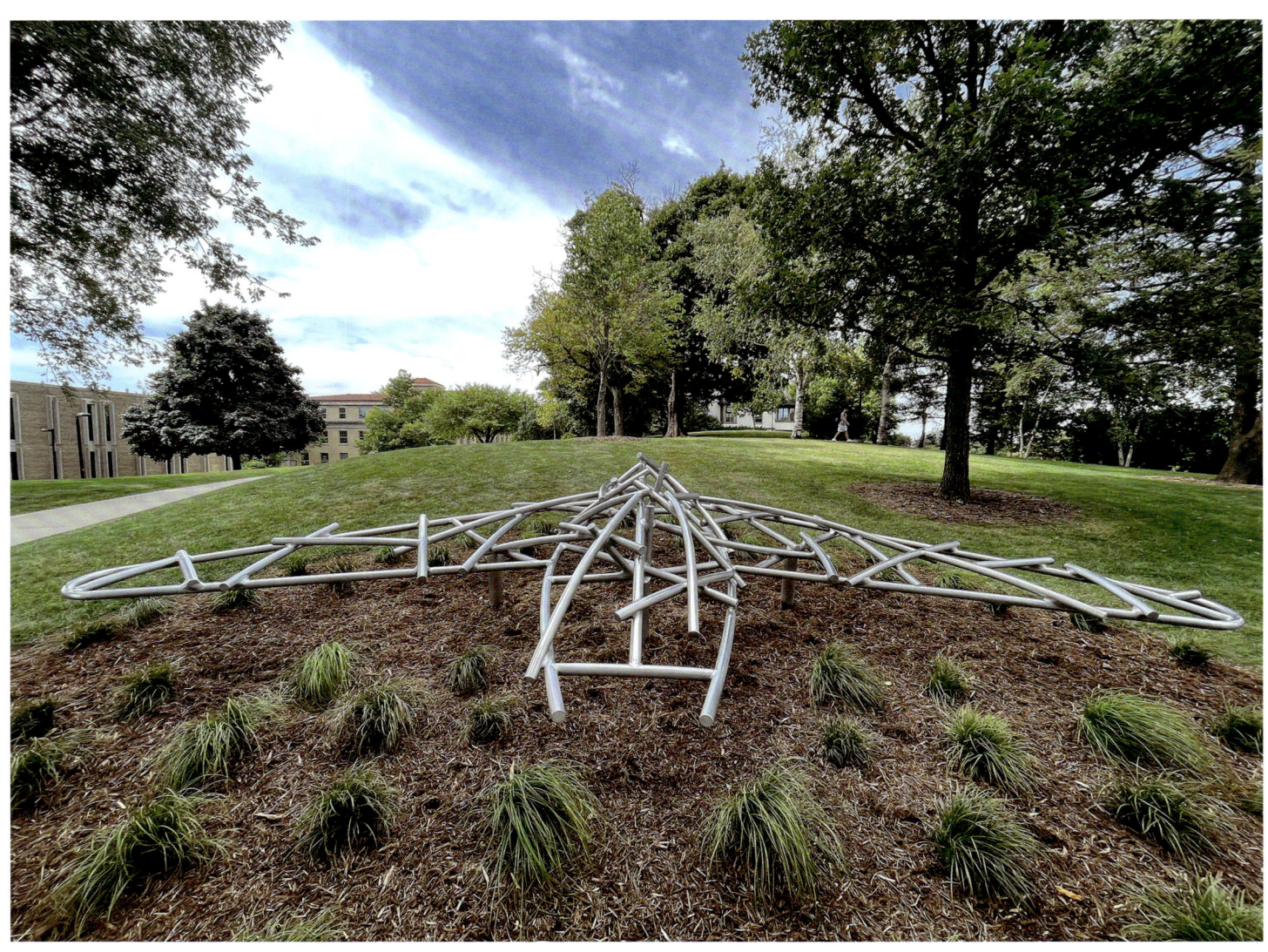

91. *Effigy: Bird Form,* 1997. Aluminum, 3 ½ x 20 ½ x 11 ft. University of Wisconsin–Madison

Patricia Marroquin Norby

IT WAS A SUNNY, BREEZY, early autumn morning on September 15, 2023, when a large group of people gathered at Observatory Hill on the University of Wisconsin–Madison campus just steps away from the Lake Mendota shoreline. They were there to honor the renowned Hoocąk (Ho-Chunk) sculptor Truman Lowe (Wakąjahųkga) and welcome home his sculpture, *Effigy: Bird Form* (fig. 91). Created in 1997, the smooth, metallic, winged sculpture speaks to seasonal migrations, effigy mounds, and bodies of fresh water adjacent to the UW–Madison campus. The Hoocąk community aptly named the place Teejop, or "Four Lakes," which references the Mendota, Monona, Waubesa, and Kegonsa lakes. To live in Madison, or any part of the Great Lakes region, means to live with respect for the freshwater bodies and local environments, which all impact daily life. This September gathering was a day of community and celebration that included drumming, singing, dancing, and feasting. A lineup of speakers shared stories and memories about Lowe's legacy as the premiere Hoocąk sculptor in the United States and his numerous contributions as a Hoocąk community member, father, teacher, colleague, curator, and friend. On that early autumn day in 2023, as the leaves on the ancient oak trees danced in the dappled sunlight, there was a tangible warmth among the many people gathered who had known and embraced the artist as one of their own.

EARTH, WATER, AND SKY

Effigy: Bird Form was originally exhibited in the Jacqueline Kennedy Garden at the White House in Washington, DC, from 1997 to 1998. It was included in a celebration of twentieth-century American sculpture at the White House, which highlighted twelve works by contemporary Native American artists. This was part of a series of exhibitions organized by then-First Lady Hillary Clinton. *Effigy: Bird Form* was inspired by the ceremonial effigy mounds found in the upper Midwest and throughout the Great Lakes region.[72] Lowe explained at the time, "Being from the woodlands, I wanted the influence to come from woodlands, from a culture that inhabited this area one time or another and left their mark with earth mounds, or effigies."[73] He said further, "It was really a unique way this culture had of showing respect and living with the earth. This is an attempt on my part to represent the many pieces that have disappeared—to pay my respects to that culture."[74]

Lowe's sculptures reveal an aesthetic reverence for the ancestral mounds and lush landscapes of the Hoocąk homelands. To fully appreciate his artwork requires embracing both the artist's and the Hoocąk people's deep understandings of the inextricability of earth, water, and sky—a theme Lowe continually explored in his larger body of work through titles, materials, and subject. He consistently expressed personal and ancestral connections to the effigy and other earthen mounds of Wisconsin and across the midwestern United States. At the same time, his work would allude to bodies of fresh water significant to the Hoocąk people—waters that over the course of centuries witnessed numerous cultural ceremonies and historical events and, ultimately, became sites of preservation for Hoocąk oral histories and material culture. Throughout his career, Lowe created hundreds of drawings, prints, sculptures, and environmental installations that paid homage to the human-made earthworks, local woodlands, and thick forests, as well as the streams, rivers, and lakes that are contiguous to them.

Across the Midwest are thousands of extant mounds and mound groupings built approximately four hundred to three thousand years ago. They include effigy, elongated, conical, stepped, and burial mounds of various sizes. These earthen sculptures had multiple purposes, and their relationship to water is culturally and historically indisputable.[75] Many were once activated as directional maps marking the locations of freshwater sources that have nourished, provided sanctuary, offered transportation, and delineated political boundaries for the Hoocąk and other Indigenous peoples of the region. In interviews, Lowe emphasized his fascination with the ever-changing interconnections between earth and water, in particular moving water and its impact on the landscape. "You never know where the water is going to travel next as it begins to overflow its banks or begins to move its channel. You never really know what's going to happen. . . . That's the best way to describe it really."[76] Strikingly minimal, *Effigy: Bird Form* elegantly intersects complex histories and the layered elements of the earth, water, and sky through its site-specific and cultural references, its intentions as an environmental installation, and its avian shape. Notably, on the UW–Madison campus, the sculpture is positioned on the eastern side of Observatory Hill, flying directionally toward other mounds located on the campus and toward an important ancestral mound grouping just three miles northwest on Lake Mendota, at a site now known as the Blackhawk Country Club, also in Madison, Wisconsin.[77]

The Blackhawk mounds date from between AD 650 to 1200. According to the Wisconsin State Historical Society,

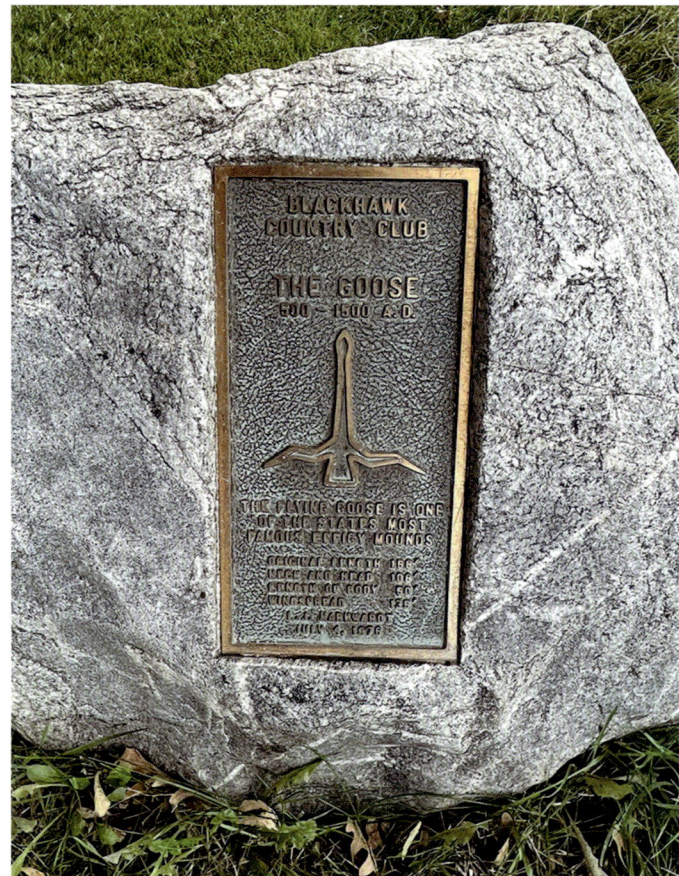

92. "Flying Goose" or migrating bird placard identifying the bird effigy mound at Blackhawk Country Club in Madison, Wisconsin

collectively, the grouping includes three bears, one panther, three conical, two elongated, and one large flying bird or migrating goose mound (fig. 92). Remarkably more massive in scale than Lowe's *Effigy: Bird Form*, this large earthen bird mound demonstrates a wingspan of 135 feet. Significantly, as educator Janice Rice (citizen of the Ho-Chunk Nation) once noted, the bird points directionally south toward the Effigy Mounds National Monument in Iowa, where the states now known as Wisconsin, Illinois, and Iowa all meet at the confluence of the Mississippi and the Wisconsin rivers. According to historian Patty Loew (Mashkiiziibii, Bad River Band of Lake Superior Ojibwe), around 1570 it was along the Wisconsin River that the ancestral Hoocąk divided into separate communities now known as the Hoocąk, Iowa, Otoe, and Missouria, after being pushed southwest from their territory once located at the confluence of Lake Michigan and Lake Superior.[78]

Water confluences are meaningful to ancestral mound sites, and this relationship between earth and water is present in Hoocąk oral histories and in Lowe's work. For instance, approximate to the Blackhawk mounds, a freshwater spring identified by the Hoocąk as Mąąką Mąą'íí, or "Medicine Spring," gently trickles into Lake Mendota where a stand of willow and cottonwood trees leads to the water's shoreline (fig. 93). It was near this place where multiple Hoocąk dugout canoes, carved from white oak

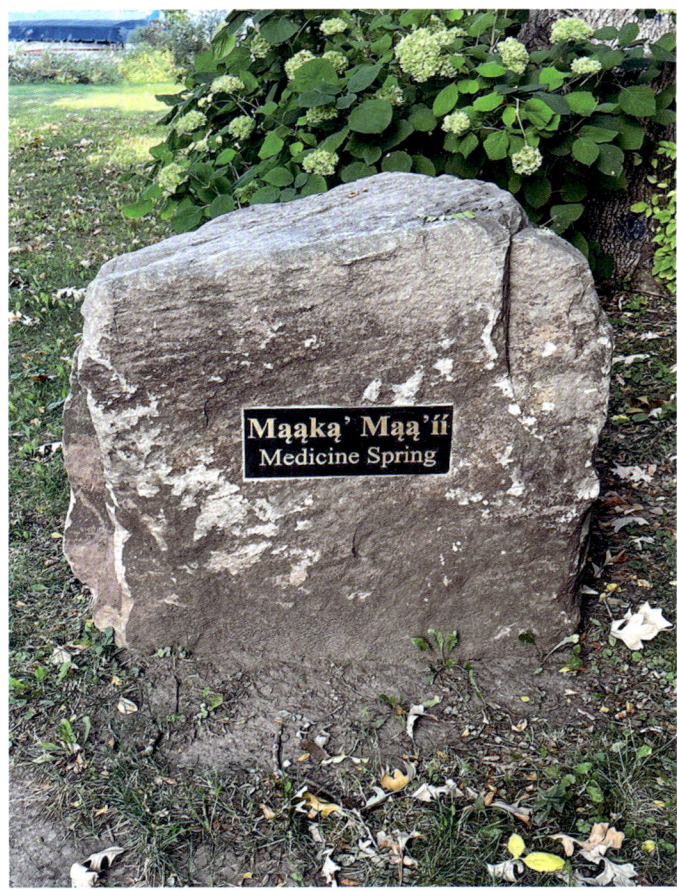

93. Mąąką Mąą'íí, or "medicine spring," located on the shoreline of Lake Mendota in Madison, Wisconsin

and dating back 1,200 to 3,000 years, were excavated from Lake Mendota's waters in 2021 and 2022 by Wisconsin state archaeologists, volunteers, and members of the Ho-Chunk Nation and Bad River Band of Lake Superior Chippewa. The collaborative recovery of the vessels, preserved in the ancient lake's waters for centuries, helped to tangibly affirm oral histories about the significance of water and maritime life to the ancestral Hoocąk and their intergenerational presence at Teejop (Madison). As Mollie Pauliot (Ho-Chunk Nation, Buffalo Clan) succinctly puts it, "Madison is the water."[79]

CONFLUENCES OF PEOPLE, PLACE, AND TIME

Lowe's respect for the seasonal shifts of the Great Lakes regions and the interconnections of natural forces are present in his environmental installation *Ke-Chunk Ciporoke* (2019) (figs. 94 and 95). The painted steel and copper wire sculpture, which was installed posthumously at Keecąk Ciinąk (Turtle Village), is located at the confluence of Turtle Creek and Rock River in South Beloit, Illinois. Ciiporok'e translates to "round-shaped house or dwelling." Lowe's aesthetic interpretation of this word features an open dome-shaped armature that echoes the form of Hoocąk ciiporok'e constructed from flexible wood poles and branches lashed together and then covered with bark and grasses. Lowe's sculpture marks the site where, from 1822 to 1832, Keecąk (or Ke-Chunk) was one of the most prosperous Hoocąk villages and supported thirty-five lodges and seven hundred Hoocąk community members. It was a place of seasonal gatherings for ceremony and for hunting, fishing, and raising crops along the banks of the area's waterways.

Drawing on the architectural knowledge of his community, Lowe echoed the long-standing practice of joining together individual branches of willow, or other tree saplings, in order to shape and hold his sculptural forms. He also used copper wire, leather thongs, or rawhide to secure them. These material selections were deliberate. His keen interest in regionally harvested willow saplings, copper wire, leather, and feathers emphasized Lowe's fascination with the ecological histories of diverse Indigenous peoples

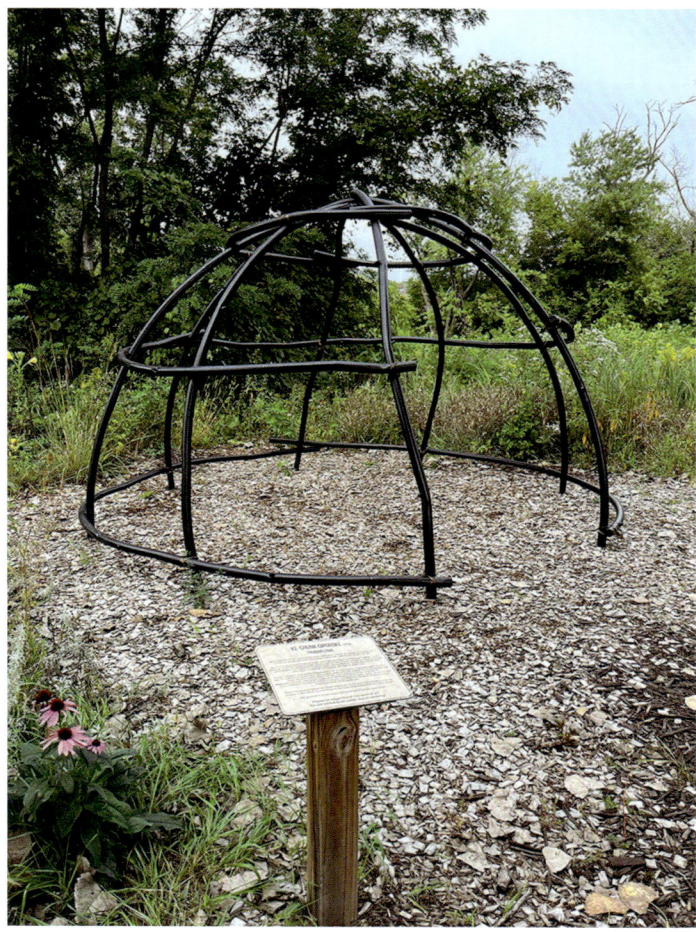

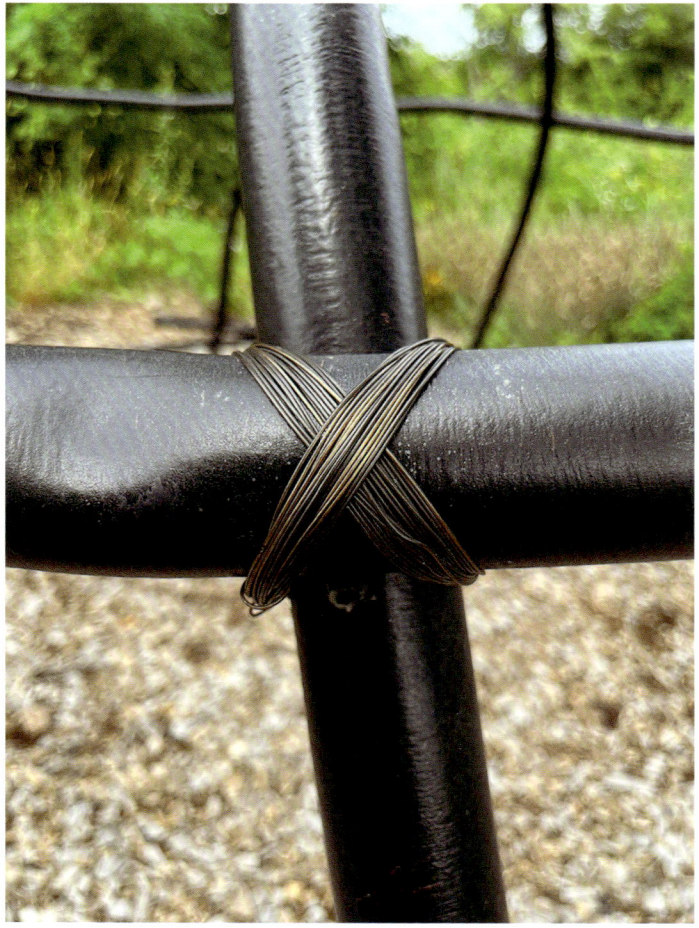

94. *Ke-Chunk Ciporoke*, 2019. Lowe's final sculpture was installed posthumously at Turtle Creek and Rock River in South Beloit, Illinois.

95. Detail of *Ke-Chunk Ciporoke*, 2019

of the Woodlands and Great Lakes regions. Narrow wooden strips of milled pine, which he frequently used to replicate cascading or falling water, materially alluded to the aesthetic expressions of Hoocąk makers. These techniques tangibly referenced the intergenerational production and sale of splint-plaited black-ash baskets—an economic and creative endeavor that helped to support Lowe's own family financially for generations.

THE MAGIC OF WATER MEMORIES AND FLYING CANOES

In 2021, I had the honor of welcoming one of Truman Lowe's original works, *Feather Canoe* (1993), to the Metropolitan Museum of Art for our Native American collection in the American Wing (fig. 40). At that time, I was a new curator to the museum, and *Feather Canoe* was one of my first official acquisitions. I was thrilled to bring Lowe's art into the Met's collections, which added important representation of the Ho-Chunk Nation and community as well as midwestern Native American peoples to an East Coast institution. As an Indigenous curator, I am honored to help spotlight the art and creative expressions of Native American and other Indigenous artists. Welcoming *Feather Canoe* was especially meaningful for me both personally and professionally.

I first met Truman Lowe at UW–Madison. He was my professor from 1999 to 2003. I remember that Truman's teaching style was very open. He believed in giving young

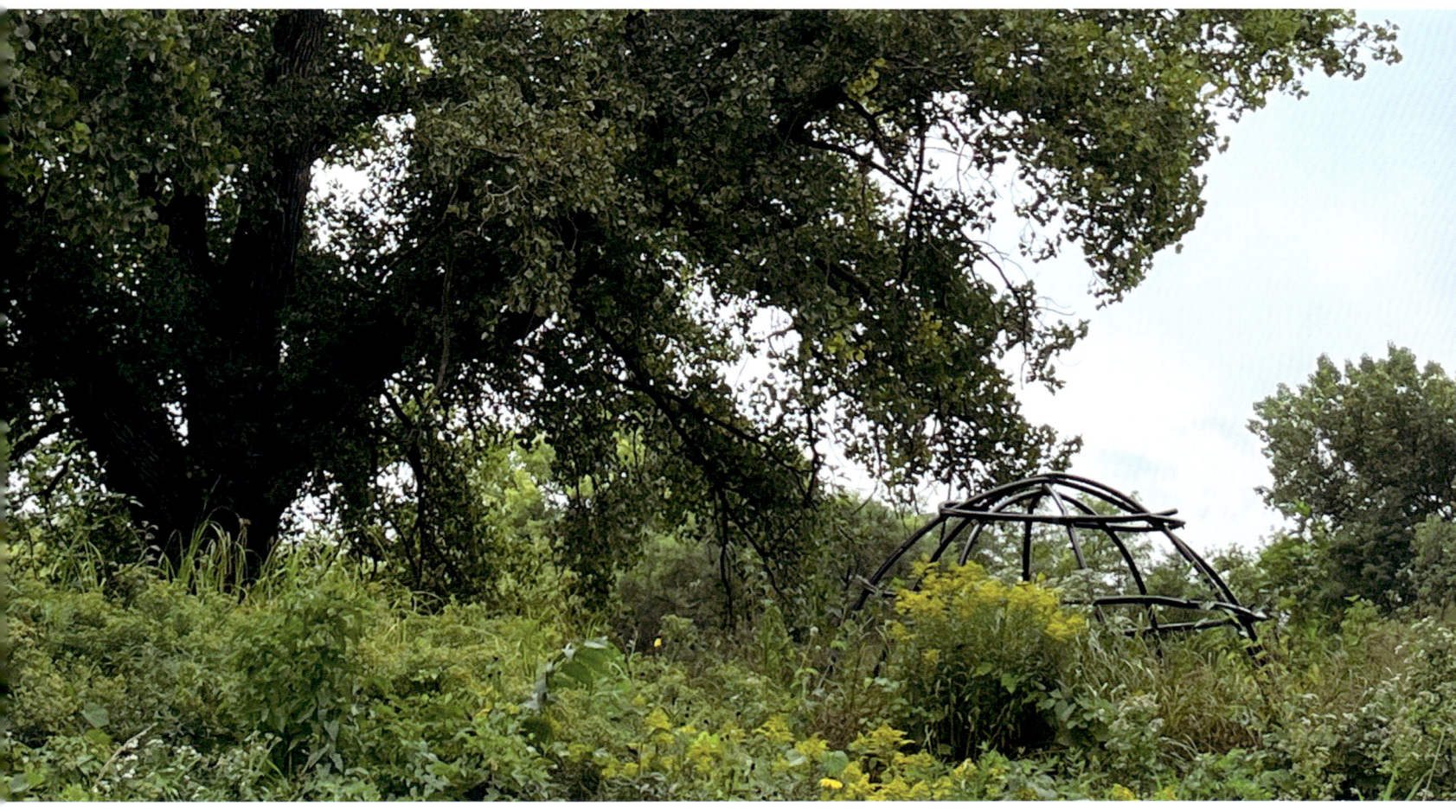

96. *Ke-Chunk Ciporoke*, 2019

artists the space and time to work out their aesthetic challenges. Later, Lowe was also my professional mentor as I was first navigating the museum world. From 2000 to 2008, he took a leave of absence from teaching at UW–Madison to serve as curator of contemporary art at the Smithsonian's National Museum of the American Indian in Washington, DC. Lowe helped to open the museum on the National Mall in 2004 and, for nearly a decade, worked diligently to foreground the artwork of modern and contemporary artists. In 2003, I served as a summer intern at the National Museum of the American Indian in Washington, DC, and shadowed Truman and his curatorial research team, which included the curator of *Water's Edge*, Rebecca Head Trautmann. My time with Truman helped to ignite my museum career and my love for museums, which has now lasted more than twenty years.

Feather Canoe became the centerpiece of the Met's 2022 exhibition *Water Memories*, a project which highlighted Indigenous people's personal reflections and community stories associated with oceans, lakes, rivers, and streams. Created with hand-harvested and stripped willow, copper wire, and white feathers, *Feather Canoe* held an ethereal presence in the gallery space. Much like *Effigy: Bird Form*, it too integrates layered elements of the earth, water, and sky. During its presentation, some truly incredible moments occurred as we carried out plans to install the canoe.

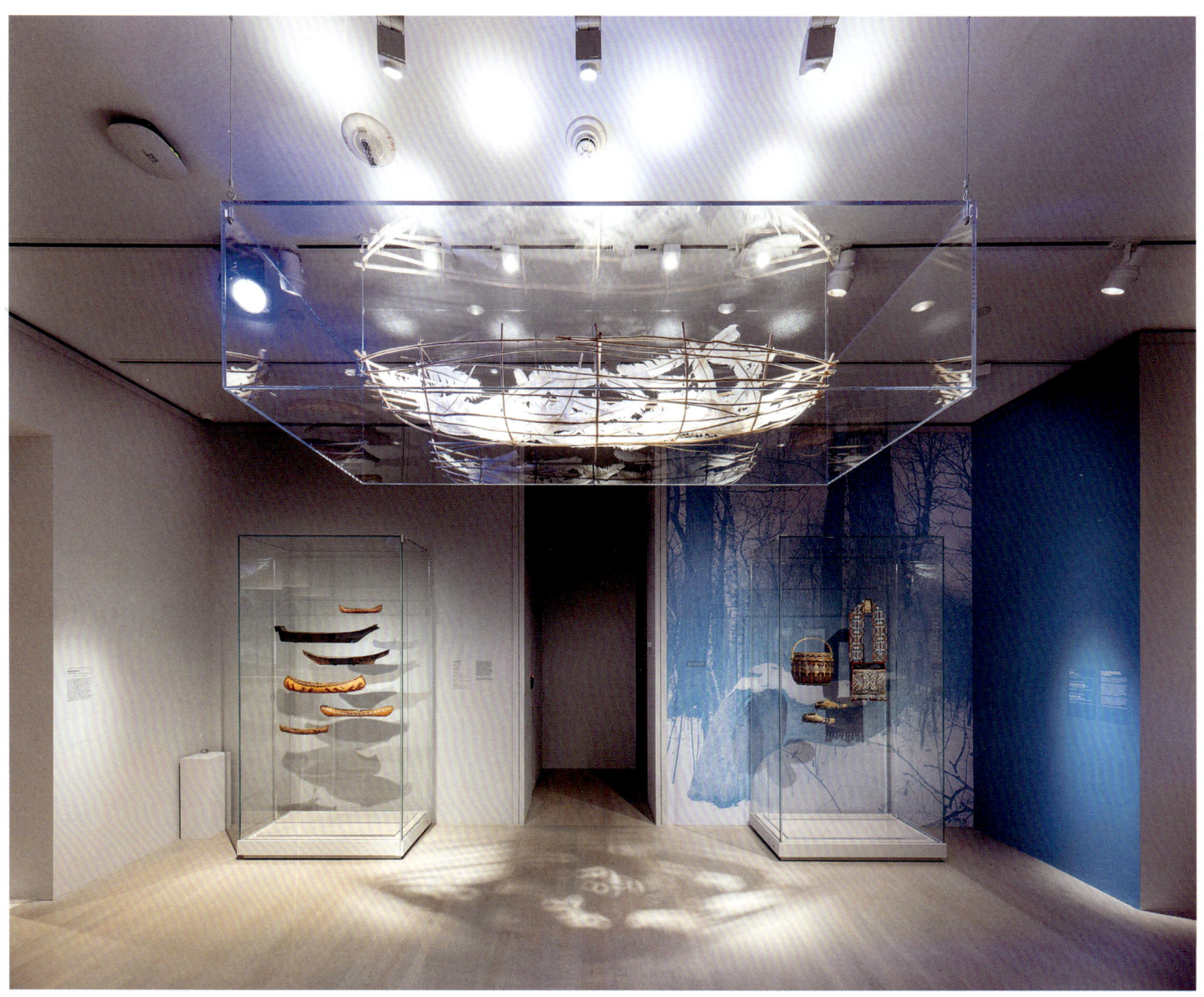

97. *Feather Canoe*, featured in the Metropolitan Museum of Art's exhibition, *Water Memories*, 2022–23. Unexpectedly, the plexiglass around the sculpture reflected the work from all sides, allowing visitors seemingly endless views of the "floating" artwork.

Originally, I had envisioned the in-gallery presentation of *Feather Canoe* as open and atop a platform so that audiences could engage with it in the round and closely view the soft white feathers lining its hull. Our exhibition designer shared some news that changed the trajectory of the exhibition installation: Not only could the canoe not be in the open because of its delicate willow branches, which visitors would surely be drawn to touching, it also required a plexiglass case to protect it from environmental elements. I remember feeling disappointed that my original vision for the canoe was not to be. However, something magical unfolded that has now led me to believe that the artist may have had *his own ideas* for how the canoe should be shown at the Met.

In addition to installing the canoe in a clear plexiglass case, we had also decided to suspend it from the gallery ceiling so that viewers could engage with it from below, and to recreate Lowe's personal memory of being "suspended above" the water while canoeing on the Wisconsin River.[80] Special lighting was installed to give the canoe the appearance of gently floating on air and water. On the day of its installation, as our team finished securing the work, we realized that the lighting combined with the smooth reflective surface of the plexiglass case created an optical effect that reflected the canoe from every possible angle; and not just once, but a mirrored infinity of feather canoe reflections. When audiences stood under the canoe in its case, they were able to view the vessel flying from below,

above, from the stern, from the bow, and from the hull. True to Lowe's aesthetic, it was a breathtaking moment of patterned light, shadows, and reflection. Throughout the run of the show, viewers were captivated by the flying canoe and would often stand underneath it for extended periods of time while gazing at its infinite reflections. The canoe had taken on its own life. It became a visual highlight in photographs and articles in the *New York Times* and other high-profile reviews of the exhibition (fig. 97).[81]

There is a certain kind of magic that happens when an artist's work comes from within but also has the ability to speak to diverse audiences. Lowe's art is deeply personal and grounded by his love for his family and community, as well as for the natural elements of his ancestral homelands at Teejop. Although intentionally specific to the Hoocąk and other Native American communities of the Woodlands and Great Lakes regions, his art conveys an elegance and refined presentation that gracefully calls on us to remember our natural surroundings of earth, water, and sky and our very human reliance upon them. Intentionally minimal and deceptively simple, Lowe's work demands much from his viewers. He asks us to appreciate the graceful curve of a bird's wing. He invites us to pause on moments of dappled light and elongated shadows. But he never *tells* us what to do. Instead, he encourages us to activate *our own* imaginations and histories in order to honor the truest, most streamlined form of our original selves, and to simply love this place.

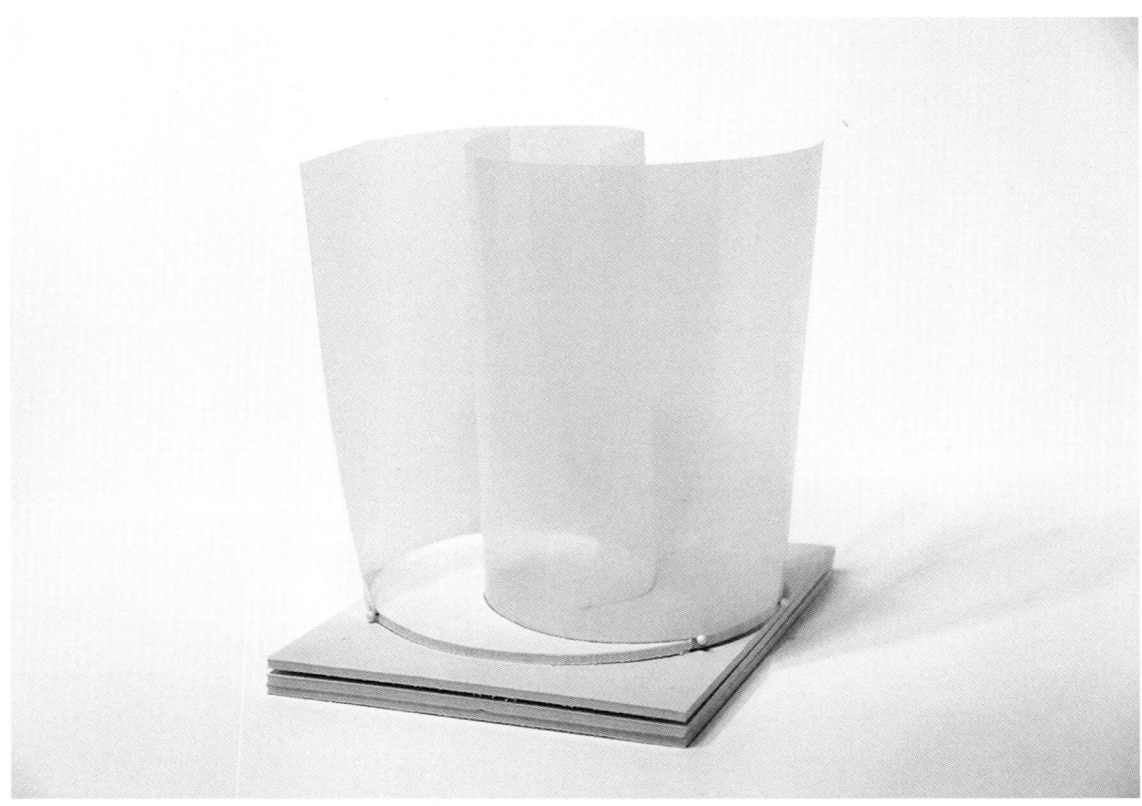

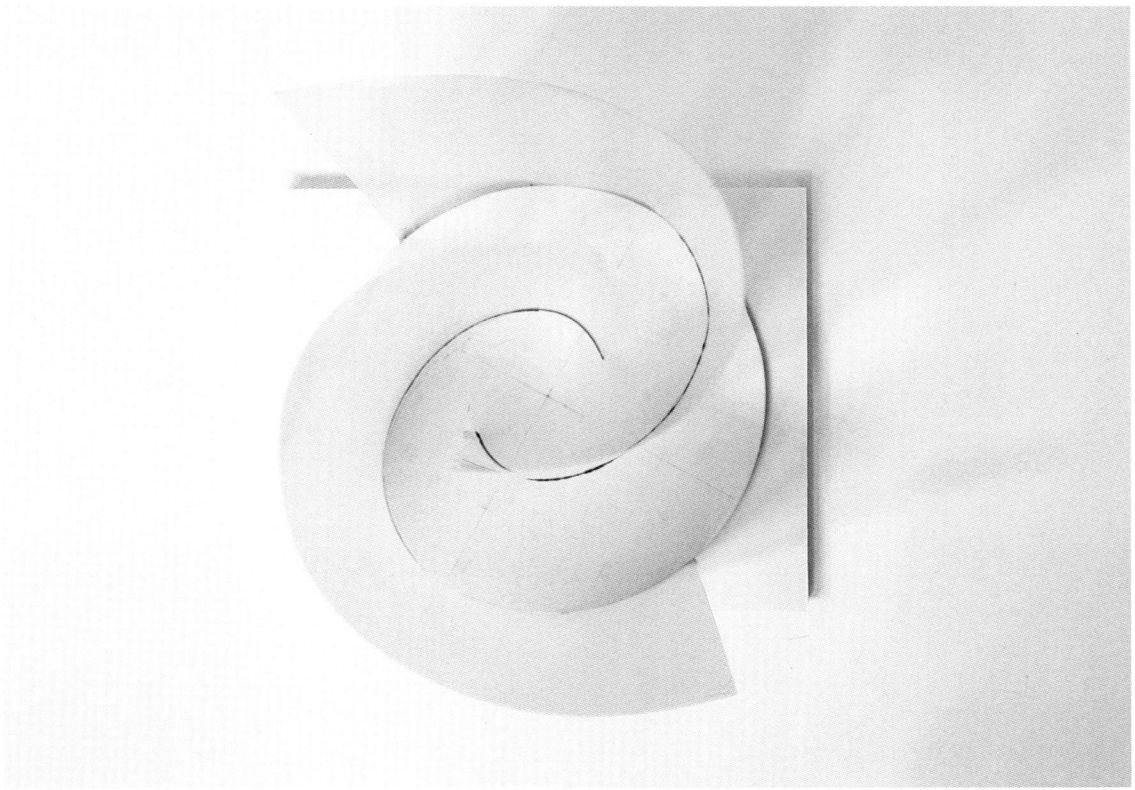

98. Lowe's conceptual model for the collaborative artwork *Approaching Silence*

Approaching Silence: A Collaboration

Andrea Reynosa

I HAD THE GREAT HONOR of studying and eventually collaborating with Truman Lowe for thirty-three years. From 1986 to 1989, I was his teaching assistant in the sculpture department at the University of Wisconsin–Madison while pursuing my bachelor of fine arts in sculpture. In 1991, he recommended me for a foundry tech position so I could obtain my master of fine arts in sculpture. He subsequently served as an advisor while I formulated Smack Mellon, a nonprofit art space in Brooklyn. Finally, we collaborated closely on Truman's visionary artwork *Approaching Silence* from 2009 to 2019. This relationship kindled not only a unique artistic path but a deeply spiritual one. Truman taught me that the power of art and the role of the artist are a sacred obligation, not a privilege. And for that wisdom, I am eternally grateful.

In 2009, there was a call for entries at the newly renovated Archway of the Manhattan Bridge on the Brooklyn side. I approached Truman to see if he had any ideas for an art piece at the Archway while he was in town giving a lecture at the Museum of Art and Design about the exhibition *Fritz Scholder: Indian/Not Indian*, which he had co-curated with Paul Chaat Smith for the National Museum of the American Indian. Truman proposed to create a "pillar of silence" and developed the concept into *Approaching Silence*—a collaborative project singularly focused around perceptual sound through sculptural interaction.

The piece offers an unparalleled lens through which to recognize and understand noise pollution, an overlooked but pervasive source of environmental stress. It gathered together an assemblage of remarkable talent in art,

acoustics, engineering, and technology. I served as the artist and facilitator. Joe Levine and Troels Heiredal of Bone/Levine Architects provided the architectural expertise. Raj Patel of ARUP Engineering offered innovative engineering solutions. The project also featured the precise fabrication of SITU Fabrication's Wes Rozen and the insightful perspective of art historian Lucy Lippard. *Approaching Silence* invites participatory public engagement: an opportunity to experience a moment of silence in an immersive structure, illuminating the imperceptible and empowering a movement for change.

This conical structure allows participants to perceive invisible noise waves and the associated biological, social, and environmental effects by transitioning in and out of

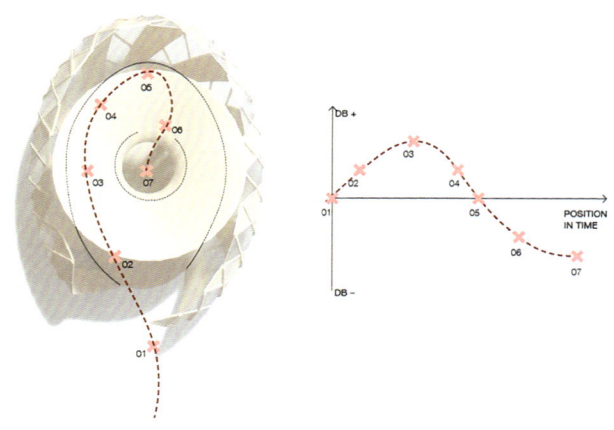

99. *Approaching Silence,* plan and sound level diagram.

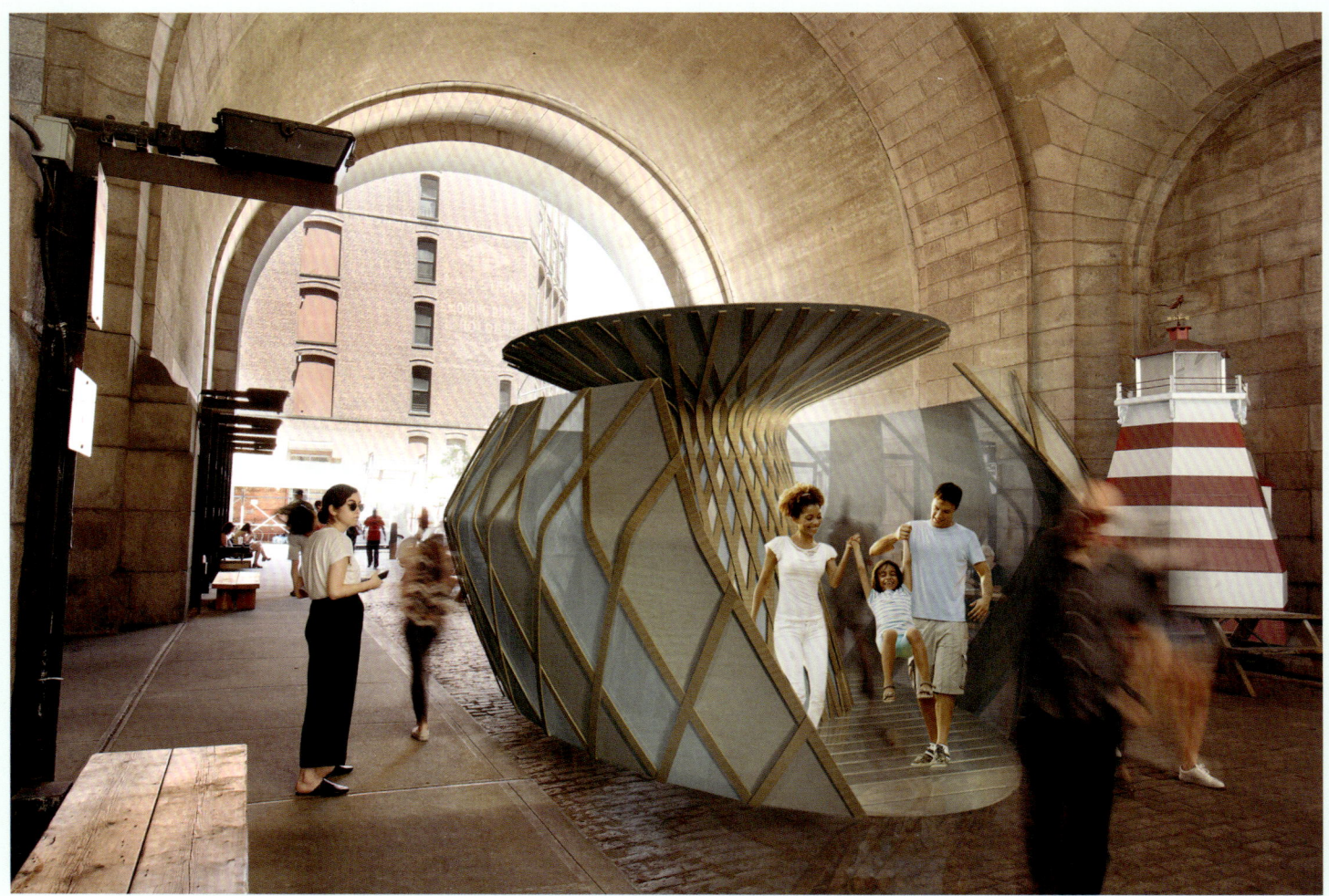

100. Rendering showing the entrance to *Approaching Silence*

the piece and experiencing the noise adjustment of -10 decibels. Participants' awareness of sound is heightened, leaving them with a greater appreciation of how noise impacts individuals. The structural concept of *Approaching Silence* is a contemporary reflection of traditional willow saplings twisted and bent into sections of a wood frame. The slight rotation of the straight pieces creates the illusion of a curved surface. The interlocking structural pieces create a rigid framework upon which panels of various acoustic properties are hung to enhance the soundscape. One experiences the structure from both sides with its opaque and transparent panels.

In her description of the artwork, Lippard writes, "Truman Lowe developed a sure and subtle sculptural identity, grounded by trees and streams. Storyteller, eco-artist, and quiet activist, he opened up a new, firmly Ho-Chunk view of the natural world. His work with wood was never wooden, admitting light and air and a fresh perception of forms we take for granted."[82]

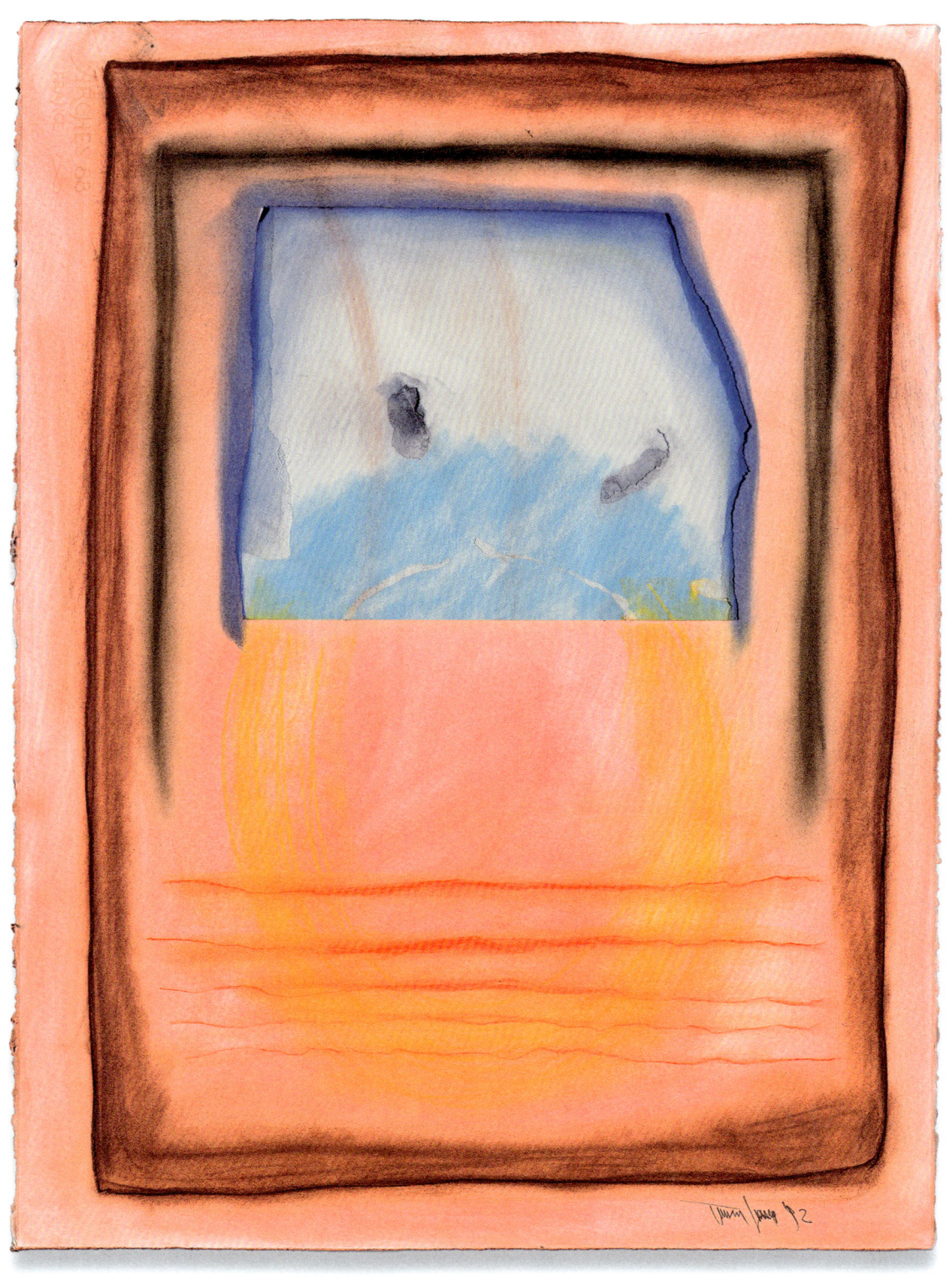

101. Untitled, 1992. Pastel and collage on paper, 30 x 22 ½ in. National Museum of the American Indian 26/9770, gift of John and Meryl Lipton Lavine

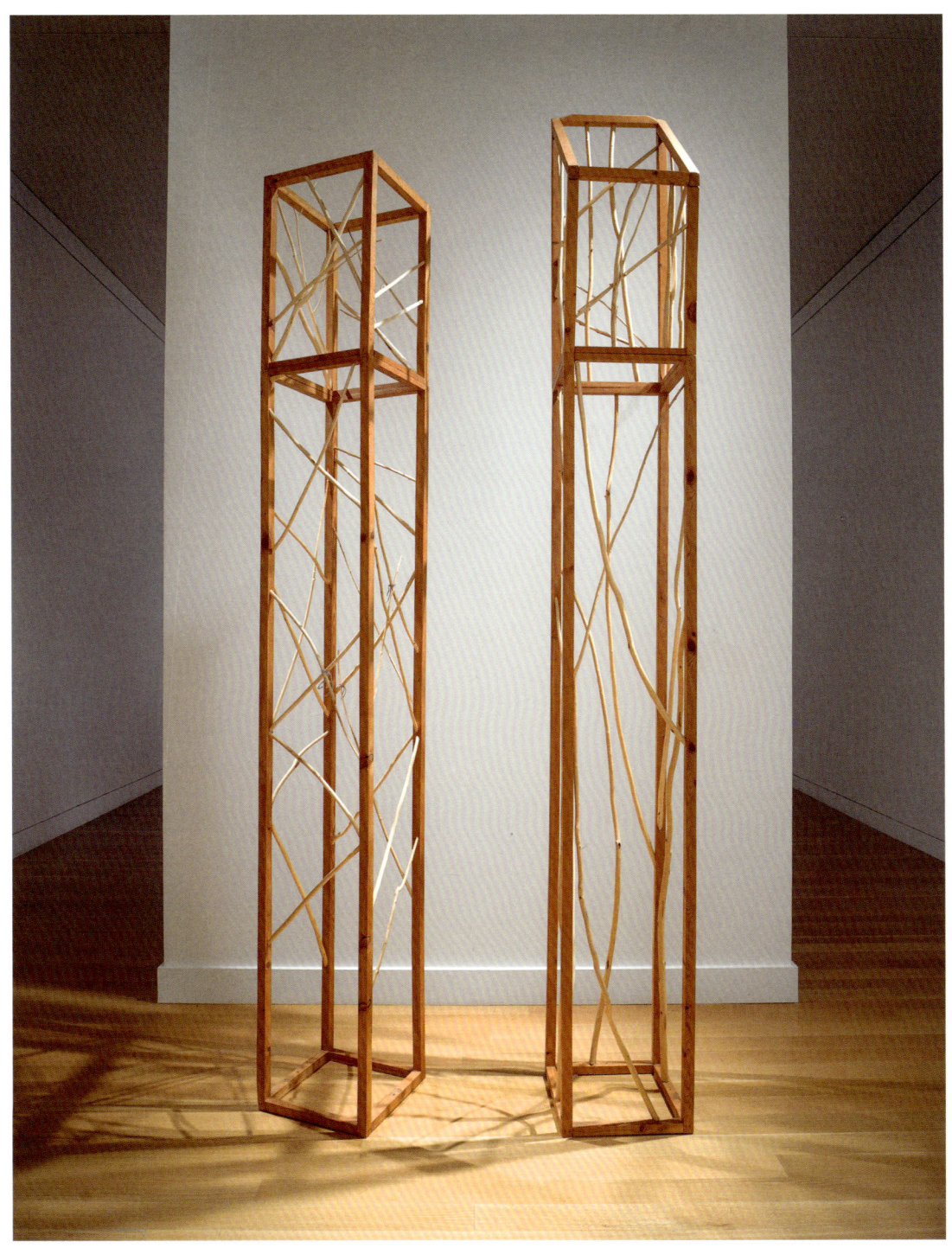

102. *Totem for Kunu (First Son)*, 1985. Pine, peeled willow saplings, 114 x 15 x 15 in.; *Totem for Henu (First Daughter)*, 1985. Pine, peeled willow saplings, 126 ½ x 15 x 15 in. Smithsonian American Art Museum, museum purchase made through the Luisita L. and Franz H. Denghausen Endowment, 2022.9.2–3

Truman Lowe at the Smithsonian American Art Museum: Notes from the Galleries

Karen Lemmey

IN SEPTEMBER 2023, the Smithsonian American Art Museum reopened its renovated galleries for modern and contemporary art and reinstalled several iconic sculptures from its permanent collection, the largest public collection of sculpture of its kind. These galleries also featured two new acquisitions, Truman Lowe's *Totem for Henu (First Daughter)*, and *Totem for Kunu (First Son)*, which the museum acquired in 2022, along with *Ne Pu Saka (Sand on Water)* and *Waterfall* (figs. 109, 111, 103, and 104).

Every addition to the collection introduces new ways of seeing the other artworks on view, and this was apparent while installing Lowe's two *Totems* alongside Louise Nevelson's *Sky Cathedral* (1982). All three sculptures are made of wood, a material both artists favored (fig. 106), but Lowe's choice of materials—peeled willow branches and untreated milled pine—hews closer to their natural origins. Seeing *Totems* next to *Sky Cathedral* encourages us to look closely at the material choices of both artists, and underscores how far removed Nevelson's medium is from an actual tree. Like many of Nevelson's sculptures, *Sky Cathedral* is made from salvaged pieces of wooden furniture that she assembled and painted a uniform black. Significantly, Nevelson might have used another material to create her monumental frieze; by contrast, the peeled willow Lowe used for *Totems* is core to their meaning in several ways.

The slender, flexible willow directly evidences a tree's new growth, making this material an apt metaphor for the rising generation after which *Totems* are titled. But the material also gestures to past generations of Lowe's family. Willows grow predominantly in wetlands and therefore recall the riverbanks of Lowe's own childhood, the place and time in which he first learned to work with wood by observing his parents creating splint-plait baskets and other handmade articles. Lowe conceived of the two *Totems* as distinctly separate sculptures, but when shown together they form an abstract intergenerational family portrait that specifically refers to Lowe's children while also acknowledging his parents (grandparents of Hiinų [Henu] and Kųnų [Kunu]) and the knowledge they shared with him as makers. The interwoven willow branches of *Totems* convey the notion of family not by rendering the likenesses of its specific members, but rather by pointing to the waterways and woodlands that Lowe held dear and that have been intimately connected to lifeways passed across generations of his kin.

Each of Lowe's four sculptures in the museum's collection is a beautifully made physical construction, but they are fundamentally conceptual artworks. That is to say, they aim to convey ideas rather than faithfully depict things. They do not replicate nature but instead invoke it as a means of inviting viewers to consider relationality, how entities come together and how we situate ourselves within the natural world of which we are a part. They communicate what we might learn, for example, by thinking about how sand and water form mounds when they encounter one another in the shallows of a river (*Ne Pu Saka*) or the dynamism and awe conveyed by falling water (*Waterfall*).

As sculptures about ideas, Lowe's works share a common ground with those of Martin Puryear, who for decades has also used wood and attentively studied Indigenous materials and methods of construction across

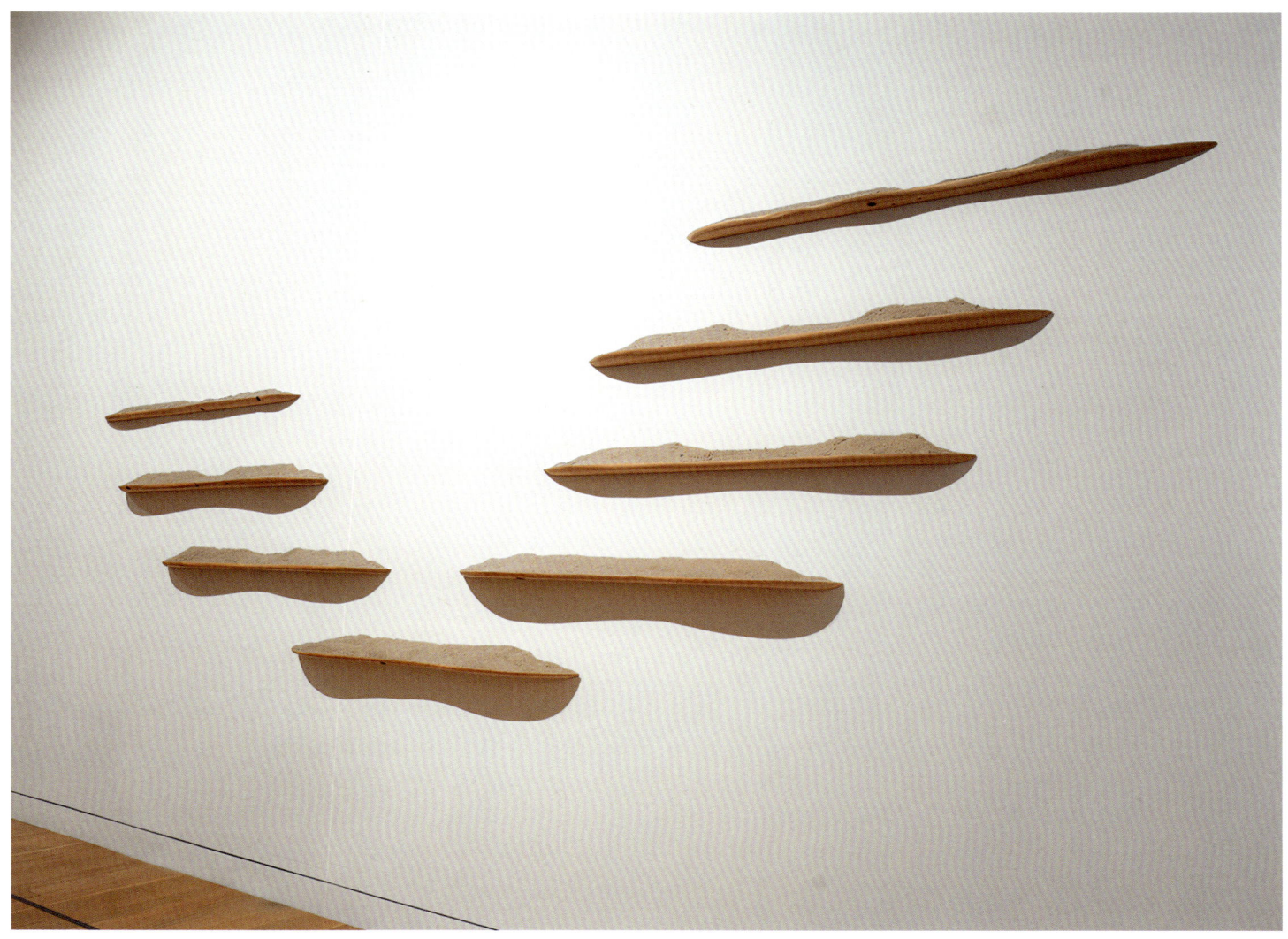

103. *Ne Pu Saka (Sand on Water)*, 1996. Pine, sand, 96 x 144 x 8 in. Smithsonian American Art Museum, museum purchase made through the Luisita L. and Franz H. Denghausen Endowment, 2022.9.1A-H

the globe (fig. 105).[83] Puryear's *Vessel* (1997–2002) stands within sight of Lowe's *Totems* in the museum's reinstalled galleries. It, too, is made of unfinished wood that has been structured into an openwork frame around an interior volume of space, which visitors can look through but never enter. Together these transparent structures challenge viewers to think of sculpture not just as a three-dimensional mass that occupies our space, but also as an art form that guides us to pay attention to the space between things, such as the spaces Lowe often observed between trees in a forest.

In time, all four of Lowe's works at the Smithsonian American Art Museum will rotate into the galleries, introducing additional narratives, sight lines, resonances, and provocations that we cannot yet anticipate.

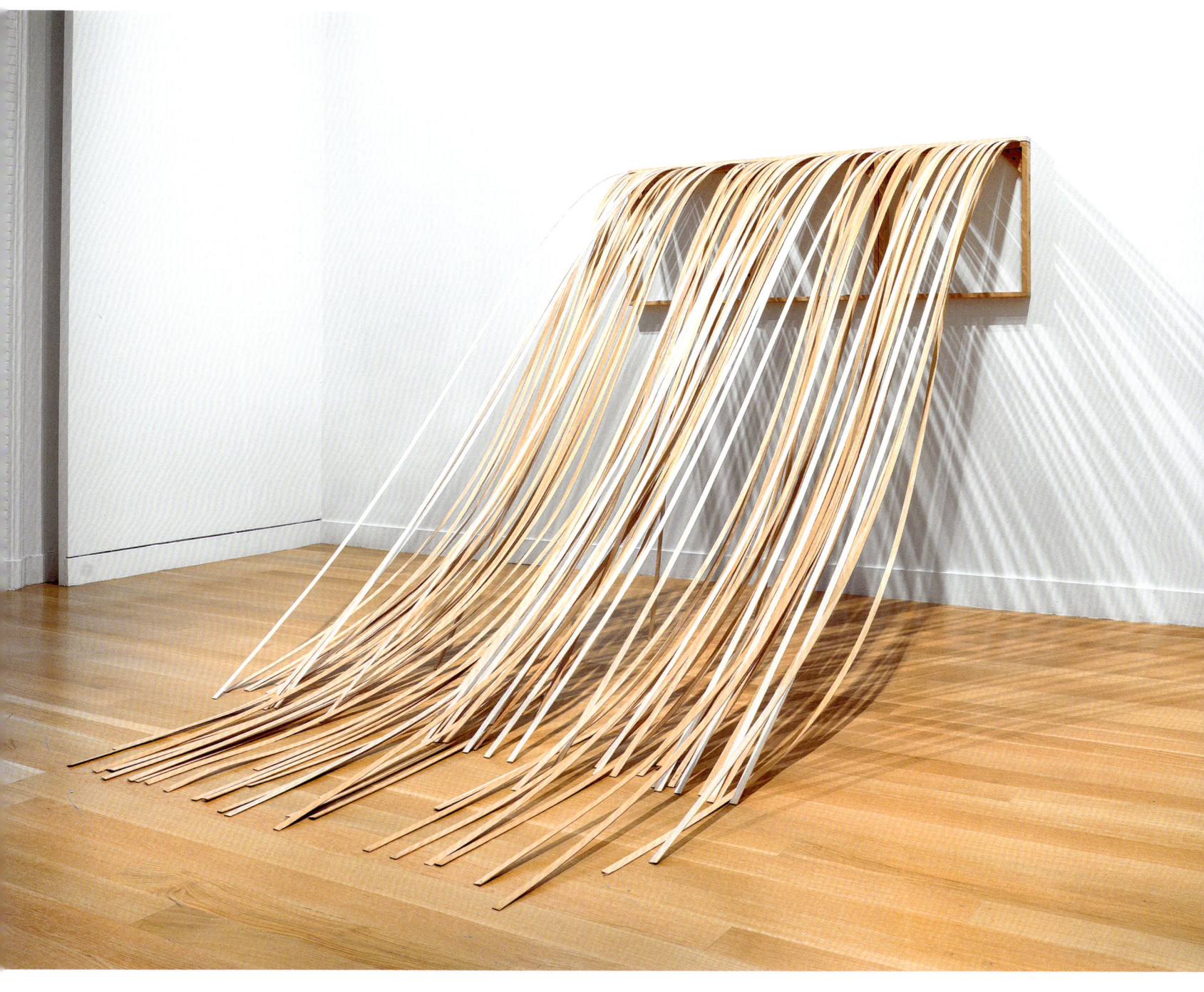

104. *Waterfall*, 1993. Pine, metal fasteners, 74 x 72 x 67 in. Smithsonian American Art Museum, museum purchase made through the Luisita L. and Franz H. Denghausen Endowment, 2022.9.4

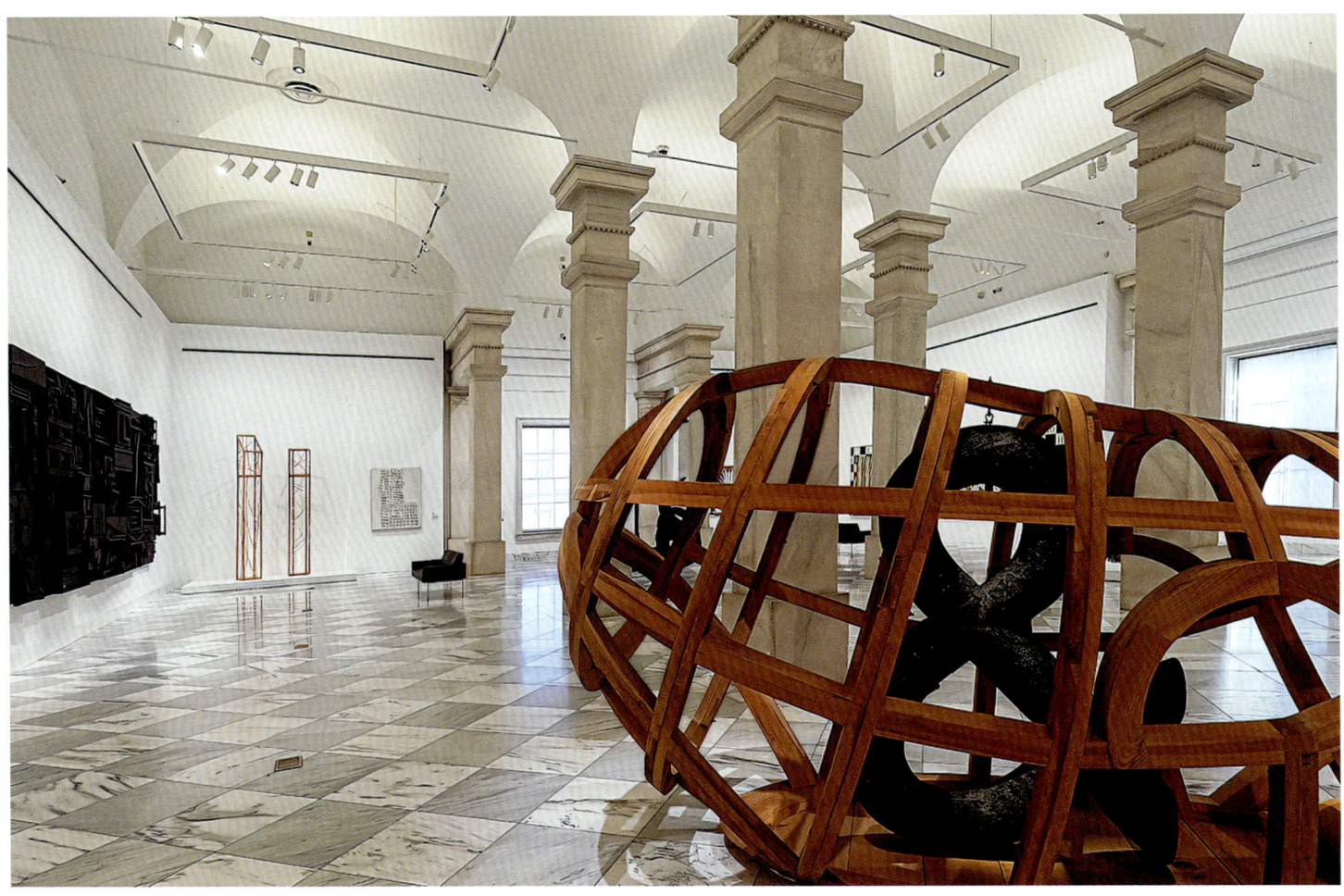

105. Martin Puryear's *Vessel* (foreground) with, from left, Louise Nevelson's *Sky Cathedral*, Truman Lowe's *Totem for Henu (First Daughter)* and *Totem for Kunu (First Son)*, and Chryssa's *White Relief* in the Smithsonian American Art Museum's modern and contemporary art galleries, 2024

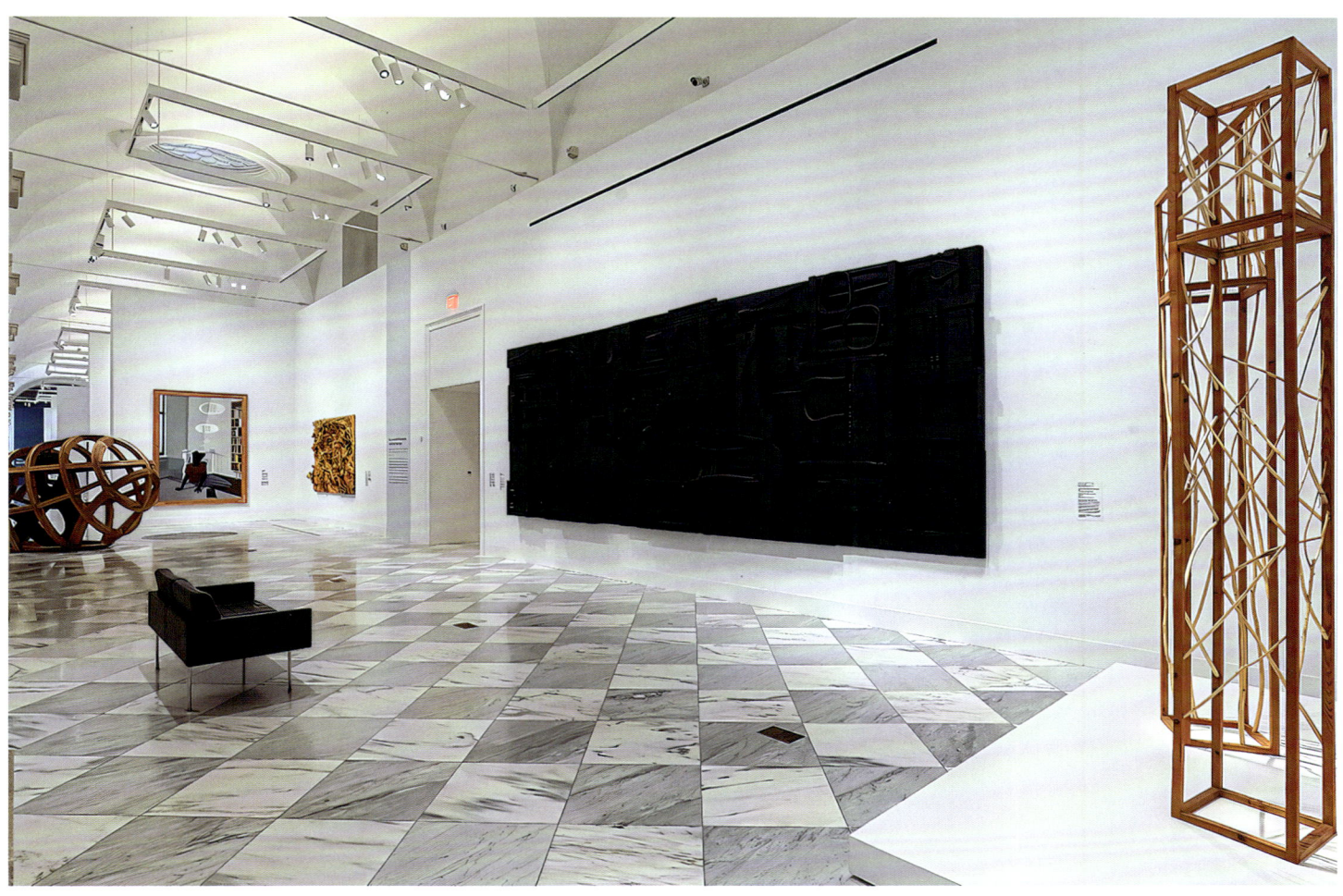

106. From left, Martin Puryear's *Vessel*, Kerry James Marshall's *SOB, SOB*, Thornton Dial Sr.'s *The Beginning of Life in the Yellow Jungle*, Louise Nevelson's *Sky Cathedral*, and Truman Lowe's *Totem for Henu (First Daughter)* and *Totem for Kunu (First Son)* in the Smithsonian American Art Museum's modern and contemporary art galleries, 2024

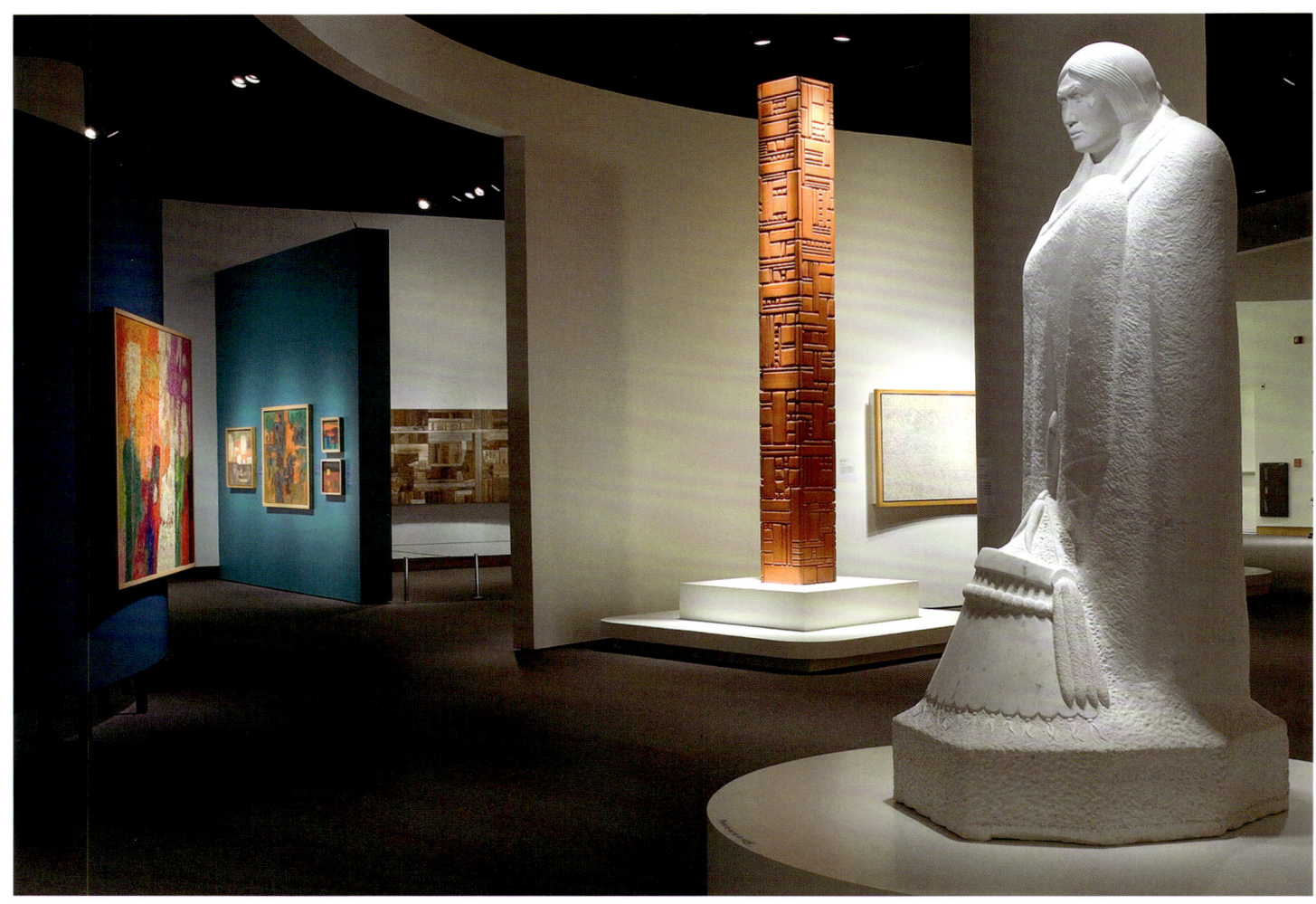

107. Works by George Morrison and Allan Houser in *Native Modernism: The Art of George Morrison and Allan Houser* at the National Museum of the American Indian, 2004

Last of the Mohicans

Paul Chaat Smith

IN AUGUST 2001 I was a brand-new federal employee of the aching to be, yet so far from finished, National Museum of the American Indian in Washington, DC. I always wondered if they hired me because I was giving talks and drafting essays dissing the entire enterprise. That's how Washington works sometimes. Trash the establishment, they offer you a job.

I called the new museum "a bad idea whose time has come." My gang would amuse ourselves about the name: the curious decision to make "Indian" singular rather than plural. Speculating on which Indian, of all the Indians on Turtle Island, they would choose. Yes, there were self-nominations. This was back when I lived in New York. Everything about the Indian is ridiculously complicated, so naturally there already was a National Museum of the American Indian, opened in lower Manhattan back in 1994. It was fine, but nobody cared. The New York museum was Apollo 10, testing out equipment and maneuvers. All that mattered was landing on the moon.

Was I nervous? Sure. I was no astronaut, and in fact had not received any astronaut training whatsoever. On the other hand, I also knew very little about creating expensive exhibitions on the National Mall, so there's that.

In those innocent days, people called the National Mall "America's Main Street." All that is gone now. It was phony, even then, but it was something at least. One talking point was how a new Smithsonian museum is a once-in-a-generation event. Another is how the museum of the Indians would rise on the last open site on the National Mall. (That used to be the case. Since 2004, 46 additional Smithsonians have opened and 237 more are planned.[84])

Nervous yet excited, I was a fake curator assigned to the grammatically confusing *Our Peoples* exhibition. (We must not have hired copy editors yet. Indian is singular, and People is plural? Seriously?) It was about the history of half the world from the beginning of time to the present. The museum was an excavation site, mostly dirt and big ideas. All the action was in office buildings downtown and at the Cultural Resources Center across the Anacostia River in Maryland—the home of curators, both fake and real, and the massive collection.

Four big galleries. All racing to meet the immovable deadline of the first day of autumn, 2004. Competitive? Hell yes. The exhibition called *Our Universes* was in the pole position; they had their act together before anyone else and hoovered up all the money. Jealous, we called it the Taj Mahal since every element was custom designed and hardwired into the goofy building architecture. *Our Universes* had tons of messages. One of them was, Hey, good luck ever changing this.

Truman Lowe was a semi-famous artist on loan from Wisconsin's flagship university. His exhibition was called *Native Modernism: The Art of George Morrison and Allan Houser*. People loved Truman. He was the coolest professor in the faculty lounge, always chill. Treated people right. Short hair. Eyeglasses. Not the BIA cat eye ones, or super expensive, just a handsome style you'd get from Lens Crafters. Wore blazers. People who are actually cool never have to dress for the part. He drove a late model Audi. Gorgeous next-level instrumentation, damn those Germans . . . always wished I had a car like that. Kind, funny, never mean. You can see why I didn't like him. Not

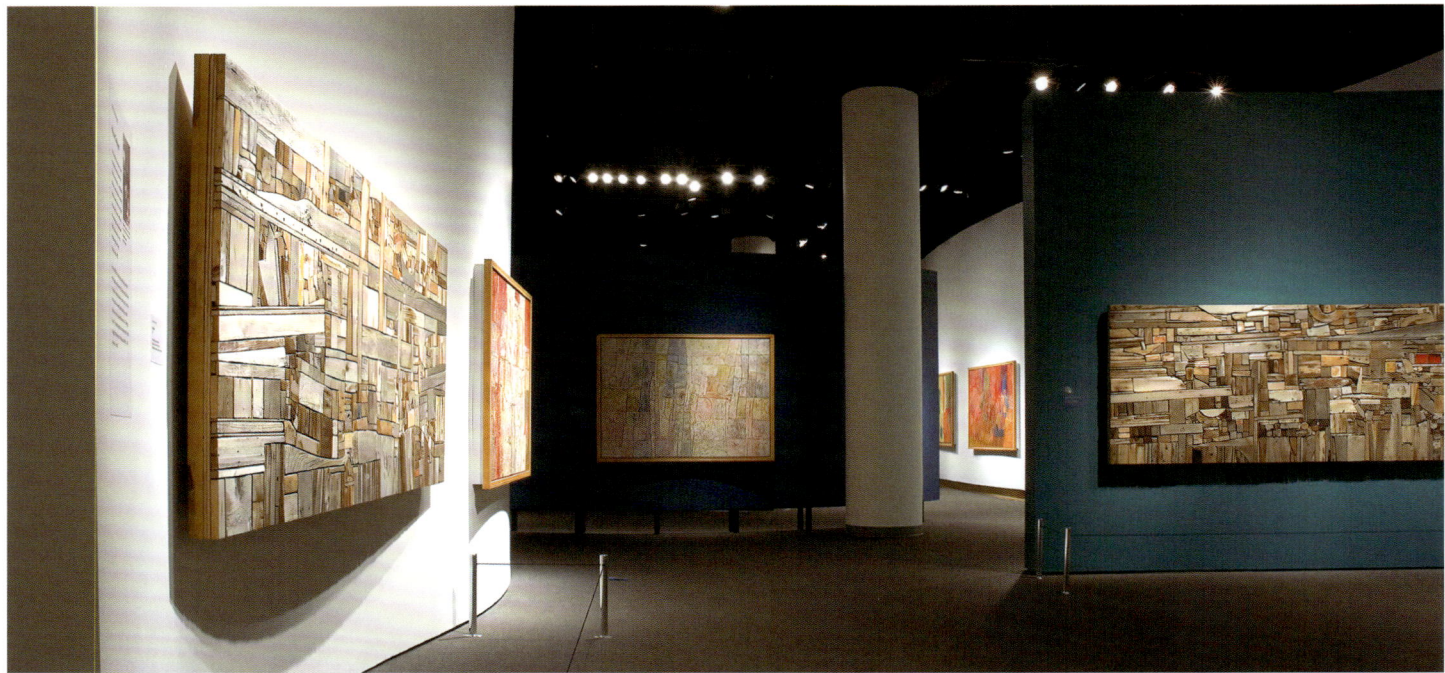

108. George Morrison's paintings and wood collages in *Native Modernism,* 2004

at first, anyway. But people like that tend to wear you down if you give them half a chance.

Our Universes, Our Lives, and *Our People*, or *Peoples,* whatever; they were Very Important. Morrison and Houser, okay if you like that kind of thing, but not Very Important.

Lowe knew things. He serenely tracked all that was going on in the mad rush to open the museum, high above the fray. This was because nobody cared what he was doing. He explained to me that he wanted to give visitors a space that wasn't so noisy and crammed with objects and images and floor-to-ceiling text. I'm not a human voice recorder, so I don't remember his exact words, but they were free of snark, because Truman was Never Mean®. At the same time, he understood that *Our Peoples, Our Universes, Our Lives* (the "Big Three"), were going to be received by many as inescapably ponderous, for the simple reason they couldn't help but be precisely that. *Native Modernism* flew below the radar, free of the impossible expectations that weighed down the others. *Native Modernism* was not ponderous. You could exhale.

Consider the museum of the Indian(s) as an art project, organized around a powerful idea. That idea is not the messages we assault the public with, messages that tend to be vague and boring. At the center of this art project is this: the Indian world is immense. It is full of beautiful and amazing contradictions. The museum's job is to resolve the contradictions, which in museum language is about interpretive plans and messaging and thematics. Museums like things to be clear, to make sense. Problem is the Indian world doesn't actually make sense, any more than the ocean makes sense. Resolving the contradictions is impossible. On some level, the museum knows this. But it has no alternative. It tries to do this impossible thing.

For America's Indians, the central contradictions say that we are fully modern and ancient. We have always been here. We are the land, the land is us. Except few of us live where our ancestors did three hundred years ago. We suffered inconceivable loss. We're still here. Most of us were wiped out. Our cultures are vibrant and intact. Our cultures were decimated by governments out to kill us. We love America. We're not really Americans. We live in the twenty-first century, in cities and suburbs and towns and reservations. We are everywhere. We're just like you. We're nothing like you.

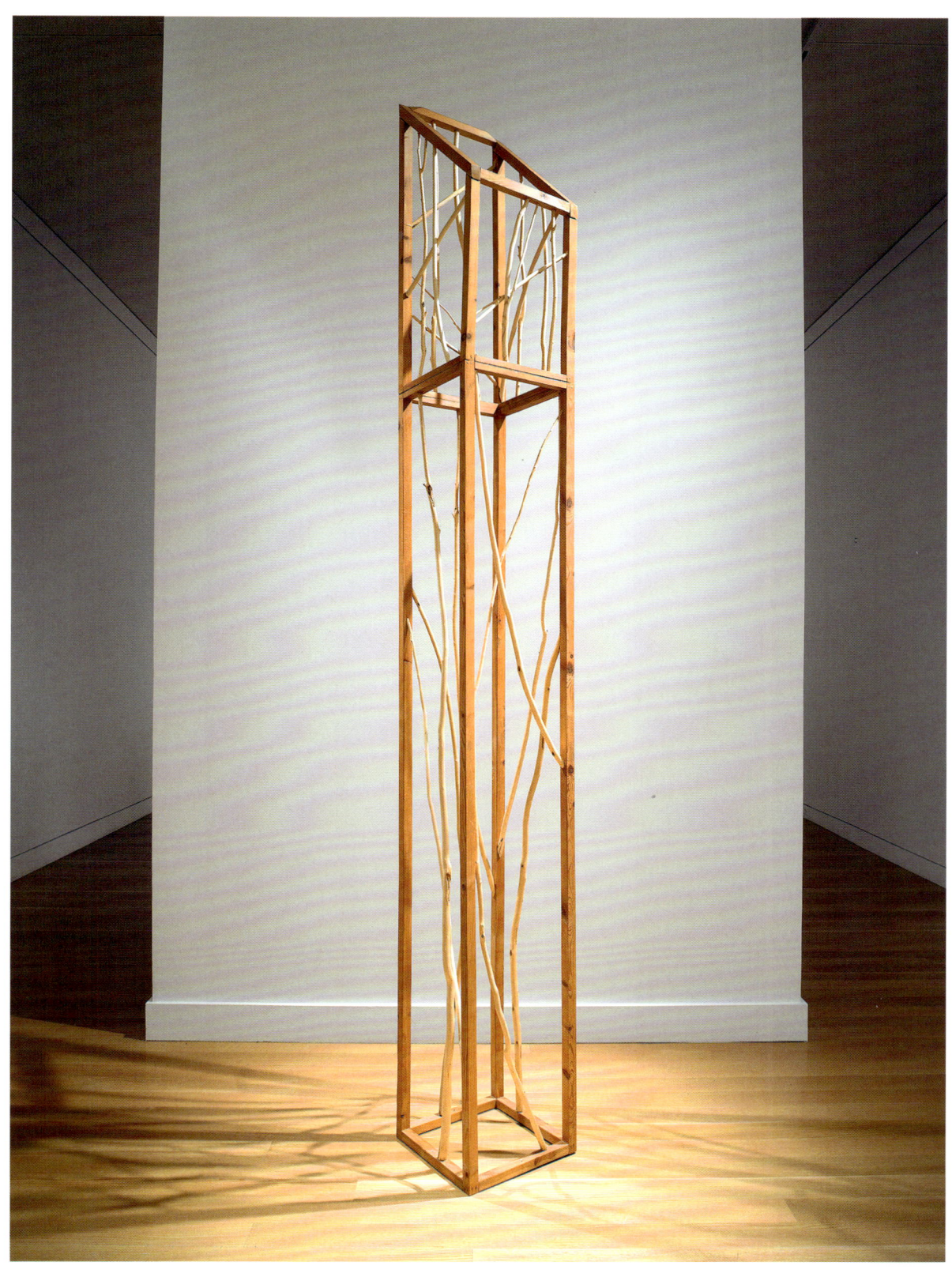

109. *Totem for Henu (First Daughter)*, 1985. Pine, peeled willow saplings, 126 ½ x 15 x 15 in. Smithsonian American Art Museum, museum purchase made through the Luisita L. and Franz H. Denghausen Endowment, 2022.9.3

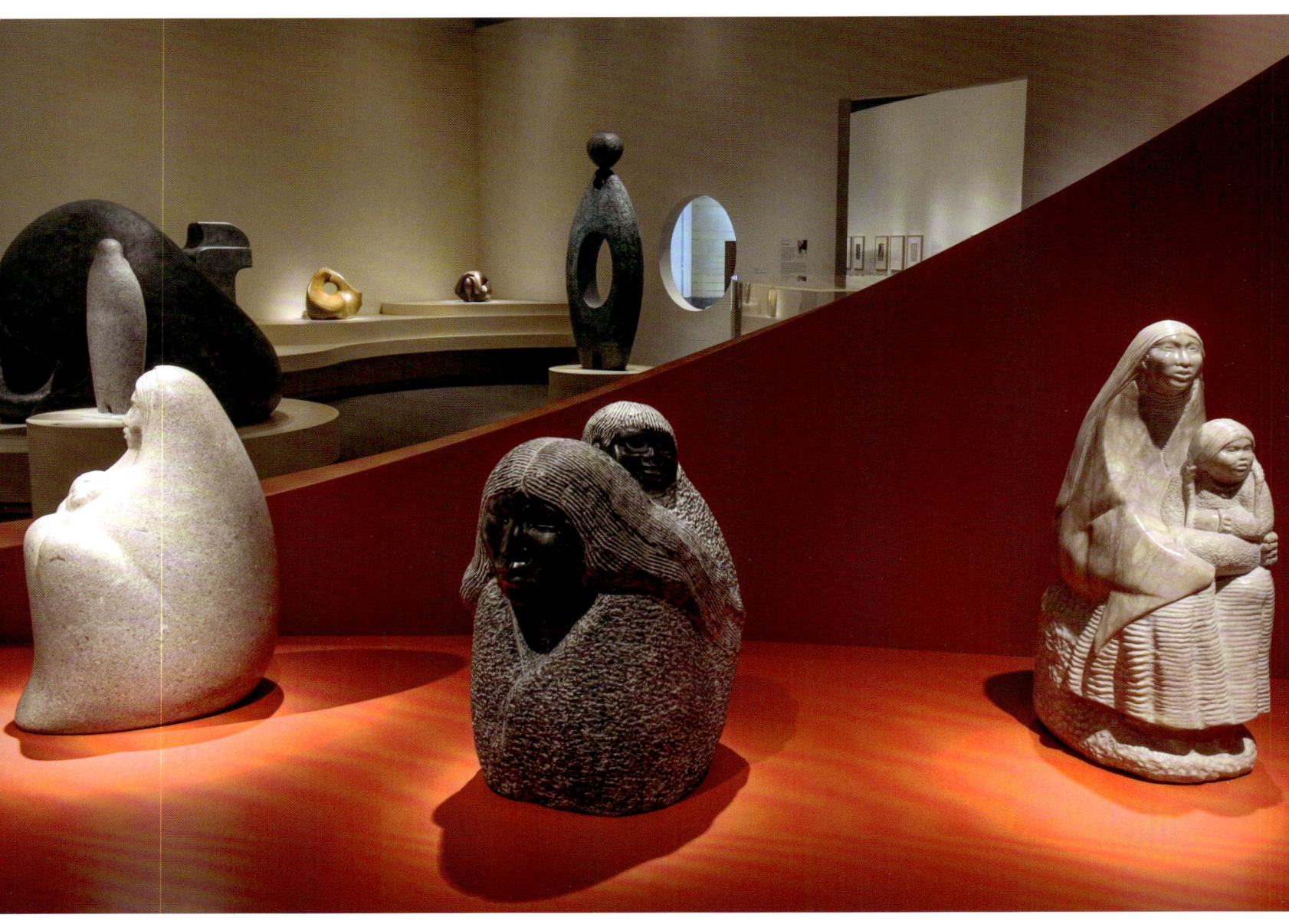

110. Allan Houser's sculptures in *Native Modernism*, 2004

The messages and narratives all engage and circle the central dialectic of immensity, difference, complexity.

If you look for consistency and a unified field theory of the Indian at the museum of the Indians, you will be disappointed. If you read the museum as a text, I have good news: You will be rewarded with profound insights. Tragedy, comedy. World-class performances, both actual performances and performative performances, often revealing far more than they intend. The contradictions are the real message.

And the point? That out of these engagements with impossible contradictions, sometimes, answers emerge. Insights. New stories to replace the old stories.

Let's go.

Our text is the catalog for the Truman Show, *Native Modernism: The Art of George Morrison and Allan Houser*. It opens with an introduction by the museum's founding director, W. Richard West Jr., titled *The Art of Contradiction*. You read of cubism and James Joyce, William Blake ("Without Contraries there is no progression"), and dadaism. There is nothing like this anywhere in the thirty thousand square feet of exhibitions in the museum itself. Interesting. West throws down a marker. He says this too is Indian experience. If you thought Director West's name-dropping of superstars of Western culture was an outlier, you were right. Discordant, yes. Intentionally so.

Lowe's essay is called *The Emergence of Native Modernism*. Like his boss, Lowe knew the museum would have to lead with strategically essentialist notions of cultural authenticity. Both West and Lowe trusted that some visitors would find ways to read the museum, and their texts are a guide to doing just that.

The radicalism of Lowe's exhibition is his unwavering commitment to naming the thing, to say, Yes, you may think it's a White-Eyes term, but I'm here to show that Native Modernism is the correct way to think about these artists. He tells us, This is where it starts. Pay attention.

Now comes Gerald Vizenor writing about George Morrison. These guys all know each other and are roughly the same age. The story of George Morrison is peppered with shrines of postwar American art: the Cedar Tavern, the Art Students League, Fulbright, Pollock, de Kooning,

John Hay Whitney. Oh, and Morrison's son's godfather was Franz Kline. Vizenor recounts a conversation with Morrison about whether the two of them might have crossed paths in Greenwich Village in 1955.

Lowe decides to enlist the most famous Native writer on the planet to write about Allan Houser. That would be Pulitzer Prize winner N. Scott Momaday. Houser's art features Indians who look like Indians, unlike Morrison's abstractions, but they prove to be two sides of the same Native Modernist coin. There's Houser in Mexico City in 1966, looking just like any other international art superstar. Differences for sure: Houser worked in a refinery in Los Angeles, went to Haskell, Indian Country's national high school. He also won a Guggenheim. And he joined the Institute of American Indian Arts in Santa Fe in 1962. The old guard meets the new guard. One narrative says nothing much happened before that government art school took flight. Lowe tells us, Not so fast.

Gail Tremblay contributes a stellar essay and gives us a welcome distance from the Great Men and Their Talented Lives. For sure, Lowe, Morrison, Houser, West, Vizenor, Momaday are a blast, there at the Cedar Tavern's corner table. And yet, after a while, the clubbiness can feel oppressive. We need some air, and Tremblay takes us outside for a smoke.

Here's the thing: when you are coming up and enthralled with the Now, you tend to regard yesterday's vanguard as, well, just that. They were fine, met their moment one supposes, though their moment is now gone. You tend to think they have little to offer.

And then you are no longer coming up, you are there, and not so enthralled with the Now, because the Now is past, and maybe not as amazing as you thought. And you revisit the played-out vanguard from the middle of the last century, and you are embarrassed by your earlier take. They had no vanguard to lead the way. They were the way.

The show *Native Modernism* and its catalog are a time capsule, full of things we forget. That, in the early 2000s, language was sprinkled with obsolete words and phrases that were still hanging around. Multiculturalism. Winnebago. Chippewa. Dominant culture.

And you notice the words that are absent. Decolonization. Settler Colonialism. Genocide. Appropriation. Postcolonial.

Also, regular colonial and other flavors. It would be remarkable to find a Native art catalog, conference, or curriculum in the 2020s where these terms were not in heavy rotation.

How is it that decolonization is indispensable now, and wasn't just a few decades ago? Do we think the Fab Five thought colonialism was not real or wasn't important? The correct answer is no. These were sophisticated cosmopolitans who read widely across many disciplines. They knew the score.

I find it hard to imagine our vanguard plotting to decolonize the universities, museums, and foundations they knew so well. When they talk about their careers, they sound pretty much like most artists who achieved success after the usual trials. They note the barriers posed by racism and move on. They lived in large worlds and knew that the vocations of art and prose are a gamble; nothing is promised. And if it wasn't ridiculous art competitions where you might be disqualified for not painting in a manner your Winnebago ancestors would approve (who, umm, didn't actually paint), it would be something else. Dust off their shoulders.

Everyone I know (and probably everyone you know) talks about how time has become twisted, shortened, a baffling smoke monster that has us genuinely unsure whether an event took place three years ago or twelve. That makes it harder to remember the conventional wisdom you held close, and how much is no longer part of your conventions. But we should try anyway. Because what tends to happen is the things we were sure of become things we doubt. And usually that happens in darkness, no witnesses.

Others in this volume will write about the art of Truman Lowe. I have focused on his curatorial work because I have come to believe that however much he has been underestimated as an artist, it's even more true of his accomplishments as a curator.

Native Modernism was a bold stand against rising essentialism, brilliantly executed as an exhibition, with a brilliantly organized catalog. I can imagine Lowe wondering if it was all a bit much, loading all these giants of Indian art and prose into one canoe. If so, I am certain he knew it was required in order to build a project that would prove its relevance two decades later. With this show,

spotlighting two legendary artists, chronicled by Momaday and Vizenor—two reigning philosopher kings of a fading era—Lowe built a stealth canoe designed to push Native art down waters that understood, welcomed, even thrived on complexity. And away from the growing chorus that was even then doubling down on essentialism.

Lowe and Momaday and Morrison and West and Houser and Vizenor were a bridge. I always admired the way they held their tongues as other Indian artists in the 1980s and 1990s lectured everyone on the ways of their people and the importance of community. These guys must have found it all hilarious. Well, except for Vizenor, he let them have it. But by then, Vizenor, the seasoned, often furious intellectual who would write about born again, super traditional, super Indians as fascists (yes, he used the word) had been replaced by "Vizenor," the beloved elder statesman who could be appropriated by everyone for any reason. His most famous creation, the tricky concept of survivance that makes Derrida seem simple, became an outfit that could be worn for any occasion.

But dammit, they tried. Not many exhibitions have things to teach us twenty years later. This one does.

My favorite new hangout in Washington is the reimagined *American Art Since 1945* (now called *American Voices and Visions)* at the Smithsonian American Art Museum. Truman Lowe's there, with a whole bunch of other red people. Right next to those white dudes from the Cedar Tavern. In the same space, the same air.

Finally. Finally. Finally.

Lowe's works are two totems, effortlessly spectacular. One is called *Totem for Kunu (First Son)*. The other is *Totem for Henu* (*First Daughter*) (fig. 102). Truman Lowe had thoughts about totems, and here they are: "We have no concrete evidence that Woodland Indians built totems." Musing, he says, "Perhaps they did, but none have endured or survived. I am sure we had them, though. If we did not, then I think we might need them. Totems tell us a lot."[85]

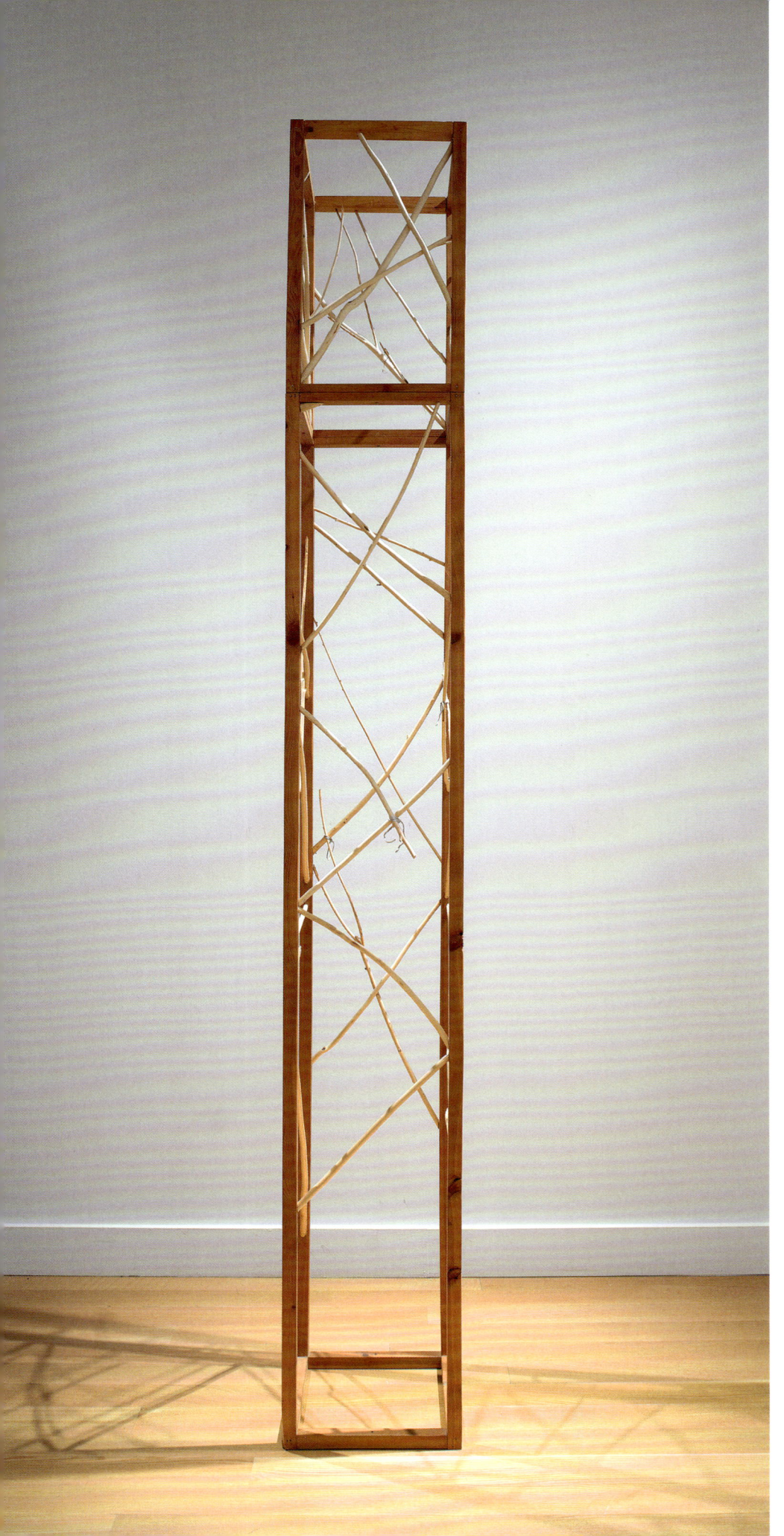

111. *Totem for Kunu (First Son)*, 1985. Pine, peeled willow saplings, 114 x 15 x 15 in. Smithsonian American Art Museum, museum purchase made through the Luisita L. and Franz H. Denghausen Endowment, 2022.9.2

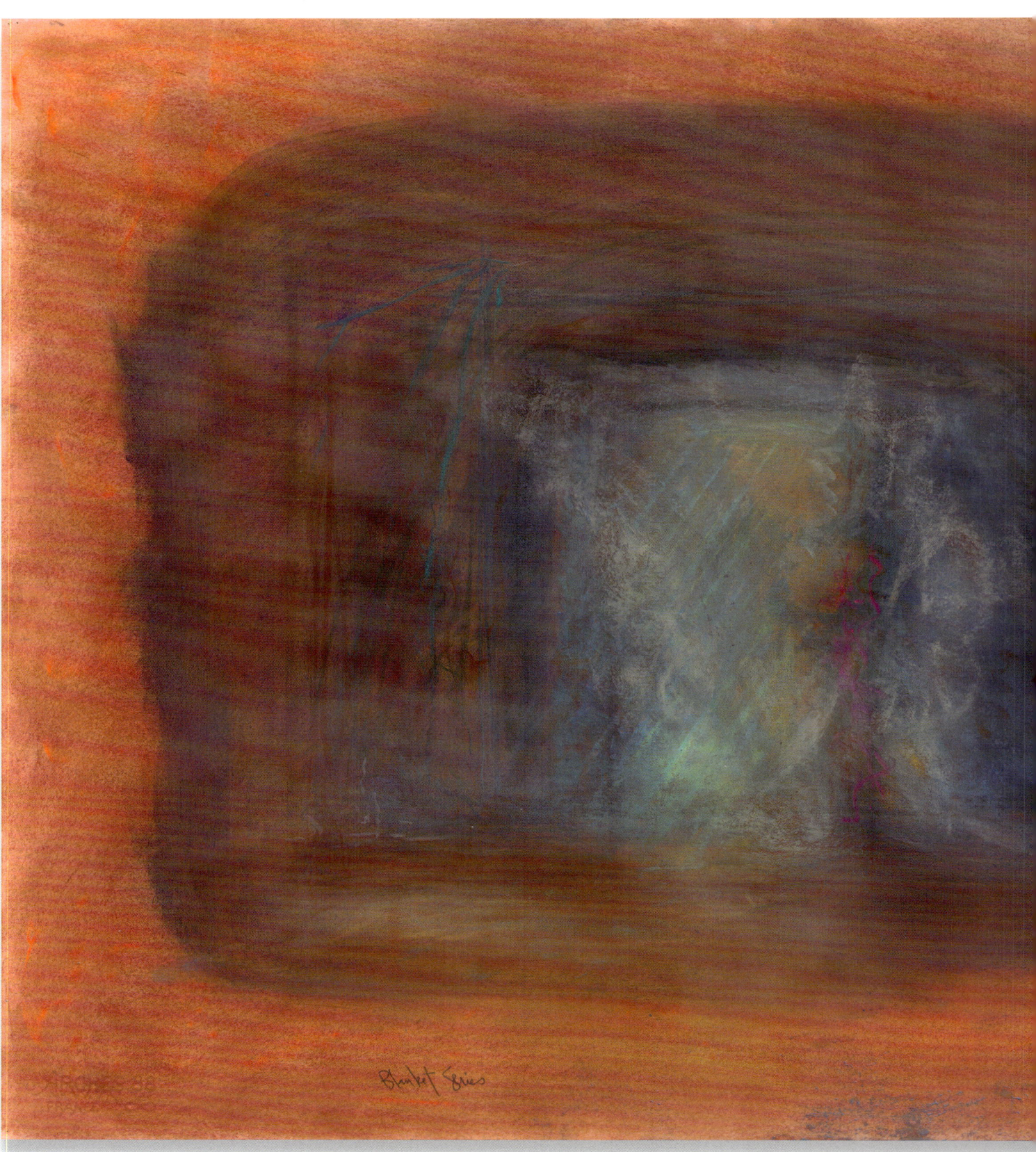

Blanket Series

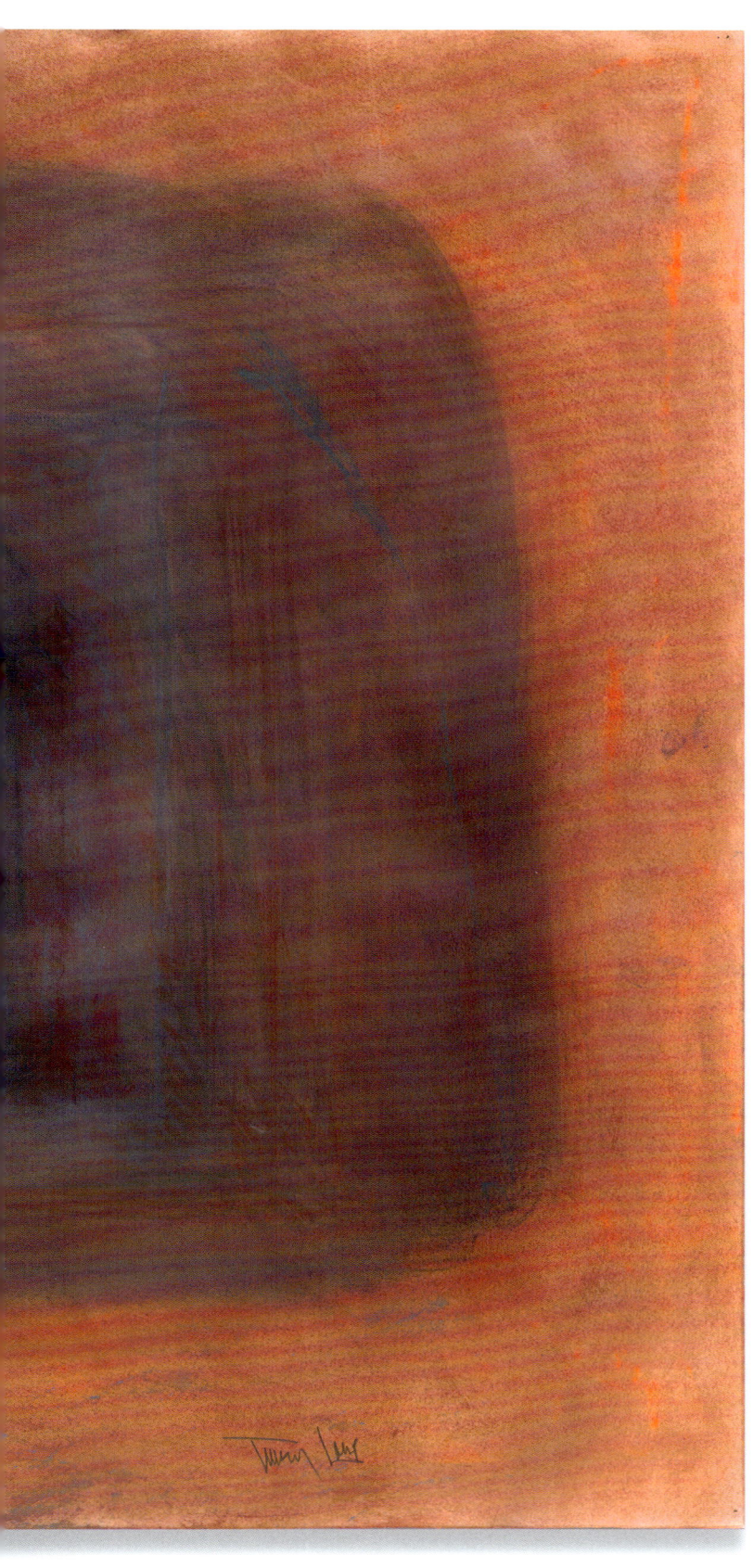

112. *Blanket Series (Red Purple)*, 1994. Brushed powdered pigment and pastel on paper, 30 x 42 in. National Museum of the American Indian 27/616

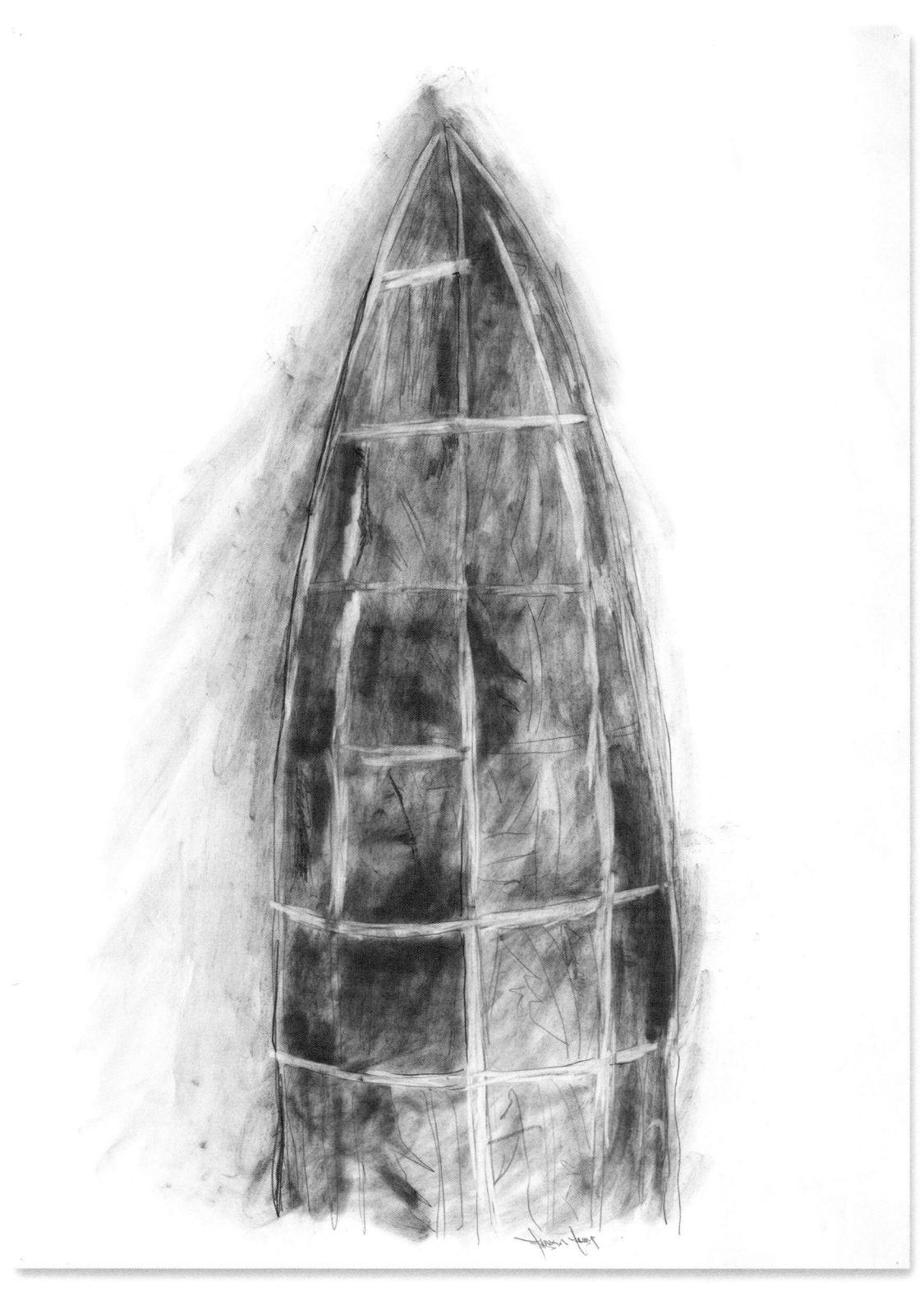

113. Untitled (Canoe Form), ca. 2010. Charcoal on paper, 42 x 30 in. National Museum of the American Indian 27/614

Tonia Lowe

ODDLY ENOUGH, MY FIRST MEMORY is of almost drowning. The details of the swimsuit I was wearing that day are seared into my mind. It was bright spring green on the bottom, with green and white vertical stripes on top, red straps, and three red buttons. I was taking a group swimming lesson at the local YMCA. The swim instructor told us to hold on to the wall and not let go under any circumstances until she came to help each of us individually. She explained that she would show us how to kick with our legs, float on our backs, and practice all the other fundamental elements of swimming. But showing a tendency toward oppositional defiant disorder from an early age, I launched off the wall as soon as the instructor's back was turned. It's hard to say exactly what was going through my three-year-old mind, but there is a kind of messy swirl of emotions that comes back to me every once in a while. The enormous struggle to breathe, the terror of not knowing whether I would make it back to the wall, the realization that my headstrong decision might turn out to be my last. Finally, there was blessed relief when the instructor scooped me up and put me back on the wall. For some, this experience might have led to a lifelong fear of water. However, as fortune would have it, I was the daughter of Truman Lowe—a reality that would send me on a completely different trajectory.

When I first watched the regional Emmy-winning video, "Exploring the Artistic Process of Truman Lowe: A Journey Through Native Art & Education," created by Discover Wisconsin in collaboration with the Ho-Chunk Nation, I was reminded—with the clarity of spring water bubbling up from the ground—that my dad is the reason I love being in and around water as much as I do. So many memories of him and so many of the things I learned from him are inherently intertwined with the life-giving flow of water. He was particularly drawn to moving water. Rivers, streams, and creeks were endless sources of fascination, as was the movement of water: ripples, currents, waves, and waterfalls. Of all the different types of bodies of water, rivers were his favorite. In many ways, my dad was like the rivers he loved so much. He was a steady, constant force. He was always moving, sometimes at a gentle pace on the surface but swiftly in the depths. One moment, he would be carving surprising new channels; the next pausing to swirl briefly in an eddy, but always advancing.

One of my dad's greatest skills was supporting people by believing in their ideas. He helped people take the seed of an idea and nurture it until it thrived, by listening empathetically and offering gentle guidance, often delivered with a poignant story and a much-needed dose of humor. He nurtured so many people's ideas over the years—family, friends, colleagues, students—he was like an idea-protecting force of nature. With my dad at your side in the currents of life, you would find yourself reassured that you were heading in the right direction, confident that you would arrive, even if your precise destination was not yet clear.

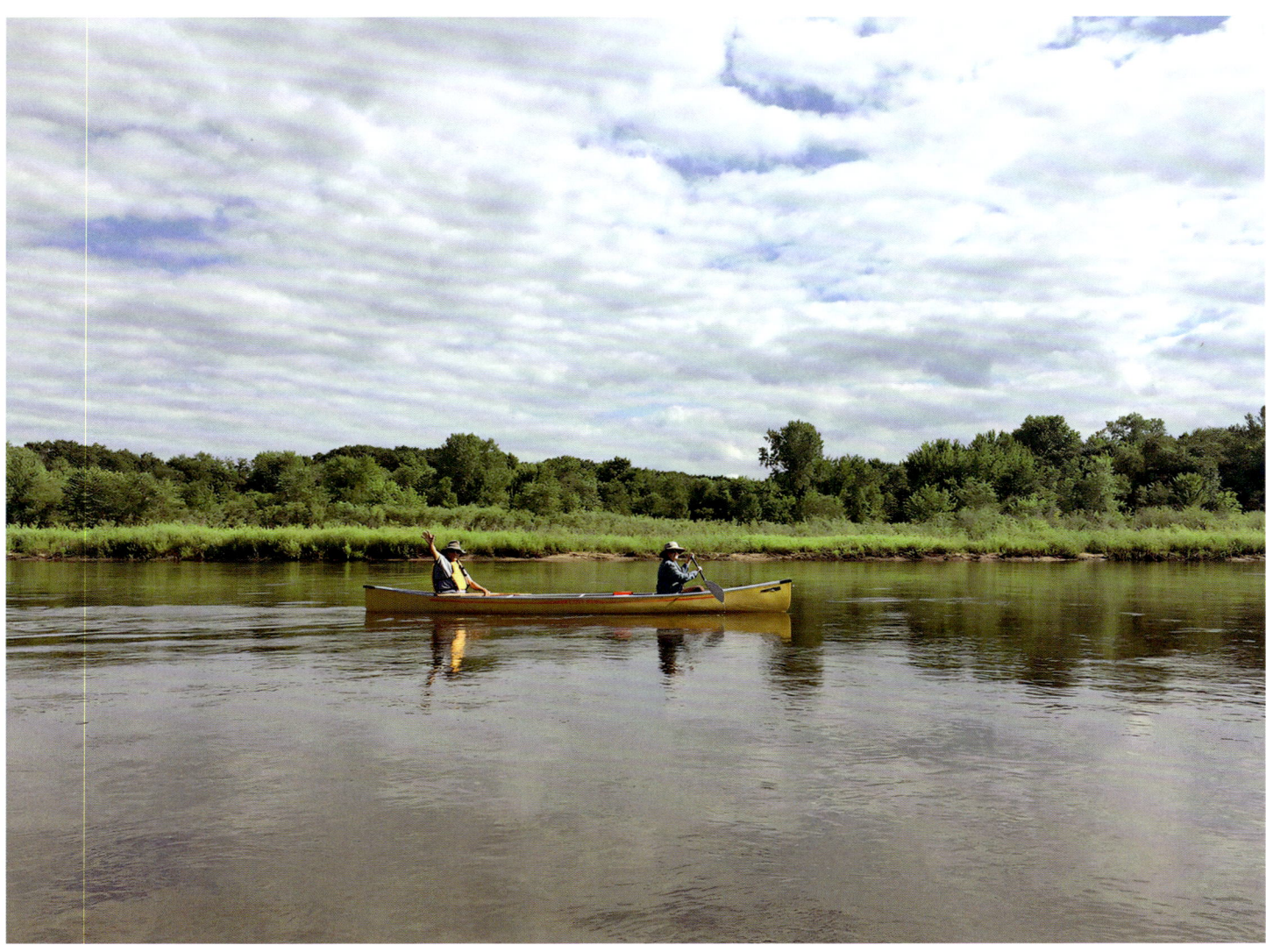

114. Nancy and Truman Lowe canoeing on the Wisconsin River, 2016

My dad grew up swimming in Hall's Creek at the Indian Mission near Black River Falls, Wisconsin. On summer days he and other kids at the Mission would spend hours playing in the swimming hole and along its banks, entertained by the endless stream of moving water. My dad was especially entranced by the white chalky rocks he found, which he used to draw pictures on other rocks. Whenever he talked about time spent playing at the creek, a deep, satisfied smile would emerge on his face. He couldn't possibly have known it at the time, but those early memories would form the foundation of his creative life. It was clear that moving water provided him a sense of freedom and joy, opening the door to a future of inspired artistic endeavors. It was a place he would turn back to again and again in his mind to relive that early source of joy.

Years later, when my parents bought their first house, my dad convinced my mom that it was a great time to buy a canoe since they finally had a place to store it. After some careful consideration, they decided on a beautifully elegant, seventeen-foot Sawyer canoe. It was a decidedly inelegant banana-yellow color with an orange stripe. The color was my dad's choice. We can only imagine that it was an aesthetic decision that was perfectly obvious to him if baffling to us. What was evident is that my dad

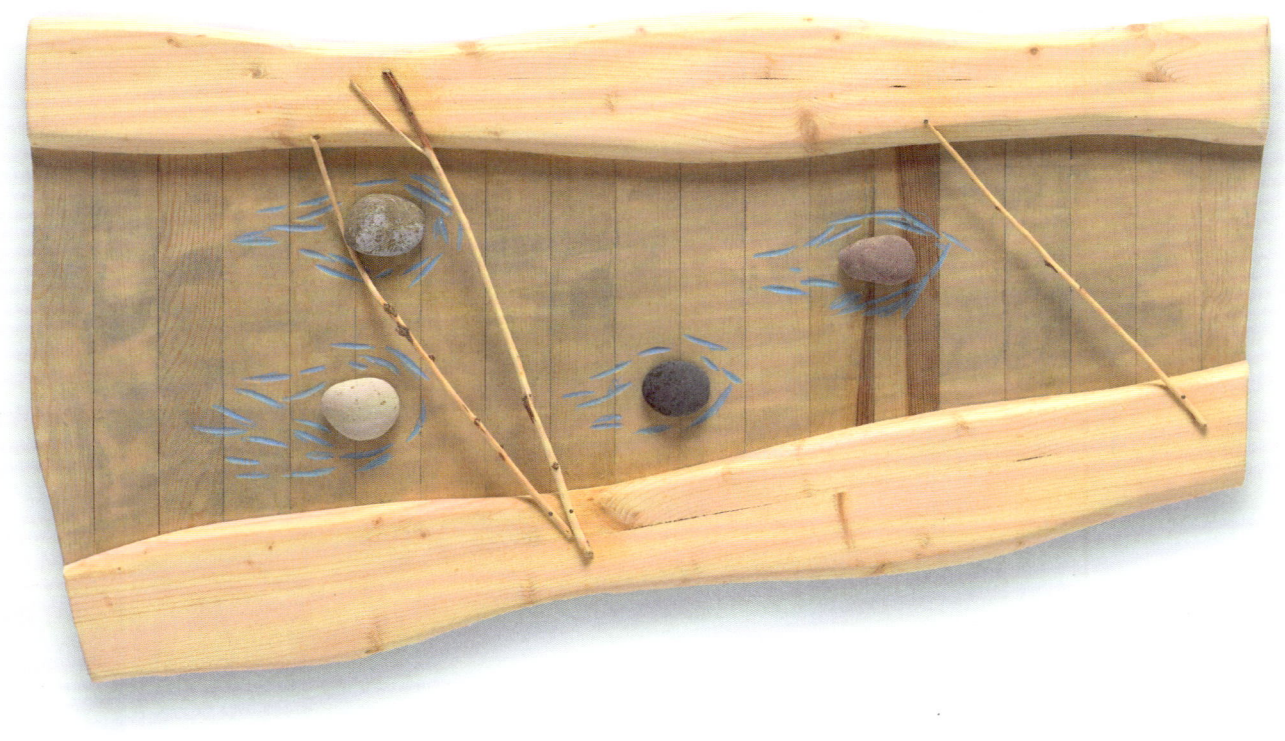

115. *Stream II*, ca. 1990–91. Pine, peeled willow sticks, watercolor, stones, pastel, 18 x 32 ¼ x 1 in. National Museum of the American Indian 27/608

absolutely loved that canoe. My mom, Nancy, my brother, Kųnų (Hoocąk hoit'e for firstborn son), and I all learned to love it, too, after we got over the surprising color choice. That canoe took us on countless family adventures on rivers and lakes throughout Wisconsin. One of my all-time favorites was canoe-camping on the Wisconsin River with family friends. This meant spending nearly three days paddling down the river, plus two nights camping on sandbars along the way. If we were really lucky, we would find a nice long sandbar that would allow us kids to jump in the water at one end and float along in the current down to the other end where we would get scooped up by an adult. Then we'd run up the sandbar and do it all over again until we were exhausted. It wasn't Hall's Creek but I like to think it was my dad's way of giving us the same experience he'd had when he was young—that special kind of joy and freedom that can only be found floating untethered in aqueous surrender. It's a joy you hold on to and never want to forget, because even as a kid you somehow know that you're going to need it to sustain yourself throughout your life.

After my brother died in an accident, the three of us spent time canoeing together. Weighted down with grief, paddling through the water helped us feel a little bit lighter. It gave us time to reflect, reminisce, and appreciate what had been and accept what would be. To be thankful for the time we'd had with Kų́nų́ and start to imagine what our lives would be like without him, both collectively and individually. So many things about canoeing made their way into my dad's artwork: the canoe form, the water compositions, and even the sandbars. But it wasn't until my brother's death that I could finally *feel* the real significance of my dad's connection to canoeing. The canoe is a magic vehicle that can transport a person to a liminal state, floating weightlessly between water and sky. And sometimes, that's exactly what you need, even if it's just for a moment (fig. 114).

Of course, my dad didn't always have to be in the water or floating on it to recognize its magnificence. Throughout our lives, he would often pause beside a river or stream and watch the surface of the water. He would point out the movement, the light, and the color—emphasizing how different the water can look as it flows. There were so many moments when we stood together, watching the water falling, meandering, rippling, knowing that it was eternal, always moving, always changing. It was there long before us and would remain long after us. We were simply witnesses to a particular moment in time. It was mesmerizing and, to this day, I find watching the surface of water to be one of the most relaxing things in the world. My dad spent much of his life trying to capture those fleeting moments in his work. His work reminds us that there is natural beauty all around us. You simply have to pause and learn how to see it. And once you see it, once you experience that awe and wonder, you realize how precious it really is.

I think my dad would be happy to know how much time I spend in and around water. I swim regularly with a group of masters swimmers at a nearby community pool and a group of open-water swimmers in the San Francisco Bay. I always enjoy a good pool swim, but swimming in the bay is an other-worldly experience. The weather, the water temperature, the light, the waves, and the tides make each swim different. Sometimes it's calm; other times it's positively wild. You never quite know what you're going to get. I make a point of pausing during bay swims to take my goggles off and look around, consciously trying to absorb as much of the view of the world from the water as possible, willing myself to remember every last detail of that specific moment so I can add it to all the other memories of water that I've been accumulating over a lifetime. It's in those moments that I am reminded of the lessons I've learned from my dad. Always keep moving, revel in currents of joy, keep paddling when things get hard, and never forget how precious our connections to the natural world are.

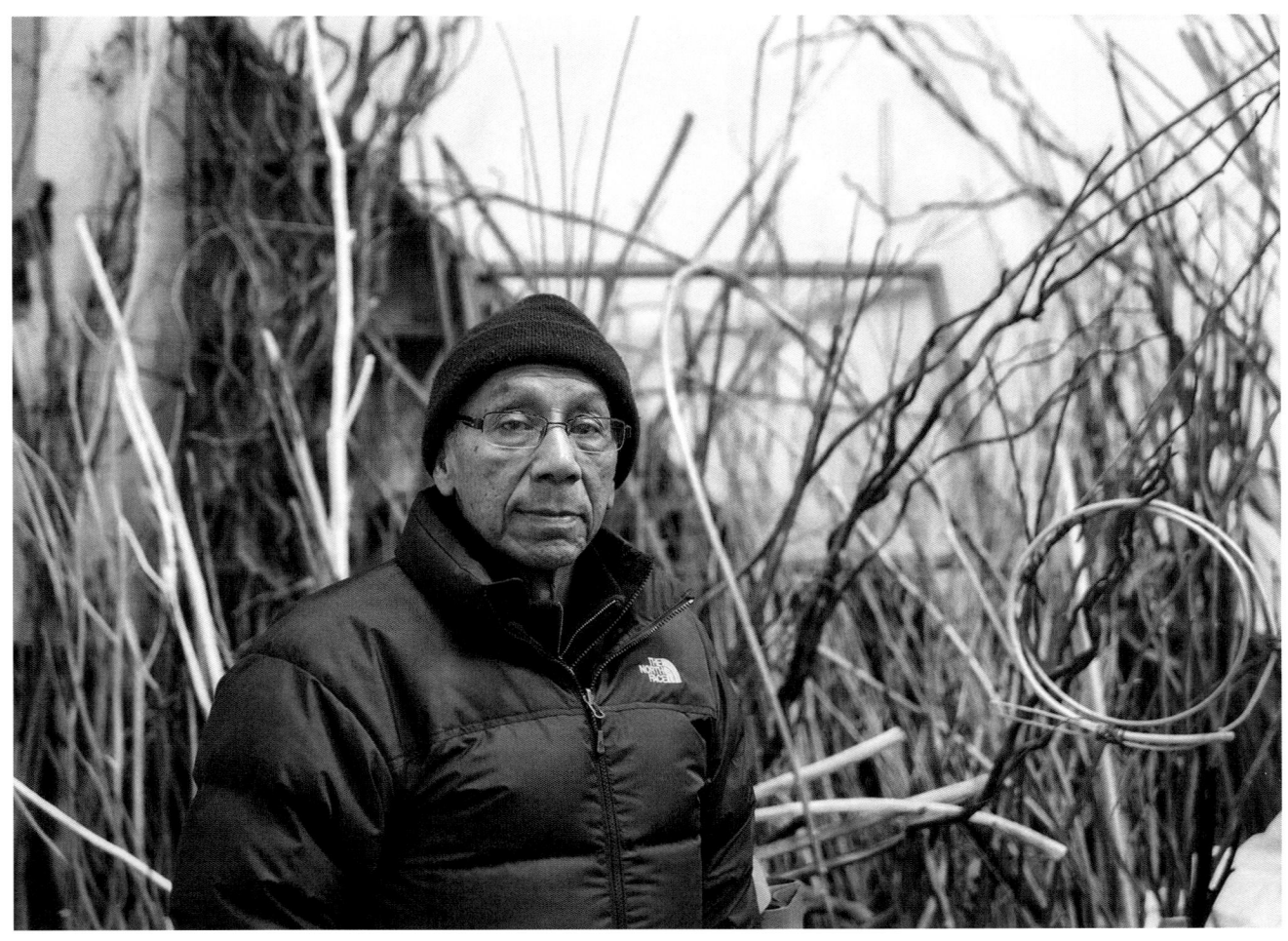

116. Truman Lowe in his studio, Middleton, Wisconsin, ca. 2018

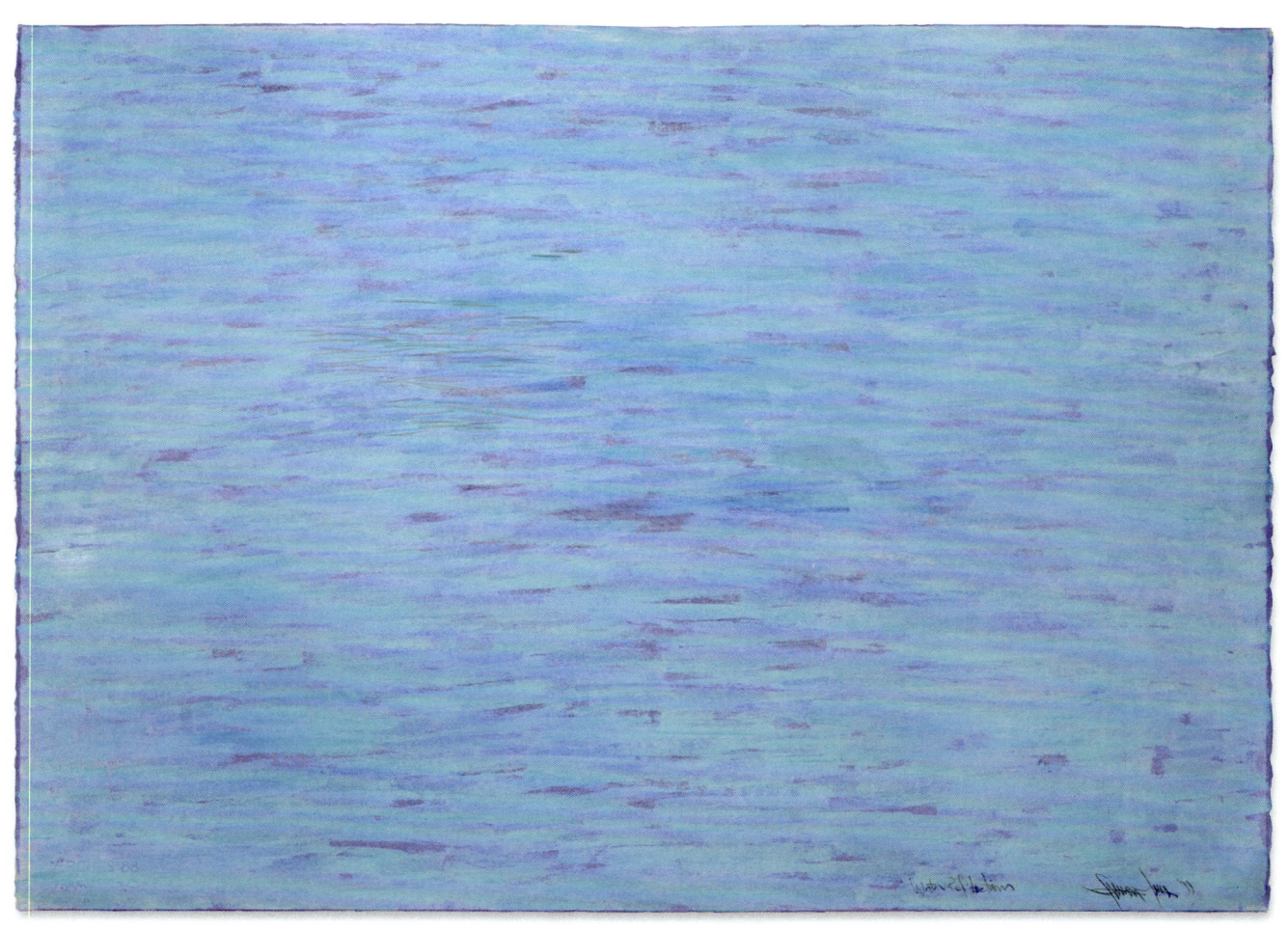

117. *Water Reflections I*, 1999. Acrylic, chalk pastel, graphite, and colored pencil on paper, 30 x 42 ¼ in. The Rockwell Museum, Clara S. Peck Fund. 2000.34.1

118. *Water Reflections II,* 1999. Chalk pastel and paint on paper, 30 ½ x 42 ½ in. The Rockwell Museum, Clara S. Peck Fund. 2000.34.3

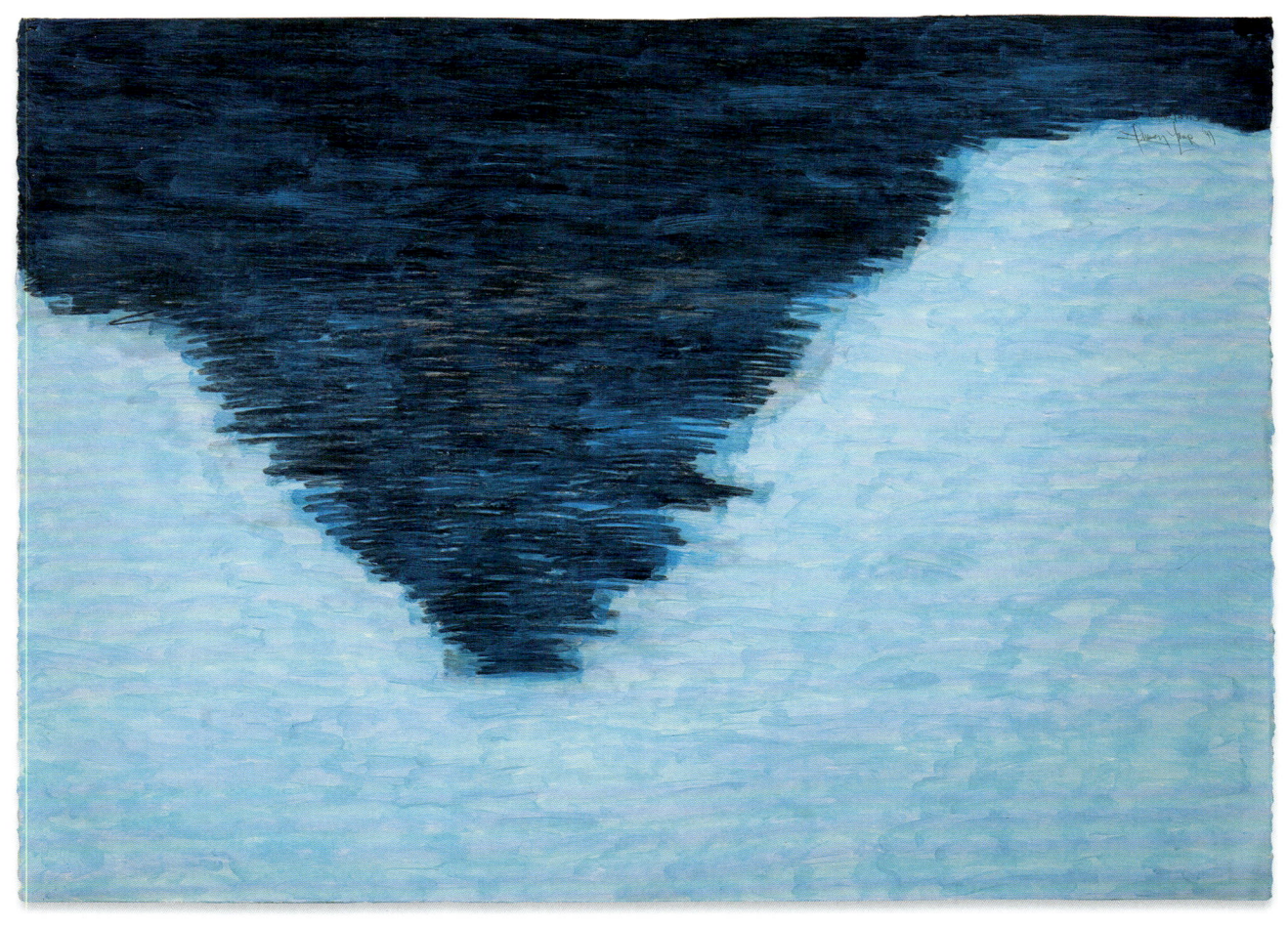

119. *Water Reflections III*, 1999. Chalk pastel and paint on paper, 30 ½ x 42 ½ in. The Rockwell Museum, Clara S. Peck Fund. 2000.34.2

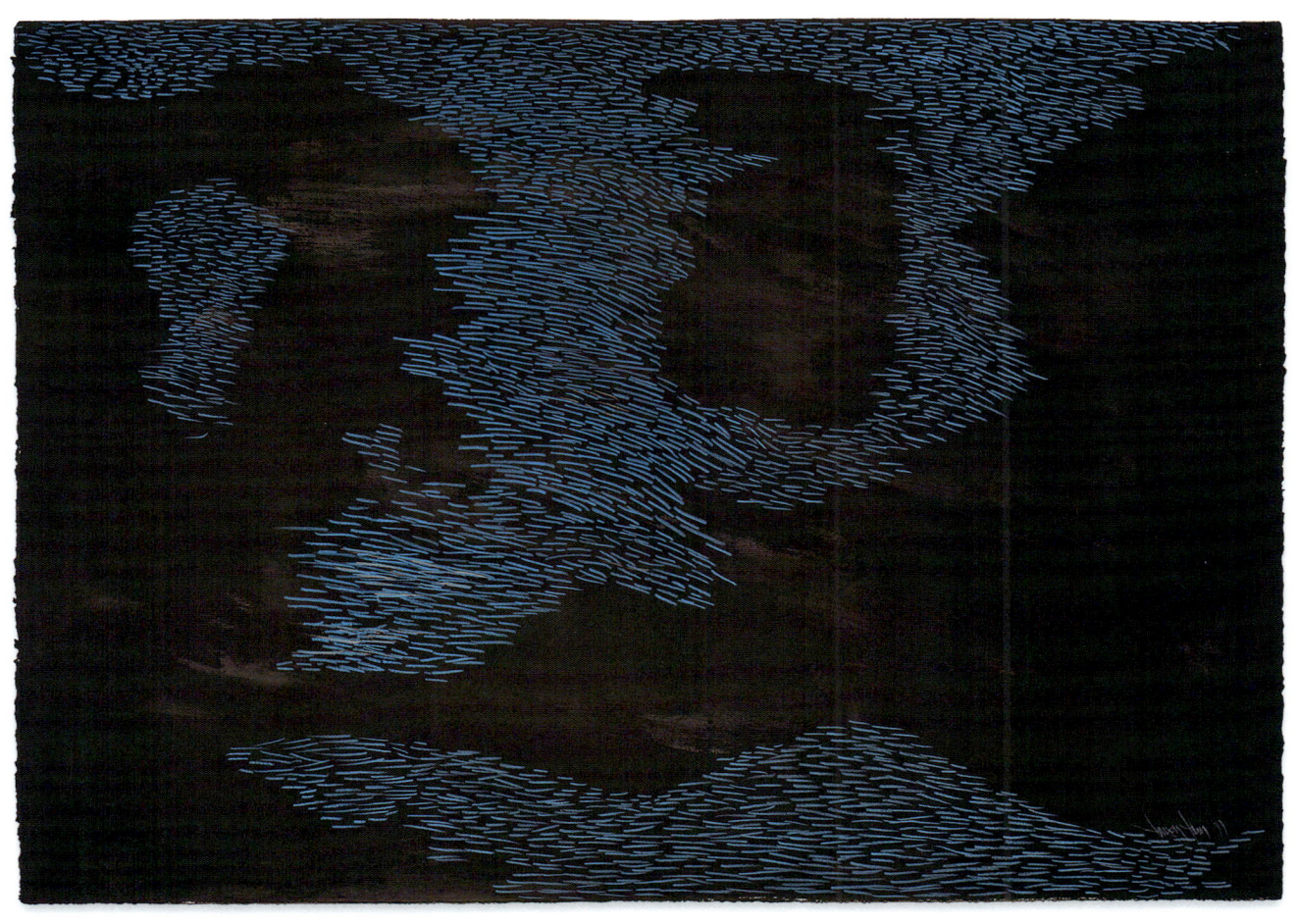

120. *Water Reflections IV*, 1999. Gesso, chalk pastel, colored pencil, and graphite on paper, 30 ½ x 44 in. The Rockwell Museum, Clara S. Peck Fund. 2000.34.4

Notes

INTRODUCTION

1   Hayward Allen, *Truman Lowe: Streams* (La Crosse: University Art Gallery, University of Wisconsin–La Crosse, 1991), 23.

2   "Truman Lowe: Spirits All Around Us," (in University of Wisconsin–Madison Art Department Newsletter, 1995), 3.

3   Allen, *Streams,* 22–23.

4   Jennifer Complo, *Haga (Third Son): An Exhibition of Sculpture, Drawing and Painting by Winnebago Artist Truman Lowe* (Indianapolis: Eiteljorg Museum of American Indians and Western Art, 1993), 22.

"WOOD . . . LAND . . . WOODLAND . . ."

5   Traditional Hoocąk society is organized around twelve clans, each bearing certain responsibilities within the community and distinct traditions and customs. The upper clans ("those who are above the earth") include the Thunder (or Thunderbird), Eagle, Hawk, and Pigeon clans. The lower clans ("those who are on the earth") include the Bear, Wolf, Water Spirit, Deer, Elk, Buffalo, Fish, and Snake clans. The clan structure continues to this day.

6   In 1970, the Winnebago Indian Mission Church became the Winnebago United Church of Christ. Today, the church is widely called the Hoocąk United Church of Christ.

7   At the time Lowe enrolled, the university was called Wisconsin State College–La Crosse. In 1964, it became part of the Wisconsin State University system and was renamed Wisconsin State University–La Crosse. When the Wisconsin State University system merged with the University of Wisconsin system in 1971, Lowe's alma mater was renamed the University of Wisconsin–La Crosse.

8   Nancy Knabe grew up in Nelson, Wisconsin. She attended what today is called University of Wisconsin–Stout. From 1955 to 1964, the school was named Stout State College. When Nancy graduated in 1966, the school was called Stout State University.

9   The couple was married in the church of Nancy's youth, Lyster Lutheran Church in rural Nelson, Wisconsin.

10 *A Plastic Presence* was organized by the Jewish Museum, New York, in 1969. It then traveled to the Milwaukee Art Center, now the Milwaukee Art Museum, where it was on display from January 30 to March 8, 1970. From there, the show traveled to the San Francisco Museum of Art.

11 Vince Gotera, "What's Really Crucial: An Interview with Truman Lowe," *Minorities Fellows Network/The Committee on Institutional Cooperation (CIC)* 5 (1987).

12 Robert Morris, "Anti-Form," *Artforum* 6, no. 4 (1968): 33–35.

13 Lowe was hired as a visiting lecturer in art at Emporia State University, now Kansas State University–Emporia.

14 I provide more detail about the post and surrounding circumstances in my book, *Woodland Reflections: The Art of Truman Lowe* (Madison: University of Wisconsin Press, 2003), 44–45.

15 *Hiinų* is the Hoocąk word for first-born daughter, which Tonia was sometimes called within the family. In 1985, Lowe made a totem for each of his children using their Hoocąk birth order names.

16 Lowe helped recruit Deer (1935–2023) to teach at the University of Wisconsin–Madison in 1977. Because she did not have a PhD and, as she wrote in her memoir, had "no intention of writing or doing research. I'm busy doing something about the problems in society," she was hired into a joint appointment as a lecturer in the School of Social Work and part of the American Indian program. Ada Deer with Theda Perdue, *Making a Difference: My Fight for Native Rights and Social Justice* (Norman: University of Oklahoma Press, 2019), 128.

17 The US Department of Agriculture Natural Resources Conservation Service describes sandbar willow as "a common native suckering shrub 3 to 20 feet high found throughout the Northern Great Plains and the Northeast United States. It quickly forms thickets on sand or gravel deposits along streams, roadside ditches, sloughs, and other places frequent to flooding." The NRCS also indicates that it is "an aggressive spreader." Source: plants.sc.edgov.usda.gov/home/plantProfile?symbol-SAIN3. Accessed July 9, 2024.

18 As quoted in Warren Moon, "Department Provides Diversity," *Wisconsin Academy Review* 31, no. 2 (March 1985): 50.

19 As quoted in Hayward Allen, "The Spirit Moves: Essay on Truman Lowe's Exhibition," in *Truman Lowe: Streams* (La Crosse: University Art Gallery, University of Wisconsin–La Crosse, 1991), 5.

20 Multiple conversations with the author.

21 Jane Ziebarth, "Art Comes Naturally," *Wisconsin State Journal* (April 3, 1986).

22 Lowe often likened the sensation of canoeing to flying on water. In his essay "The Spirit Moves," in *Truman Lowe: Streams*, 16, Hayward Allen quotes Lowe: "To be in a canoe is to be able to fly on water." Art critic Lucy Lippard in turn used the phrase "flying on water" for the title of her foreword to my book, *Woodland Reflections*.

23 Mylene Hengen, "Networking a native arts force: ATLATL, National Service Organization for Native American Arts," *Settler Colonial Studies* 3, no. 2 (2013): 180.

24 Gotera, "What's Really Crucial," 1987.

25 In 1984, Lowe was promoted to associate professor of art. His earlier appointment as assistant professor, which had begun in January 1976, was split at 50 percent in the department of art and 50 percent in the dean's office as director of the Native American Studies program; these split responsibilities continued until 1988. In 1985, Lowe was awarded the chancellor's Faculty Development Grant for the Creative Arts. Created in 1982 to encourage talented young creative arts faculty members, the award provided recipients with $5,000 per year for five years. In 1989, Lowe was promoted to full professor of art, and when he retired in 2010, he was awarded emeritus status.

26 Carolyn Shoulders, "With Respect for the Natural World," *Research Sampler 1992*, University of Wisconsin–Madison, 37.

27 Lowe would continue to collaborate with the Eiteljorg Museum on many projects over the next twenty years.

28 *From the Shadows of the River*, produced and directed by Janet Whitaker (Lexington: Kentucky Educational Television, 1996).

29 John Aehl, "UW professor's sculpture soars in White House garden," *Wisconsin State Journal* (November 18, 1997). In 2023, *Effigy: Bird Form* found its permanent home on the UW–Madison campus, overlooking Lake Mendota and in proximity to some of the ancient earthen mounds Lowe so revered.

30 Lowe served on the Chancellor's Scholarship Committee at UW–Madison from its founding in 1984 to 2004, and for a number of years he chaired the committee, one of the university's most successful initiatives providing substantial financial support to under-represented students. He also served for twenty years on the university's Committee for the Academic Affairs of Minority and Disadvantaged Students.

31 Lowe received the award in 2007. In 2008, he was one of five UW–Madison alumni who received the Wisconsin Alumni Association's Distinguished Alumni Award. (He had already received the Outstanding Alumni Award from his undergraduate alma mater, UW–La Crosse, in 1999.)

32 Shoulders, "With Respect for the Natural World," 37.

33 Truman Lowe, artist's statement in Jaune Quick-to-See Smith, *We, The Human Beings: 27 Contemporary Native American Artists* (Wooster, OH: The College of Wooster Art Museum, 1992), 29.

TRUMAN LOWE: ASSEMBLING A PRACTICE IN THE EARLY 1980S

34 For more on the Chandler/Pohrt collection, see David W. Penney, *Art of the American Indian Frontier: The Chandler/Pohrt Collection* (Seattle: University of Washington Press, 1992).

35 Elizabeth Weatherford and Emelia Seubert, eds., *Native Americans on Film and Video* (New York: Museum of the American Indian/Heye Foundation, 1981).

36 Lloyd Oxendine, "Twenty-Three Contemporary Indian Artists," *Art in America* 60, no. 4 (July/August): 1972.

37 Edwin L. Wade and Rennard Strickland, *Magic Images: Contemporary Native American Art* (Tulsa: Philbrook Art Center and Oklahoma University Press, 1981), 75–100.

38 See Jo Ortel, *Woodland Reflections: The Art of Truman Lowe* (Madison: University of Wisconsin Press, 2003).

39 Robert Houle, "The Emergence of a New Aesthetic Tradition," in *New Work by a New Generation* (Regina, Saskatchewan: Norman MacKenzie Art Gallery, 1982).

40 George C. Longfish and Joan Randall, "Contradictions in Indian Territory," in *Contemporary Native American Art* (Stillwater, OK: Gardiner Art Gallery, 1983).

41 Truman Lowe, artist statement in Longfish and Randall, *Contemporary Native American Art*.

42 Hayward Allen, "The Spirit Moves: Essay on Truman Lowe's Exhibition," in *Truman Lowe: Streams* (La Crosse: University Art Gallery, University of Wisconsin–La Crosse, 1991), 8–10.

43 Ortel, *Woodland Reflections*, 47, 72.

44 Rebecca Trautmann, personal communication, February 2024; Lowe's quote is from Allen, *Streams*, 6.

45 Diana Nemiroff, Robert Houle, and Charlotte Townsend Gault, *Land Spirit Power: First Nations at the National Gallery of Canada* (Ottawa: National Gallery of Canada, 1992), 182–89.

46 Charles Pomeroy Ottis, trans., *Voyages of Samuel de Champlain*, vol. 3 (Charleston, SC: Bibliobazaar, 2006), 58, 76.

47 "'Ke-Chunk Ciporoke' sculpture by Wisconsin Ho-Chunk artist Truman Lowe," https://natureattheconfluence.com/ke-chunk-ciporoke-sculpture-by-wisconsin-ho-chunk-artist-truman-lowe/.

48 Truman Lowe, artist's statement in Longfish and Randall, *Contemporary Native American Art.*

49 Nemiroff et al., *Land Spirit Power,* 188.

TRUMAN LOWE AND A HOOCĄK HERITAGE OF RESILIENCE

50 Tom Jones, Michael Schmudlach, Matthew Daniel Mason, Amy Lonetree, and George A. Greendeer, *People of the Big Voice: Photographs of Ho-Chunk Families by Charles Van Schaick, 1879–1942*, foreword by Truman Lowe (Madison: Wisconsin Historical Society Press, 2011).

51 Truman Lowe, foreword, in Jones et al., *People of the Big Voice*, vii.

52 Jo Ortel, *Woodland Reflections: The Art of Truman Lowe* (Madison: University of Wisconsin Press, 2003), 19.

53 Ortel, *Woodland Reflections*, 12–14, 18.

54 Ortel, *Woodland Reflections*, 19.

55 "Survivance" is an appropriate term to use when describing Hoocąk history, as the word "survival" does not sufficiently encompass the strength and perseverance that it took for our people to remain intact as a tribal nation in the aftermath of colonial violence and oppression. Gerald Vizenor defines survivance as "more than survival, more than endurance or mere response; the stories of survivance are an active presence. . . . [S]urvivance is an active repudiation of dominance, tragedy, and victimry." Gerald Vizenor, *Fugitive Poses: Native American Indian Scenes of Absence and Presence* (Lincoln: University of Nebraska Press, 1998), 15.

56 In my essay published in *People of the Big Voice*, I provide an overview of Hoocąk history with particular attention given to the mid-nineteenth-century forced removals and assimilation era policies of the late nineteenth and early twentieth centuries that were in place when a majority of the images were taken. Some of the historical discussion that follows draws from that earlier work. See Amy Lonetree, "Visualizing Native Survivance: Encounters with My Ho-Chunk Ancestors in the Family Photographs of Charles Van Schaick," in Jones et al., *People of the Big Voice*, 15–20; and Amy Lonetree, "A Heritage of Resilience: Ho-Chunk Family Photographs in the Visual Archive," *The Public Historian* 41, no. 1 (2019): 36–38.

57 Jason Tetzloff, "The Diminishing Winnebago Estate in Wisconsin: From White Contact to Removal" (MA thesis, University of Wisconsin–Eau Claire, 1991), 1.

58 Grant Arndt, *Ho-Chunk Powwows and the Politics of Tradition* (Lincoln: University of Nebraska Press, 2016), 37.

59 For a lengthier discussion on the Hoocąk leader's negotiations for a new reservation, see Edward J. Pluth, "The Failed Watab Treaty of 1853," *Minnesota History* 57, vol. 1 (Spring 2000): 2–22.

60 For a longer discussion of Hoocąk history in Minnesota and the Knights of the Forest, see Cathy Coats, *To Banish Forever: A Secret Society, the Ho-Chunk, and Ethnic Cleansing in Minnesota* (Saint Paul: Minnesota Historical Society Press, 2024).

61 Steven Hoelscher, *Picturing Indians: Photographic Encounters and Tourist Fantasies in H. H. Bennett's Wisconsin Dells* (Madison: University of Wisconsin Press, 2008), 58.

62 In Article II, the Ho-Chunk Constitution outlines membership requirements: "(a) All persons of Ho-Chunk blood whose names appear or are entitled to appear on the official census roll prepared pursuant to the Act of January 18, 1881 (21 Stat. 315), or the Wisconsin Winnebago Annuity Payroll for the year one thousand nine hundred and one (1901), or the Act of January 20, 1910 (36 Stat. 873), or the Act of July 1, 1912 (37 Stat. 187); or (b) All descendants of persons listed in Section 1(a), provided, that such persons are at least one-fourth (1/4) Ho-Chunk blood." Ho-Chunk Nation Official Government Website, "Constitution of the Ho-Chunk Nation," https://ho-chunknation.com/wp-content/uploads/2019/10/Final-HCN-Constitution-July-2019-1.pdf (accessed June 11, 2024).

63 Quoted in Jo Ortel, *Woodland Reflections*, 52–53.

NURTURING *COO*: CONCEPTUALIZING A HOOCĄK COLOR THEORY IN THE WORK OF TRUMAN LOWE

64 PBS LearningMedia, "Truman Lowe: Contemporary Native American Artist | Native American Culture," accessed May

21, 2024. https://www.pbslearningmedia.
org/resource/natam.arts.visarts.truman/
native-american-culture-truman-lowe-
contemporary-native-american-artist/.

65 Jo Ortel, *Woodland Reflections: The Art
of Truman Lowe* (Madison: University
of Wisconsin Press, 2003), 11.

66 *Exploring the Artistic Process of
Truman Lowe: A Journey Through
Native American Art & Education*,
2023. https://www.youtube.com/
watch?v=oBltTFXKNLw.

67 Karen Martin, conversation with author,
May 20, 2024.

68 Interview with Truman Lowe,
Museum of Wisconsin Art, October
6, 2015. https://www.youtube.com/
watch?v=pkcJYCqDTxo.

69 Joe Keenan, conversation with author,
May 25, 2024.

70 Truman Lowe, conversation with Jo
Ortel, June 14, 1999.

71 Tony Thayer, conversation with author,
May 25, 2024.

**WATER MEMORIES: EARTH, WATER, AND SKY
IN THE ART OF TRUMAN LOWE**

72 Lowe frequently singled out one mound
in particular, the bird effigy located on
Observatory Hill. As he told Mary Lynn
Kotz, "On the University of Wisconsin
campus, there's a bird-mound with a
wingspan of 50 feet and a length of 30
feet, head-to-tail. I wanted to create
something out of respect for that
particular culture, from 2,000 to 3,000
years ago." (Mary Lynn Kotz, "At the
White House: The First Lady's Sculpture
Garden," *Sculpture* Magazine 17, no. 6
(July/Aug. 1998): 29.) According to Jo
Ortel, Truman would be deeply honored
to know that the university chose to give

his sculpture a permanent home nearby.

73 John Aehl, "UW professor's sculpture soars in White House garden,"
Wisconsin State Journal, November 18,
1997.

74 Gwen Carlson, "UW sculptor's work
at White House," *The Capital Times*,
November 19, 1997.

75 Robert A. Birmingham and Katherine
H. Rankin, *Native American Mounds in
Madison and Dane County* (Madison,
WI: City of Madison and State Historical
Society of Wisconsin, 1996), 3–5, in
addition to the author's conversations
with Hoocąk community elders and
members while living and studying in
Wisconsin.

76 "Exploring the Artistic Process of
Truman Lowe: A Journey Through
Native American Art & Education,"
Discover Wisconsin, April 19, 2023,
YouTube https://www.youtube.com/
watch?v=oBltTFXKNLw.

77 Art historian Jo Ortel has stated that
this orientation of the sculpture was
unintentional and was not directed by
the artist. Jo Ortel, conversation and
correspondence with the author,
June 2024.

78 Patty Loew, *Indian Nations of
Wisconsin: Histories of Endurance and
Renewal* (State Historical Society of
Wisconsin, 2001 and 2013), 40–53.

79 Megan Provost, "Land of The
Ho-Chunk" *OnWisconsin* (Fall 2022),
onwisconsin.uwalumni.com. See also
Sarah Kuta, "3,000-Year-Old Dugout
Canoe Recovered From Wisconsin
Lake," *Smithsonian* Magazine,
September 27, 2022, https://www.
smithsonianmag.com/smart-news/3000-
year-old-dugout-canoe-recovered-from-
wisconsin-lake-180980843/.

80 Quoted in Jo Ortel, *Woodland
Reflections: The Art of Truman Lowe*
(Madison: University of Wisconsin
Press, 2003), xii.

81 Holland Cotter, "At the Met, Protest and
Poetry About Water," *New York Times*,
July 3, 2022.

**APPROACHING SILENCE:
A COLLABORATION**

82 Lucy Lippard, personal communication
to the author, July 2024.

**TRUMAN LOWE AT THE SMITHSONIAN
AMERICAN ART MUSEUM: NOTES FROM THE
GALLERIES**

83 Martin Puryear, in conversation with
the author at the Smithsonian American
Art Museum, May 2016.

LAST OF THE MOHICANS

84 As of 2025, the Smithsonian Institution
comprises twenty-one museums (the
National Museum of the American
Latino and the Smithsonian American
Women's History Museum are in
development), twenty-one libraries, the
National Zoo, numerous research centers, and several education units and
centers.

85 As quoted in Hayward Allen, "The
Spirit Moves: Essay on Truman Lowe's
Exhibition," in *Truman Lowe: Streams*
(La Crosse, University Art Gallery,
University of Wisconsin–La Crosse,
1991), 5.

Selected Exhibition History and Collections

SELECTED SOLO EXHIBITIONS

Movement: Water into Wood: The Art of Truman Lowe, Edith Farnsworth House, Plano, IL, 2025

Elements, The Green Gallery, Milwaukee, WI, 2025

Origin, Vision, Place, Voice: The Art of Truman Lowe, Chazen Museum of Art, University of Wisconsin–Madison, Madison, WI, 2021

Changing Currents: The Art of Truman Lowe, UWL Art Gallery, University of Wisconsin–La Crosse, La Crosse, WI, 2020

Cultural Confluence: Work by Truman Lowe, Plains Art Museum, Fargo, ND, 2017

Truman Lowe: Spiritual Migrations, Museum of Wisconsin Art, West Bend, WI, 2014–15

Between the Real and the Imagined: Installation by Truman Lowe, Denver Botanic Gardens, Denver, CO, 2011

Truman Lowe: Limn, Museum of Wisconsin Art, West Bend, WI, 2010

Truman Lowe: Remembrance, Madison Art Center, Madison, WI, 2001

Nigachiwong: Swirling Waters, Tweed Museum of Art, University of Minnesota Duluth, Duluth, MN, 2001

Truman Lowe: Neo-Xahnee, John Michael Kohler Arts Center, Sheboygan, WI, 1999–2000

University of Wisconsin–Milwaukee Art Museum, Milwaukee, WI, 1997

Ma-Shu, Jan Cicero Gallery, Chicago, IL, 1997

From the Shadows of the River, Clara M. Eagle Art Gallery, Murray State University, Murray, KY, 1996

The Canyon Series, Jan Cicero Gallery, Chicago, IL, 1995

Haga (Third Son): An Exhibition of Sculpture, Drawing, and Painting by Winnebago Artist Truman Lowe, Eiteljorg Museum of American Indians and Western Art, Indianapolis, IN, 1994

Truman Lowe: Red Ochre Series, Tula Foundation Gallery, Atlanta, GA, 1991

Streams, University Art Gallery, University of Wisconsin–La Crosse, La Crosse, WI, 1991

Red Banks: An Installation, Lawton Gallery, University of Wisconsin–Green Bay, Green Bay, WI, 1991

Truman Lowe: Sculpture, Kathryn Sermas Gallery, New York, NY, 1991

School of the Arts, Rhinelander, WI, 1990

American Indian Community House Gallery, New York, NY, 1989

Truman Lowe: Sculpture and Works on Paper, Signature Gallery, Stoughton, WI, 1988

Emporia State University, Emporia, KS, 1988

American Indian Center, Minneapolis, MN, 1987

University of Minnesota, Minneapolis, MN, 1987

United States Embassy, La Paz, Bolivia, 1985

United States Embassy, Cotonou, Benin, 1985

Trail Marker, Mid-America All-Indian Museum, Wichita, KS, 1981

Constructions, University of Wisconsin–Madison, Memorial Union, Main Gallery, Madison, WI, 1980

M.F.A. Exhibition, University of Wisconsin–Madison, Madison, WI, 1973

SELECTED GROUP EXHIBITIONS

Sculpture Milwaukee, Milwaukee Symphony Orchestra, Milwaukee, WI, 2024–25

Native Prospects: Indigeneity and Landscape, Thomas Cole National Historic Site, Catskill, NY; Florence Griswold Museum, Old Lyme, CT; Farnsworth Art Museum, Rockland, ME, 2024–25

Honoring Truman Lowe, Promega Art Showcase, Fitchburg, WI, 2023

Monarchs: Brown and Native Contemporary Artists in the Path of the Butterfly, Bemis Center for Contemporary Arts, Omaha, NE; Museum of Contemporary Art North Miami, Miami, FL; Blue Star Contemporary and Southwest School of Art, San Antonio, TX; The Nerman Museum of Contemporary Art, Overland Park, KS, 2017–19

Changing Hands: Art Without Reservation 3, Contemporary Native North American Art from the Northeast and Southeast, Museum of Arts and Design, New York, NY, 2012; traveled in the United States and Canada, 2013–14

Shapeshifting: Transformations in Native American Art, Peabody Essex Museum, Salem, MA, 2012

Vantage Point: The Contemporary Native Art Collection, National Museum of the American Indian, Washington, DC, 2010

Tradition and Change: A Survey of Contemporary American Indian Art, Northwest Museum of Arts and Culture, Spokane, WA, 2008

Between the Lakes: Artists Respond to Madison, Madison Museum of Contemporary Art, Madison, WI, 2006

All My Life: Contemporary Works by Native American Artists, Peabody Essex Museum, Salem, MA, 2005–10

Power and Beauty, Peabody Essex Museum, Salem, MA, 2003–05

Holponiyochi: Contemporary Native American Sculpture, Wright State University Art Galleries, Dayton, OH, 2003

Contemporary Masters: The Eiteljorg Fellowship for Native American Fine Art, Eiteljorg Museum of American Indians and Western Art, Indianapolis, IN, 1999

Powerful Images: Portrayals of Native America, National Cowboy & Western Heritage Museum, Oklahoma City, OK, 1998

Twentieth Century American Sculpture at The White House: Honoring Native America, The White House, Washington, DC, 1997

We Are Many, We Are One, University Art Gallery, University of Wisconsin–La Crosse, La Crosse, WI, 1997

Gifts of the Spirit: Works by Nineteenth Century & Contemporary Native American Artists, Peabody Essex Museum, Salem, MA, 1996–97

Native Streams, Jan Cicero Gallery, Chicago, IL; Turman Art Gallery, Indiana State University, Terre Haute, IN, 1996–97

Indian Humor, American Indian Contemporary Arts, San Francisco, CA; Cheney Cowles Museum, Spokane, WA; National Museum of the American Indian, New York, NY, 1994–98

Sixth Quadrennial Exhibition of the UW–Madison Department of Art Faculty, Elvehjem Museum of Art, University of Wisconsin–Madison, Madison, WI, 1994–95

Artists Who Are Indian, Denver Art Museum, Denver, CO, 1994

Jan Cicero Gallery, Chicago, IL, 1994

Melange, Walker's Point Center for the Arts, Milwaukee, WI, 1993–94

Land, Spirit, Power: First Nations at the National Gallery of Canada, National Gallery of Canada, Ottawa, Ontario, Canada, 1992; traveled in Canada and internationally 1993–94

We, the Human Beings: 27 Contemporary Native American Artists, College of Wooster Art Museum, Wooster, OH; Krannert Art Museum and Kinkead Pavilion, University of Illinois, Champaign, IL; Museums at Hartwick College, Oneonta, NY; Eiteljorg Museum of American Indians and Western Art, Indianapolis, IN; The Riffe Gallery, Columbus, OH; Gibson Gallery, State University of New York–Potsdam, NY, 1992–94

Without Boundaries, Jan Cicero Gallery, Chicago, IL, 1992

Shared Visions: Native American Painters and Sculptors in the Twentieth Century, Heard Museum, Phoenix, AZ; Thomas Gilcrease Institute of American History and Art, Tulsa, OK, 1991–92

Portfolio III: Ten Native American Artists, American Indian Contemporary Arts, San Francisco, CA, 1991

Elvehjem Museum of Art, University of Wisconsin–Madison, Madison, WI, 1991

Without Boundaries: Contemporary Native American Art, Jan Cicero Gallery, Chicago, IL, 1991

Artifacts for the Seventh Generation: Multitribal-Multimedia Visions, American Indian Contemporary Arts, San Francisco, CA, 1990

Walker's Point Center for the Arts, Milwaukee, WI, 1990

8 Native American Artists, Fort Wayne Museum of Art, Fort Wayne, IN, 1987–88

Lowe/Fedderson [sic]*: Works by Truman Lowe and Joe Fedderson* [sic], Beloit College Museums, Beloit, WI, 1987

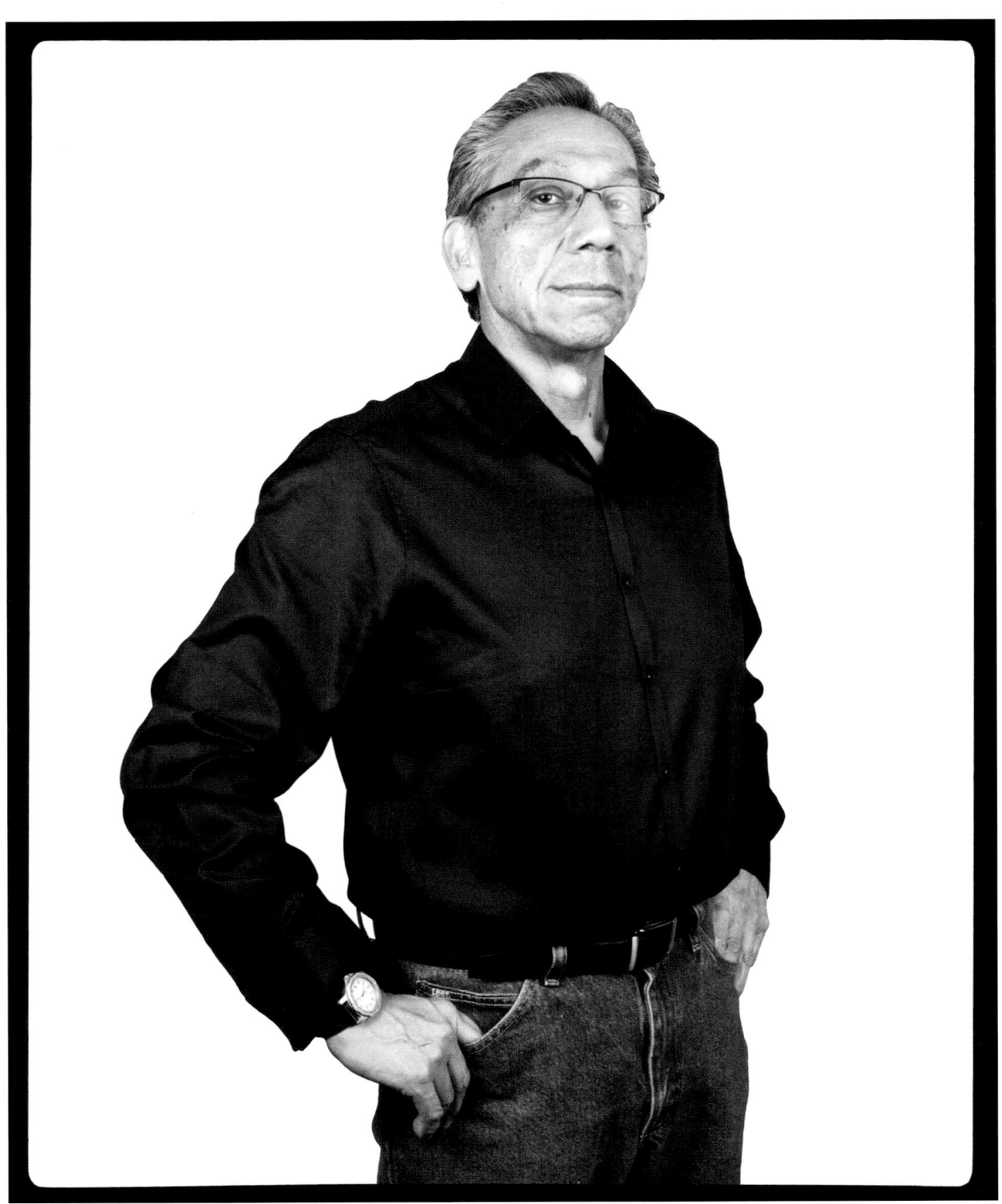

121. Rosalie Favell (Métis, b. 1958), *Truman Lowe, Washington, D.C., 2010*, from the *Facing the Camera* series, 2008–18

What Is Native American Art?
Philbrook Art Center, Tulsa, OK, 1986

The Second Biennial Native American Fine Arts Invitational, Heard Museum, Phoenix, AZ, 1985

Wisconsin Directions 4, Milwaukee Art Museum, Milwaukee, WI, 1984

Contemporary Native American Art, Gardiner Art Gallery, Oklahoma State University, Stillwater, OK, 1983

SELECTED PERMANENT INSTALLATIONS

Ke-Chunk Ciporoke, Nature at the Confluence, South Beloit, IL, 2019

Water Whispers, Eiteljorg Museum of American Indians and Western Art, Indianapolis, IN, 2005

Restful Place, Indianapolis Art Center, Indianapolis, IN, 2004

Effigy: Bird Form, University of Wisconsin–Madison, Madison, WI, 1997; installed 2023

Ojibway Stream, Fond du Lac Tribal and Community College, Cloquet, MN, 1992

SELECTED COLLECTIONS

Chazen Museum of Art, University of Wisconsin–Madison, Madison, WI

Denver Art Museum, Denver, CO

Des Moines Art Center, Des Moines, IA

Eiteljorg Museum of American Indians and Western Art, Indianapolis, IN

Fort Lewis College Center of Southwest Studies, Durango, CO

Fort Wayne Museum of Art, Fort Wayne, IN

Heard Museum, Phoenix, AZ

Hood Museum, Dartmouth College, Hanover, NH

Kellogg School of Management, Northwestern University, Evanston, IL

Madison Museum of Contemporary Art, Madison, WI

McCormick Place, Chicago, IL

Metropolitan Museum of Art, New York, NY

Milwaukee Art Museum, Milwaukee, WI

Minneapolis Institute of Art, Minneapolis, MN

Montclair Art Museum, Montclair, NJ

Museum of Contemporary Art Chicago, Chicago, IL

Museum of Contemporary Native Arts, Institute of American Indian Arts, Santa Fe, NM

Museum of Fine Arts, Boston, Boston, MA

Museum of Wisconsin Art, West Bend, WI

National Museum of the American Indian, Smithsonian Institution, Washington, DC

Peabody Essex Museum, Salem, MA

Plains Art Museum, Fargo, ND

Portland Art Museum, Portland, OR

Rockwell Museum, Corning, NY

Saint Louis Art Museum, Saint Louis, MO

Smith College Museum of Art, Northampton, MA

Smithsonian American Art Museum, Washington, DC

Spencer Museum of Art, University of Kansas, Lawrence, KS

Stanley Museum of Art, University of Iowa, Iowa City, IA

Tucson Museum of Art, Tucson, AZ

Tweed Museum, University of Minnesota Duluth, Duluth, MN

Whitney Museum of American Art, New York, NY

Wright Museum of Art, Beloit College, Beloit, WI

Exhibition Checklist

Mimi, 1979
Pine, peeled willow sticks, blue jay
feathers, leather, glass beads
18 x 16 x 16 in.
National Museum of the
American Indian 26/9773,
gift of John and Meryl Lipton Lavine

Ribbon Appliqué, ca. 1980
Pastel on paper
22 x 30 in.
National Museum of the
American Indian 27/621

Untitled (Ribbonwork), ca. 1980
Pastel on paper
22 x 30 in.
National Museum of the
American Indian 27/622

Untitled, from the *Artifact Series*,
ca. 1980–90
Pine, peeled willow sticks, leather,
glass beads on mat board
19 x 16 in.
National Museum of the American
Indian 26/9252, gift of John
and Meryl Lipton Lavine

Totem for Henu (First Daughter), 1985
Pine, peeled willow saplings
126 ½ x 15 x 15 in.
Smithsonian American Art
Museum, museum purchase made
through the Luisita L. and Franz H.
Denghausen Endowment, 2022.9.3

Totem for Kunu (First Son), 1985
Pine, peeled willow saplings
114 x 15 x 15 in.
Smithsonian American Art
Museum, museum purchase made
through the Luisita L. and Franz H.
Denghausen Endowment, 2022.9.2

Canoe Form, ca. 1985–90
Peeled willow saplings, leather
25 x 191 x 25 in.
National Museum of the American
Indian 26/9766, gift of John
and Meryl Lipton Lavine

Mask, 1985–90
Leather, pine, peeled willow sticks
and bark, brushed powdered pigment
26 ½ x 12 x 2 ½ in.
National Museum of the American
Indian 26/9255, gift of John
and Meryl Lipton Lavine

Mnemonic, ca. 1985–90, 2013
Peeled willow, leather, paper
37 x 90 x 3 in.
National Museum of the American
Indian 26/8988, gift of John
and Meryl Lipton Lavine

Stars, ca. 1985–90
Pastel on paper
22 x 30 in.
National Museum of the
American Indian 27/617

Untitled, from the *Artifact Series*,
ca. 1985–90
Feathers, wood, thread, copper wire
on mat board
12 x 10 in.
National Museum of the American
Indian 26/9765, gift of John
and Meryl Lipton Lavine

Untitled, from the *Artifact Series*,
ca. 1985–90
Peeled willow stick, feather, stone,
copper wire on mat board
8 x 11 in.
National Museum of the American
Indian 26/9253, gift of John
and Meryl Lipton Lavine

Skychart III, 1986
Pine, peeled willow saplings,
leather, watercolor
24 x 60 x 4 in.
Collection of Linda Nix and Neil Short

Chief Takes His Dog for a Ride, 1989
Pine, peeled willow sticks, leather,
copper wire, brass nails
11 ¾ x 16 ½ x 3 ⅜ in.
National Museum of the
American Indian 27/609

Mnemonic Canoe, 1989
Bronze and rawhide
36 x 19 ½ x 12 ¾ in.
Chazen Museum of Art, University of
Wisconsin–Madison, Frank R. Horlbeck
Endowment Fund purchase, 2020.44.2a-b

Stream II, ca. 1990–91
Pine, peeled willow sticks,
watercolor, stones, pastel
18 x 32 ¼ x 1 in.
National Museum of the
American Indian 27/608

Water Spirit #1, 1991
Pine, peeled willow saplings,
watercolor, leather
94 ¼ x 49 ½ x 32 in.
Milwaukee Art Museum,
gift of Jan Serr & John Shannon

Hoounch II, 1992
Pine, peeled willow,
leather, powdered pigment, and ink
75 x 72 x 3 ½ in.
Museum of Wisconsin Art, gift of
James and Judith DeStefano

Ottawa, 1992
Pine, peeled willow saplings
5 ¾ x 8 x 30 ft.
Truman T. Lowe Estate

Sauninga, 1992
Pastel on paper
30 x 22 ¼ in.
National Museum of the
American Indian 27/628

Tobacco Pouch, 1992
Chalk pastel on paper
30 x 22 ½ in.
National Museum of the
American Indian 26/9771, gift of
John and Meryl Lipton Lavine

Untitled, 1992
Pastel and collage on paper
30 x 22 ½ in.
National Museum of the
American Indian 26/9770, gift of
John and Meryl Lipton Lavine

Feather Canoe, ca. 1993
Peeled willow saplings,
feathers, copper wire
22 x 74 x 12 in.
National Museum of the
American Indian 27/607

Mnemonic, 1993
Brushed powdered pigment
and pastel on paper
11 x 14 in.
National Museum of the
American Indian 27/626

Blanket Series (Red Purple), 1994
Brushed powdered pigment
and pastel on paper
30 x 42 in.
National Museum of the
American Indian 27/616

Feather and Lightning, 1995
Pine, peeled willow sticks, leather, paint
26 ¹⁵⁄₁₆ x 16 ¾ x 1 ⁷⁄₁₆ in.
Milwaukee Art Museum, gift of
Jan Cicero Gallery M1997.55

Hoounch III, 1995
Pine, leather
73 x 72 ¼ x 3 ½ in.
Museum of Wisconsin Art, gift of
James and Judith DeStefano

Untitled #3, from the *Petroglyph Series*,
1995
Peeled willow sticks, pine, leather,
powdered pigment
17 ½ x 14 x 5 in.
Truman T. Lowe Estate

Untitled #4, from the *Petroglyph Series*,
1995
Peeled willow sticks, pine, turkey
feathers, powdered pigment
23 x 13 ½ x 5 in.
Truman T. Lowe Estate

Ne Pu Saka (Sand on Water), 1996
Pine, sand
96 x 144 x 8 in.
Smithsonian American Art Museum;
purchase made through the Luisita
L. and Franz H. Denghausen
Endowment, 2022.9.1A-H

Shadow Canoe, 1996
Charcoal and pastel on paper
30 x 80 in.
National Museum of the
American Indian 27/615

Untitled, 1996
Brushed powdered pigment and
pastel on paper
30 ¼ x 79 ½ in.
National Museum of the
American Indian 27/611

Wa-Du-Sheh (Bundle), 1996
Peeled willow saplings, paper, wax, leather
24 x 18 x 3 ft.
National Museum of the
American Indian 26/7724

Wach-Nee (Canoe Form), 1996,
reworked 1999
Pine wood, peeled willow saplings,
twine, leather, iron screws
8 x 24 x 4 ft.
Eiteljorg Museum of American Indians
and Western Art 1999.6.1 A–B. Museum
purchase from the Eiteljorg Fellowship
for Native American Fine Art

Winter Structure, 1997
Pastel on paper
30 ¼ x 42 ¼ in.
National Museum of the
American Indian 27/618

Untitled, ca. 1999
Gesso and chalk on canvas
72 x 24 in.
National Museum of the
American Indian 27/610

Waterfall '99, 1999
Pine, peeled willow saplings
96 x 144 x 4 in.
Eiteljorg Museum of American Indians
and Western Art 1999.6.4 A–C. Museum
purchase from the Eiteljorg Fellowship
for Native American Fine Art. Additional
funding provided by Mike and Juanita
Eagle, Roger and Mindy Eiteljorg, Stan
and Sandy Hurt, Arnold and Carol Jolles,
Jay Peacock and Carolyn Kincannon

Water Reflections I, 1999
Acrylic, chalk pastel, graphite,
and colored pencil on paper
30 x 44 ¼ in.
The Rockwell Museum, Clara
S. Peck Fund. 2000.34.1

Water Reflections II, 1999
Chalk pastel and paint on paper
30 ⅜ x 44 ½ in.
The Rockwell Museum, Clara
S. Peck Fund. 2000.34.3

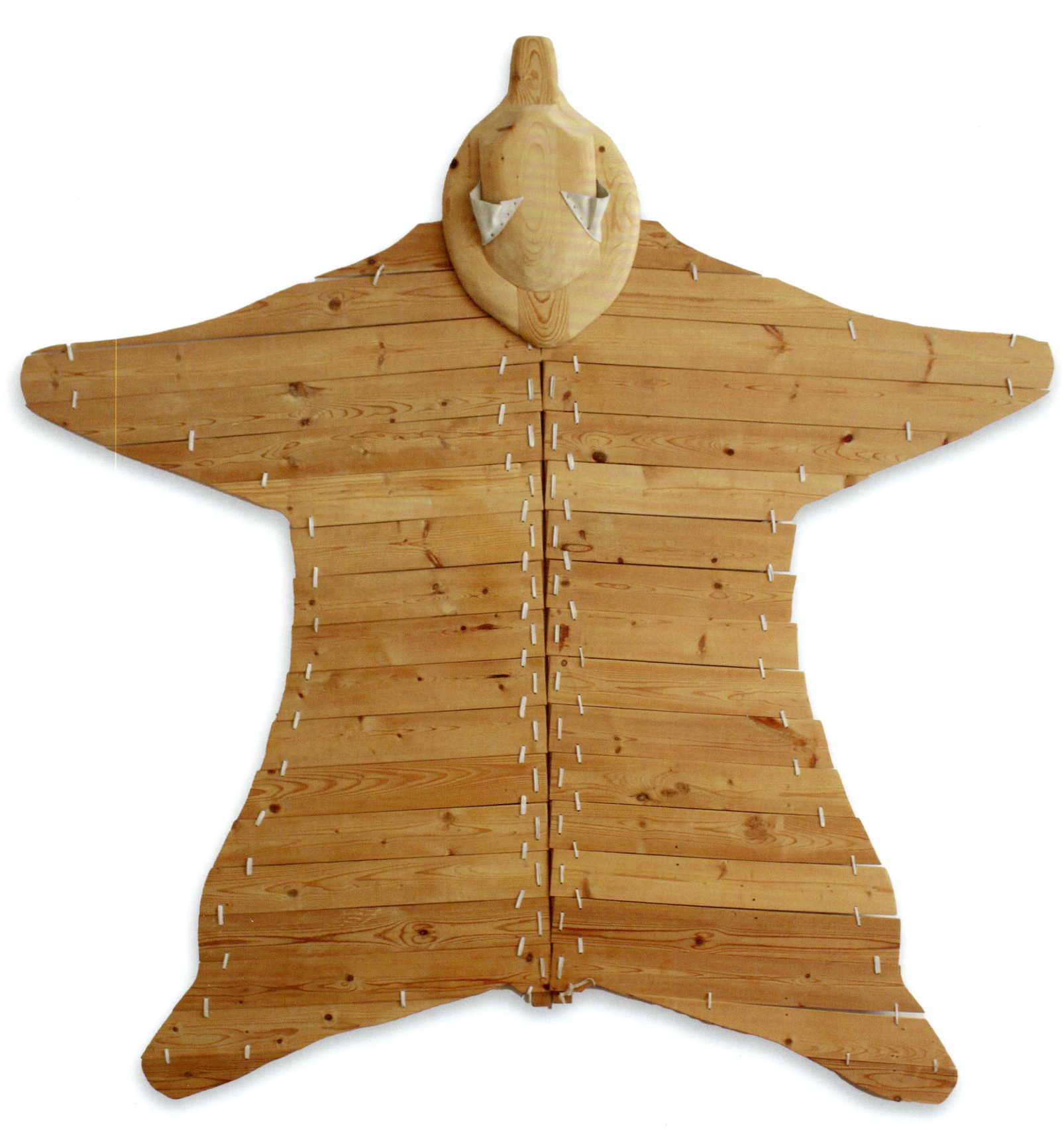

122. *Hoounch III*, 1995. Pine, leather, 73 x 72 ¼ x 3 ½ in. Museum of Wisconsin Art, gift of James and Judith DeStefano

Water Reflections III, 1999
Chalk pastel and paint on paper
30 ½ x 42 ½ in.
The Rockwell Museum,
Clara S. Peck Fund. 2000.34.2

Water Reflections IV, 1999
Gesso, chalk pastel, colored pencil
and graphite on paper
30 ½ x 44 ½ in.
The Rockwell Museum, Clara
S. Peck Fund. 2000.34.4

Wána (Cascade), 2002
Aluminum
48 x 128 x 1 ⅝ in.
Northwestern University,
Kellogg School of Management

Untitled (Canoe Form), ca. 2010
Charcoal on paper
42 x 30 in.
National Museum of the
American Indian 27/614

Untitled, ca. 2010–15
Gesso and pastel on paper
11 x 30 in.
National Museum of the
American Indian 27/627

Untitled (Stream), ca. 2010–15
Gesso and pastel on paper
30 x 11 in.
National Museum of the
American Indian 27/613

Waterfall VIII, 2011
Pine, metal fasteners
82 x 80 x 64 in.
Denver Art Museum: Native Arts
acquisition fund, 2011.430A-N

Untitled, n.d.
Charcoal and graphite on paper
11 x 30 in.
National Museum of the
American Indian 27/612

Untitled (Sauninga), n.d.
Chalk pastel on paper
11 x 14 in.
National Museum of the
American Indian 27/619

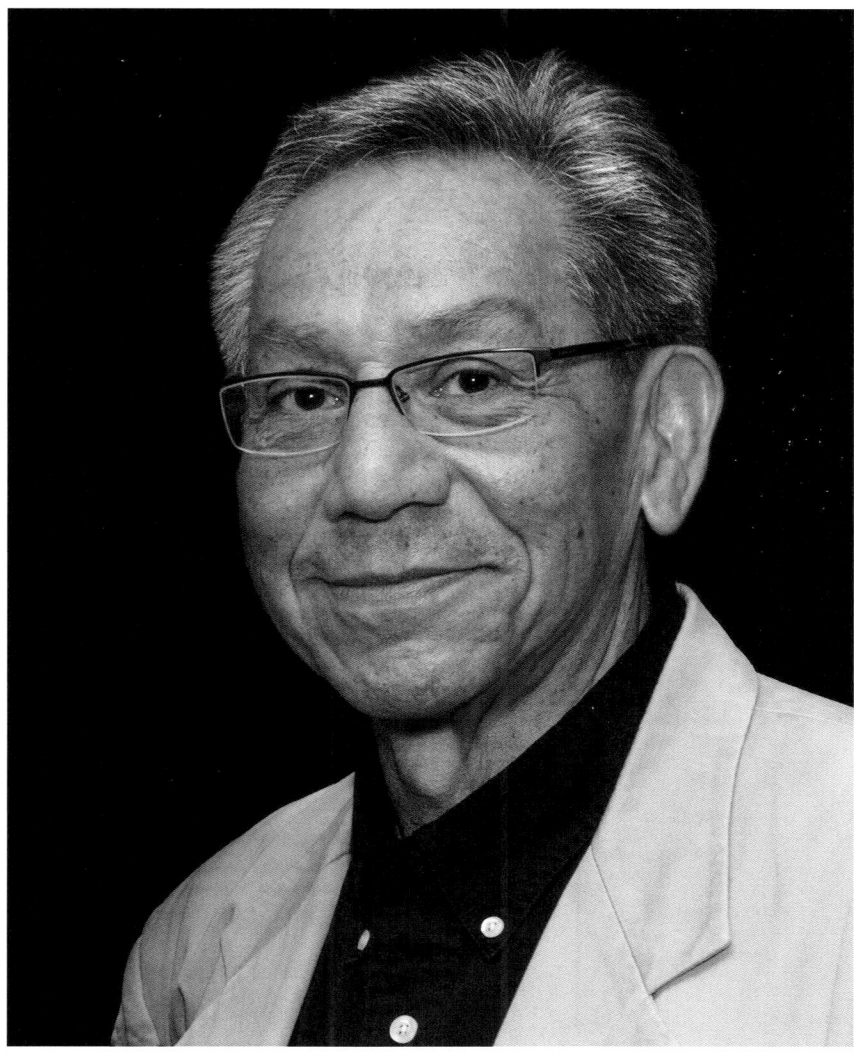

123. Truman Lowe, 2010.

Contributors

RACHEL ALLEN (Nimiipuu [Nez Perce Tribe]) is the curator of modern and contemporary art at the Northwest Museum of Arts and Culture (MAC) in Spokane, Washington. Most recently, she cocurated *Joe Feddersen: Earth, Water, Sky* (2024) and coedited the accompanying catalog, organized by the MAC. Prior, she was an assistant curator at the Peabody Essex Museum in Salem, Massachusetts. Allen is a PhD candidate at the University of Delaware.

MICHAEL BELMORE (Anishinaabe) employs a variety of materials and processes that may appear disjointed; the reality is that together his work and processes reflect on the environment, land, water, and what it means to be Anishinaabe. A graduate of the Ontario College of Art & Design, he completed his Master of Fine Art at the University of Ottawa in 2019. Practicing for over twenty-five years, Belmore is an internationally recognized artist and is represented in the permanent collections of various institutions including the National Gallery of Canada, the Art Gallery of Ontario, and the Smithsonian's National Museum of the American Indian.

JOE FEDDERSEN, member of the Confederated Tribes of the Colville Reservation (Okanagan and Arrow Lakes), is an artist and professor emeritus at the Evergreen State College in Olympia, WA. His work has been featured in numerous exhibitions, including *Continuum 12 Artists: Joe Feddersen* (2003) curated by Truman Lowe at the National Museum of the American Indian, and *Sharing Honors and Burdens: Renwick Invitational 2023* at the Smithsonian American Art Museum. He was the subject of a major survey exhibition and monograph, *Vital Signs* (2008), organized by the Hallie Ford Museum of Art, and his career retrospective and monograph, *Joe Feddersen: Earth, Water, Sky* (2024), was organized by the Northwest Museum of Arts and Culture. Feddersen earned his MFA from the University of Wisconsin–Madison, where he studied with Truman Lowe.

KENDRA GREENDEER, a citizen of the Ho-Chunk Nation and descendant of the Red Cliff Band of Lake Superior Ojibwe, is the Ihlenfeld Curator of Collaborative and Community Exhibitions at the Weisman Art Museum in Minneapolis, Minnesota. Her research and curatorial projects explore the work of contemporary Native American women artists who enact rematriation as a method, Indigenous museum practices, and land and materiality relations. Dr. Greendeer received her PhD in art history from the University of Wisconsin–Madison, her MA in art and museum studies from Georgetown University in Washington, DC, and her BFA in museum studies from the Institute of American Indian Arts in Santa Fe, New Mexico.

JOHN HITCHCOCK is a contemporary artist and musician. Hitchcock is an enrolled member of the Kiowa Tribe of Oklahoma, and also is of Comanche and northern European descent, based out of Madison, Wisconsin. Hitchcock currently works in multimedia, including neon, textiles, printmaking, sound, and video to reclaim narratives of resilience and survival. He uses visual storytelling to understand his relationships to community, land, and culture. He earned his MFA in printmaking and photography at Texas Tech University and his BFA from Cameron University. He has been the recipient of the Robert Rauschenberg Foundation Artistic Innovation and Collaboration grant, New York; Jerome Foundation grant, Minnesota; and the Creative Arts Award and Emily Mead Baldwin Award in the Creative Arts at the University of Wisconsin. He is currently an artist and the Vilas Distinguished Achievement Professor at the University of Wisconsin–Madison where he teaches screen printing, relief cut, and installation art.

SKY HOPINKA (Ho-Chunk Nation/Pechanga Band of Indians) was born and raised in Ferndale, Washington, and Palm Springs, California. His video, photo, and text work centers around personal positions of Indigenous homeland and landscape, designs of language as containers of culture expressed through personal, documentary, and nonfiction forms of media. His work has played at various festivals including Sundance, Toronto International Film Festival, and the New York Film Festival. His work has been part of multiple solo and survey exhibitions in the United States and internationally. His works are in the collections of the Museum of Modern Art, the Guggenheim Museum, the San Francisco Museum of Modern Art, Museum für Moderne Kunst in Frankfurt, Germany, and others. He received the 2022 Infinity Award in Art from the International Center of Photography, is a 2022 MacArthur Fellow and was a winner of the 2023 Baloise Art Prize at Art Basel. He currently is an assistant professor in the department of Art, Film, and Visual Studies at Harvard University.

KAREN LEMMEY is the Lucy S. Rhame Curator of Sculpture at the Smithsonian American Art Museum; she joined the museum's staff in 2012. Lemmey is responsible for research, exhibitions, and acquisitions related to the museum's extensive sculpture collection, which is the largest collection of American sculpture in the world. Her research interests include public art and monuments, the history of materials and methods, American artist colonies in nineteenth-century Italy, the construction of race in American sculpture, the history of sculpture conservation and direct carving. Lemmey earned a bachelor's degree in art history from Columbia College, Columbia University and she holds a doctorate in art history and certificate in American studies from the Graduate Center of the City University of New York.

AMY LONETREE is an enrolled citizen of the Ho-Chunk Nation and a professor of history at the University of California, Santa Cruz. Her scholarly research focuses on Native American history, public history, visual studies, and museum studies, and she has received fellowships in support of this work from the School for Advanced Research, the Newberry Library, the Georgia O'Keeffe Museum Research Center, the Institute of American Cultures at UCLA, and the University of California, Berkeley Chancellor's Postdoctoral Fellowship Program. Her publications include *Decolonizing Museums: Representing Native America in National and Tribal Museums* (2012); a coedited book with Amanda J. Cobb, *The National Museum of the American Indian: Critical Conversations* (2008); and a coauthored volume, *People of the Big Voice: Photographs of Ho-Chunk Families by Charles Van Schaick, 1879–1942* (2011). She is currently working on a book focusing on the history of the Ho-Chunk Nation that explores family history, tourism, settler colonialism, and Hoocąk survivance through an examination of two exceptional collections of studio portraits and tourist images taken between 1879 and 1960. She is also pursuing research on the history of Indigenous child removal in the United States.

TONIA LOWE (Hoocąk) is Truman Lowe's daughter. Growing up, she was often recruited to help peel willow for her dad's installation sculptures. Inspired by her father's work, she studied art history, earning a BA at the University of Wisconsin–Madison, and an MA at the University of Colorado Boulder where she wrote her thesis on Edgar Heap of Birds's public artworks. She has been working in advertising in the San Francisco Bay Area for the past twenty-five years and is now making her way back to the art world.

PATRICIA MARROQUIN NORBY (Purépecha descent) is the associate curator of Native American art at the Metropolitan Museum of Art. An award-winning scholar and museum leader, she previously served as senior executive and assistant director of the Smithsonian's National Museum of the American Indian in New York and as director of the D'Arcy McNickle Center for American Indian and Indigenous Studies at the Newberry in Chicago. Her forthcoming book, *Water, Bones, and Bombs* examines twentieth-century American Indian art and environmental disputes in northern New Mexico. She coedited "Aesthetic Violence: Art and Indigenous Ways of Knowing," *American Indian Culture and Research Journal* (2015). She earned her PhD at the University of Minnesota–Twin Cities.

JO ORTEL is the author of *Woodland Reflections: The Art of Truman Lowe* (2004). She has published exhibition reviews, articles, and essays on a range of topics related to contemporary Native American art. At Beloit College, where she taught for more than twenty years, Jo held the Richard K. and Gloria I. Nystrom Chair in art history. In 2003, she won the Underkofler Award for Excellence in Undergraduate Teaching. Since her retirement in 2020, Jo has worked tirelessly to secure Lowe's legacy, facilitating museum acquisitions, loans, and exhibitions of his art. She is currently completing an expanded edition of *Woodland Reflections*. She received a BA from Smith College, MA from Oberlin, and PhD from Stanford University.

DAVID W. PENNEY is the former associate director of Museum Research, Scholarship, and Public Engagement at the National Museum of the American Indian and an internationally recognized scholar of American Indian art history. Penney arrived at the Smithsonian in 2011 after a thirty-one-year career at the Detroit Institute of Arts, where he last served as vice president of Exhibitions and Collections Strategies. The author of numerous publications, Penney's most recent work includes essays for the exhibition catalogues *Unbound: Narrative Art of the Plains* (2024), *Shelley Niro: 500 Year Itch* (2023), and *Robert Houle: Red is Beautiful* (2022). He produced "Native North American Art: Pre-Contact" for the acclaimed online

Oxford Bibliographies in Art History and authored the art history textbook *Native North American Art*, published by Thames & Hudson in 2004. His essay "Siyosapa: At the Edge of Art" for the online publication *Arts* earned a Secretary's Research Award from the Smithsonian Institution's Congress of Scholars in 2020.

ANDREA REYNOSA is a multidisciplinary artist, activist, and farmer. She practiced sculpture at University of Wisconsin–Madison, where she was mentored by Truman Lowe, and received her MFA from the University of Arizona working closely with Harmony Hammond. Later, she collaborated with Lowe on *Approaching Silence*, an environmental sound sculpture. In 1996, Reynosa founded the Brooklyn arts space Smack Mellon before moving to Narrowsburg, New York. She blended permaculture and forest stewardship after establishing SkyDog Farm in 2000. As a councilwoman and grant writer for Tusten, New York, she blended food and environmental justice projects with youth workforce development. Reynosa has received grants from the Warhol, Pollock/Krasner, and Ford Foundations. Her projects explore Indigenous pre-contact farming technology and cultural exchange, inspiring *First Suppers of San Fidel*, which promotes food sovereignty and orchard revitalization.

PAUL CHAAT SMITH is a Comanche author, essayist, and curator. He joined the Smithsonian's National Museum of the American Indian in 2001. His exhibitions include *Americans*, James Luna's *Emendatio*, *Fritz Scholder: Indian/Not Indian*, and *Brian Jungen: Strange Comfort*. His books include *Everything You Know about Indians Is Wrong* (2009), and with Robert Warrior, *Like a Hurricane: the Indian Movement from Alcatraz to Wounded Knee* (1996). Smith lives in Baltimore, Maryland.

REBECCA HEAD TRAUTMANN is an assistant curator of contemporary art at the Smithsonian's National Museum of the American Indian, where she's worked with modern and contemporary art since 2003. She curated the exhibitions *Vantage Point: The Contemporary Native Art Collection* and *Making Marks: Prints from Crow's*

Shadow Press, and cocurated *Stretching the Canvas: Eight Decades of Native Painting*. Trautmann served as curator for the National Native American Veterans Memorial, which opened in 2020. She previously held positions at the Museum of Indian Arts and Culture in Santa Fe, New Mexico, and at the University of New Mexico's Maxwell Museum of Anthropology. Trautmann earned a BA in humanities at the University of Texas at Austin before doing graduate work in Native American art history at the University of New Mexico.

KAY WALKINGSTICK (Cherokee Nation) has had over thirty solo exhibitions in the United States and Europe. Her work is in the collections of numerous museums, including the National Museum of the American Indian. WalkingStick taught painting and drawing at Cornell University for seventeen years before retiring as professor emerita in 2005. She has received honorary doctorates from Pratt Institute and Arcadia University and is a fellow of the National Academy of Design and the American Academy of Arts and Science. In 2015, the National Museum of the American Indian organized the traveling retrospective *Kay WalkingStick: An American Artist*.

DYANI WHITE HAWK (Sičáŋǧu Lakota) is a multidisciplinary artist based in Minneapolis. White Hawk was featured in the 2022 Whitney Biennial and recent solo exhibitions *Reflections* at Various Small Fires, Los Angeles, and *Speaking to Relatives* at the Museum of Contemporary Art Denver and Kemper Museum of Contemporary Art. She has received awards from the Guggenheim Foundation, the MacArthur Foundation, Creative Capital, Anonymous Was a Woman, Joan Mitchell Foundation, and McKnight Foundation. Her work can be found within collections such as the Guggenheim, Brooklyn Museum, Hirshhorn Museum, Minneapolis Institute of Art, Museum of Modern Art, Walker Art Center, and Whitney Museum of American Art.

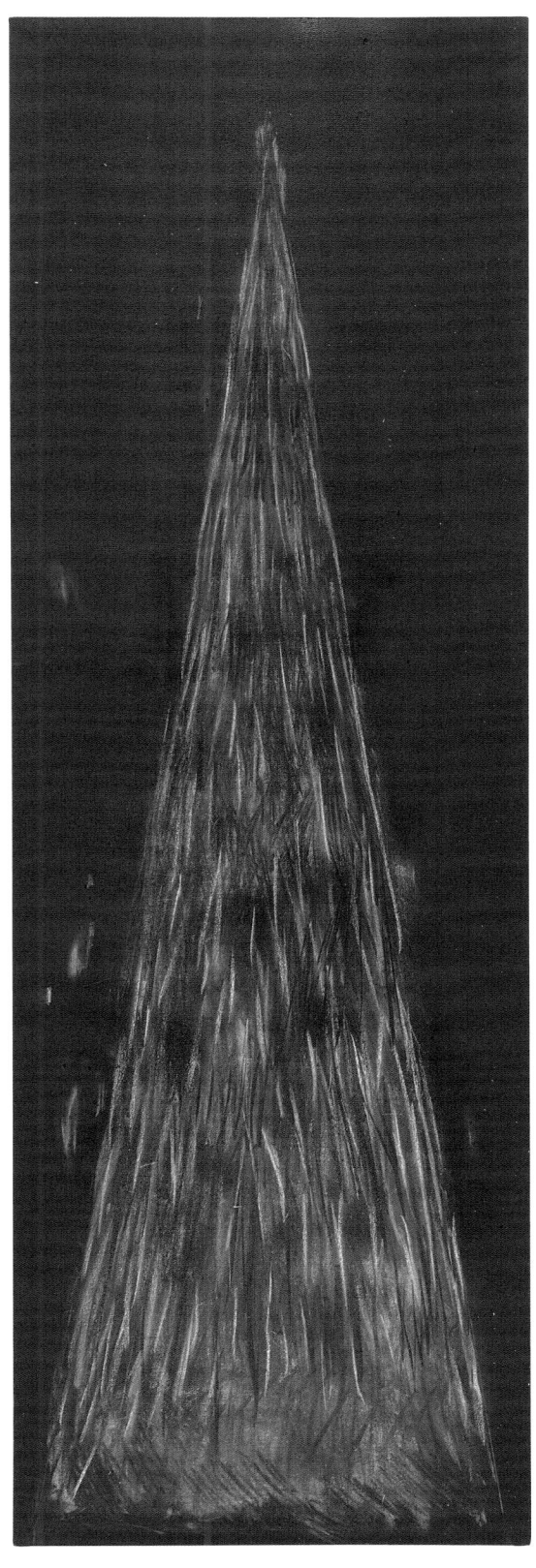

124. Untitled, ca. 1999. Gesso and chalk on canvas, 72 x 24 in. National Museum of the American Indian 27/610

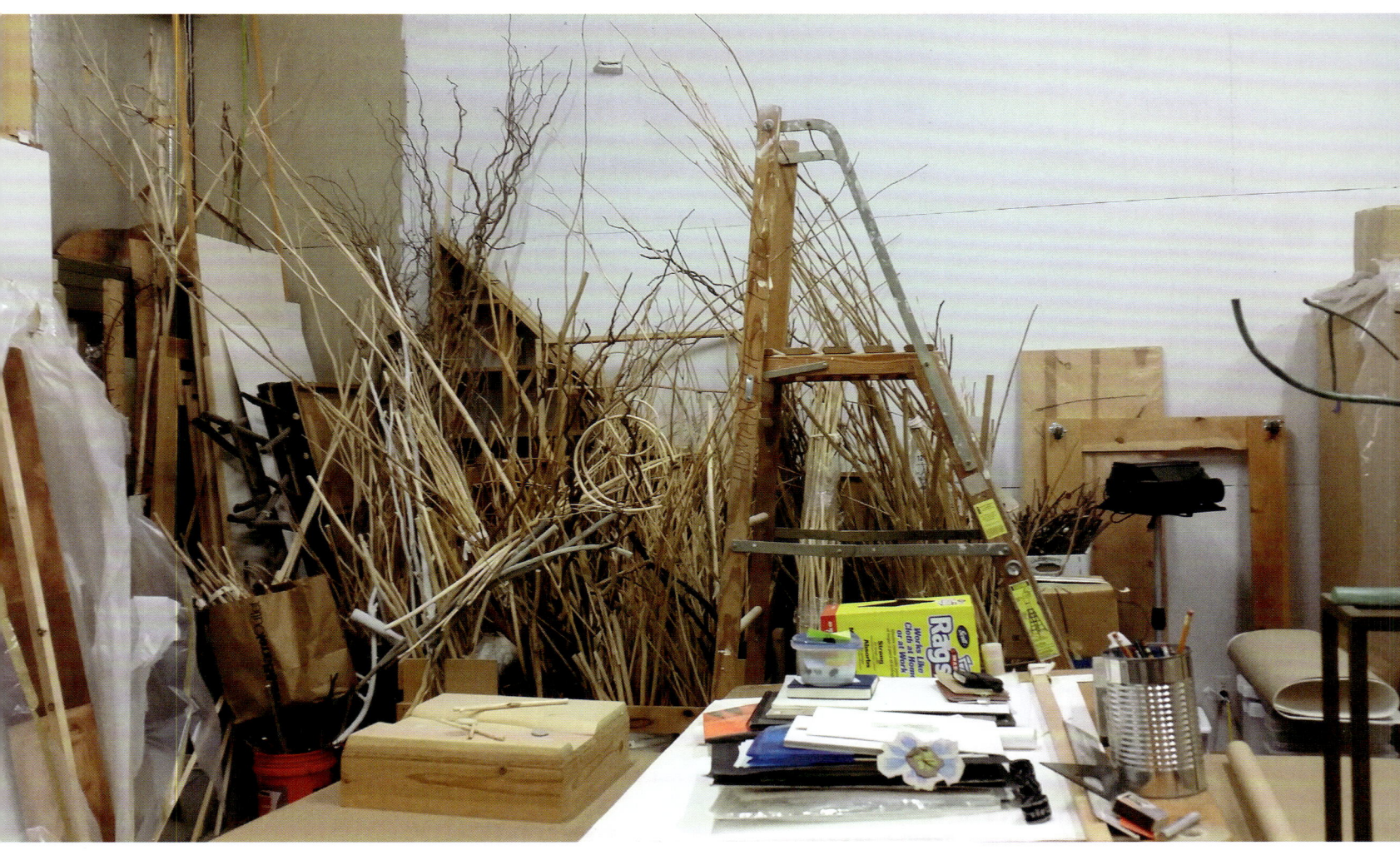

125. Truman Lowe's studio, Middleton, Wisconsin, 2018

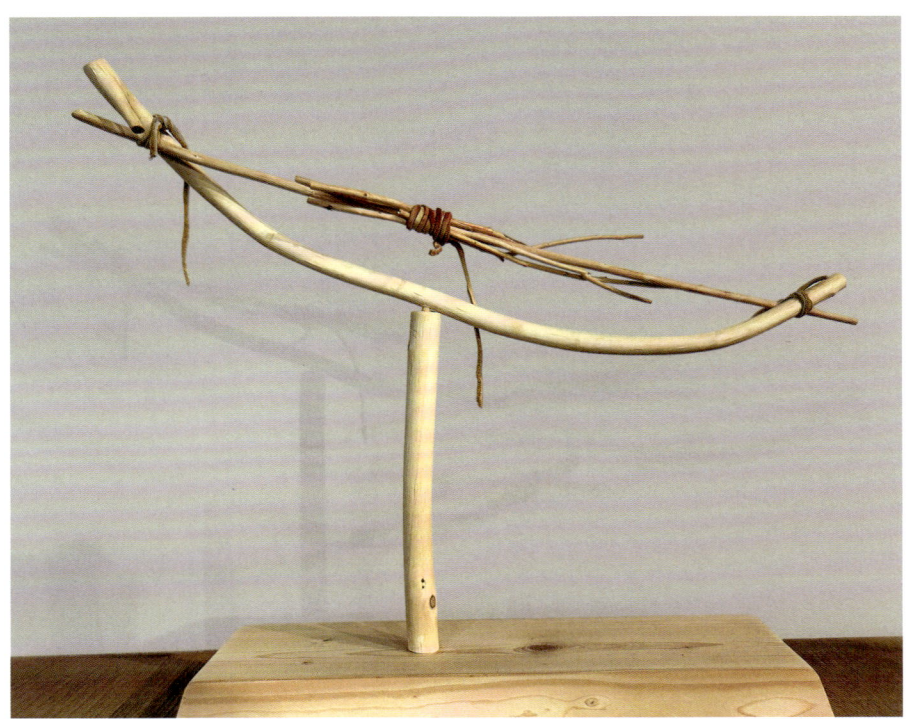

126. Untitled #3 from the *Petroglyph Series*, 1995. Peeled willow sticks, pine, leather, powdered pigment, 17 ½ x 14 x 5 in. Truman T. Lowe Estate

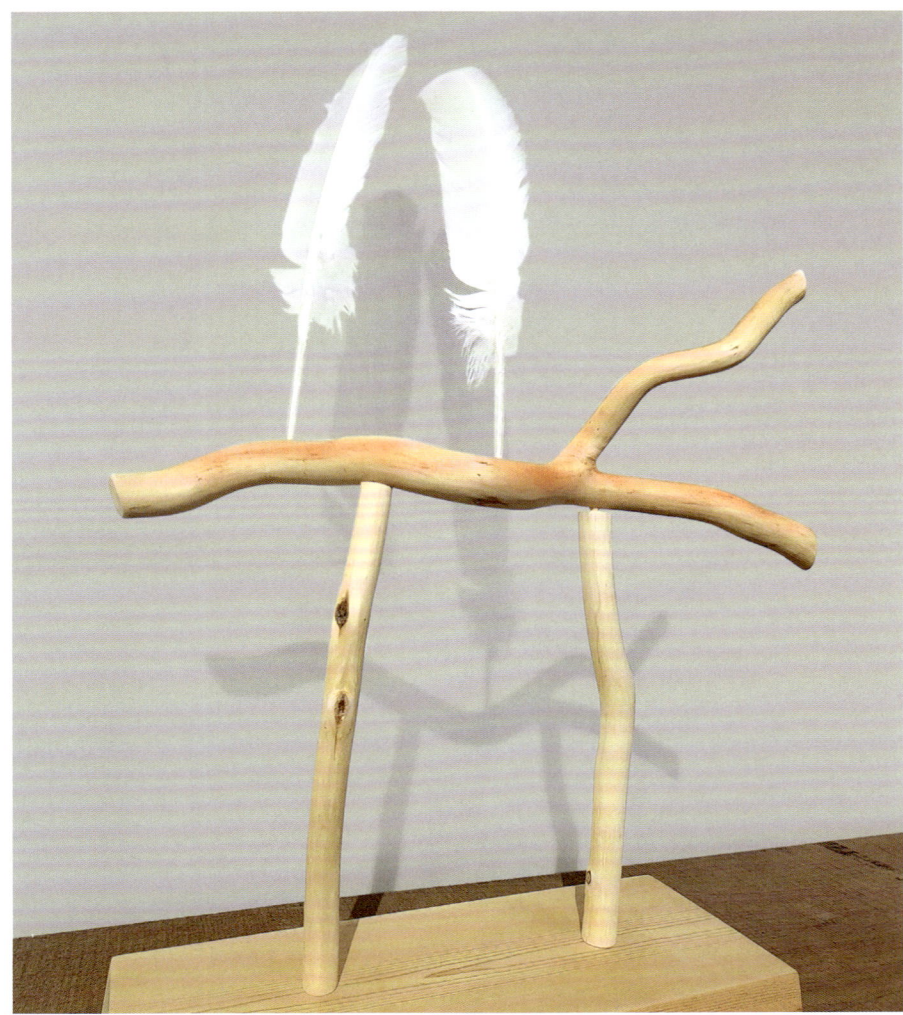

127. Untitled #4 from the *Petroglyph Series*, 1995. Peeled willow sticks, pine, turkey feathers, powdered pigment, 23 x 13 ½ x 5 in. Truman T. Lowe Estate

Index

Page numbers in *italics* indicate illustrations; n indicates a note.

Credits

Credits listed by figure number.
All artworks by Truman Lowe appear courtesy of the © Truman T. Lowe Estate. All works are by Lowe unless otherwise noted.

1–2: National Museum of the American Indian (NMAI). **3**: Courtesy of Rebecca Head Trautmann, photo by NMAI staff. **4**: Chazen Museum of Art, University of Wisconsin–Madison. **5–7**: NMAI. **8**: Northwestern University, Kellogg School of Management. **9**: M1997.25. Photographer credit: John R. Glembin. Image Courtesy of the Milwaukee Art Museum. © Truman T. Lowe Estate. **10**: Gift of Tonya Lowe. Courtesy of the Eiteljorg Museum of American Indians and Western Art, Indianapolis. **11**: NMAI. **12**: Eiteljorg Museum of American Indians and Western Art, Indianapolis. **13**: NMAI. **14**: Museum of Fine Arts, Boston, John Wheelock Elliot and John Morse Elliot Fund and Harriet Otis Cruft Fund, 2022.180. **15–18**: © Truman T. Lowe Estate. **19**: Wisconsin Historical Society, image 129477. **20**: © Truman T. Lowe Estate. **21–23**: Photographer unknown, courtesy Truman T. Lowe Estate. **24**: © Truman T. Lowe Estate. **25–26**: Photographer unknown, courtesy Truman T. Lowe Estate. **27**: Museum of Contemporary Art Chicago, gift of Katherine S. Schamberg by exchange. **28**: Courtesy of Madison Museum of Contemporary Art, Wisconsin. Photographed by Paige Holzbauer. **29**: Photographer unknown, courtesy Truman T. Lowe Estate. **30**: © William J. Lizdas – USA TODAY NETWORK. **31**: Photography © Denver Art Museum. **32–33**: © Truman T. Lowe Estate. **34**: Photo by Jeff Miller, courtesy of University of Wisconsin–Madison. **35**: Western Michigan University. Photography by Mary Whalen. **36**: © Truman T. Lowe Estate. **37**: Jeff Miller / University of Wisconsin–Madison. **38**: Installation view of *Cultural Confluence: Work by Truman Lowe*, February 9–September 16, 2017, Plains Art Museum, Fargo, North Dakota. Photo by Cody Jacobson. **39–42**: NMAI. **43**: Photographer unknown, courtesy Truman T. Lowe Estate. **44**: Truman Lowe, Detroit River, 1983, wood, rawhide. Detroit Institute of Arts, lent by the artist, T1983.147. **45**: © Truman T. Lowe Estate. **46–50**: NMAI. **51**: © Truman T. Lowe Estate. **52**: Collection of Linda Nix, photography by Ben Winkler. **53**: NMAI. **54**: © Truman T. Lowe Estate. **55–56**: NMAI. **57**: Photographer unknown, courtesy Truman T. Lowe Estate. **58**: Courtesy of the Eiteljorg Museum of American Indians and Western Art, Indianapolis. **59**: Denver Art Museum: Native Arts acquisition funds, 1994.469. Photography © Denver Art Museum. **60**: Photographer unknown, courtesy Truman T. Lowe Estate. **61**: Wisconsin Historical Society, WHI-60881. **62**: Wisconsin Historical Society, WHI-3691. **63**: Wisconsin Historical Society, WHI-62265. **64**: Wisconsin Historical Society, WHI-61600. **65**: Map of Ho-Chunk Migrations by Amelia Janes, Earth Illustrated, Inc. Reprinted with permission of the Wisconsin Historical Society. **66**: Photo courtesy of the Warehouse Art Museum (WAM), Jan Serr & John Shannon Collection. Photographed by Avery Pelekoudas. **67**: Photographer unknown, courtesy Truman T. Lowe Estate. **68**: Courtesy of John Hitchcock. **69**: Truman Lowe, Remembrance, June 3–August 19, 2001. Exhibition organized by the Madison Museum of Contemporary Art. Courtesy of the Madison Museum of Contemporary Art, Wisconsin, Photographed by Jessie Cork. **70–72**: NMAI. **72**: Photograph by Andrea Waala, Museum of Wisconsin Art. **73**: NMAI. **74**: Kendra Greendeer. **75**: NMAI. **76**: Courtesy Truman T. Lowe Estate. **77**: Wisconsin Historical Society, WHI-1981.57.1. **78–84**: NMAI. **85**: Milwaukee Art Museum. **86–87**: NMAI. **88**: Courtesy of the Peabody Essex Museum. **89**: Photographer unknown, courtesy Truman T. Lowe Estate. **90**: NMAI. **91–96**: Photo by Patricia Marroquin Norby, 2023. **97**: © The Metropolitan Museum of Art. Image source: Art Resource, NY. **98**: Bone/Levine Architects. **99**: Scale Model by Koroglu Model Makers / Photo of model and Graphics by Bone/Levine Architects. **100**: Bone/Levine Architects. **101**: NMAI. **102**: Smithsonian American Art Museum, Museum purchase made through the Luisita L. and Franz H. Denghausen Endowment, 2022.9.3, © 2021, Truman Lowe Estate. **103**: Smithsonian American Art Museum, Museum purchase made through the Luisita L. and Franz H. Denghausen Endowment, 2022.9.1A-H, © 2021, Truman Lowe Estate. **104**: Smithsonian American Art Museum, Museum purchase made through the Luisita L. and Franz H. Denghausen Endowment, 2022.9.4, © 2021, Truman Lowe Estate. **105–106**: Martin Puryear, *Vessel*, 1997–2002, Eastern white pine, mesh, tar, 84 × 181 ½ × 68 in. (213.4 × 461.0 × 172.7 cm), Smithsonian American Art Museum, Gift of Nion McEvoy and Leslie Berriman in memory of Nan Tucker McEvoy, gift of Lucy S. Rhame, and museum purchase through the Luisita L. and Franz H. Denghausen Endowment, 2017.18, © 1997–2002, Martin Puryear; Louise Nevelson, *Sky Cathedral*, 1982, painted wood, overall: 104 ⅜ x 288 ⅜ x 15 ¾ in. (265.1 x 732.5 x 40.0 cm), Smithsonian American Art Museum, Gift of an anonymous donor, 1994.85A-AA; Truman Lowe, *Totem for Henu (First Daughter)*, 1985, pine and peeled willow, 126 ½ x 15 x 15 in. (321.3 x 38.1 x 38.1 cm), Smithsonian American Art Museum, Museum purchase made through the Luisita L. and Franz H. Denghausen Endowment, 2022.9.3, © 2021, Truman Lowe Estate; Truman Lowe, *Totem for Kunu (First Son)*, 1985, pine and peeled willow, 114 x 15 x 15 in. (289.6 x 38.1 x 38.1 cm), Smithsonian American Art Museum, Museum purchase made through the Luisita L. and Franz H. Denghausen Endowment, 2022.9.2, © 2021, Truman Lowe Estate; Chryssa, *White Relief*, 1960, gesso over plaster on wood, 59 ¼ x 44 ¾ in. (150.5 x 113.6 cm.), Smithsonian American Art Museum, Gift of Mr. and Mrs. David K. Anderson, Martha Jackson Memorial Collection, 1980.137.18; Kerry James Marshall, *SOB, SOB*, 2003, acrylic on fiberglass, 108 x 72 in. (274.3 x 182.9 cm), Smithsonian American Art Museum, Museum purchase through the Luisita L. and Franz H. Denghausen Endowment, 2010.29, © 2003, Kerry James Marshall; Thornton Dial, Sr., *The Beginning of Life in the Yellow Jungle*, 2003, plastic soda bottles, doll, clothing, bedding, wire, found metal, rubber glove, turtle shell, artificial flowers, Splash Zone compound, enamel, and spray paint on canvas on wood, 75 x 112 x 13 in., Smithsonian American Art Museum, Partial gift of Debbie Simon and Tim Grumbacher and museum purchase, 2020.80. **107–108**: NMAI. **109**: Smithsonian American Art Museum, Museum purchase made through the Luisita L. and Franz H. Denghausen Endowment, 2022.9.3, © 2021, Truman Lowe Estate. **110**: NMAI. **111**: Smithsonian American Art Museum, Museum purchase made through the Luisita L. and Franz H. Denghausen Endowment, 2022.9.2, © 2021, Truman Lowe Estate. **112–113**: NMAI. **114**: Tonia Lowe. **115**: NMAI. **116**: Photographer unknown, courtesy Truman T. Lowe Estate. **117–120**: The Rockwell Museum. **121**: © Rosalie Favell. **122**: Photograph by Andrea Waala, Museum of Wisconsin Art. © Truman T. Lowe Estate. **123**: Photo by Jim Escalante. **124–125**: NMAI. **126–127**: © Truman T. Lowe Estate.